THE CHOCTAWS IN OKLAHOMA

American Indian Law and Policy Series
Lindsey G. Robertson, General Editor

THE CHOCTAW NATION IN OKLAHOMA

From Tribe to Nation, 1855–1970

Clara Sue Kidwell

Foreword by Lindsay G. Robertson

University of Oklahoma Press : Norman

Also by Clara Sue Kidwell

(with Charles Roberts) *The Choctaws: A Critical Bibliography*
(Bloomington, Ind., 1980)

Choctaws and Missionaries in Mississippi, 1818–1918 (Norman, 1995)

(with Homer Noley and George E. "Tink" Tinker) *A Native American Theology*
(Maryknoll, N.Y., 2001)

(with Alan Velie) *Native American Studies* (Edinburgh, U.K., 2005)

Library of Congress Cataloging-in-Publication Data

Kidwell, Clara Sue.
   The Choctaws in Oklahoma : from tribe to nation, 1855–1970 / Clara Sue
Kidwell ; foreword by Lindsay G. Robertson.
      p.   cm.—(American Indian law and policy series ; v. 2)
   Includes bibliographical references.
   ISBN: 978-0-8061-4006-3 (paper)
   1. Choctaw Indians—Oklahoma—History.   2. Choctaw Indians—
Oklahoma—Government relations.   3. Choctaw Indians—Oklahoma—
Treaties.   4. Oklahoma—Ethnic relations.   5. Oklahoma—History—19th
century.   I. Title.
   E99.C8K526 2007
   976.6004'97387—dc22

                                                                              2006034695

The Choctaws in Oklahoma: From Tribe to Nation, 1855–1970 is Volume 2 in the
American Indian Law and Policy Series.

The paper in this book meets the guidelines for permanence and durability of
the Committee on Production Guidelines for Book Longevity of the Council on
Library Resources, Inc. ∞

To the memory of my parents
Hardin Milton Kidwell
Martha Evelyn Kidwell

CONTENTS

List of Illustrations   ix
Series Editor's Foreword   xi
Acknowledgments   xiii
Introduction   xv

  1. The Choctaws in 1855   3
  2. The Treaty of 1855   15
  3. "Embarrassments and Perplexities":
      The Church, the Nation, and Slavery   30
  4. The Constitutional Crisis of 1858:
      The Politics of Change   41
  5. The Civil War in Indian Territory   57
  6. The Treaty of 1866   72
  7. Little Strings of Houses   87
  8. Iron Horses and Indian Maidens   102
  9. The Net Proceeds Case   121
 10. Selfishness and Civilization   137
 11. The Leased District Claim   151
 12. The Issue of Citizenship   162
 13. A Family History   176
 14. Oklahoma!   183
 15. After Statehood   193
 16. Terminating the Choctaws   206
Epilogue   219
Notes   225
Bibliography   285
Index   311

LIST OF ILLUSTRATIONS

PHOTOGRAPHS

Choctaw Lighthorsemen, 1893   115
Enrollment of citizens of Choctaw Nation, 1899   116
Senate of the last Choctaw Council, ca. 1905   116
Choctaws and Chickasaws registering for government
     allotments of land, ca. 1900   117
Gilbert Webster Thompson family, ca. 1905   118
Susie Thompson, ca. 1915   118
Peter Pitchlynn   119
Gilbert Dukes   119
Green McCurtain   119
Choctaw Council House, Tuskahoma, Oklahoma, 1909   120

MAPS

Indian Territory, 1855   17
Choctaw Nation, 1866   74
Indian Territory, 1889   140
Political Districts of Indian Territory, 1907   172

SERIES EDITOR'S FOREWORD

Begin text

ACKNOWLEDGMENTS

I would like to thank the Tribal Council of the Choctaw Nation for its endorsement of this project. I hope it will be of interest to both the government of the Nation and the approximately 175,000 Choctaws who are currently on the rolls (many of whom are probably too young to read it but who may find it useful in the future). I would like to thank the Newberry Library in Chicago for a ten-month fellowship during the 2003–2004 academic year that allowed me to complete the first draft of the manuscript. My special thanks to Brian Hosmer, director of the D'Arcy McNickle Center for the Study of American Indian History at the Newberry; to Dan Cobb, assistant director of the center during the time of my stay at the Newberry; and Olivia Littles, administrative assistant of the center, for hospitality, generosity, and good humor. Dr. James Grossman, vice president for research, and Sara Austin, assistant director, were also very helpful. John Aubrey, who is legendary among scholars of American Indian history, was unfailingly knowledgeable in pointing me to sources. The group of long-term fellows at the Newberry during my stay provided a congenial atmosphere and lively discussion of a multitude of topics. Thanks also to John Lovett, Josh Clough, and the student assistants in the reading room of the Western History Collections at the University of Oklahoma.

Alessandra Jacobi-Tamulevich guided the manuscript through the review process at the University of Oklahoma Press, and Kate Babbitt did a meticulous job of copyediting. I thank them both.

I appreciate the interest and discussions over the years with Fred Hoxie (who invited me to meet with his graduate seminar at the University of Illinois at Urbana-Champaign) and for his and his students' comments about the issue of Choctaw nationalism. Don Fixico, R. David Edmunds, Patricia Galloway, Ray Fogelson, Michael Green, and Theda Purdue have inspired me over the years with the quality of their scholarship and their interest in my work. Valerie Lambert works on Choctaws from an anthropological perspective, and our exchange of ideas has been fruitful for my work.

Finally, I would like to thank my family—my late parents, to whom this work is dedicated, my sister Mona Hatfield and her husband Bill, and my brother John and his family—for their love and support. My father said when I began this project, "Well, baby. Whatever you do, make it interesting." I hope I have lived up to his expectations. And finally, my gratitude to Betsy, Bob, and Jane, who sat patiently shedding cat hair into the hard drive and occasionally helping with the typing while I labored over the manuscript.

INTRODUCTION

In 1822, a Choctaw leader named Hoolatahomba promulgated a set of written laws for the Six Towns District of the Choctaw Nation in Mississippi. The crimes it listed were stealing cattle, infanticide, importing and using whiskey, neglecting one's crops, and being drunk in public, and the prescribed punishment was public whipping. Hoolatahomba's code is significant because it declared public authority over behaviors that had previously been regulated privately by kin groups.[1] Cyrus Kingsbury, who had established the first mission of the American Board of Commissioners for Foreign Missions in Choctaw territory in 1818, lauded Hoolatahomba's code of laws as a sign of the civilizing effects of Christian missionary activity, but the U.S. government would ultimately come to regret the Choctaws' mastery of the law.[2] To prove that they could live peacefully with their white neighbors and function on an equal basis with the United States and the state of Mississippi, the Choctaw Nation adopted a written constitution in 1826.[3] The Nation established a general council for decision making and asserted its sovereign power of self-government.

The relationship between the Choctaws and the United States was colored also by the fact that the Nation owned a large area of land west of the Mississippi River in fee simple, the form of legal title that prevailed in the United States. By the Treaty of Doaks Stand in 1820 the Choctaws had exchanged much of their land in central Mississippi for lands west of the river and received title in fee simple to them.[4] Choctaw leaders, having been civilized by missionaries, understood the significance of private property, and the U.S. government, having determined to civilize the southeastern Indians, had to treat them as land holders on the same basis as American citizens. The Choctaws' fee simple title to their western lands would complicate their relationship with the U.S. government throughout the twentieth century. They owned their land, albeit collectively, in a way that gave them total control over it. Most did not choose to occupy it, instead opting to remain in their homes in Mississippi.

The U.S. government and white settlers were, however, determined to force the Choctaws out of Mississippi. In 1830, the state legislature extended its laws over the Choctaw Nation, making it a crime for a man to be a chief. Confronted with the conundrum of remaining in their homeland as individuals subject to state law or moving to the western lands to preserve their sovereignty, a small group of Choctaw leaders signed the Treaty of Dancing Rabbit Creek, in which they agreed to move west. As the rabbits danced at the creek, the Choctaw Nation's leaders began a long and complicated engagement with the U.S. government.

In 1832, the chief justice of the U.S. Supreme Court, John Marshall, enunciated a principal that became entrenched in federal Indian law into the twenty-first century. Marshall declared in his decision in the case of *Worcester v. Georgia* that the relationship of tribes to the U.S. government was that of a ward to its guardian. His decision was a product of the fierce debate over states' rights and the power of the federal government in America. It was not so much an affirmation of Indian rights to land as it was a politically motivated decision. Although the legal argument behind Marshall's decision is flawed, it created the unique fiduciary relationship between modern tribes and the U.S. government.[5]

Choctaw politicians quickly learned to use the rhetoric of dependency on the government, but they also demanded justice in the form of fulfillment of their treaty rights. The Choctaw Nation confronted the government as a legal adversary to achieve its own ends. With the assistance of lawyers and lobbyists, it established a presence in Congress and ultimately in the courts of the United States that gave it a political status well beyond that of mere wards. Choctaw delegates in

Washington became adept at playing the three branches of the federal government against each other, appealing to the president, to Congress, and ultimately to the U.S. courts for justice before the law. Their first issue was an appeal for the proceeds of the sale of their eastern lands. The Net Proceeds Case, as it came to be called, would occupy the Nation throughout most of the nineteenth century.

From 1855, when the Choctaw national government appointed a delegation to initiate negotiations for a new treaty that would redefine its relationship with the U.S. government, to 1970, when the federal government acknowledged the right of tribal members to choose their own leaders by popular election, the Choctaw Nation underwent a transition from a tribal society whose cultural values were based on communal land-holding, obligations to kin, oral traditions and language, and traditional food and game, to a political, corporate national entity that in 2001 had a budget of over $300 million dollars; whose tribal leaders traveled regularly to Washington, D.C., to lobby for legislation favorable to the tribe; and whose membership included approximately 128,000 people living in all fifty of the United States.[6] From the painful period of the Civil War in the 1860s through the development of a full-fledged market economy in the form of railroads, the coal-mining industry, and the flood of white entrepreneurs in the 1870s, Choctaw leaders faced the challenge of maintaining control of communal resources in an era of increasing individualism. In the 1880s, they were confronted with and were forced to accede to the federal policy of allotment of their lands as private holdings, the ultimate step to assimilate them into American society. Ultimately, however, the Choctaw Nation has endured.

Throughout the nineteenth and twentieth centuries, through shifts in federal Indian policy and political interpretations of the law, the Choctaws dogged the U.S. government to live up to its obligations to the tribe. From the primacy of treaty rights over federal law in the early nineteenth century to the end of treaty-making in 1871 and in the face of the doctrine of plenary powers—that is, the doctrine that Congress had the power to abrogate treaty provisions at will—the Choctaws pleaded their cases and badgered congressmen to rise to some level of moral behavior with regard to tribal rights.[7]

The Nation's success in asserting its claims against the U.S. government under various treaties led inevitably to a new source of Choctaw identity. Land translated to money, and individual claimants looked to their share of the tribal estate. Money judgments led to per capita payments. The Net Proceeds Case and the Leased District claims reveal both how the traditional value of land as communal property was converted into the value of money and how the value of community was converted to that of self-interest. Choctaws had learned the importance of private property and self-interest from their first contacts with the federal government, and Choctaw lands were distributed under federal policy in the early twentieth century. The sources of Choctaw identity changed, but they did not disappear.

In the early twentieth century, a shadow Choctaw government remained to deal with remnants of communal property, and Choctaw-speaking communities survived in the reaches of the hills and forests of southeastern Oklahoma. But by the 1960s, the tenor of American society was challenging the federal government with issues of anti-war activism and civil rights. For American Indians, the challenge was to assert their treaty rights and political and cultural identities as contemporary nations.

The history of the Choctaws illuminates a key point in contemporary scholarship on the history of American Indians: they were not passive victims of American colonization and they did not assimilate quietly into American society.[8] In this book I argue that Choctaws adapted certain practices in American society to preserve their tribal, then national identity. Rather than maintaining an unchanging stance and intact culture in the face of the pressure for change, they found ways to use the rhetoric of treaty rights to argue their cases and create a particular political identity in the face of a federal policy of assimilation. Europeans brought new ways of understanding the world. They made treaties with Indian tribes in order to exploit land and its resources, but Choctaws learned to use the structures imposed on them by their colonizers—courts and laws—to their own ends. They were indefatigable contestants in Congress and the courts who demanded their rights under treaties. Harvey Rosenthal has noted that "no single tribe was more tenacious in its relentless drive for satisfaction than the Choctaws. From the mid-1830s into the 1880s no Congress was without a bill, a memorial, an internal report, or an executive recommendation whose intent was to meet and resolve a tribal claim rooted in the many treaty infractions."[9]

The contemporary Choctaw Nation has political relationships with both the U.S. government and the state government of Oklahoma. Many of its citizens identify themselves as members by such political acts as voting in elections for national officers. Choctaws have made the transition from a sense of tribal identity in the mid-nineteenth century to a national identity in the latter half of the twentieth century.

For the Choctaws, as for other tribes in the United States, the transition has been marked by contradictory federal policies designed both to assimilate tribal members as individuals into American society and segregate them from contact with the larger society. At the same time, American Indians have had to adapt to the profound political and economic changes taking place in American society. The history of the Choctaws depends on unique circumstances, as each tribe's history is unique, but it illuminates the way in which tribal societies have dealt with federal policy and economic forces in American society.

THE CHOCTAWS IN OKLAHOMA

CHAPTER 1

THE CHOCTAWS IN 1855

In 1830, on the bank of Dancing Rabbit Creek in northwest Mississippi, about 5,000 Choctaws gathered to hear the words of a commission sent by the U.S. government to ask the Choctaws to give up their lands in Mississippi and move west of the Mississippi River. Seven elderly Choctaw women sat in the center of the treaty grounds while the commissioners, John Coffee and John Eaton, presented the government's arguments for removal. If the Choctaws did not give up their lands, the commissioners would sign a treaty with the Choctaws who had moved west after the Treaty of Doaks Stand in 1820, when the Choctaws had first ceded eastern lands for lands west of the Mississippi. If the Choctaws moved west, they would be able to govern themselves without interference from the United States.[1]

The commissioners' proposals confronted tribal members with a profound choice, or perhaps it was a foregone conclusion. They could remain in their homeland in central Mississippi, where they had homes and fields and livestock but where they would have to live as citizens of the state, which had extended its laws over the Choctaws in that year. Or they could give up the homeland and move west of the Mississippi River to new lands where they could maintain their identity as a sovereign nation.

The choice presented in 1830 would compel removal, and it caused deep divisions within the Nation. Many Choctaws, living in their villages and relatively unaffected by the activities of Christian missionaries, were probably unaware of the pressures being exerted on their leaders to give up the homeland. The missionaries of the American Board of Commissioners for Foreign Missions and the Methodist Church, who had worked among the Choctaws since 1818 and 1823, respectively, decried the injustice of the government's action in passing the Indian Removal Act and seeking to expel Indians from their homes east of the Mississippi River. They feared the disruption that removal would bring to their carefully nurtured converts and congregations. Although some Choctaw leaders resisted removal, others realized pragmatically that the government would have its way despite Indian resistance and sought to protect the integrity of the Choctaw Nation as a self-governing entity.[2]

The Treaty of Dancing Rabbit Creek represented the final acquiescence to the government's removal policy. Although the majority of the approximately 5,000 Choctaws who attended the treaty council rejected the federal commissioners' proposals and left the treaty grounds, a small group remained to sign the final document, ceding their remaining eastern lands and agreeing to move to the west. The U.S. government thus acquired the Choctaw lands for the use of American citizens and guaranteed to the Choctaws, in fee simple, title to the western lands they had acquired by the Treaty of Doaks Stand.[3] Fee simple meant that the Choctaws owned their land, albeit communally, on the same basis as American citizens owned property. That title would have significant consequences for future Choctaw claims against the government.

The Choctaws had been adapting to European and American society since their first contacts with French colonists, who established the towns of Biloxi in 1699 and New Orleans in 1701, and English traders based in Charles Town (established in 1670). French Jesuits in the mid-eighteenth century and missionaries of the American Board of Commissioners for Foreign Missions and the Methodist Church in the early nineteenth century had brought Christian teachings to the Nation.[4] Livestock (cattle, horses, and swine) had become a major source of subsistence and economic activity in the Nation. Many Choctaws engaged in an active trade economy during the colonial period and soon learned the meaning of debt, although many others still relied on subsistence hunting. The U.S. government maintained the economy with guarantees of annuities of goods and money in various treaties. The Treaty of Fort Dexter in 1805 was the first in which land cessions were in part driven by trade debts amassed by Choctaw leaders. The Choctaws were succumbing to Thomas Jefferson's plan to drive Indians into debt so that they would "lop off" sections of their lands to sell to pay those debts.[5] As cash replaced barter and debt became a reality, individual interest became a fact of life, challenging traditional values of reciprocity and communal responsibility.

With the removal, the Choctaws had to adapt to a new environment, although the new land bore certain similarities to their eastern lands. Low hills and mountains were interspersed with areas of prairie. Rivers cut the land and defined discrete districts. The South Fork of the Canadian, the Kiamechi, the Blue Water, and the Boggy were major waterways in the territory. The Choctaw territory was defined by the Red River on the south, the Arkansas River and the Canadian Fork to its source on the north and west, and a line along the western boundary of Arkansas. The vagueness of the eastern and western boundaries of the territory would have significant import for the future history of the tribe.

Choctaw families in the territory lived on widely dispersed farms rather than in compact villages, as they had in the east.[6] This dispersion of the population gave a different character to Choctaw life, emphasizing economic self-sufficiency, but the values of hospitality and sharing maintained the sense of community. As Presbyterian missionary John Edwards noted, "They have no system of exchange of visits and calls; but each goes and comes as he chooses. And when one goes to another's house, he does not have to ask for food; but the best they have is set before him. . . . One result of this is that they have no need of poorhouses." Such hospitality, however, "militates very strongly against accumulation of property."[7] The value of sharing distributed resources throughout the community, and those in need could always depend on their neighbors. Sharing is a very Christian value on the one hand, but it conflicted strongly with the flourishing American ideal of capitalism.

The Choctaws brought their traditional tripartite form of government to their western territory. The three districts—Apukshunnubbee, centered on Fort Towson; Mushulatubbee (Skullyville was its capital); and Pushmataha (Boggy Depot)—perpetuated the tradition of those three great leaders who had governed in the East prior to removal. The Choctaws also brought their form of constitutional government, which had originally been adopted in Mississippi in 1826 and revised in 1834. It institutionalized the three districts as separate entities with their own leaders, and it established representation from each of those districts in a national legislature.[8] The constitutional nature of the Choctaws' government was both a sign of civilization to U.S. officials and a measure of their adaptation to the political forces that surrounded them.

American Board missionaries Cyrus Kingsbury and Cyrus Byington followed them west and reestablished mission churches and schools. Kingsbury established his mission at Pine Ridge in the Indian Territory in 1832[9] and Byington established his at Stockbridge in 1835.[10] By 1855, the American Board had missions at Stockbridge, Yazoo Creek, Wheelock, Pine Ridge, Good Water, Good Land, Bennington, Mount Pleasant, and Lenox and outstations at Mt. Zion and Bok Chito.[11]

Many Choctaws by the 1850s lived much as white families did in rural areas in the southeast—in clay-floored log cabins on small farms ranging generally from one to ten acres. With schools, churches, and a government that resembled that of the United States, their society resembled that of their non-Indian neighbors. Men cleared the land and women hoed the crops. Choctaw farmers still employed rainmakers who promised relief when drought threatened.[12] On larger farms in the prairie areas, the fields were often tended by a few slaves. Choctaws in the Kiamichi River basin raised corn and potatoes, sometimes supplemented with pumpkins, peas, melons, and yams, and occasionally tobacco, and along the Red River some Choctaw entrepreneurs, such as Peter Pitchlynn, raised cotton on larger plantations using slave labor. Fields were tilled with iron plows, albeit "one-pony" plows that drew only a shallow furrow.[13] Karl von Möllhausen, who accompanied a railway surveying party across Indian Territory in 1853, observed numbers of Indian cattle roaming in the woods, and Josiah Marcy made similar observations in his travels through the territory.[14] Möllhausen observed "blooming farms, . . . luxuriant crops, and a general prosperity."[15] Cattle were becoming important not only for food but also for sale.

One Choctaw man was reported to have sold $5,000 worth of stock annually.[16] Fences, which were unknown before the introduction of domesticated animals in the late eighteenth century, became a matter regulated by law in the mid-nineteenth century.[17] In some parts of the Choctaw territory, cattle and cotton plantations had virtually replaced agriculture. A passenger on the first Butterfield Overland Mail coach to travel through Indian Territory in October 1858 reported that many of the Choctaws were "quite wealthy, their property consisting chiefly in cattle and negroes," but he did not see much farming. He observed that their treatment of slaves was "generally more lenient than the white slaveholders."1 Hogs, cattle, and poultry provided meat for many families, while those who did not raise livestock still had abundant wild game to hunt. Corn was still the agricultural staple, although the frequent heat and drought conditions in the Indian Territory led to an increasing dependence on wheat.[19] Although subsistence farming was still the major occupation of the majority of Choctaw families, the presence of cotton plantations and cattle herds indicated a growing entrepreneurial spirit in the Nation.

Some Choctaws, mainly mixed-bloods, were not only consumers of trade goods but also suppliers who found markets for their goods both within and outside the Nation. The growth of the market economy within the Nation led to interesting confusions of values. The Christian missions depended on Choctaw suppliers for food. Robert Jones, a Choctaw, sold beef to missionary families in the Mushulatubbee District but was "greatly confused" because they would not buy from him on Sunday. He could not "ascertain how it could be right to buy beef on <u>Saturday</u> wrong on <u>Sunday.</u>"[20]

Choctaw society was becoming increasing diverse, both physically and economically. White traders and settlers had fathered children with Indian women, giving rise to a division between full-bloods and mixed-bloods that was cultural, economic, and political as well as biological. The slave population constituted a third element of Choctaw society, not only in an economic sense but also in a cultural sense because slaves were often important mediators between Choctaws and whites as translators, church members, and laborers.[21] Choctaw men did not farm. That was women's work.

Slaves could replace female labor, although certainly women were not equated with slaves. The presence of slaves indicated not only Choctaw acceptance of aspects of white civilization but also portended the Choctaws' future involvement in one of the negative consequence of their contact with white society, the Civil War.

To white observers, the distinction between full bloods and mixed-bloods was dramatic. John H. B. Latrobe, a man who would play a significant role in later Choctaw history, commented upon the distinction in the east during the time of removal:

> If you can see a nice farm in the Nation you are told that it is the property of a half breed; fine cattle, they are the same. If you hear any name more often than others in the mouths of the people, it is that of a half breed. The Indians of the full blood care for nothing but their personal ease; and are satisfied, so long as they have game in plenty, and can procure those articles with facility, which their intercourse with the whites has made necessary to them.[22]

Mixed bloods were also the primary traders in the Nation, ordering goods from major commercial centers and selling them to their fellow tribesmen.[23] The prominent mixed-blood families—the LeFlores, the Folsoms, the Pitchlynns, the Nails, and others—had come to dominate Choctaw politics in the East, and they continued to do so in the West.[24] In the newly established Choctaw Nation in Indian Territory, there was a growing distinction between the more acculturated class that was accepting Christianity and the trappings of civilization and those who held to the old ways of funerals, ball plays, subsistence hunting and farming, and courtship and marriage. The distinctions between full blood and mixed blood had significant political consequences within the Nation and have continued to have political ramifications throughout Choctaw history.

In 1837, the leaders of the Choctaw Nation agreed to share their lands with the Chickasaw Nation, which would hold joint title.[25] Their reasons for doing so were both cultural and practical. According to one version of their origin tradition, Chata and Chicksa were brothers who, with their followers, were led on a westward migration by a sacred pole that leaned in that direction. At some point in the migration, the brothers and their followers either had a falling out or were separated in a thunderstorm.[26] Historically, the Choctaws and Chickasaws were separate groups that had made their own treaties with the United States.[27] In uniting them, the Treaty of 1837 established a problematic identity for the Chickasaw Nation as a political division within the Choctaw Nation. The Choctaw Nation revised its constitution in 1838 to accommodate the Chickasaws.[28]

The year 1842 was significant because the yearly annuities for education guaranteed in the Treaty of Washington in 1825 expired in 1841. Peter Pitchlynn appealed to President John Tyler to allow the tribal government direct control of its schools.[29] Although Choctaw parents who owned slaves might resent the missionaries' criticism, they valued the education their children received in reading, writing, and arithmetic and they depended on the missionaries as teachers. They did, however, demand control over their schools.

The Nation also revised its constitution once again. The new constitution established a bicameral legislature and a Supreme Court comprised of a national judge and the superior court judges of each district. It was particularly notable for its commitment of $18,000 a year to education. It empowered the General Council to make regulations and appoint officers for "the promotion and advancement of all the schools in the Nation."[30] The leaders of the Nation embraced education wholeheartedly. Reading, writing, and arithmetic in English would be the tools of the rising generation in its dealings with American society.[31]

On November 29, 1842, the General Council adopted a school law, written by Pitchlynn, that established an elaborate system of schools. Spencer Academy, which was located on the military road about nine miles north of Doaksville, became the training ground for future national leaders. Fort Coffee Academy in the Mushulatubbee District and Nanawaiya Academy near the national council house were for male students. Four schools for girls were also established—Koonsha Female Seminary in the Pushmataha District; Chuwala Female Seminary in Apukshunnubbee District; and Wheelock Female Seminary and Ayanubbee Female Seminary near Eagletown in the Mushulatubbee District.[32] The education of females was important because, as Israel Folsom pointed out, "If we have our girls educated, civilized, christianized, enlightened, when they are grown up to become wives & mothers, they will put a stamp in society & character & weight to our nation, & their offsprings will be considered civilized as soon as they are born—O, what advantage."[33] Land for the schools came from the public domain and funds from the annuities provided by the Treaty of Washington. Teachers lived at the schools and received room and board and a salary of $400 per year.

Although the General Council retained direct control of Spencer, which it viewed as the training ground for its future leaders, it contracted with the Methodist Episcopal Church to operate Fort Coffee and Nanawaiya, and the American Board of Commissioners for Foreign Missions operated the four girls' schools, Koonsha, Wheelock, Chuwala, and Ayanubbee. The contracts called for the missionary organizations to pay $1,000 toward the support of each school in addition to providing the staff. Although the General Council retained control of Spencer Academy by appointing a Board of Trustees for the school, it nevertheless sought the help of the American Board of Commissioners for Foreign Missions to find a superintendent for it.[34]

The year 1842 was also noteworthy because President John Tyler finally issued to the Nation the official patent to its lands. Although the patent had been guaranteed in the Treaty of Dancing Rabbit Creek, its formal issuance reinforced the fact that the Choctaw Nation held its land as property on the same terms as American citizens held title to their lands.[35]

Despite the Nation's apparent advances in civilization, however, Choctaw cultural identity was still largely intact in two of its most important indicators, language and kinship systems. Christian missionaries in Mississippi had confronted the problems of trying to translate Christian concepts into the Choctaw language. Cyrus Byington and Loring Williams had learned the language and translated the New Testament into Choctaw and produced textbooks in Choctaw for mission schools, and in so doing they tried to introduce changes in values and gave the Choctaws access to literacy in their own language, which reinforced its persistence. Although a number of Choctaws were "men of good, practical, English educations"36 throughout the first half of the nineteenth century, Choctaw was the language of everyday life, and, in a longer view, the Choctaw legislature continued to do business in Choctaw and English and to publish digests of its laws in both languages.[37] Two newspapers appeared in the Nation, the *Choctaw Telegraph* in 1848–1849, and the *Choctaw Intelligencer* in 1850–1852.[38]

Social and kinship relations were beginning to change. The Choctaws were a matrilineal society, tracing kinship through the female line in a moiety system, the two parts of which were called *iksas*. A person was either an *in hulatah* (younger brother) or an *imoklasha* (elder brother). Reciprocal relationships between family groups were dictated by the *iksa* rule of exogamous marriage. That rule had been repealed, however, by the Choctaw legislature in 1836.[39]

Men hunted and women farmed. As white men married into Choctaw society during the nineteenth century, they were accepted into Choctaw society as the husbands of their wives. Since they brought new resources—trade goods and intercourse with white society—their presence began to impact social and cultural values. The Nation institutionalized intermarriage in its laws by giving white men married to Indian women the privileges of citizenship.[40]

Gender roles had begun to change under Christian influence. John Edwards noted the traditional way in the Choctaw family: "If they have but one horse, the man rides; the woman walks and carries the child or bundle." If, however, the woman rode while the man walked, "we then take it for granted at once that they have received the gospel."[41] Even though Christianity had begun to change social values, women were still the main carriers of the culture, and despite Choctaw laws governing marriage, the matrilineal system persisted. Choctaw mothers were still the predominant influence on their children.

Most Choctaws still retained distinctive customs. Some remembered an origin tradition about a great flood that destroyed the whole nation except for a few families. The flood story had certain Christian overtones: "There reigned, 'they say,' an impenetrable darkness over the whole world and the wise medicine men tried all kinds of methods to overcome this gloom, and looked long for returning daylight." Another tradition was a story about the craw-fish people who lived in a cave but were finally smoked out and convinced to become part of the tribe.4 Moral concepts of reward and punishment appeared in the story of the slippery log over which the deceased had to pass. If the person had led a good life, he or she would cross the log to a land of fat deer and abundant crops. If not, the person would slip into the river below, which contained rotten fish, and the land on the other side was barren and the deer thin.[43]

Funerals were one of the most telling signs of both change and persistence in the Choctaw Nation. The practice of exposing the body of the dead on a scaffold to decay had been largely abandoned by the early 1800s, to be replaced by burial and the erection of poles around the grave where monthly "wailes" were held, but by the mid-nineteenth century, even the practice of setting up poles had been abandoned.[44] The funeral ceremony had previously been an occasion for "mirth and revelry, drinking and dancing" but it was becoming more an occasion for preaching. It was still a custom, how-ever, that personal property was buried with the deceased. Although the practice was diminishing as material property became more abundant, it still persisted. Edwards reported that "it is less than 20 years since a woman of wealth died, and her wardrobe, pony, some furniture and food, her watch, her portrait, and various articles of value, including $300 in money, were buried with her." Offerings of food and personal clothing were still placed in graves. Although cemeteries were coming into use, most burials were still made near the home of the deceased.[45]

Ball games remained an essential and distinctive part of Choctaw culture, and Möllhausen's 1853 description of a game—the center pole and goal post, the singing of the women to encourage their men, and the incantations of the medicine men who invoked spiri-tual power for their team—was very similar to what George Catlin had recorded in 1838.[46]

Although the American ideal of civilization—Christianity, for-mal education and government, and the English language—had been woven into the fabric of Choctaw life, the cultural identity remained strong. According to one observer, the Choctaws had "amalgamated less with whites than any other tribes who have lived so long on reserved lands." The observer added that "having witnessed so little in the white people to impress them favorably, they were resolute in their purpose to maintain lives of wild, exciting, and unfettered independence."[47]

Changes in Choctaw society were apparent primarily in the extent to which laws began to supplant custom and formal education influenced children. By the early years of the 1850s, punishment for murder was administered by courts rather than through the old system of private revenge by family members, although isolated incidents of revenge killing still occurred.[48] The General Council of the Nation legislated inheritance, decreeing that a man's property should go to his wife and children instead of being distributed by the family as was customary.[49] Marriage, traditionally an affair that was formalized between families, was now regulated by law, especially with regard to intermarriage, and marriage ceremonies had to be performed by a judge or a Christian minister. Polygamy was prohibited. The custom by which men avoided any contact with their mothers-in-law had been undermined among the Sixtowns people at the insistence of the chief of the southern district and the audacity of a young man who was inspired to rush up to his mother-in-law in public, uncover her head, and seize her hand.[50]

In lifestyle and appearance, many Choctaws of the mid-nineteenth century were virtually indistinguishable from white Americans settling in new lands, but some "old-fashioned of the men" wore buckskin leggings and some men still wore moccasins, although most wore pantaloons and shoes. Long sashes ornamented with beadwork were popular. Shirts were worn with "capes" ornamented with braid or fringe, generally in bright shades of pink or red. Men frequently wore their hair long, but some older men cut their hair close to the head, leaving a single strip over the top of the head. Feathers were used as an adornment, although Edwards noted that "it is now, however, a sign of a rowdy to wear them, and Christians avoid them." Face paint and feathers were also considered signs of "rowdyism." Women wore long dresses "after the manner of white ladies" and scarves on their heads and generally went barefoot or wore moccasins. Older people often had zigzag lines tattooed on their faces, although the custom was no longer practiced by younger people.[51]

The stable homes and subsistence agriculture in the Choctaw Nation promoted generally good health, but Choctaws suffered from the kind of diseases that afflicted Americans generally—trachoma (a disease of the eyes), scrofula (a form of glandular tuberculosis), tuberculosis, malaria, and gastrointestinal conditions. A number of herbal medicines were used for minor ills—boneset, burnweed, blackroot, and Mayapple, among others. Some remedies were obviously of European origin, notably the use of rusty water in which iron chains had been soaked as a kind of tonic.[52] Medical practices to alleviate pain and physical distress included cauterizing, sweat bathing, massage, and bloodletting by cupping. Belief in witchcraft as a source of illness was still prevalent, and the "witchball" that had been injected by a witch had to be removed by a man who learned the skill from the *kowi-anu'k asha* (something in the woods). The fear of witches led to the killing of individuals suspected of being witches, a practice that was finally prohibited by law, although Edwards reported an occasion of the killing of a woman suspected of witchcraft in the winter of 1857–1858.[53]

At the same time, however, Choctaws were also espousing Christianity. Church membership grew and the number of churches increased. In 1854–1855, 236 new members were accepted in the churches of the American Board of Commissioners for Foreign Missions.[54] In 1857, the Board reported 1,222 members in its churches.[55] By 1860, there were fourteen ministers and sixteen churches.[56] By 1859, Cyrus Kingsbury could declare that the Choctaw Nation was a Christian one. Council meetings were opened and closed with prayer, and no one who did not espouse a belief in a supreme being could hold office.[57] The Nation's schools operated under contract with missionary societies. If many Choctaws were becoming virtually indistinguishable from Americans, they still enjoyed the distinctive status of a sovereign Indian Nation with ties to the federal government through treaties.

CHAPTER 2

THE TREATY OF 1855

In 1855, the Choctaws signed a treaty that fundamentally reoriented the Nation's relationship with the U.S. government. As Peter Pitchlynn, the main architect of the treaty, envisioned it, the treaty would "reduce into one simple code, easily understood and administered, all the crude, inharmonious, and in some cases inconsistent stipulations of our various existing treaties."[1] The treaty was the result of the ongoing efforts of the Choctaw Nation to recover the proceeds of the sale of its eastern lands to the U.S. government in 1830, the Net Proceeds Case. The case hinged on the interpretation of one sentence in the eighteenth article: "And for the payment of the several amounts secured in this Treaty, the lands hereby ceded are to remain a fund pledged to that purpose, until the debt shall be provided for and arranged."[2] But what were the amounts and how were they to be paid? The treaty itself was not clear, and its ambiguity was specifically acknowledged in the last line of the eighteenth article of the Treaty of Dancing Rabbit Creek: "In the construction of this Treaty wherever well founded doubt shall arise, it shall be construed most favorably towards the Choctaws."

Pitchlynn's strategy in pursuing a new treaty was to consolidate all the Nation's annuity payments from previous treaties and the Net Proceeds claims against the government into one monetary judgment that would be paid to and then controlled by the Nation. He also envisioned not just payment for unfilled treaty obligations but a whole reorientation of the relationship between the Choctaw Nation and the federal government. If the Choctaw government took over the responsibility for administering individual claims established under the Treaty of Dancing Rabbit Creek, it would strengthen its political position vis-à-vis both the federal government and its own citizens and provide greater autonomy to the Choctaw Nation. By challenging the federal government's will and/or ability to carry out its treaty obligations, Pitchlynn hoped to present the Choctaw government as the responsible party. He was to be a major political force in the Choctaw nation.[3]

The Net Proceeds claim stemmed from the choice that faced individual Choctaws in 1830—to keep their lands and homes in Mississippi by living as citizens of the state or move west as citizens of a sovereign nation. The choice appeared in the fourteenth article of the Treaty of Dancing Rabbit Creek. Choctaws who wished to keep their lands could take them as individual allotments of 640 acres and remain as citizens of the state of Mississippi.[4] This provision, an attempt to convince Choctaw leaders that their followers had a choice, encapsulates the much larger and more significant choices that American Indian nations faced in the early national period in America. The futility of either choice for the Choctaws emerged in the subsequent history of the Net Proceeds Case.[5]

The efforts of many Choctaws to register for individual claims were thwarted by the federal Indian agent for the tribe, William Ward. Ward was instructed to register fourteenth article claimants, but his instructions reached him only two months before the deadline for registration set out in the treaty.[6] Of those who made application for allotments, Ward sent the war department the names of only sixty-nine heads of families, of whom fifteen were white men with Choctaw wives and twenty-four were half-bloods. Ward rejected, destroyed, or lost a large number of applications, telling the Choctaws to emigrate instead. Ward himself later testified that when upward of 200 persons from one section of the country applied for registration, he refused to register their claims, saying that they were incited to the action by designing men who were opposed to the treaty.[7] In short, many people who should have gotten individual allotments failed to do so, and after two government commission investigations and a series of legislative actions, their claims were converted into the cash payment of

Indian Territory in 1855. (Adapted from Charles Robert Goins and Danney Goble, *Historical Atlas of Oklahoma*, 4th ed. [Norman: University of Oklahoma Press, 2006].)

$872,000 that the Nation received in 1852, ostensibly as a final settlement of all the Choctaw claims against the government.

In 1833, George Martin was appointed special agent to locate and record the allotments claimed by Choctaws, but initially he could not get the government plat maps for the ceded lands. When he finally did and traveled through the countryside to mark the claims, he heard many complaints from individuals who had tried unsuccessfully to register. He submitted a report listing their names, but the government put the Choctaws' ceded lands up for public sale beginning in October of 1833 without investigating Martin's reports.[8] Several Choctaws protested the sale and rejected the proposal that they be given money instead of the lands that had been promised to them.[9] The complaints finally led Congress to appoint a commission in 1837 to investigate the situation.[10]

Almost all the claimants before the commission were represented by lawyers who had signed contingency contracts giving them half of the land they could win for their clients. The situation cast a cloud of suspicion over the claims. Since land speculation was rampant in the state of Mississippi, it appeared that the Choctaws were pawns of speculators.[11] The commission was presented with a total of 1,426 claims.[12] As it held hearings from 1837 to 1845, Congress passed a series of laws that effectively dispossessed most of the applicants. The act that extended the life of the commission in 1838 excluded claims by any Choctaws who had moved west. Congress also acknowledged existing Choctaw claims but allowed white preemption claims to supersede them.[13] In 1842, it imposed an elaborate set of conditions on the claims that went far beyond the language of the treaty. In addition to proving that they had signified intent to remain in Mississippi, claimants had to own an improvement and have lived on it for five years. White men with Indian families were ineligible to claim land, although a number of them had appeared on Ward's original registers. In cases where claimants' land had been sold by the government, they would receive scrip (certificates for public lands in Mississippi, Louisiana, Alabama, and Arkansas), but they would receive only half while they remained in Mississippi and the other half when they had moved west. It was clear that the federal government and state citizens wanted the Choctaws out of Mississippi.[14]

Scrip had little value to Choctaws who had no knowledge of land law, little ability to move freely to find new lands, or the capital to develop new farms. Its only value was that it could be sold to speculators. The lives of individual Choctaw families were thus subsumed in the larger financial issues of a money economy they did not understand. Moreover, if they did understand, they could collect only half the scrip in Mississippi; they had to go to Indian Territory to collect the other half. In November 1852, Thompson McKenney and Forbis LeFlore negotiated the final settlement of fourteenth article claims and received a payment of 5 percent of the settlement.[15] The Choctaw General Council passed an act accepting the payment as "a final release of the claims of such parties under the fourteenth article of said treaty."[16] The act, however, was not the final settlement of the tribe's claims in Mississippi; it was only the beginning of the protracted legal and political struggle that was the Net Proceeds Case. The case and the Treaty of 1855 demonstrate how the value of Choctaw land was being converted into money.

The major provisions of the Treaty of 1855 granted rights of way to railroads, leased land to the government for the settlement of the Wichita Indians and related tribes, and gave the Chickasaws political autonomy by creating a separate district for them. Although the first railroad did not arrive in Choctaw territory until 1870, the Treaty of 1855 provided the opening wedge. Although the lease was initially only that, it would ultimately turn into a cession, and although the Chickasaws gained self-government, the land continued to be communally held by the Choctaws and Chickasaws together, a situation that continued to complicate the relationship of the two tribes.

The Treaty of 1855 was negotiated against the national backdrop of the Kansas-Nebraska Act, which opened the Central Plains to white settlement by extinguishing Indian land claims; the increasingly acrimonious debate over slavery, which would ultimately draw the Choctaws and Chickasaws into the Civil War; and the expansionist economic ambitions of men who desired an intercontinental railroad to link eastern and western American ports to those of Asia and Europe. The treaty, then, involved the Choctaws in the affairs of the American nation even as they asserted their own political rights.

The Chickasaws, who had bought the right to settle in the Choctaw Nation in 1837 for $530,000, were increasingly dissatisfied with their political representation in the Choctaw government. When they first arrived in the Nation they were given the political status of a district in the far western part of the territory, but because Comanches, Kiowas, and Apaches regularly used that area, many Chickasaws settled in the Choctaw districts, where they had little political power. As a nation of about 6,000 people, they were also a minority among the more numerous (about 12,000) Choctaws. In 1854, the Chickasaws insisted on a survey to establish the physical boundaries of their district, although it remained clear that the Choctaws adamantly refused to cede any of their territory to the Chickasaws.[17] The Chickasaws, meanwhile, did their own lobbying in Congress and went so far as to threaten war if they did not get their political autonomy.[18] Chickasaw nationalism was running rampant in Choctaw territory. For its part, the federal government could settle the problematic claim that the Choctaws still maintained to lands beyond the 100th meridian, the western part of Choctaw and Chickasaw territory could become a home for Texas Indians, the Chickasaws could achieve their independence, and, most important from Peter Pitchlynn's point of view, the Choctaws could assert their claims to the money from the sale of their southeastern lands.

In 1853, after a protracted series of protests and investigations, the General Council accepted a payment from the federal government of $872,000 to settle claims of individual Choctaws to lands in Mississippi. On November 9, 1853, the Choctaw council appointed Peter P. Pitchlynn, Israel Folsom, Dixon W. Lewis, and Samuel Garland as delegates "fully empowered to represent and to institute . . . a claim upon the United States" for the lands east of the Mississippi. They were charged to "protect and defend all and every right and interest of the Choctaws, arising under treaty stipulations or otherwise." The delegates were "clothed with full power to settle and dispose of by treaty, or otherwise, all and every claim and interest of the Choctaw people against the Government of the United States, and to adjust and bring to a final close all unsettled business of the Choctaw people with the said Government of the United States."19 The act gave the delegates a contingency fee of 20 percent of the proceeds they were able to collect.[20]

The Choctaw delegation was, in effect, a fourth branch of the Choctaw government, an autonomous body with wide-ranging powers to negotiate complex agreements with representatives of the U.S. government. Its actions were, of course, subject to approval by the General Council, but it operated at a distance from the Nation and with significant independence. It was the voice through which the Choctaw Nation presented its issues to the federal government. By their persistent presence in Washington and their voluminous correspondence (particularly Pitchlynn's) with congressmen, the president, and various government officials, the Choctaw delegates maintained the strong identity of the Choctaw Nation as a sovereign nation meeting the U.S. government on its own terms. It is unlikely that Pitchlynn and his fellow delegates, as they set out for Washington, could have foreseen the duration of their task in bringing the Net Proceeds Case to a close. Indeed, its membership changed over time and came in several instances to be viewed with suspicion by the General Council, particularly when the collection and distribution of funds from the federal government were at issue in the 1870s. Autonomy and distance had their price.

The Choctaw delegation proceeded to Washington in the winter of 1853–1854. Pitchlynn and Garland sought advice from two well-placed men in Washington, John T. Cochrane, a lawyer, and Robert W. Johnson, a U.S. senator from Arkansas, about how to proceed. Both advised them to seek out some man of influence to assist them with treaty negotiations. The man they found was Albert Pike, an attorney from Arkansas, a minor poet, and a man already acquainted with Indian claims through his work on behalf of the Creek Nation.[21] If the Choctaws gained a reputation for both political acumen and litigiousness, it began with these negotiations. Pike agreed to take the Choctaw claim for a contingency fee of 25 percent, and he in turn enlisted other influential men, notably Douglas H. Cooper, the U.S. Indian agent for the Choctaw and Chickasaw tribes, who had accompanied the Choctaw delegation to Washington. He also engaged John T. Cochrane and Luke Lea, former commissioner of Indian affairs and then Chickasaw national attorney. Pike agreed to rebate 5 percent of the 25 percent fee to Pitchlynn, Cooper, Cochrane, and Lea, thus splitting his fee five ways to create his legal team.[22] Pike, however, left Washington in 1854 and appeared to have abandoned the claim. The delegates then drew up a new contract with John Cochrane, this time for a 30 percent contingency fee. Cochrane agreed "to manage and prosecute the claims of said Nation and individuals thereof against the United States" and to rebate half of his contingency fee back to the Choctaw delegates. The Choctaw national council approved a payment of $100,000 as an advance on Cochrane's fee, and Cochrane paid the delegates their shares. Pitchlynn received one-sixth, and Luke Lea and Douglas Cooper also received shares.[23] Pike was not mentioned in this new contract, although Cochrane led him to believe that it simply substituted names from the existing agreement.[24] The preliminary meetings between Pitchlynn and Pike, however, planted seeds of suspicion regarding the Net Proceeds Case that would become full blown in the minds of the Choctaw Council and members of the U.S. Congress as the case progressed after the Civil War. Was Pitchlynn acting out of self-interest rather than that of the Nation? The issue would emerge again with Pike's claims against the Nation for legal fees.

The agreement with Cochrane established the basis of operations of the Choctaw delegation throughout its tenure in Washington. The original appointment by the national council had given the delegates a contingency fee of 20 percent of what they could recover. Contingency fees were necessary because the delegation received no direct funding from the Choctaw government. Delegates essentially gave up significant amounts of their own funds and spent much time away from home to engage in long drawn-out efforts to win justice and payments from a government whose vagaries of politics made the outcome of claims cases very uncertain. Contingency fees were the usual practice for lawyers who paid their own expenses in researching and representing cases. Pike's decision to subcontract with other influential men by splitting his fee among them enhanced his chances of getting a favorable judgment, but the split was a sub rosa agreement that ultimately weakened the case its makers were putting forth.

Pitchlynn chose to lay the Choctaw case directly before President Franklin Pierce for immediate action in February 1854 rather than face an unsympathetic Congress, first in a letter and then in a public address reported in the *Washington Union*. Pitchlynn's rhetoric was masterful. He called on the federal government to fulfill its obligations so that the Choctaws could indeed become civilized:

> Our progress is too slow, and we are almost disheartened; but, let our affairs with the government be properly and kindly adjusted—let only simple justice be done to us . . . and we believe a new and brighter day will soon dawn upon us; that the dark clouds which have so long obscured our future will pass away, and the sunlight of hope will gladden our hearts, exciting and encouraging us to renewed efforts and still nobler aims."[25]

But he also used more pointed language with regard to the obligation of the federal government to the Choctaws. He suggested that a new treaty was necessary as a matter of right and justice in order to settle the claims of the Choctaw since the records concerning the sale of land and the circumstances of individual claims were inadequate to make a fair determination. He chided Pierce for referring the Choctaws' claims to Congress. He cited Choctaw claims "for a redress of grievances, arising out of the non-fulfillment of treaty stipulations" and declared that the president, as the executive branch of the federal government, could not put aside the Choctaw claims "without a manifest disregard of its just obligations." He declared that it was the president's obligation to carry out the laws "promptly, justly, and, in the case of a feeble Indian tribe, magnanimously," and he called for a new treaty. Amid his rhetoric of achieving the government's objectives to enlighten and civilize Indians, he also suggested that it was impossible to investigate anew every fourteenth article claim. As an alternative, he suggested that the U.S. Senate allow a gross sum as final settlement of all claims.[26]

The Choctaw delegates next directed a letter to Commissioner of Indian Affairs George Manypenny, who then referred it to Secretary of the Interior George McClelland, who rejected any notion of revisiting Indian treaties but was anxious to quiet the Choctaw claims. McClelland authorized Manypenny to proceed with determining what it would take to settle the claims, and Manypenny, in turn, although he was aware of Cooper's financial interest in the legal contract the

Choctaw delegation had with John Cochrane, instructed him to confer with the delegation, which he had accompanied to Washington at the tribe's request.[27]

Cooper's estimate of the net proceeds, based on the records of the Department of the Interior, was an amazing $2,380,701. Obviously surprised by the size of the potential payment, the secretary of the interior suggested that the commissioner of Indian affairs refer the matter of unpaid annuities to Congress for an appropriation.[28]

There were many reasons for the government to wish to settle Indian claims. It was trying to redraw the boundaries of Indian Territory in order to clear the way for white settlement and the development of railroads. As the admission of Texas to the Union in 1845, the subsequent war with Mexico, and the signing of the Treaty of Guadalupe Hidalgo in 1848 opened the Southwest and California to exploration and settlement, the prospects of a rail line linking the eastern railroads with the West Coast became increasingly important politically. The idea of an intercontinental line appeared in its most grandiose form in a pamphlet published by Asa Whitney in 1849. As Whitney envisioned it, the line would do more than link the coasts of America; it would make America a bridge across which the wealth of the Orient could travel to the East Coast and the goods of Europe to the West Coast. For him, the railroad was the key to America's economic domination of the entire world.[29] The organization of the Territory of New Mexico in 1850 gave the South an advantage by creating the possibility of a southern route for the railroad.[30] In an ironic twist of fate, however, Indian tribes relegated to the hinterlands west of the Mississippi to clear the way for colonization of the eastern United States now stood athwart the passage to the West, and their rights to their lands, guaranteed by treaties with the U.S. government and by the Indian Removal Act of 1830, blocked the way of a transcontinental railroad.

As the wealth of the West beckoned with the discovery of gold in California, Congress in 1853 authorized the exploration of possible routes for a transcontinental railroad.[31] Amiel Weeks Whipple was sent to explore the 35th parallel, a route that took him through the Choctaw Nation.[32] The building of new rail lines across the Plains would, however, necessitate the admission of the western territories as new states if the builders were to have the necessary governmental support and protection for their efforts, and the admission of new states raised two major political issues: the status of slavery in those states and the status of the Indian tribes whose treaties guaranteed them undisturbed possession of their lands. The political compromises of 1820 and 1850 had attempted to deal with the issue of slavery, intensifying the conflict between North and South. The debate over rail lines contributed to the conflict since the presence of a transcontinental line would bring economic benefit to the section of the country in which it was built.

The economic welfare of California and Oregon also depended on the development of settlement on the Plains. But what of the rights of the Plains tribes? Their possession of the land blocked white settlement, but as Congressman Hall queried, "In the name of God, how is the railroad to be made if you will never let people live on the lands through which the road passes?" (His question ignored the fact that Indians are people.)[33] The solution to the problem was to extinguish Indian title to their lands, and the Indian appropriation bill passed on March 3, 1853, authorized the president to negotiate with tribes west of the states of Missouri and Iowa for that purpose.[34]

The hostilities between Texans and Indians were intense and ongoing, and Texans called for the removal of Indians from their territories. The formation of Kansas Territory went on despite the existence of significant Indian reservations in the eastern part of the state, and federal commissioners scrambled to negotiate new treaties by which Indians would cede their lands and move to Indian Territory.[35]

Apart from Pitchlynn's rhetoric of justice, the Choctaws brought to the bargaining table two important political chips. One was the land west of the 98th meridian and the other was the Chickasaw problem. In order to open the Kansas and Nebraska territories, the federal government had to find permanent settlements for Plains Indian tribes in order to clear the way for railroads and white settlement. The U.S. government and the Choctaws both were also anxious to deal with the Wichitas, who had been a consistent thorn in the side of the Choctaws and Chickasaws as raiders into the nations' territories. Indeed, Pitchlynn had suggested to Cooper that the arid western lands beyond the 98th meridian could be used for the settlement of the Wichitas. The

Chickasaws had never settled in those lands because of Wichita incursions and, indeed, the area was of virtually no use to either Choctaws or Chickasaws because of incursions by various tribes—Wichitas, Kiowas, Comanches and Apaches. Characterizing the "Witchitaw and other bands of Indians" as "a nuisance" and declaring that "we had far rather be rid of them altogether," Pitchlynn nevertheless suggested that the Nation would "consent to [leasing the land] on fair and reasonable terms, if it can be made a part of a just and equitable adjustment of all the matters involved in the existing controversy between the Choctaws and the government."[36]

When the total amount of the possible net proceeds amount hit the negotiating table and was rejected, the Choctaw delegates put this bargaining chip on the table.[37] In the early 1850s, the whole sweep of the Central Plains, from the Dakotas to the Red River, was still Indian Territory, but the doctrine of manifest destiny and the burgeoning U.S. population threatened its integrity. The government adopted a policy of consolidating Indians into the area between the 37th parallel and the Red River as part of its strategy to develop the Kansas and Nebraska territories and clear a path for the development of an intercontinental railway system. Not only was the Indian Territory the logical place for Indians but it also offered an attractive economic opportunity for the Choctaws. Agent Cooper proposed to the Choctaw delegates that the negotiation of the new treaty would "open a rich field for the Choctaws, with their extensive territory, for realizing large profits from their wild lands, without parting with the ownership and sovereignty over an acre of it. . . . Your treasury would overflow from the tribute, paid individually, by these tribes for the privilege of living on your land."[38]

They put a second chip on the table when they suggested their willingness to settle their differences with the Chickasaws over governance in order to negotiate a lease of the western lands for the settlement of the Wichitas.[39] They intimated that they would agree to a separate boundary and political autonomy for the Chickasaws. Although they protested to Cooper that they did not consider a settlement of their claims in regard to the Treaty of Dancing Rabbit Creek a condition for settling their dispute with the Chickasaws and providing land for the Wichitas, it seems obvious that they were linking the issues in a way that would make it difficult to separate them entirely.[40] Although Manypenny balked at the $800,000 demanded by the Choctaws and Chickasaws for the lease and at their demand that no tribes be moved from north of the North Fork of the Canadian River, he finally conceded these points.

Secretary of the Interior George McClelland was adamantly opposed to reopening the issue of the fourteenth and nineteenth article claims, but he was nevertheless aware that the larger issues of finding land for Indians displaced from the new territories of Kansas and Nebraska and from Texas depended on the Choctaws.[41] Pitchlynn stated as much to Acting Commissioner of Indian Affairs Charles Mix: "If the Choctaws refuse accommodation for their Indians, it is not likely it can be had from the other tribes."[42]

Using the political leverage of their land claims and the secretary of the interior's urgent desire to avoid the open warfare the Chickasaws threatened against the Choctaws over their demand for their own government, the Choctaw delegation got the attention of the U.S. government.[43] During the spring of 1855, the Choctaws adamantly refused to cede land to the Chickasaws but agreed to their political autonomy in return for a payment of $150,000. The Chickasaws had their own political leverage against the Choctaws because without a guarantee of political autonomy, they would not agree to the cession of the lands beyond the 100th meridian and the lease of the lands between the 98th and 100th meridian. The monetary value of the lease, $200,000 to the Chickasaws and $600,000 to the Choctaws, would remain a point of contention in future dealings between the Choctaws and the U.S. government. The Choctaws also agreed to sell their claims to the lands beyond the 100th meridian that were included in their original land grant in 1820 but that were truncated by the sale of those lands to Spain in 1821. The treaty was signed on June 22, 1855.[44]

The delegates hurried home to assure its ratification by the Choctaw legislature, but instead they found strong opposition. Cochrane attributed the opposition to certain headmen who acted from "selfish motives."[45] The Treaty of 1855 created a new basis for the political identity of the Choctaw Nation, a troubling prospect for many. The new status of the Chickasaws deprived the Choctaw Nation of political control over a significant part of its territory.[46] The subsequent reorganization of the Choctaw Nation raised significant issues of political power, legal jurisdiction over non-Indians, and the role of slavery in the Nation. The delegates had not won a final settlement of the Net Proceeds Case. They could only agree that the question, "together with the whole subject-matter of their unsettled claims . . .shall be referred to the Senate of the United States for final adjudication and adjustment."[47] The case would drag on until 1886.[48] The Choctaws gave up their rights to lands west of the 100th meridian (which had effectively been relinquished for them in a U.S. treaty with Spain in 1821) and leased the western lands to accommodate the government's policy of settling "wild" Indians.

Other articles of the treaty reaffirmed general principles of interaction between the Choctaws and the government. The fourteenth article affirmed that the United States would protect the nations from domestic strife and hostile invasion.[49] It confirmed earlier treaties that established the general principal that Indian criminals were to be prosecuted in tribal courts and white criminals were to be turned over to U.S. forces for prosecution. This provision was consistent with the Indian Trade and Intercourse acts, but it was to be a crucial element in debate over the status of the Nation and its jurisdiction over non-Indians in Indian Territory after the Civil War.[50]

The eighteenth article gave railroads virtually unlimited rights of way across the Choctaw Territory. Politically astute enough to recognize the significance that white men gave to railroads, the Choctaw delegates probably saw this article as a trade off for other things that they desired. Being businessmen, Pitchlynn (a plantation owner who raised cotton) and Samuel Garland (who had a mercantile business in Columbus, Mississippi) realized the potential economic benefit of the railroad to the territory.[51] At the same time, they sought to regulate the activities of non-Indians in the territory. The seventeenth article allowed military roads, railroads, and agencies into the Choctaw and Chickasaw territory, but it limited the amount of land and timber that could be used for these enterprises and it limited farming and stock-raising to people who were subject to the laws of the Nation.[52]

The treaty also raised an important new issue for the Nation, the eastern boundary claim, based on the Nation's eastern boundary with Arkansas Territory. The line had been run in 1824 to define a cession of Choctaw lands that had been guaranteed by the Treaty of Doaks Stand in 1820 but upon which whites had settled.[53] Over time, however, the original boundary markers had largely disappeared, leaving the Nation "liable to disputes" with its Arkansas neighbors. The subsequent establishment of the Chickasaw District (1837) and its separation (1854) required that the boundary between the Choctaws and Chickasaws be clearly defined.[54] It was also time to mark the western boundary, which had been defined as the 100th meridian but which needed to be in a "proper and durable manner." Based on the 1830 treaty, the admission of Arkansas Territory as a state in 1836, the formal Choctaw patent to its lands in 1842, and the Treaty of 1855, the boundaries of the Nation needed to be redrawn.[55]

The survey of Choctaw boundaries was finally begun in 1858. To keep the process honest, U.S. government surveyors A. H. Jones and H. M. C. Brown were accompanied by commissioners from the state of Arkansas and the Choctaw Nation to assure agreement on the starting point. That point was finally determined to be a line beginning 100 paces from Fort Smith, proceeding to where it crossed the Arkansas River.[56] When the survey was complete, Jones and Brown reported to the commissioner of Indian affairs that the line drawn from that point put approximately 161,000 acres of Choctaw land into the state of Arkansas. The secretary of the interior, however, instructed the surveyors simply to retrace the 1824 line. The secretary's directive caused "great dissatisfaction" among the Choctaws,[57] and the Choctaw delegation had another claim for lost lands.[58]

The Treaty of 1855 looked back to the rights guaranteed to the Choctaw Nation by the treaties of Doaks Stand and Dancing Rabbit Creek and forward to new economic opportunities in the form of railroads. In opening the Nation to railroads and in leasing land for the settlement of western tribes, the treaty represented a new emphasis on monetary gain. It embodied new ways of viewing communal values and self-interest. In doing so, it set the Choctaw Nation on a new path toward self-determination.

CHAPTER 3

"EMBARRASSMENTS AND PERPLEXITIES"
THE CHURCH, THE NATION, AND SLAVERY

On December 28, 1858, Richard Harkins, brother of George Harkins, was ostensibly drowned trying to ford the Little River, about ten miles from the Stockbridge missionary station. There was suspicion, however, that he had actually been murdered by one of his slaves, a man named Prince. Confronted with the crime, Prince in turn accused a slave named Lucy of instigating the murder. The two were seized and tortured until Prince led his accusers to the place where Harkins's body was submerged, tied to a large rock. He then escaped his captors, threw himself into the river, and drowned. Lucy, who consistently protested her innocence, was seized by a "lawless mob" and burned alive in the presence of her mistress, Richard Harkins's widow, Lavinia. Crucial to the situation was the fact that both mistress and slave were members of the Stockbridge Mission church and that Mrs. Harkins, although she was present at the burning and probably instigated it, upon examination and her explanation of the matter, was continued in good standing in the church.[1]

The incident raises important questions about the changing nature of Choctaw society in the mid-nineteenth century. How did the incident reflect the cultural values and political identity of the Choctaw Nation, which Cyrus Kingsbury had confidently characterized as Christian in 1859?[2] What did it say about the significance of Christian missionary activity in the Choctaw Nation? Did the missionaries' continued acceptance of Mrs. Harkins as a Christian condone the institution of slavery?

Slavery was firmly entrenched in the Choctaw Nation and was regulated by legislation. The missions of the American Board of Commissioners were also firmly established, and missionaries operated schools for the Nation. But Christian idealism clashed dramatically with the practice of slavery, and the relationship between the Choctaw Nation and the American Board foundered. The General Council assumed control over its schools amid internal political struggles, and the Choctaws took another step in the development of their Nation.

The incident of Lucy's death confronted the missionaries with a moral dilemma. Lavinia Harkins was Peter Pitchlynn's daughter, and George Harkins, Richard's brother, was a district headman. In the eyes of the U.S. government and the missionaries, they were acculturated Christians who represented the achievement of American policy, but they were also politically powerful slave owners, and the American Board missionaries depended upon them to sanction their efforts. The missionaries confronted the reality that coming to terms with slavery was a part of the process of civilizing Indians. Although the missionaries taught the Christian value of agricultural self-sufficiency, American society was promoting large-scale exploitation of land and labor.

Lucy's death represents major forces that were not only at work in the Choctaw Nation but were also impelling the United States with seeming inevitability toward civil war. Lavinia Pitchlynn Harkins remained a Christian despite her role in Lucy's death, and although the missionaries raised moral objections to the practice of slavery, they implicitly acknowledged that they had no legal power to forbid it in the face of Choctaw law.[3] And if they were to continue their work among the Choctaws and bring more converts to Christianity, they could not afford to antagonize the leaders of the Nation with whom they had contractual obligations to operate its schools.

As the ostensibly free territory of Kansas became Bleeding Kansas, the specter of similar conflicts in Indian Territory reared its ugly head. The prospect of violent conflict appalled the peaceful missionaries who had accompanied their slaveholding converts to the territory after 1830. They also confronted doctrinal conflict in the Presbyterian Church over the issue. The missionaries had consistently preached against slavery, but their basic need for physical labor to sustain their mission establishments led them to hire slaves. The fact that many of their major supporters in the nation were slaveholders confronted them with a conundrum. If they abandoned the institution of slavery, they would lose the allegiance of their supporters. If they followed church doctrine, they would have to abandon their commitment to a Christian mission in the Choctaw Nation.

The Nation depended on missionaries to provide education for their children, something that they valued highly, and the issues of slavery and education became intertwined. As the Choctaws legislated the status of slaves and assumed control over their own educational system, Cyrus Kingsbury and his fellow missionaries confronted their dilemma.

Slavery as an institution had become deeply entrenched among the leading men of the Choctaw Nation long before the removal to Indian Territory. It was not, for the most part, an economic institution but rather was an adaptation to farming, which had largely replaced hunting as a subsistence base. Farming was traditionally women's work, but it could be done equally well by slaves. With the notable exception of Greenwood LeFlore, who established a major cotton plantation in the Mississippi delta and had several hundred slaves, Choctaws, primarily but not exclusively mixed-bloods, used slave labor to sustain small farms that supported their families.

The practices of slavery in the Choctaw country were, by one report, more lenient than those of slavery in the United States. Despite the restrictive laws the Choctaw Nation passed, in a settlement in the Chickasaw District that included about 150 slaves, "the privileges granted by a large portion of the Chickasaws to their slaves, has enabled some of them to dress quite as well as their masters, and to make a very respectable appearance at religious meetings." Slaves could ride horses to meetings even if they didn't own them.[4]

Slaves were more likely to be treated as members of the family. Because they spoke English, they often could translate in negotiations between Choctaws and whites. Slaves could farm and raise their own livestock, and they were the earliest converts in the Christian missionary churches established among the Choctaws and Chickasaws in the southeast in the early nineteenth century.[5]

For one Choctaw leader, the evil of slavery was that it fostered indolence among Choctaws, especially in the younger generations. George Harkins lamented that "we Choctaw half bloods don't raise up our children aright—we show them to [sic] much indulgence—if we would make them work in the corn field, from the time they are able to do anything and at the same time give them the hickory every time they transgressed they would be some account when they grow up." The problem was that Choctaws depended on slaves to do the work, not their own children.[6] Cyrus Kingsbury echoed the sentiment: "A great proportion of the red people, who own slaves, neglect entirely to train their children to habits of industry, enterprise & economy."[7] Slaves thus relieved their owners of the burden of labor that the Christian missionaries believed was necessary to a true Christian lifestyle, although Kingsbury considered the slaves of Choctaw owners to be nearly as indolent as the owners themselves.[8]

In the Indian Territory, however, racial attitudes hardened into law. Although very few Choctaws ever entered the economic system that sustained slavery in the southern states, Choctaw leaders were aware of attempts to abolish the institution, and as early as 1836, the General Council enacted a law against the expression of "the most fatal and destructive doctrine of abolitionism" by citizens of the United States in the Choctaw Nation. It forbade teaching slaves to read, write, or sing hymns or allowing them to sit at table with their masters. Anyone guilty of such acts would be banished from the Nation. Although aimed primarily at missionaries, the law was made to apply to all U.S. citizens in the Nation. The Constitution of 1838 included the provision that "no free negro, or any part negro, unconnected with Choctaw and Chickasaw blood, shall be permitted to come and settle in the Choctaw nation."[9] It confirmed not only the Choctaw leaders' proslavery attitudes but also their sovereignty to control the practice.

The American Board missionaries depended on slave labor to maintain their missions. Although Cyrus Kingsbury sent heartfelt pleas for additional helpers to the American Board, the number who came was disappointingly small and the labor associated with building and maintaining homes, churches, and schools was great. The

agonizing of the missionaries over the issue was particularly
poignant. Kingsbury justified buying slaves on the grounds that they
would be paid wages so they could ultimately buy their freedom.[10]
They also agonized over issues raised by the Presbyterian Church, the
main supporter of the American Board. Should slaveholders who
showed signs of Christian conversion be admitted to membership in
the Church?[11] For the missionaries, the Bible was ultimate authority. If
the apostles had not openly condemned slavery in the Roman empire,
the missionaries would not condemn it in the Choctaw Nation.[12]

In 1844, the American Board issued a report that condemned slavery as wicked and the source of "disastrous moral and social influences" on the "less enlightened and less civilized communities" in
which missionaries worked. It did not condemn slaveholders as sin-
ners, but it gave its missionaries latitude to follow the example of the
apostles to "bring men to a saving knowledge of Christ" through
preaching. Missionaries were free to use their own judgment to
determine the "evidence of piety and fitness for church fellowship in
professed converts."[13]

Theologically, the principles complied with Presbyterian doctrine
and left it to the missionaries' discretion to determine whether slave
owners showed enough piety to be admitted to church membership.
But reports of slavery at the Choctaw and Chickasaw missions led
the board to send S. B. Treat, corresponding secretary of its Prudential Committee, to investigate the situation in 1848. Following Treat's
visit, Kingsbury sent him a carefully considered letter outlining the
missionaries' position on their relationship with the Choctaw government and its leaders:

> For many years it has been deemed by us, important to our usefulness in
> *our own sphere of labor*, not to agitate over our minds, nor those of our peo-
> ple with any of the great & existing topics of the day in church or state,
> such as cause debate & division & the ranging of men into parties against
> each other. We had our principles once tried in this respect, when the
> Presbyterian church was divided into two schools.

Kingsbury acknowledged that the missions hired slaves—"Good
free help for us in our situation is very rare in this land"—and that they
admitted slaveholders to their churches within the guidance of the

board's directives. He compared the missionaries to the apostles, pointing out that slavery existed in the Choctaw Nation by virtue of the constitution and laws of that Nation and that "we are in a civil respect *foreigners & tenants at will* under the officers of our Government."[14]

Treat's response to their letter, dated June 22, 1848, was a shock. It condemned the institution of slavery and demanded that the missionaries deny church membership to Choctaw slaveholders. Treat's letter seemed to deny the board's 1844 doctrine. To their defense that they were "*foreigners & tenants at will*" in the Nation, Treat responded by conceding that although the missionary could judge "the *time* and *mode*" in which slaveholders came to an understanding of the gospel, he was not justified "in closing his mouth forever." Although Treat denied that his letter was a directive, he made it quite clear that the Prudential Committee strongly questioned the suitability of slaveholders as church members and that he discouraged the hiring of slaves in strong terms.[15]

Treat's report on the Choctaw and Cherokee missions acknowledged that slaves were more leniently treated there than in the United States and that the board had failed to provide enough laborers, especially given the demands of the schools.[16] The board's annual report in 1848 concluded that churches newly established among the "heathen" should not initially be held to the same standards of Christian excellence as well-established Christian churches. But Treat's letter was a strong censure of the Choctaw missions, and Kingsbury could only reiterate the commitment of the missionaries to the principles laid out by the board in 1844 and repeat that the hiring of slaves had been "a matter of necessity."[17]

The Choctaw schools placed new demands on the missionaries' resources, and they continued to hire slaves. Kingsbury put the situation bluntly to David Green, corresponding secretary of the board: "The Churches, whose servants we are, must either release us from our present liabilities; or they must send us help to meet them; or they must let us employ such help as we can get in the country. We submit it to them, to choose the course to be pursued."[18] When Kingsbury bought a slave named Blakely with the express understanding that the value of his labor would buy him his freedom, he received a scathing letter from a northern churchman castigating him for his actions.[19]

For Kingsbury, it was a no-win situation. Israel Folsom accused him of "chilling the hearts of the Choctaw Christians, who were just beginning to improve in the Christian religion with joy," and he declared that the Choctaws "want you to stop interfering with the civil relation which exists in this nation, which has been sanctioned by the word of God, as well as by our law."[20] Folsom and George Harkins charged that the missionaries had used their influence to sway tribal leaders toward abolitionist sentiments. Newspapers in Arkansas and Texas asserted that the missionaries wanted to make the Choctaw Nation an abolitionist state.[21]

Kingsbury could only lament to his northern accuser, "So you see, that while at the North I am held up to odium as a slaveholder, here I am charged with being an Abolitionist. Will the good brother who has charged so heavily upon me in your region, tell me what I am to do in this dilemma."[22]

In 1853, an incident at the Good Water School compounded the missionaries' woes. Rumors spread that Ebenezer Hotchkins, director of the school, had fathered a child by a girl who subsequently left the school. In light of the scandal, the Choctaw school trustees suspended operations at Good Water and Kingsbury appointed a committee to investigate the reports. Upon questioning by the committee, the girl's father denied the allegations, and the committee exonerated Hotchkins of the charges, which they concluded were malicious, but the damage had been done and the school remained closed for the year.[23] The American Board discreetly concluded that the reasons for the suspension were "insufficient" and that "injustice has been done to Mr. Hotchkin, the laborious and efficient superintendent."[24]

The mission schools became pawns in political struggles within the Choctaw Nation. Peter Pitchlynn had turned against the American Board and joined the Cumberland Presbytery, a rival denomination. Kingsbury implied that Pitchlynn and his brother-in-law, Israel Folsom, had sought to discredit the Good Water School in order to divert money to a boarding school to be operated by the Cumberland Presbytery.[25] It was rumored in the Nation that Pitchlynn and Folsom were seeking to discredit missionaries so as to gain control of the Choctaw school funds.[26] George Harkins attacked the missionaries as "a treacherous hypocritical set of Yankees" and sought to discredit the schools by charging that the teachers were "too young and unexperienced—and without qualifications" and that the pay offered was not good enough to attract good teachers.[27]

In November 1853, the General Council reaffirmed the earlier law that provided that no slave or child of slaves was to be taught in any school. The Choctaw legislature extended its control more firmly over the mission schools by establishing a Board of Trustees that was empowered to judge the fitness of teachers, call for the removal of any it thought unfit, and remove known abolitionists or those espousing abolitionist doctrines, among other things. The trustees proposed that they modify the school contracts by inserting a clause that the contracts could be terminated upon six months' notice by either party.[28]

The missionaries knew that they could not operate the schools under such uncertainty, but they were also convinced that the new laws did not represent the opinion of the majority of the Choctaw people, that they were opposed by "wealthy slave owners" and "common Choctaws," as Kingsbury claimed, and that Kingsbury could get the law repealed. Indeed, by 1854 the laws were not being enforced.[29] S. B. Treat immediately protested to the General Council in a letter he sent to Kingsbury to deliver. Kingsbury refused to do it, telling Treat that although the letter might perfectly express an opinion acceptable in Boston, in the Choctaw Nation it would be seen as an attempt to incite an abolitionist movement and would undermine the missionaries' efforts.[30]

The ongoing "embarrassments and perplexities" of the Choctaw missions led the Prudential Committee of the American Board to send a second visitor to the missions in the fall of 1855.[31] George Wood arrived at Stockbridge on April 11 and spent eighteen days visiting the various Choctaw stations.[32] He found the missionaries confident that the schools laws would at least not be enforced, if not repealed, and that they could continue the schools on the same basis as they had undertaken them. But he also found some sentiment that the laws offered an opportunity for the missionaries to give up the burden of the schools:

> In the opinion of several of the missionaries, it was at least doubtful whether the cost in health, perplexity, trouble in obtaining teachers, time which might be devoted to preaching, and money, was not too great for the results; and it was suggested that an opportunity, afforded by divine

Providence for relieving us from a burden too heavy to sustain for nine years longer, should be embraced.[33]

The actions of the Choctaw council in asserting its control over the management of the schools and proposing to modify the American Board's contract were "portentous of increasing embarrassment from other causes than the new school law." Wood concluded that "grave objections exist to the connection with civil government of any department of missionary operations."[34]

The missionaries, for their part, asserted that they were responsible "not for correct views and action on the part of . . . church members, but only for an honest and proper endeavor to secure correctness of views and action under the same obligations and limitations on this subject as on others." They had "nothing to do with political questions and agitations." Their responsibility was to deal only with "what is morally wrong" and to assure that "people of God may separate themselves therefrom, and a right standard of moral action be held up before the world." They summarized their position thus: "When [slavery] is made unavoidable by the laws of the State, the obligations of guardianship, or the demands of humanity, it is not to be deemed an offence against the rule of Christian right."[35]

The missionaries hoped to clarify their position vis-à-vis the "suggestions" offered in Treat's letter of 1848, and Wood's visit seemed to indicate that the board had modified the position that Treat spelled out. But when Wood presented his report to the board at its meeting at Utica, New York, in September 1855, he made it appear that the missionaries had instead acceded to Treat's advice to exclude slave owners from church membership. Kingsbury immediately protested that "we cannot consent to be thus made to sanction principles & sentiments which are contrary to our . . . deliberate, & settled convictions of right, & to what we understand to be the teachings of the word of God." And the missionaries made the fateful decision that their relationship with the board "may be dissolved in a way that will do the least harm to the Board & to our Mission."[36]

By thus forcing the issue, the missionaries provoked a conciliatory response from the Prudential Committee, but they raised the stakes in their bid for autonomy.[37] "If the Board will withdraw all past legislation on the subject of slavery, give up all control of it to the missionaries, to act according to the instructions of the New Testament & their own best judgment, & make distinct public announcement of this, we will withdraw our resignation," they wrote.[38] The Prudential Committee agreed implicitly, if not explicitly, to continue its relationship with the missionaries by paying their estimated expenses for the next year.[39]

In 1858, a committee recommended to the American Board meeting in Detroit that the board "should be relieved as early as possible from the increasing embarrassment and perplexities connected with the missions in the Indian territory."[40] Kingsbury made conciliatory gestures to forestall the potential severance: "We see nothing in our present circumstances requiring a separation." The missionaries had made their position on slavery clear in their letter of September 6, 1856, and they wrote that "we apprehend no such difficulty from the Choctaw people, or from others in their region."[41]

Even as Kingsbury predicted no difficulty, he could not have foreseen the murder of Richard Harkins and the burning of the slave Lucy. Although written evidence of the episode did not appear until 1860, it is likely, given the prominence of the families involved, that other prominent and not-so-prominent members of the Choctaw Nation had become aware of it. Certainly Cyrus Byington's action in questioning Mrs. Harkins and keeping her as a member of the church at Stockbridge was known to his parishioners, and given the prominence of the families involved, the incident was probably fairly widely known in the Nation. Although there is no specific evidence that Lucy's death and Kingsbury's action were among the "embarrassments" cited for the final dissolution of the American Board's relationship with its Choctaw missions, the incident provided evidence that slavery in the Choctaw Nation was sometimes vicious.[42]

Upon learning of the proposed action of the American Board, the school trustees of the Choctaw Nation, Robert W. Nail, George Folsom, and Kennedy McCurtain, wrote to S. B. Treat offering the American Board its "desired relief" by terminating the board's contracts.[43] The General Council, however, repudiated their action, and Joseph Folsom, national secretary, characterized them as "having been elevated into that office in consequence of our political difficulty, and

being bitter enemies of the missionaries of the American Board."
Despite Folsom's comments, the threat to the schools and the status of
the missionaries was nevertheless very real.[44]

The final break came in July of 1859. The "embarrassments" of the
Choctaw mission were affecting "injuriously" both the work of the
missionaries and the board's relations with its "friends and patrons."
The board resolved on July 16 that "it is incumbent on the Prdl. Com.
to discontinue the Choctaw mission, and the same is hereby discontinued."[45] The Choctaw Mission did not, however, end with the American Board's decision. Kingsbury and his fellow missionaries had too
much invested spiritually to give up their work. Kingsbury appealed
to and was accepted by the Board of Foreign Missions of the Presbyterian Church, and the work continued. The threat of civil war, however, precipitated a split over slavery in the Board of Foreign Missions,
and Kingsbury and his colleagues associated themselves with the
proslavery Southern Assembly of the Presbyterian Church.[46]

The missionaries were still entangled in an immediate way with
the economics of slavery. When they hired slaves, it was the owners
who ultimately profited financially. If they bought slaves with the
intention of freeing them when they had worked off the purchase
price, they became actively engaged in the slave trade. No matter
how noble their motives, the missionaries depended on slaves to
sustain their efforts to undermine the institution of slavery. And they
were attacked from both sides. When they attempted to preach to
slave owners about their responsibilities to their slaves, they were
viewed as abolitionists. Choctaw Christians who read the *Missionary
Herald*, the organ of the American Board, knew the board's stance
full well.[47] Christians in the North who learned that the missionaries
actually hired slaves were outraged.[48]

Much as the missionaries in the 1840s tried to distance themselves
from the politics of the Choctaw Nation, their position in the schools
and the known position of the American Board on the issue of slavery drew them into political controversies and undermined their
position. Ultimately, the experience of the ABCFM missionaries in
the Choctaw Nation demonstrated the futility of trying to separate
the church from the state in the matter of slavery.

CHAPTER 4

THE CONSTITUTIONAL CRISIS OF 1858
THE POLITICS OF CHANGE

The Treaty of 1855 totally reoriented the relationship between the Choctaw Nation and the federal government. The Choctaw delegation established a new rhetoric of Choctaw rights based on the failure of the federal government to meet its treaty obligations. If the Choctaw Nation was to challenge the government successfully, it needed to have a strong basis for its own government. It had written laws and a constitution that represented its evolution, but the new treaty confronted the Choctaws with a major crisis that moved the Nation toward a more centralized power in a new constitution as the basis for that relationship.

One revision was required by the Chickasaws' new autonomy. The Nation also wanted to exert stronger control over the institution of slavery to protect its rights. The formation of a new constitution, however, created a crisis of confidence in government in the Choctaw Nation. The crisis stemmed from the rise of partisan politics and power struggles within the Nation. It also marked increasing social and economic divisions within the Nation—full-bloods and mixed-bloods, progressives and conservatives, slave owners and missionaries, political elites and the common people. It crystallized deeply held divisions of opinion about the federal government's efforts to make Indian Territory a territory of the United States. It raised complex questions about the relation of the individual to the national government. As the

Choctaws began to wield political power through formal institutions rather than public consensus, the stress points in the society often ruptured in open conflict, and the resolution of those conflicts reshaped the society.

The changing nature of the political process for the Choctaws is one of the most significant factors in their transition from an egalitarian community-based tribal society to a nation with a representative form of government with centralized authority. If the constitutions in 1826, 1834, 1838, and 1842 indicated a growing sense of Choctaw national identity, the constitutional crisis of 1857–1858 led Sampson Folsom to declare that "Choctaw Nationality is almost gone of sight, never to regain its former vigor and health & standing among the nations of the Earth."[1] That the Nation survived the crisis is evidence that its processes allowed it to adapt to its changing circumstances.

The traditional form of tribal government was basically egalitarian. Each community had its *mingo* (chief), whose *tichimingo* (speaker) assisted him. Adult males who had killed an enemy in battle were designated by the suffix *ubbee* appended to their names. Politically, the three separate districts into which the communities were divided, the *okla falaya*, *okla tanap*, and *okla hannali*, were autonomous units, each with its *mingo*. Except for a separate territory for the leading men of the tribe, the *chunka*, there is no evidence that centralized government played a role in Choctaw thinking.[2] After European contact, however, village leaders were thrust into new roles as negotiators in diplomatic relationships, and French and English colonial governors created "medal chiefs" to satisfy their need for identifiable leadership among the Choctaws. Throughout the processes of treaty negotiation and signing in the early nineteenth century, the U.S. government promoted the idea of centralized and authoritarian government, but except for the Treaty at Hoe Buctinoopa in 1803, which dealt with land only in the district bounded by the Tombigbee River, it was always the chiefs of the three districts who signed the treaties.[3]

The threat of removal to the West, however, created growing tensions within the Choctaw Nation between full-blood and mixed-blood elements. Apukshunnubbee and Pushmataha, two of the three full-blood chiefs whose leadership had been recognized since the early 1800's1800s, died in 1824. Apukshunnubbee died after falling from a cliff in Ohio during the journey to Washington, D.C., and Pushmataha died mysteriously during the negotiations of the treaty signed in Washington in 1825. These losses opened the way for a new generation of leaders, scions of mixed-blood families, notably David Folsom and Greenwood LeFlore, to assume positions of leadership.[4]

Folsom and LeFlore wrote the Nation's first constitution in 1826. It provided for a council that met annually and the election of the chiefs, but it maintained the traditional tripartite government and left the three districts of the nation largely self-governing. The crisis over the prospect of removal to the land west of the Mississippi that the tribe had acquired by the 1920 Treaty of Doaks Stand almost precipitated a civil war within the tribe between David Folsom and Mushulatubbee, the full-blood chief of the northeast district.[5] By 1830, David Folsom asserted his leadership of the Mushulatubbee District, but he and Samuel Garland, of the Pushmataha District, stepped aside so Greenwood LeFlore, the elected chief of the Apukshunnubbee District, could serve as the sole chief of the Choctaws in the negotiation of the Treaty of Dancing Rabbit Creek.[6]

In 1834, in their new lands, they wrote a new constitution that retained the three district chiefs and added a formal court system whose judges were appointed by the chiefs of the districts.[7] The customs of justice among the Choctaws had been based on family and *iksa* relationships and dealt primarily with the taking of human life. If a person killed another person, whether intentionally or accidentally, the relatives of the deceased avenged the death by killing the killer. With the introduction of the court system, justice was converted from a private matter to a matter of public law and punishment.[8]

In 1838, the Choctaws revised their constitution to integrate the Chickasaw Nation into their territory as a separate political district.[9] This constitution was also an attempt to demonstrate the Nation's ability to adapt to American society. Its preamble—"In order to establish justice, insure tranquility, promote the general welfare, and secure to ourselves and our posterity the right of life, liberty and property"— adopted language from the U.S. Constitution. It formed a "free and independent Government" over the Choctaw territory, including the new Chickasaw District.[10] The new constitution maintained the district form of government. There were now four district chiefs answering to the General Council. Any two of them could serve as executive when the General Council met, but there was no principal chief. All answered to the General Council. Each district chief had his speaker and his secretary, and each district had its own supreme court and from one to three inferior courts. National identity now resided in the name of the nation's capital—Nunihwayah, or Bending Mountain, the name the Choctaws had given the sacred mound in the southeast that marked their former home.[11] The key meaning of the constitution was that the Choctaws were independent of control by the U.S. government. They had given up their Mississippi homeland in order to protect their right to govern themselves, and the 1838 constitution was as much a declaration of independence as it was a document of governance.

The 1842 constitution was prompted by the expiration of the school annuities in the 1825 treaty. It expanded the Choctaw government by adding a senate to create a bicameral legislature. Each district had three senators, and the number of representatives was established on the basis of 1 per 1,000 persons. Elections were held by district. It also established the Nation's control of its own schools, authorizing the expenditure of tribal funds for public education and committing $18,000 of the interest money from the Chickasaw fund to "educational purposes." The additional $7,000 generated by the fund was to be spent on "blacksmith shops and other national purposes."[12]

A new constitution in 1850 significantly expanded Article II, the Declaration of Rights. Sections on freedom of the press, security from unreasonable search and seizure, security in judicial proceedings with regard to "life, liberty and property," and acknowledgement of private obligation in the form of contracts were added.[13] It also included provisions for the General Council to set salaries for chiefs and their speakers.

The changes in 1850, however, called attention to other parts of the constitution that inspired significant discontent among some leading men of the Nation. The chiefs of the Nation, George W. Harkins, Cornelius McCurtain, and George Folsom, in a special message to the General Council in November of 1853, declared that the constitution was "imperfect and . . . dangerous to the interest and welfare of the people." That assessment would prove prophetic. It was difficult to amend—two-thirds of the members of the General Council could propose amendments, which then had to be ratified by four-fifths of the next council. The chiefs also cited unequal representation by counties, imperfections in the judiciary, and dissatisfaction with Nuniwayah as the seat of government.[14]

There was much for people to be dissatisfied about in the Nation besides the location of the capital. Farming, the great civilizing force promoted by the U.S. government, often failed in the face of the forces of nature. Even the weather challenged the Choctaws. Drought plagued the countryside, lowering the levels of the Arkansas and Red rivers to the point that supplies could not be brought in by boat, leaving families destitute. Choctaw men of "wealth and public spirit" turned their attention to the possibility of railroads as a means of transport; for them it was as much a matter of personal interest as of public good.[15]

White settlers in Indian Territory were beginning to monopolize large tracts of land, and Thomas Pitchlynn wrote to his brother Peter, "I am in hopes that the government will put a stop to all the settlers at the Fourts [sic] in this nation, of making farms and rasing [sic] corn and stock on the reserve, here are white men living in our country making large farmers, takin [sic] all the corn tracks, and no chance for the Choctaws."[16] Comanche raiders came from the west to steal Indian cattle, mostly from the Chickasaws but sometimes from Choctaws.[17] And Choctaws increasingly used laws to assert individual rights. As Thomas Pitchlynn informed his kinsman Peter Pitchlynn, "There is more seuing [sic] for property now than a little."[18] Social unrest was rampant. Peter Pitchlynn's son Leonidas reported to him that "I have no news to tell you only the Indians are killing one another up like dogs upon a fox down on the line."[19]

The 1855 treaty crystallized the need for constitutional reform, and on November 12, 1856, the General Council authorized the convening of a constitutional convention comprised of delegates elected by the voters of each county of who were "empowered to amend the old or frame a new constitution for the government of the Choctaw Nation." The delegates met at Skullyville to carry out their work.[20]

The new constitution that emerged at Skullyville initiated a radical change in Choctaw government by creating a single governor
who in turn appointed the three district chiefs. This centralized government significantly altered the tripartite system of autonomous
districts, the only form of government with which most Choctaws
were familiar, and the response was, predictably, a strong antipathy
to the new constitution. Other changes initiated in the Skullyville
Constitution were about the style of voting. The customary manner
spelled out in the 1838 constitution was for voters simply to line up
behind the candidate they supported and be counted. The new constitution specified election by ballot.

Other changes were more routine. Terms of representatives were
set at two years rather than one, and the operations of the legislature
were set out in much greater detail than they were in the 1850 constitution. Section 27 provided that no one paid by the tribe could
serve on the General Council. It also created a probate court as part
of the judicial system that had "jurisdiction in all matters testamen-
tary and of administration in orphan's business, and the allotment of
dower in cases of idiocy and lunacy, and of persons 'non compos
mentis.'" The Nation had begun to define its power over the property of the deceased and their heirs.[21]

The constitution regulated slavery by giving the General Council
"power to pass laws to permit the owners of slaves to emancipate
them" and "power to pass such laws, regulating or prohibiting the
introduction of slaves into the Nation, as may be deemed proper and
expedient." The constitutional provisions opened the door to abolition, but they were dangerous. As Tandy Walker warned, "We have
Arkansas on one side and Texas on the other, both slave holding
states, whose people would not sit quietly by and permit another
Canada, or runaway harbor, to be established upon their borders."
Walker declared that "we are too weak to resist such force and the
inevitable result would be that we should be overrun and our
Nationality destroyed and our country taken away from us and our
people forced to find homes in the barren plains west of us."[22] His
words were prophetic.

Despite its assurances in numerous treaties that Indian Territory
would remain the domain of Indian tribes, the U.S. government was

determined to bring the territory under federal control. Its position was that Indian land had to become private property and Indians had to become land owners like other Americans. Territorialization became the new political watchword in the Choctaw Nation. Many Choctaws were beginning to accept that idea. George Harkins declared that "I find nearly every man of the Skullyville party is in favor of sectioning the country," although he feared that "it will not suit our common Tubbees."[23]

The issue marked the growing division between the political leadership and the ordinary citizens of the Choctaw Nation. The Choctaws had to grapple with the possible division of their land. Israel Folsom noted "a great stir now among the people of all parties about the subject of sectionizing the land—some bitterly opposed to it & some for it—but I am surprised to find so great a number of the people in favor of it than I thought they would." Private property would enable the Choctaws to exclude non-Indians from their lands, but many of the Choctaws were "not prepared in point of civilization & education for the system proposed." The sentiment for private property was strongest in the district along the Red River, where a number of Choctaws had cotton plantations, but even there Choctaws were adamant that individuals should be prohibited from leasing or selling the residue of that land "to improper persons."[24]

About the only satisfaction with the new constitution was expressed by the commissioner of Indian affairs, who saw it as a remedy for the bureaucratic "inconveniences" of having to obtain the signatures of three district leaders on documents. In the Nation, the constitution became a major source of political conflict.[25] Its result was "Confusion! Yea, worse than Confusion! Strife and Contention for Power."[26]

Lycurgus Pitchlynn, who managed his father Peter's farm, essayed a very pragmatic view of Choctaw politics. The constitution was too complex:

> This country is in a terrible pickle, a deep rooted hostility exists against this new Constitution. It can't stand. It is not suited to the philosophy of the Choctaw mind. We have legislated beyond the march of their intellect. . . . The Choctaws want a practical man—a real common sense legislator, one who understand their thoughts—their wants—and necessities."

The Skullyville Constitution was "a beautiful one in theory, suited to a civilized and refined state of society, but decidedly inappropriate to the condition of the Choctaws." In a burst of enthusiasm, the younger Pitchlynn proposed that he write an entirely original constitution: "Greece but one Solon, The Roman Republic but one Remus, the empire but one Justinian and England but one Alfred, and why not the Choctaw Nation have but one Pitchlynn." His constitution would be called the Pitchlynn Code.[27]

Distinction by blood was a growing issue, Pitchlynn claimed: "Under the new Constitution the full bloods say that [they] have no share at all. All the officials are taken from them & given to a select few. . . . The full blood Indians have and begin to lose confidence in the half breeds."[28] Douglas Cooper, the U.S. agent, attributed the situation to "party spirit."[29] Whether based on blood or politics, the emotions dividing Choctaws were strong.

The proposed constitution divided Choctaw sentiment regarding the issue of a centralized government. The division coalesced into "progressive" and "conservative" factions.[30] Tandy Walker, chief of the Nation when the council called for the constitution and leader of the constitutional convention in Skullyville, and Sampson Folsom, attorney general of the tribe, were the leading "progressives." George Harkins, former chief of the Apukshunnubbee District, and Peter Pitchlynn represented the "conservatives." Harkins supported the amendment of the constitution, but Walker's Skullyville Constitution, with its radical reorientation of the government, represented a whole new form of government that he could not condone.

The crux of the political crisis of 1857 was itself a constitutional one. Did the power to form a new constitution lay with General Council or did the council's action need to be approved by a vote of the people? The 1850 constitution provided for a very cumbersome process of amendment subject to council approval. George Harkins argued that the General Council's action in 1856 authorizing a convention with the power to "frame a new constitution" was basically unconstitutional because it contravened the process of amendment in the 1850; for him, the Skullyville Constitution was not a valid document.[31]

Harkins's challenge set the stage for a major crisis both within the Choctaw Nation and in its relations with the U.S. government. He accused certain members of the council, Daniel and Jacob Folsom, Adam Nail, and "Peter Folsom perhaps more to blame than all of them," for trying to "force a constitution down the throats of a majority." He blamed Douglas Cooper for urging the General Council to ratify the new constitution without advising its members to submit it to the vote of the people. He derided Tandy Walker's political supporters in the Skullyville District, and he objected to the fact the General Council had "laughed at" a petition of some 1,800 voters in the Pushmataha and Apukshunnubbee districts that rejected the Skullyville Constitution and called for a new one.[32] Walker defended the constitution, arguing that the vote for delegates to the constitutional convention under the General Council resolution constituted a grant of power from the people to form a new constitution. The vote implicitly, if not explicitly, approved the constitution drawn up by the delegates.[33] In the end, what was at issue was the power of the people versus the power of the government.

Having formulated an essentially new document in January 1857, the Skullyville delegates called for the election of officials to implement it without submitting it to a vote of the people. Harkins encouraged his supporters to boycott the elections. On March 2, 1858, he and a large number of his followers met at the Apukshunnubbee District council ground and agreed to hold elections under the Constitution of 1850 and to abide by that constitution until a new one could be drawn up.[34] Joseph Dukes, noting that "an overwhelming majority are opposed to the New Constitution," joined Harkins in asserting that it had been unconstitutionally adopted.[35] In the tribal elections of 1858, only one district, "the Arkansas District" (the Mushulatubbee District, where Skullyville was located), voted under the Skullyville Constitution. In the two districts bordering the Red River (Pushmataha and Apukshunnubbee), only about 100 out of some 1,600 voters cast ballots under the new constitution, while the rest of the votes were cast under the 1850 constitution.[36] The failure of Harkins's followers to vote in the election for national officers led Walker to believe that they had acquiesced to the Skullyville constitution. Harkins, however, still supported the 1850 constitution. The Nation now labored under two constitutions, the 1850 one and the Skullyville one, each with its own supporters.

To Sampson Folsom, the "old chiefs" represented the past, an "oligarchical system," and he chided Peter Pitchlynn as being "behind the true times" for corresponding with them rather than with Alfred Wade, the man elected as governor under the Skullyville Constitution.[37] Tandy Walker reported to Pitchlynn that "Col. Harkins is still opposing the new Constitution and is now wishing to get up a convention to frame another Constitution."[38] When Wade called for county elections, no candidates for office appeared in Red River, Eagle, Bok Tuklo, and Neshoba counties in Pushmataha District. Pitchlynn had decided that no vote should be taken in Eagle County, and Harkins instructed the voters in Towson County that "unless we were united we could not effect anything so we did not vote—the largest error I ever made."[39] Folsom attributed the lack of candidates to the $1,500 bond required of them, but the result was that those three counties were not represented at all in the General Council.[40]

The political division rendered the General Council powerless. As Kingsbury observed, "The government, if it deserves the name, is without strength." Alfred Wade resigned as governor early in 1858 and Tandy Walker replaced him, but the Choctaw Nation was without an effective constitutional government.[41] Sampson Folsom commented, "It appears to me that we are on the verge of anarchy and God alone . . . can bring us out of our present difficulties."[42] The Skullyville Constitution was perceived as representing a mixed-blood minority. Cyrus Kingsbury characterized the new council as "mostly half breeds" who were "very much under the influence of Arkansas lawyers." The issues, in the eyes of both Kingsbury and Lycurgus Pitchlynn, were those of blood and were outside the realm of political influence.[43]

The conflict also had implications for the financial interests of the Nation. Any signs of internal turmoil would undercut Pitchlynn's attempt to recover the net proceeds of the land sales of 1831–1832. Harkins realized the implications and denied to Pitchlynn that he was actively trying to undercut the claim.[44]

The only entity that sanctioned the Skullyville Constitution was the U.S. government. Douglas Cooper assured Commissioner of Indian Affairs Charles E. Mix that "the Choctaw government represented by Gov. Walker is beyond question the only legal authority in the Choctaw Nation" and that he had given it government recognition by giving it the treaty annuities.[45] Walker's assertion that Harkins had agreed to the Skullyville Constitution by not voting provoked Harkins to convene his own constitutional convention in May at Doaksville.[46] The Doaksville Convention proceeded without the General Council's sanction and concluded its work in mid-May. The new document included the three district chiefs and a fourth chief. The delegates agreed to submit their document to a popular vote, to be held on the first Wednesday in July 1858. The Choctaw Nation now labored under the weight of three competing constitutions: the 1850 constitution, which some considered to be still in effect; Walker's Skullyville Constitution; and Harkins's Doaksville Constitution. And so the Nation found itself with two constitutions and two governments.[47] Harkins challenged the advocates of the Skullyville Constitution to put it up for a vote so people could make a choice.[48] The vote on the Skullyville and Doaksville constitutions was held on July 4, 1858. It effectively constituted a national referendum on governance, but once again it did not settle the matter because Harkins and his followers would not accept the result.

Harkins maintained that "Towson County has never once agreed to surrender, we shall vote for the Doaksville constitution. . . . News may reach you that we have given up, but it is no such thing. We are as determined as ever and will not yield one inch." He admitted that he had blundered in calling for the boycott of the earlier elections for General Council, and he promised to proceed with an election of officers under the Doaksville Constitution."[49]

News of the situation caused alarm in Washington. The commissioner of Indian affairs wrote to Nation leaders asking that the matter not be taken to extremes. Peter Folsom, one of the Choctaw delegates in Washington, D.C., was asked to return to the Nation to try to mediate between the two factions, and Harkins and his supporters "gave up the voting" in the hope that Folsom would be able to settle the difficulties.[50]

The constitutional crisis brought government in the Nation to a standstill. Reports of violence and bloodshed were rife, evidence of an apparent breakdown in respect for law and order. "Murder, manslaughter, stealing, lieing, drinking whiskey (rot gut) assault &

battery are an everyday occurrence. Person & property is considered without protection," Folsom reported to Peter Pitchlynn.[51] "People . . . drinking, fighting and killing each other," George Hudson wrote.[52] "Lawlessness—murder and violence are common things in this nation," Lycurgus Pitchlynn told his father.[53] Joseph Dukes reported "nearly a whole year a total suppression of laws throughout the Nation." He expressed his "thankfulness that we are no worse off than we are," a situation that he attributed to "the good effect of the gospel."[54]

The situation appeared to warrant federal military intervention. Douglas Cooper suggested to Charles Mix that if the Doaksville "party" tried to establish a separate government, the "effect of the presence of a sharp force of U. States troops in the country would prevent a collision. And, if unfortunately a conflict should take place they would be necessary to restore order."[55]

Chief Tandy Walker sent a message to the Doaksville Convention "which we construed as an overature [sic]for a compromise," but compromise was not possible. The Skullyville government seemed totally unwilling to bend in its June session. It castigated Harkins and his followers as "revolutionaries" and strongly admonished them to submit to "the present legal government."[56] The opponents, of course, ignored the admonition and attacked the Skullyville government where it could actually hurt, in its pocketbook.

On July 3, just before the vote on the two constitutions, Harkins and his followers submitted a petition to the commissioner of Indian affairs that asserted that the Nation was "in a most deplorable and confused state; owing to the fact that a small minority has assumed the reins of the Government, contrary to the wishes of a large majority of the people." The Skullyville government was "squandering the money of the Nation, and effecting no good whatever." The document echoed Lycurgus Pitchlynn's rhetoric: "That Constitution does not suit our present condition. It will do for Civilized people. We want something that is plain and simple. All we ask is the rights and privileges of a Free people." The petition asked that no future funds be given to the Nation until its political difficulties were settled.[57]

Harkins's petition threw the Nation on the mercy of the U.S. government, but his strategy backfired. On October 13, Elias Rector, superintendent of the southern superintendency of the Office of Indian Affairs, met with representatives of both factions. Rector was accompanied by Albert Pike, who was very familiar with Choctaw affairs. Pike lectured the assembly on "how ruinous to their prosperity, how insane, how discouraging to their friends were their dissensions." He threatened that U.S. forces might be called in and that bloodshed might follow. The Skullyville representatives were intransigent. Any call for a new constitution would lead "the mass of these people" to consider the Skullyville Constitution invalid, and "the officers under it would resign, and the Government would fall into anarchy." Five counties were in open revolt, and until they submitted, any concession to the Doaksville demand for a vote would be "a confession of Weakness and an act of imbicilety."[58]

The Skullyville representatives, however, assured Superintendent Rector that they would submit any amendment desired by "any portion of the Choctaw people, to the existing constitution" to a vote. Rector was satisfied with the apparent fairness of this act and directed that the Choctaw annuities be paid to the council, thereby giving what Tandy Walker described as "a just rebuke to the disobedient portion of our people and, an act of the Supt. Necessary to sustain the position of the existing government of the Nation." Rector thus affirmed the legitimacy of the Skullyville Constitution and the council's earlier censure of the dissenters, labeling them "rebels and traitors."[59]

On October 16, the council, acting under the constitution, passed an act restoring the offices of the district chiefs, although it was clear that the bulk of the power would remain in the hands of an elected governor. The council's action was an attempt to "restore peace, quietude and conformity to law and its authorities."[60] On October 26, it passed the crucial resolutions that it had promised Rector, submitting the question of a new constitutional convention to a vote of the people.[61] At last, the people could vote on their future government.[62]

The General Council did not act in deference to Rector's wishes. Its resolutions on a vote on the new constitution were aimed not at conciliation but "to vindicate the justice and wisdom of the General Council and the Executive officers of the government" in delaying a vote on the expediency of a new convention. The council declared that

Harkins and his followers had created an "agitated state of the public" and pointed out that the president of the United States, the secretary of the interior, and the commissioner of Indian affairs had recognized the council by its payment of annuities. Having thus established its pedigree, the council asserted that the leaders elected under the Doaksville Constitution had "yielded their opposition . . . and now submit to the Skullyville Constitution" and went on to assure the Choctaw people "that the course of the existing government . . . and the party controlling it, has been solely for their good, in preventing anarchy and misrule, by delaying the reference of so great and important a question to their suffrages, until all the counties in the Nation were organized and the public mind quieted." The actions of the council were also presented "as an assurance to the government of the United States, our great monitor and friend, that the government of the Choctaw Nation are mindful of their teachings, ready to preserve the domestic peace they desire and to observe their counsels."[63]

The council's resolutions were not a bow to public opinion but rather an assertion of political power. It sought to vindicate its actions and coerce the dissidents into a formal political organization; that is, the "disorganized" counties had to organize before an election would be held. It held out the notion that it acted for the public good in not submitting the Skullyville Constitution to a public vote, while in truth what emerged from Rector's account of the October 13 meeting was a fear that its legitimacy would be questioned and anarchy would result.

Although Elias Rector took the position that the only "substantial difference" between the Skullyville and Doaksville constitutions had to do with the matter of the executive power—that is, whether to have a single governor or a principal and district chiefs—the dissatisfaction with the Skullyville Constitution may be seen in broader terms as a culturally based reaction to political change. The tribal tradition was tripartite governance and district autonomy. Power in the hands of a single individual was a foreign notion. Although Rector assumed that the council's willingness to pass a resolution reinstating the office of district chief would solve the problem of the Nation, the council used it not to recognize the legitimacy of the cultural issue but to assert its own power.

The conflict crystallized a number of issues—full-bloods versus mixed-bloods, "progressive" versus "conservative" political parties, respect for law and order versus disrespect for organized government, Choctaw self-government vis-à-vis the U.S. government, and, ultimately, whether power resides in an elected government or in the people collectively. Peter Pitchlynn, for instance, felt that the General Council acted appropriately in establishing the Skullyville Convention, while Sampson Folsom argued that power resided in the people.[64]

Rector dismissed the conflict as "on the part of the leaders of the opposition, a contest for power and the control of money."[65] But it was not just the leaders of the opposition who were contesting power. It was a contest of wills between two opposing forces, and it is impossible to take sides when the issue at stake is the identity of the Choctaw Nation as a sovereign entity. There were, however, issues of the utmost importance to the future of the nation embedded in the Skullyville Constitution. One was slavery and the other was the extension of a territorial government over Indian Territory by the U.S. government. On the slavery issue, the language of the Skullyville Constitution allowed the General Council to regulate the importation of slaves into the Nation by "emigrants." Although regulation might allow non-Indians to bring slaves into the Nation, it might also prohibit them from doing so, and the language was widely interpreted as an abolitionist stance against slavery.[66] Lycurgus Pitchlynn declared that "we have now a regular abolition constitution. I think I must turn abolitionist."[67]

On the issue of territorialization, as it was generally termed, Kingsbury expressed the opinion that "our fear is that Congress may at an early Day pass the Territorial Bill, & that it will be approved by the present Council. . . . If the Territorial Bill passes it will be carried over the heads of the great majority of the nation as was the case in the Dancing Rabbit Creek Treaty." He continued, "It is doubtful, with the present Constitution, whether white emigrants with slaves could be kept out of the country."[68]

The vote was held, and "the voice of the people through the ballot box [was] almost unanimous in favor of a convention," which the General Council called for January 11, 1860, at Doaksville.[69] The struggle had had the positive effect of providing a mechanism for expressing political opposition. The constitution framed at Doaksville in 1860 and approved by the voters restored the system of elected district chiefs, although it vested authority in a principal chief elected nationally. District chiefs were charged primarily with maintaining law and order, and thus they had the power to appoint and supervise the lighthorsemen in their districts.

The 1860 constitution remained the governing document of the Choctaw Nation. Although the powers of the Nation were supplanted by the federal government in the late nineteenth century, the congressional act in 1906 that called for the final disposition of the affairs of the Five Tribes in Indian Territory provided for the continuation of the government until Congress should dissolve it, which it never did. The Constitution of 1860 thus, at least symbolically, represented the power of the Choctaw Nation. The dispute over its passage touched, however, on the deeper issue of the political process by which the competing constitutions came about and ultimately, on the ways in which Choctaw people were adapting to the notion of representative government.

CHAPTER 5

THE CIVIL WAR IN INDIAN TERRITORY

In 1860, William H. Seward declared in a ringing speech to the Republican Party Convention in Chicago that "the Indian Territory, also, south of Kansas, must be vacated by the Indians." Southern white and Indian ears may well have prickled at his suggestion that the Republican Party, if elected, would dispossess the Indians of their lands.[1] Abraham Lincoln's election in November 1860 brought to a head national issues of slavery, tariffs, and states' rights. When South Carolina seceded from the nation on December 20, 1860, the first crack in the Union appeared. By early February 1861, seven states had seceded and established the Confederate States of America. U.S. forces attacked the new Confederate post at Fort Sumter in Charleston, and its surrender on April 13 precipitated Abraham Lincoln's proclamation raising a federal militia. The fracture was complete.

The Civil War confronted the Choctaws with a conundrum. The political identity of the tribes in Indian Territory depended upon their treaty relationship with the U.S. government, which guaranteed that the government would protect them from foreign invaders.[2] Some Choctaws, however, were slaveholders and had political ties with Arkansas, which joined the Confederacy on May 7, 1861. It was almost a foregone conclusion that the Indian Territory would join the Confederacy.[3] When federal troops abandoned Indian Territory in 1861, the U.S. government abrogated its treaty obligations. When Confederate troops attacked Fort Cobb, Fort Arbuckle, and Fort Washita, which had originally been established to guard the western reaches of the Choctaw-Chickasaw country from incursions by Kiowas and Comanches, federal forces mounted a brief defense but fled to Fort Leavenworth in Kansas.[4] When Confederate forces captured Fort Smith, Arkansas, in May 1861, they effectively closed the lower Mississippi River to the Union and isolated Indian Territory from the North. Although the sympathy of many Choctaw slave owners lay with the South, the Choctaw Nation had little choice under the circumstances but to sign a treaty with the Confederacy. In doing so, it essentially abrogated its allegiance to the United States. The Choctaws could argue that they were defenseless against the Confederacy because the federal government had not upheld its treaty obligation to protect them.[5] On the other hand, the Union could argue that the Choctaws abrogated the treaties by allying with the Confederacy, and it suspended their annuity payments under treaties.[6] Peter Pitchlynn expressed the dilemma eloquently:

> But the Choctaws are completely tied up, by Treaties, with the government of the United States, which Texas & Arkansas and all of our Southern friends had a hand in making. By these very same treaties, we have a complete title & right to the land we now live on and all our invested funds are now in the hands of President Lincoln. These treaties are the only guarantees we have for our country & our monies. If we now violate them by joining the secessionist, we lose that guarantee for our country & our monies. Still we cannot and must not oppose our Southern friends, and all we now ask of them is to wait upon us, and by no means to doubt our friendship, for their friendship is dear to us. Their interest is our interest, their prosperity is our prosperity. But how can we forfeit all of our rights without first having guaranties made to us for our future security?[7]

Pitchlynn walked a tightrope between his awareness of the Indian Territory's vulnerability to the powers of its Texas and Arkansas neighbors and his own interests, which were tied firmly to the Net Proceeds Case. A break with the federal government would threaten all that he had worked for in the settlement of the claim.[8]

The loss of Indian Territory to the Confederates was a major blow to the Union. If the Union could control the territory, it could isolate

Texas and its rich food resources from the rest of the Confederacy.[9] The territory was crucial to the Confederacy because of the natural resources of the area—agricultural land, coal, stone, and minerals. Confederate leaders would have been content simply to annex it and make it a kind of protectorate, but Indian Territory was still the home of sovereign nations whose political power could not be discounted.

Many Choctaws had reason to reject an alliance with the South. Those who had endured the rigors of removal in the 1830s might well have remembered that it was the state of Mississippi that had insisted on their removal and that Andrew Jackson had coerced the Nation's leaders to accept the provisions of the Treaty of Dancing Creek by supporting the right of the state to extend its jurisdiction over the Nation.[10] The Choctaw alliance with the Confederacy was, however, inevitable. As the Commissioner of Indian Affairs observed,

> Cut off from all intercourse with loyal citizens; surrounded by emissaries from the rebels, who represented that the government of the United States was destroyed, and who promised that the rebel government would assume the obligations of the United States and pay their annuities; assailed by threats of violence, and seeing around them no evidence of the power of the United States to protect them, it is not surprising that their loyalty was unable to resist such influences. Many white men of far greater intelligence have joined the insurrectionists against their own convictions of right, under much less pressure.[11]

The Choctaws, believing that the U.S. government had collapsed and learning that they would no longer receive their annuity payments, put their faith in two men they knew well—the quixotic Albert Pike, the Arkansas lawyer who had first pursued the Net Proceeds Case for the tribe, and the ambitious Douglas Cooper, their U.S. Indian agent. Jefferson Davis had delegated Pike to gain the allegiance of the tribes in Indian Territory for the Confederacy because of his previous legal dealings with them.[12]

Pike convinced Davis that the Indians would have to be guaranteed weapons and military and financial assistance in order to secure their allegiance.[13] Cooper quickly abandoned his allegiance to the United States and declared his sympathies with the South.[14] He was commissioned by the Confederate secretary of war, L. P. Walker, to "cultivate the most friendly relations and the closest alliance" with the Choctaws and other tribes in the Indian Territory and to protect them from "the agrarian rapacity of the North" and "unjust designs against the Indian country."[15] He began seriously recruiting troops for the Confederacy after he received implied authorization from Secretary Walker on May 13. He may have been too eager to do his task; he had already begun enlisting Choctaw troops in April at the very outbreak of the war, while he was still an official of the U.S. government.[16] On July 25, he reported that the organization of the Choctaw and Chickasaw Regiment of Mounted Rifles would be completed during the week, but his statement that "Choctaws and Chickasaws can furnish 10,000 warriors if needed" seems overly optimistic in light of his estimate of a total population of the two tribes of 23,000. Most important for their effectiveness as a fighting force was the fact that they had not yet been furnished with guns and ammunition.[17]

Pike's primary direction from the Confederacy was that he should make no financial commitment to the tribes, but his orders were otherwise vague when he set out for the Indian Territory in May 1861. When he reached North Fork Village on the Canadian River, he finally received a directive that he should tell the Indians that the Confederacy would establish "well defined laws" so that they would receive individual tracts of lands and would form a territorial government for them but without any guarantee of statehood or independence.[18] Both of these ideas were anathema to the majority of the Choctaws, a fact of which Pike was aware.[19] Pike could ask Jefferson Davis for options or he could ignore the orders. He chose the latter course.[20]

Acting on his own initiative, Pike signed a treaty with the Choctaws and Chickasaws on July 12, 1861, agreeing that the Confederacy would assume the obligations that the Union had failed to fulfill and provide the protection the Union had withdrawn. The obligations included the payment of the Net Proceeds Case, in which Pike still believed he had a claim. His interests were, in part at least, self-serving. The Five Civilized Tribes, on their part, were moving to take their own initiative by presenting a unified front in the form of a General Council. They maintained internal self-governance, but the council signed a document on July 1, 1861, that granted right of way through Indian Territory to the Confederacy and empowered each tribe to issue its own call for troops.[21]

The agreements Pike negotiated with the Five Civilized Tribes reaffirmed the terms of treaties they had signed with the U.S. government (thus protecting the Net Proceeds Case), included guarantees of their internal sovereignty, and agreed to assume the payment of annuities due to the tribes from those treaties, even though he did not have the authority to commit the Confederacy to these financial obligations. As part of the treaty, the Choctaws agreed to provide a regiment of ten companies of mounted men to fight in the Confederate Army for a year, but they expected only to defend their own territory. The Confederacy would provide the arms and pay for the soldiers, who would act as home guards. The Five Tribes had insisted in their treaties that they would not go beyond their own boundaries.[22] And indeed, despite the Indian Territory's geographical position as a buffer against the Union, the Confederacy never saw it as a major area for military operation.

Pike's treaty also guaranteed that the Choctaw and Chickasaw territory could become a Confederate state and that the Confederacy would establish a court at Boggy Depot to try cases. Choctaws had long complained about the fact that the U.S. district court in Fort Smith that had jurisdiction over cases involving Indians and non-Indians was both distant and unfair because the juries were composed of white men.[23] Pike was not authorized to obligate the Confederacy to accept the tribes as states, but to accomplish his ends, he made that promise.

By December, Choctaw troops were armed and in service with Confederate troops under Cooper's command in the campaign against the Creek leader Opothleyahola and some 7,000 of his followers. Opothleyahola had rejected the treaty with the Confederacy signed by Creek leaders and had determined to take refuge in Kansas. Cooper and his troops pursued them during November and December. In three major engagements, at Round Mountain on November 19, 1861; at Caving Banks on Bird Creek on December 9; and finally, at Chustenahlah on December 26, 1861, Cooper's troops routed them, and the Creeks fled for their lives through the bitter cold and snow-covered forests to the relative safety of a Union military camp just beyond the Kansas border. Although General David Hunter, commander of the camp, did what he could for the Creeks, many of whom were malnourished, sick, and nearly naked, their suffering was intense, and national publicity about their plight cast a dark pall on Confederate actions in Indian Territory.[24]

There is a curious historical echo in the Choctaw role in the campaign against Opothleyahola. As they had fought with Andrew Jackson's troops against Creek warriors at the Battle of Horseshoe Bend in Alabama in 1813 and won a major victory, so now they fought for the Confederacy against Opothleyahola and his people, mostly women, children, and older men. As a "civilized" people, they again fought an ancient enemy in a white man's war. Creek troops allied with the Confederacy also fought against their fellow tribesmen, as they had in the war of 1813. The Creek Nation was familiar with the agony of civil war well before the American conflict. The consequences would be as disastrous for the Creeks in the 1860s as they had been in their earlier war.

Albert Pike was rewarded for his efforts with an appointment as commander of a newly constituted Department of Indian Territory on November 22, 1861, but he had no respect for the Indian troops under his command. He felt that Indians lacked discipline if they were not influenced by white soldiers.[25] Pike's command did not last long under the demands of the war. It was quickly subsumed under the Trans-Mississippi District of Department 2, which was created by the Confederate government on January 29, 1862, under the command of Earl Van Dorn.[26] The new district encompassed Arkansas, Missouri, Louisiana, and Indian Territory, and its creation directed the Confederacy's military focus to the defense of northwestern Arkansas and the taking of Missouri.

Indeed, Indian Territory seemed an afterthought for the Confederacy. Pike was not formally dismissed when Van Dorn was appointed, and the ensuing conflict between the two men over command had significant repercussions for the Indian Territory.[27] Van Dorn's immediate charge was to gain Missouri for the Confederacy. He ordered General Benjamin McCulloch and his forces to prepare for an advance and ordered Pike and his Indian troops to join them, but four divisions of federal forces were already advancing from Rolla, Missouri, into Western Arkansas, driving McCulloch's troops back, and what had been intended as an advance became a Confederate last stand.

McCulloch's Confederate forces made a stand at Pea Ridge, near Leetown, Arkansas, on March 6, 1862. The battle continued through March 8.[28] Pike's Indian troops arrived after the battle had begun. He had recruited among the Choctaws, Chickasaws, and Creeks, but he had trouble getting the new recruits organized and moving because they had not been paid and had not been furnished with weapons and uniforms. He took three days to issue the payroll and then delayed another day waiting for additional Choctaw and Chickasaw troops to join him. When they did not appear, he marched into Arkansas, where he and Cherokee leaders Stand Watie and John Drew and their forces joined the battle.[29] The Indian troops fought from the trees behind the front, and Drew's men, the mainly full-blood First Cherokee Mounted Rifles, used bows and arrows and tomahawks, following Pike's encouragement to fight "in their own fashion."[30] Stand Watie and his Cherokee troops, mainly mixed-bloods, were actively engaged throughout the last two days of the battle, but the Choctaws and Chickasaws under Cooper's command and the Creeks under McIntosh did not receive word to advance, and they remained in the rear as the battle drew to a disastrous con-clusion for the Confederate troops. Overwhelmed by the superior Union numbers and demoralized by the deaths of their command-ers, McCulloch and General James McIntosh, the Confederates abandoned the field, with Stand Watie and his Cherokees largely covering the retreat as a rear guard.[31]

Pike's action following the battle was bizarre. He gathered what scattered forces he could and retreated rapidly some 100 miles to the far southern part of Indian Territory, camping finally at a point about twenty miles north of the Red River. There he ordered his men to build a fort, which he named Fort McCulloch, where he intended to mount a final defense of Indian Territory and the Confederacy.[32] His pleas for help from the Choctaws were met with "burlesque," and Texans ignored his "patriotic call."[33] By this point, no one could take Pike seriously. When the corpses of Union troops were discovered tomahawked and scalped at Pea Ridge, Indians were discredited as soldiers and Pike was viciously parodied in the *New York Tribune* as a "leader of savages."[34]

Pike began a vigorous letter-writing campaign, charging Van Dorn with neglect of the Indian Territory, challenging his right of command, and calling for the separation of the Territory from Van Dorn's authority. Van Dorn ignored Pike's charges. He preempted weapons, clothing, and ammunition that Pike had gathered through his own efforts and largely with his own funds for his defense of Eastern Arkansas, and he ordered Pike to Fort Smith to defend western Arkansas, a command Pike ignored.[35]

Pike's retreat to the Red River and Van Dorn's move to eastern Arkansas left the Indian Territory largely undefended. Once again, the Indian nations found themselves abandoned by those who had sworn by treaty to protect them. As Van Dorn moved east, the defense of western Arkansas fell to Major General Thomas Carmichael Hindman, who on June 8 ordered Pike to move his white troops to Little Rock. Pike and Hindman clashed, each firmly convinced that his was the right strategy. Pike delayed and Hindman demanded. Pike explained and Hindman insisted. On July 7, Hindman sent an officer to Fort McCulloch to collect weapons that Pike had failed to send with his troops to Arkansas. On July 8 he ordered Pike to proceed to Fort Smith to take command of all troops in Indian Territory and northern Arkansas, and Pike promptly wrote a letter of resignation to Jefferson Davis and asked Hindman for a leave of absence until Davis had replied. Hindman in his turn relieved Pike of his command on July 28.[36]

Rather than reporting to Fort Smith as Hindman had ordered, Pike went to Fort Washita, where he addressed an impassioned letter to the chiefs of the Five Civilized Tribes, explaining the reasons for his resignation. He charged that Hindman and Van Dorn had largely abandoned the Indian Territory by ordering him to Arkansas and failing to provide the pay, weapons, and supplies necessary for the defense of the territory.[37] Pike had his letter printed and circulated widely in the territory, but when Douglas Cooper learned of its existence, he seized all the copies he could find and, condemning Pike as "partially deranged, and a dangerous person to be at liberty among the Indians," ordered his arrest.[38] By this time, Cooper, who had ambitions to become commander of the Indian Territory after Pike's disgrace at Pea Ridge, was perfectly willing to contribute to Pike's downfall. But Cooper had a financial interest with Pike in the Net Proceeds Case, and his ulterior motive became apparent. As Pike expressed it, "I think now, and have thought from the first, Cooper's object to be to make me unpopular with the Choctaws, so that he may when peace comes, have the sole management of the Choctaw claim, and finger most of the fee."[39]

The Confederates rallied from the disastrous defeat at Pea Ridge when Hindman staged an attack on northern Missouri, and Cooper and his Choctaw troops distinguished themselves at Newtonia on September 29, 1862. The First Choctaw and Chickasaw Regiment, led by Lieutenant Colonel Tandy Walker, entered the town at full gallop, "singing their war-songs and giving the war whoop."[40] But the Confederate rally was short lived. Cooper was ordered to invade Kansas, but at Fort Wayne, just south of the Kansas border in the Delaware District of the Cherokee Nation, his Indian troops did not appear, and he was soundly defeated by Union forces. He and his forces retreated to Fort Davis, on the banks of the Arkansas River near present-day Muskogee, Oklahoma. Cooper not only lost the battle, but he and his commanding officer were accused of being drunk, a charge that would follow him throughout his subsequent military career. Cooper tried to defend himself by pointing out that his Indian forces had not appeared at Fort Wayne as ordered because they had not been paid, but a loss is a loss, and Cooper's loss gave the Union a firm grip on the land north of the Arkansas River.[41]

In the meantime, Pike abandoned Fort McCulloch and his attempt to defend Indian Territory and went to Texas, thus beginning what one of his biographers described as "the most inexplicable adventure of his life."[42] In September, he settled in Warren, Texas, but on October 22, he declared his intention to resume command of the Indian Territory to Major General Theophilus Holmes, Hindman's successor as commander of the newly named Trans-Mississippi Department. He assumed that Jefferson Davis had not accepted his resignation, that his leave had expired, and that he should return to duty.[43] Holmes agreed with Hindman, however, that Pike's letter to the chiefs of the Five Tribes in Indian Territory criticizing the Confederacy was extremely indiscrete, if not treasonous. Pike responded with extensive charges against Hindman addressed to Jefferson Davis and another letter of resignation (the first had been lost when the courier was captured by Union forces).[44] On November 14, however, he was arrested on Hindman's orders and taken to Holmes's headquarters in Little Rock. Pike was saved from the ultimate disgrace of court martial when Holmes evidently received word that Davis had indeed accepted Pike's resignation. And although Pike tried to press charges against Hindman and Holmes through congressional action, Hindman ultimately undid himself through a disastrous Confederate loss at Prairie Grove in northern Arkansas on December 7 and was relieved of his command.[45]

Pike's troubles cost Indian Territory its only real advocate in the Confederacy. Pike alone had made the defense of the territory his main cause. He alone had argued that Indian troops should not be ordered beyond the borders of the territory without their consent. He had used his own funds in some cases to secure supplies and equipment. Where other commanders viewed the Indian Territory as a source of supplies and a staging area for advances into Kansas and Missouri, Pike had struggled to protect it for its own sake. But in the end, his commitment was not to the Indian nations of the territory but to his own ambition. He wrote a long and impassioned letter to his nemesis Theophilus Holmes after his resignation, signing it "Albert Pike, Citizen of Arkansas."

> I had, unaided and alone, *secured* to the Confederacy a magnificent country, equal in extent, fertility, beauty and resources to any of our States— nay, superior to any. I had secured the means, in men and arms, of keeping it. I knew how only it could be defended.[46]

Although the Confederate government had initially sworn to protect the tribes of Indian Territory from "Northern rapacity," as the war went on and Confederate prospects dimmed, the Confederacy wanted not Indian allies but control of Indian resources.

Through 1863, the fortunes of the Confederacy and Indian Territory declined. Douglas Cooper realized his ambition to become the

Confederate superintendent of Indian affairs and called for a program of national conscription.[47] Tandy Walker was promoted to the rank of colonel and was given the job of recruiting among the Choctaws.[48] But for residents of Indian Territory, joining the army now became a way simply of getting food and clothing. Peter Pitchlynn reported that "everybody here are in favour of going into the Con. Service—and have already done so cheerfully as the only means to save themselves having no means of supporting themselves with ammunition or bread and meat."[49]

In April 1863, Union troops under the command of Colonel William A. Phillips captured Fort Gibson, giving the Union a major outpost in Indian Territory and effective control of the area north of the Arkansas River.[50] Fort Gibson was, however, a vulnerable point for the Union because it was supplied from Fort Scott in Kansas, and the supply trains had to come down the Texas Road across a branch of the Arkansas River called Cabin Creek. The creek crossing provided a strategic location from which Confederate troops, primarily Stand Watie and his Cherokee forces, could ambush the trains. On July 1, 1863, Watie launched an attack on a train, but high water prevented coordinated action among the Confederate forces and the attempt to capture the train failed.[51] This first battle at Cabin Creek dislodged the Confederates and secured the supply route for the Union. Fort Gibson was also secure, and Phillips and General James Blunt, Union commander of the Department of Kansas, advanced against Confederate forces commanded by Douglas Cooper, including a Choctaw and Chickasaw regiment under the command of Tandy Walker, at Honey Springs, about twenty-five miles south of Fort Gibson. Cooper entrenched his Indian troops along Elk Creek (near present-day Muskogee). The battle pitted 7,000 Union troops against some 6,000 Confederates. In sheer size, the battle was the largest fought in Indian Territory. The superior numbers and firepower of the Union forces prevailed, and the Confederate line broke.[52]

The Battle of Honey Springs was a disastrous blow to Indian allegiance to the Confederacy, not only because of the loss of supplies as fleeing Confederate troops burned the commissary buildings to prevent them from falling into Union hands but also because of the psychological blow inflicted by the loss of the battle. Coming shortly after Confederate defeats in the east at Gettysburg and Vicksburg, Honey Springs had a demoralizing effect on the hope for a southern victory in the war.[53] It also paved the way for Blunt's capture of Fort Smith, which by late September placed him squarely on the doorstep of the Choctaw Nation.[54]

In early 1864, Union commander General Frederick Steele proposed a thrust through Arkansas to capture the Confederate headquarters of the Trans-Mississippi District at Shreveport, Louisiana. At Poison Spring, Arkansas, on April 14, Steele met a strong Confederate force. During the battle, Choctaw forces under the command of Tandy Walker distinguished themselves by routing an entrenched federal force and capturing a battery of four cannons and most of a Union supply train. The battle was one of a series of Confederate successes in the disastrous federal operation known as the Red River campaign. A series of Union losses in Arkansas bolstered the confidence of the Confederates.[55]

General Samuel Maxey, now commander of Indian Territory, had attempted to revitalize the Indian allegiance to the Confederacy, and in June, the entire First Choctaw Regiment reenlisted and called on the General Council to pass a universal conscription law.[56] News of the victory at Poison Spring was very encouraging, but the Choctaws were basically the only strong Indian troops left to Cooper's command.[57] Stand Watie had become commander of his own Cherokee forces and achieved the rank of brigadier general. He answered directly to General Maxey.

Although it was clear that Confederate armies were crumbling in the east, Watie and Cooper scored a last-gasp victory in Indian Territory at the second battle of Cabin Creek on September 17 and 18, 1864. Again Watie launched an attack on a federal supply train, this one carrying supplies of food and clothing for the relief of refugee Indians who had remained loyal to the Union and had congregated in areas around Fort Gibson. This time, perhaps ironically given its cargo, the Confederate forces captured the train and used its supplies to feed and clothe their own men.[58] The victory gave renewed hope to people in the Indian Territory, but it proved hollow.

Confederate command in Indian Territory was also in disarray. Douglas Cooper had once again engineered the dismissal of a Confederate commander, Maxey.[59] Cooper had been passed over for command when Maxey was first appointed. Now he had finally succeeded in gaining command of what was essentially a lost cause.

With Robert E. Lee's surrender at Appomattox on April 9, 1865, the war was over. The tribes in Indian Territory had cast their lot with Cooper and Pike, white men whose own ambitions transcended those of the tribes. With the failure of the Confederacy, the tribes confronted their own need to act as sovereign nations. Stand Watie had proposed to the leaders of the Five Tribes in August of 1863 that they form a union of their own and withdraw from the Confederacy, and the Choctaws had supported the idea at a meeting of the General Council in early February 1864.[60]

A Grand Council of tribes convened at Camp Napoleon, near present-day Verden, Oklahoma, on May 24, 1865, before news of Lee's surrender had reached Indian Territory. Tribal leaders considered the possibility that they might continue to fight the Union as an independent nation. But on May 26, Confederate general Kirby Smith surrendered the Trans-Mississippi District to Union general Edward S. Canby at New Orleans, and it was fully apparent that an independent confederation of Indian tribes, no matter how eager for revenge, could not carry on the war.[61] The Camp Napoleon meeting brought together representatives of both the Five Tribes and the so-called wild Indians in the West. In extending the invitation to all Indians, including those in Kansas and other parts of the country, the Five Tribes might have been attempting to create a united Indian confederacy, but their objectives were more focused on healing their own internal divisions between Union and Confederate factions.[62]

On June 10, the Grand Council of the Five Tribes convened again at Armstrong Academy in the Choctaw Nation, this time with knowledge of the Confederate defeat. They had allied themselves with a foreign government to preserve what they saw as their interests in a war between competing nations. They also resolved "to maintain the integrity of the Indian Territory as the present and future home of our race, to preserve and perpetuate the national rights and franchises of the several nations, to cultivate peace, harmony, and fellowship." The council authorized tribal representatives to sign treaties with the U.S. government subject to approval by the councils of the tribes.[63] They also declared that they would not surrender to the Union as part of the Confederacy but would make their own treaties as independent nations.[64]

Ultimately, Indian Territory played a role of very minor importance in a region, the trans-Mississippi West, that was itself secondary to the great struggle taking place east of the Mississippi. It was important for its land and natural resources and as a staging area for operations in Kansas, Missouri, and Arkansas. It was useful and it was exploited, and in that process, Cherokees and Creeks particularly experienced deep and lasting divisions between tribal factions, they were driven from their homes, and they suffered physical hardship.

Of all the tribes in Indian Territory, the Choctaws were probably least affected in terms of the physical devastation of their territory. W. A. Stephens declared that the war had given the land "a touch of devastation,—We are not left in half as bad a condition as some of the Southern states."[64] And Isaac Coleman, U.S. agent at the temporary agency of Choctaws and Chickasaws, noted that most of the Indians had remained near their homes in the territory and had not "suffered by the destruction of their property to the same extent as have the various tribes surrounding them."[65]

There were no major military engagements in Choctaw Territory, although Choctaw troops constituted the largest number of Indian forces in the Confederate Army after the Cherokees. According to William A. Steele, commander of the Indian Territory in 1863, there were 1,024 Choctaw troops and 200 Choctaw militia.[66] Union forces raided Choctaw territory during the latter part of the war. Essentially abandoned by the Confederacy, Choctaw territory was preyed on by "jayhawkers" from both Confederate and Union sides.[67] Peter Pitchlynn reported that "the whole line from the Arkansas and Red Rivers is in danger from jayhawkers. . . .There are more than a hundred jayhawkers in Sevier County."[68]

Probably the greatest loss for the Choctaws was livestock. Beef was necessary to feed the armies, and although much of it came from Texas, a significant amount also came from Indian territory through raiders who stole from the Indians to sell to cattle dealers in Texas, who in turn sold them to the Confederate army.[69] George Williams, who was appointed by the War Department after the war to investigate the cattle trade, estimated that "during the past four years there have been at least 300,000 head of cattle stolen from the Indian territory, a country at one time rich in their cattle possessions, and now scarcely a head can be seen in a ride of 200 miles."[70]

The real devastation of the Choctaw Nation was not physical but was a result of the punitive treaty forced upon it after the war. On June 19, Peter Pitchlynn signed the final surrender of the Choctaw Nation, setting the stage for the negotiation of the treaty that would reestablish the relationship of the Choctaw Nation to the federal government on yet another basis. The U.S. government would treat the Confederacy's Indian allies as defeated nations. The tribes had joined the Confederacy for three main reasons. They had a long history of slave-owning from their time in the southeast. Their geographical position in Indian Territory, with Kansas on the north, Arkansas on the east, and Texas on the south, put them within the southern sphere. And the Union had withdrawn its troops from Indian Territory and abandoned its treaty obligations to protect them from foreign invasion. James Harlan, secretary of the interior, declared that the tribes "in flagrant violation of treaties which had been observed by us with scrupulous good faith" and "in the absence of any just ground of complaint" had "entered into an alliance with the rebel authorities and raised regiments in support of their cause."[71] Peter Pitchlynn countered that "the several Indian Nations in the Territory were before the war, in alliance by treaties with the Federal Government, those treaties were annulled by reason of the expulsion of the Federal troops from the Territory by citizens of the Confederate States."[72] The matter was still one of treaty rights and interpretation of "good faith."

CHAPTER 6

THE TREATY OF 1866

Having cast their lot with the Confederacy, the Choctaws found themselves compelled to negotiate yet another treaty that created a new basis for their relationship with the U.S. government. The new relationship was forged in an atmosphere of antagonism, and the Choctaws had to negotiate the treaty without any of the bargaining chips they had been able to use in 1855. The defeat of the Confederacy left the tribes of Indian Territory vulnerable to the long-standing desire of the U.S. government to settle the Plains Indians, develop railroads, and, ultimately, integrate the territory as a state within the United States. The Treaty of 1866 was the instrument for reconstructing the Choctaw and Chickasaw nations as part of the United States and for imposing upon them the model of civil government and individual land-holding that would put them on an equal footing with other territories and, ultimately, bring them fully into American society. As the victor in the war, the federal government could dictate terms of the Reconstruction treaties, and the Five Tribes had no political capital.

The critical issue for all of the Five Tribes in the postwar period was the prospect of territorialization. The federal government wanted Indian Territory under its control so that it could be made a state. In order for that to happen, Indians would have to give up communal ownership and take land as private property. The specter of territorialization had emerged well before the Civil War, during the debates over the Kansas-Nebraska Act. On February 23, 1854,

Senator Richard Johnson of Arkansas introduced a bill to create three federal territories out of Indian Territory: Cherokee lands would become Chahlahkee, the Creek and Seminole land would become Muscogee, and the Choctaw and Chickasaw lands would be named Chahta. Their creation would mark the success of the federal government's policy of civilizing the Indians, prepare the way for Indians to become citizens of the United States, and vest Indians "with the highest rights of self-government."[1] Territorialization would "extend the protection of the Constitution and laws of the United States" over the tribes and would "enable them to advance in civilization, and hereafter to become citizens of the United States." Johnson described his bill as the "discharge of a debt we all acknowledge, in fulfillment of a duty to a much and long injured race of people" and as "a matter of conscience." The Five Tribes, however, saw it as yet another abrogation of treaty rights that had assured them that they would remain sovereigns over their lands and would never become part of the United States. The Choctaws and Chickasaws could resist the notion of "sectionalizing" their land—that is, dividing it into individually owned parcels—because their government held the land under fee simple title, the same kind of title the U.S. government recognized. The difference was that the title was held by the tribe as communal property.

In 1865, Senator James Harlan (R-Iowa) introduced a bill outlining a plan for the organization of Indian Territory under the U.S. government.[2] A key provision allowed tribes simply to accept the plan, a significant departure from the federal policy of treaty-making, although in debate on the bill one senator insisted that a treaty be signed with the tribes getting their assent before the bill was considered.[3] The debate finally centered on the question of whether Congress had the power to interfere with tribal government. Harlan's bill gave the president of the United States the power to appoint the secretary of Indian affairs as governor of the new territory. The tribes would have no say in the matter. The Senate passed the bill by a vote of 17 to 9, but it did not reach the House in time for debate before adjournment.

In the meantime, Senator Harlan was appointed as secretary of the interior. In that role, he sought to implement his plan for territorialization by giving instructions to the U.S. commissioners who were

The Choctaw Nation in 1866. (Adapted from Goins and Goble, *Historical Atlas of Oklahoma*, 4th ed.)

sent to negotiate the postwar treaties with the tribes at Fort Smith, Arkansas, in September 1865.[4] A treaty under Harlan's terms would meld Choctaw and Chickasaw land into a U.S. territory by sectionalizing it into private property and creating towns, schools, post offices, private property, and railroads. It would also destroy the nations' power of self-government by creating a unified government for Indian Territory.

The negotiation of new treaties with the nations of Indian Territory began on September 8, 1865, when federal commissioners and representatives of the nations met at Fort Smith, Arkansas.[5] The irony of the Fort Smith meeting (which was attended by Creeks, Choctaws, Chickasaws, Cherokees, Seminoles, Osages, Senecas, Shawnees, Quapaws, Wyandots, Wichitas, and Comanches) was that the Indian representatives were all members of the factions of the tribes that had remained loyal to the Union. The Camp Napoleon meeting the previous spring had obviously not healed the deep divisions between loyalists and Confederates within the tribes. The loyalists did not flock to Fort Smith to discuss the proposed alliance of Indian nations.

Even the location of the treaty negotiations was a political issue. Peter Pitchlynn had wanted the meeting to be held at Armstrong Academy, capital of the Choctaw Nation, where the tribes, especially the Choctaws, would have a certain "home court" advantage and where the locale was "healthier," he wrote in his call for the meeting. He had already sent out word that it would be held there when he learned that the commissioners wanted to meet at Fort Smith.[6] The result was that the representatives of the loyalist factions met the federal commissioners who appeared at Fort Smith while leaders of the Confederate factions attended Pitchlynn's meeting at Armstrong Academy to discuss their strategy.

As they had been so many times in the past, those who ostensibly represented tribes at Fort Smith were selected by federal agents. Robert Patton, who was one of four Choctaws present, declared that he did not represent the tribe but had been chosen by the Indian agent to attend the meeting. He estimated that only 212 Choctaws had remained loyal to the Union, although the agent had estimated that some 1,800 full-bloods had "remained in their homes"—that is, rejected the Confederate alliance.[7] This small group was expected to sign a new treaty establishing a new relationship with the U.S. government.

Commissioner Cooley opened the negotiations with due rhetorical force by asking the Great Spirit for wisdom in deliberations and health for the delegates and their families, but his subsequent tone must have puzzled those who considered themselves still loyal to the United States. Cooley declared that the president required the tribes to "renew their allegiance to the United States," but they also needed to settle their own internal divisions that were the result of the fact that some of their members had allied with "wicked white men." The commissioners were there to make a treaty that would establish peace and amity with "all his red children who may desire his favor and protections." The rebellious Indians had "rightfully forfeited all annuities and interests in the lands in the Indian territory." With the restoration of peace, "the President is willing to hear his erring children in extenuation of their great crime." But Cooley was preaching to those who were already loyal. The Confederate Indians at whom the speech was obviously aimed were not present to hear it.[8]

When Cooley invited the Indians present to respond to his speech and the proposals, there was a general sense of confusion over the purpose of the whole exercise. Silas Armstrong, representing the Wyandots, rose to explain that his tribe, which was located in Kansas, expected to buy land on which to settle in the Indian Territory. They had remained loyal to the Union, but, as he said, "I see, from speeches of my brothers, that we are all in the suds." None of the delegates present at the beginning of the council were prepared to sign a treaty that appeared to be binding on the entire tribe or to make immediate responses to Cooley's overtures.[9]

The Indians continued to waffle and Cooley grew increasingly impatient. He launched into a tirade against Cherokee leader John Ross, whose attempt to maintain a neutral stance had revealed the deep divisions within the tribe. He regretted that the Chickasaws and Seminoles "have not been invested with more general powers, so as to settle all their difficulties at this time by entering into a proper treaty." He urged the delegates to make "a treaty of peace and amity with the United States." When the "rebel Indians" appeared, they would be forced to sign it.[10]

Cooley already had his "treaty" written, and when he presented it to the assembled Indian representatives on September 13, it was obvious that, indeed, all the Indians, loyal and disloyal alike, were "in the suds." Its first "whereas" lumped them all together as being "induced by the machinations" of Confederate agents "to throw off their allegiance" to the United States, making themselves liable to a "forfeiture of all rights of every kind, character, and description which had been promised and guaranteed to them by the United States." In its "magnanimity," however, the United States promised to "re-establish peace and friendship" with the tribes in Indian Territory, protect their persons and property, and settle all matters growing out of former treaties.[11] Copies of the treaty were printed and distributed to the delegates, and Cooley expected them to sign it the following morning. On the 14th, with much seeming hesitation, the representatives of the Wichitas, Senecas, Shawnees, Quapaws, Seminoles, Chickasaws, Creeks, Shawnees from Kansas, and Osages signed.[12]

The Confederate representatives did not begin to arrive in Fort Smith until September 16, the eighth day of the meeting, and it was September 18 before they were ready to respond to Cooley. The opening statement was presented by Robert M. Jones, head of the Choctaw delegation. If the tone of Commissioner Cooley's speech on the first day of the meeting, with its paternalistic rhetoric of the Great Father and his red children, was meant to enforce upon its audience their dependency upon the will of the U.S. government, the tone of the Chickasaw and Choctaw response was far from submissive. Jones declared that "when we admit that we recognize the government of the United States as exercising exclusive jurisdiction over us, we do not understand the United States as meaning to assume the control or jurisdiction over our internal, local, or national affairs, except as to slavery, which is open to further negotiation."[13]

The Choctaws had not been "induced by the machinations of the emissaries of the Confederate States" to make treaties. They made them from self-interest, to preserve "our independence and national identity." The Nation considered itself "a separate political organization." The cause of the Confederate states was "just," and those states had the right to secede. The Confederacy also offered the Nation "the protection that the United States then failed to give us." The alliance with the Confederacy was made "to establish what we believed to be the great cardinal principle of republican liberty—the right of self-government." Acknowledging that the Confederacy had ceased to exist, Jones agreed that the Choctaw Nation was willing to sign a treaty to reestablish its relationship with the United States and to remain loyal, as it had done until 1861, but he closed with the hope that it would be a lasting agreement and that the Nation would "never be again forced to cast our fortunes with one of two contending sections."[14]

The defiant tone of the statement was rather breathtaking in the face of the hostile intent of the United States to punish the Indians. The assertion that the Choctaws acted of their own accord and out of self-interest, the pointed statement that the federal government had failed to honor its treaty obligations, and the implication that the stability of the United States was still questionable all were true, but the Choctaws were still on very precarious ground. They, of all the tribes, had been most overwhelmingly in favor of the Confederate alliance.

While delegations of Confederate Cherokees, Creeks, and Osages signed Cooley's document, the Choctaws and Chickasaws met separately to consider it. On the following day, September 20, they submitted a slightly modified version of the statement read by Jones, adding a phrase, "we felt that we were shut up to an alliance with the south," that softened the defiant tone somewhat. On the next day, September 21, they proposed some modifications and amendments to the treaty that the commissioners would not accept. In the end, the only Choctaw signatures on the document were those of the four loyal Choctaws.[15]

All the Fort Smith meeting produced was an agreement by the Choctaws to negotiate further, although the outlines of any treaty had already been effectively set by Harlan and Cooley. Peter Pitchlynn, who had been elected chief of the Choctaw Nation in 1864, knew that the future of the Net Proceeds Case depended on a new treaty that protected previous treaty rights, but his role as chief precluded his appointment as a treaty delegate. Pitchlynn had been pro-

Union during the war and he tried to select pro-Union delegates, but none would agree to serve.[16] The General Council also thwarted his attempt. The final delegation was composed of Alfred Wade, John Wright, Robert M. Jones, Allen Wright, and James Riley.[17]

The delegates represented an interesting cross-section of Choctaw society. Robert M. Jones, a half-blood man "of large wealth," had an outstanding claim against the United States for cotton Union forces had seized during the war. Allen Wright, a full-blood, was treasurer of the Nation and a Presbyterian minister. Alfred Wade, also a full-blood, was the former governor under the Skullyville Constitution. John Page, a full-blood, had served as an interpreter for the United States and was a minister in the Methodist Church.[18] James Riley, a property owner, had commanded a Choctaw regiment in the war.[19] Pitchlynn complained that the delegates had all served under Douglas Cooper's command in the war and were wholly under his influence, but he had to confirm them.

The treaty delegation traveled to Washington in May 1866, accompanied by Cooper and Pitchlynn, but its first stop was in Baltimore. The Choctaws would need a lawyer to assist them in the negotiations, and Cooper introduced them to his brother-in-law, John H. B. Latrobe (who was married to Cooper's half-sister). Latrobe had been a prominent Union supporter during the war, and Cooper had enlisted his assistance in 1861 to get the initial $500,000 appropriation on the Net Proceeds claim.[20] The delegates reached a verbal agreement with Latrobe that specifically charged him to prevent the abrogation of former treaties (a necessary condition to save the Net Proceeds Case), to recover the annuities and other monies whose payment the federal government had suspended during the war, and to keep the Leased District (the lands beyond the 98th meridian detailed in the 1855 treaty) out of the government's hands. It gave him a contingency fee of 50 percent of the unpaid annuities he could recover and the value of the Leased District. The agreement included a $200,000 advance on the fee ($100,000 from the Choctaw delegates and $100,000 from the Chickasaws), and Latrobe agreed to give the delegates and Cooper shares of 5 percent apiece of the advance. The agreement was confirmed in a written contract with Latrobe signed on May 16, 1866.[21]

The Latrobe contract shows how money had become a driving force in Choctaw politics. Latrobe later stated that the $100,000 advance was an unexpected offer from Peter Pitchlynn,[22] but it was probably initiated by Douglas Cooper.[23] The financial agreement with Latrobe began an intrigue that would tarnish the reputations of the delegates and serve as evidence of the growing importance of self-interest among leading men of the Choctaw Nation.

Although Latrobe took credit in his later years for sole authorship of the Treaty of 1866, he initially claimed he had prepared it in consultation with the Choctaw delegates.[24] The basic framework of the treaty was established by James Harlan, but over the early spring of 1866, Latrobe and the Choctaw and Chickasaw delegates hammered out the details. The treaty was signed in Washington on April 28, 1866, and was witnessed by Pitchlynn in his role as the principal chief of the Choctaw Nation and Douglas Cooper in his role as U.S. agent for the Choctaws and Chickasaws.[25] It was confirmed by the Senate on July 10. It did indeed redefine the relationship between the U.S. government and the Choctaw Nation, and it set the stage for major issues the Nation confronted in the latter part of the nineteenth century—the status of freedmen, the advent of railroads, and the threat of territorialization.

The treaty reaffirmed "permanent peace and friendship" between the tribes and the United States, which implicitly restored the federal trade and intercourse laws of the 1830s, and provided that the "rights, privileges, and immunities" under previous treaties remained "in full force, so far as they are consistent with the provisions of this treaty."[26] The Choctaws had preserved their right to make claims for treaty rights against the U.S. government.

In the third article of the treaty, the Choctaws and Chickasaws agreed to cede the Leased District to the United States for the settlement of the freedmen. The sixth article of the treaty provided right of way for two railroads through Indian Territory, one north-south route and one east-west route. These two provisions would give rise to new claims in the future.

The tribes agreed to abolish slavery, but they then faced the issue of what to do about the large number of black freedmen in their midst. The government's plan was to reconstruct Indian Territory by requiring the tribes to adopt the freedmen as citizens and give them forty acres of land. The government would pay $300,000 for the Leased District after the tribes passed laws giving freed slaves "all the rights, privileges, and immunities, including the right of suffrage, of citizens of said nations," forty acres of tribal land, and standing as "competent witnesses" in their courts. If the tribes failed to make such laws within two years, the money would be used to pay for the removal of the freedmen to the Leased District. Freedmen in the Nation would also have the protection of a federal policy that required contracts for black laborers.[27] The freedmen represented another wedge of federal jurisdiction into the territory.

However, the Choctaws did not finally and formally adopt freed slaves as tribal members until 1883, and blacks largely segregated themselves in separate towns. The Chickasaws, for their part, avoided making their freedmen citizens, largely through the failure of the government to ratify tribal actions in a timely manner.[28] The status of the Leased District joined the question of the eastern boundary of the Nation and the Net Proceeds Case on the list of Choctaw monetary claims against the U.S. government.

The treaty incorporated the policy of allotment of land to individual tribal members, which would promote "the general civilization" and "advance their permanent welfare and the best interests of their individual members." It laid out detailed procedures by which the land would be surveyed and individual Indians would select their lands. The freedmen would have their forty acres, and Indians from Kansas would be accepted as citizens by the Choctaw and Chickasaw nations and would be entitled to select land. But the whole plan hinged on a single phrase: "should the Choctaw and the Chickasaw people, through their respective legislative councils, agree to the survey and division of their land."[29] The profound resistance of the Choctaws to the idea of allotment essentially nullified these provisions of the treaty. It did not, however, prevent the ultimate imposition of the allotment policy some thirty years later.

The treaty imposed a plan for the governance of Indian Territory and required the tribes to agree to "such legislation as Congress and the President of the United States may deem necessary for the better administration of justice and the protection of the rights of person and property within the Indian Territory."[30] The government assured the tribes that federal legislation would not "interfere with or annul their present tribal organization, or their respective legislatures or judiciaries" and that it would not affect their "rights, laws, privileges, or customs." But the threat of congressional action threatened the sovereignty of the nations.

The treaty's plan for the new government of Indian Territory consisted of an elected council of delegates from each tribe in the territory that would legislate on matters pertaining to relationships among the tribes, including extradition of criminals, internal improvements, and common defense and safety. Tribes with at least 500 members would have one representative, and larger tribes would have one representative for each 1,000 members. Tribes could be represented by its chief or headmen if that was their custom. The council would meet annually for no more than thirty days, but the secretary of the interior could call special sessions. The superintendent of Indian affairs would serve as president of the council. A court or courts could be established, although these would not interfere with internal tribal jurisdiction. A secretary was to be appointed to assist the "governor" in executing the laws of the assembly, and a marshal with the power to appoint deputies was to enforce the laws. Preference in appointing marshals and deputies was given, "qualifications being equal," to tribal members, "the object being to create a laudable ambition to acquire the experience necessary for political offices of importance in the respective nations."[31]

The federal government was intent on using the treaty process to groom tribal members for important offices and Indian Territory for statehood, a goal tribal representatives had repeatedly and strongly opposed. The tribes of Indian Territory were not interested in a unified government, despite the treaty.[32] Although the tribes made no effort to implement the allotment and governmental provisions of the treaty, various bills were introduced in Congress proposing territorialization. All died quietly in various committees until 1870, when Representative Robert T. Van Horn of Missouri introduced a bill to organize Indian Territory under the name Oklahoma, a Choctaw term meaning "red people" that had been proposed by the Choctaw delegate Allen Wright during the negotiation of the 1866 treaty.[33]

When Van Horn's bill actually reached the floor of the House, the threat of congressional action became more real. If the tribes would not act, Congress would.

The threat mobilized a response in Indian Territory. Delegates from the Cherokees, Creeks, Ottawas, Eastern Shawnees, Quapaws, Senecas, Wyandots, Peorias, Sac and Fox, Absentee Shawnees, and Osages finally agreed to meet at Okmulgee, capital of the Muscogee (Creek) Nation on September 27, 1870. The Choctaws were conspicuously absent; the Choctaw General Council had not yet authorized the appointment of delegates.[34] The group constituted itself as the General Council of the Indian Territory and established basic rules of operation and a series of committees: Relations with the United States, International Relations, Judiciary, Finance, Education and Agriculture, and Enrolled Bills. Its first official resolution called for a memorial to the president of the United States protesting any congressional action that would impair "the obligation of any treaty provision" or try to create "any government over the Indian Territory other than that of the General Council." It also protested any attempt by the federal government to offer grants of Indian land to railroads.

The second session of the council included Choctaw representatives[35] and established three basic principles: opposition to a territorial government by congressional action, the insistence that each tribe retain its own internal self-government, and the requirement that a constitution would not be binding on any nation until it had been approved by vote of the people of that nation.[36] However, it still had to be ratified by the various tribal legislatures.

The General Council finally produced the Okmulgee Constitution. Its purpose was to draw the tribes "in a closer bond of union, for the better protection of their rights, the improvement of themselves, and the preservation of their race." These goals were certainly at odds with the objectives of the federal government's policy of assimilating Indians into the general population of the United States and creating a single unified territory. The Okmulgee Constitution strictly protected each nation's right to its own lands, funds, and other property.[37]

It generally followed the provisions laid out in the Treaty of 1866, including a legislature (called the General Assembly) composed of a

Senate and a House of Representatives that would act on intertribal matters. The assembly was specifically prohibited from making retrospective laws or laws that impaired the obligation of contracts. It could raise the revenue necessary to support its operations but no more than that, and its laws concerning revenue had to be uniform throughout the territory. The Okmulgee Constitution called for election of a governor by popular vote (a departure from the plan in the Treaty of 1866). Appointed officers included a secretary of the territory, who could also serve as treasurer; a marshal; an attorney general; and two district attorneys. The judicial branch was comprised of a Supreme Court composed of three justices, three district courts, and inferior courts as provided by law. It had jurisdiction over intertribal matters, but it was not to interfere with the jurisdiction of the separate tribal courts. The power to amend the constitution lay first with the General Assembly and then with the national councils, three-fourths of which had to ratify an amendment in order for it to be accepted.

The constitution's declaration of rights included the power of the people to alter, reform, or abolish their form of government; free exercise of religion; freedom of speech; freedom from unreasonable search or seizure; the right to a speedy trial and habeas corpus; freedom from self-incrimination, excessive bail, double jeopardy, and imprisonment for debt; and the right of free assembly. Finally, the Okmulgee Constitution reserved to the nations those rights they had reserved by their treaties with the U.S. government.[38]

The Okmulgee Constitution became a matter of ongoing debate both within the Indian Territory and in the halls of the U.S. Congress. Within the territory, the matter of representation was problematic. Smaller tribes, particularly the Chickasaws and Seminoles, objected to the formula for the number of representatives and refused to ratify the constitution. The Choctaw General Council ratified it on October 24, 1871.[39] The Okmulgee Constitution revealed political strains not only among the tribes in Indian Territory over representation but between the tribes and the Congress of the United States. The 1866 treaty had specified that the superintendent of Indian affairs would be the governor of Indian Territory, but the superintendent was appointed by the president, thereby putting the selection of an executive officer in the hands of the federal government rather than in the hands of the tribes. The Okmulgee Constitution obviously was a declaration of tribal autonomy with its specification that the governor had to be elected by a popular vote. Nevertheless, it was increasingly obvious that the General Council was simply a pro forma exercise, a way of dealing with the very real threat that Congress would impose a territorial government on Indian Territory. Although Congress had funded meetings of the General Council with the hope that the tribes would follow its agenda, it became obvious that a unified government was not going to happen, and Congress withdrew funding for delegates to attend meetings. The last formal session of the General Council was held in 1876.[40]

Ultimately, the Treaty of 1866 was not as punitive as it might have been. Although it was intended to be a blueprint for far-reaching changes in land-holding patterns and governance, these were to be made only with the consent of the tribes, and although the federal government would find ways to compel consent in the future, the tribes were able to maintain more than a semblance of autonomy. The failure of the Okmulgee Constitution revealed the divisions among the tribes and their insistence on maintaining distinctive tribal identities. Peter Pitchlynn's protests against the land survey were countered by a resolution by the Chickasaw council that agreed to it. Choctaw and Chickasaw attitudes toward sectionalizing were diametrically opposed, which vastly complicated their political alliance on a commonly held land base. The two nations ostensibly ceded the Leased District permanently to the United States, but here again, land would become be transformed into a monetary claim against the federal government.

The greatest blow to Choctaw and Chickasaw autonomy was not immediately obvious. The biggest threat was the opening the government provided for the entry of railroads into Indian Territory. With the first locomotive that steamed into the territory, the inexorable advance of technology and white settlement began. Cattle not only roamed the prairies, they rode the railroad to market.

Of primary importance for Peter Pitchlynn was the fact that the tenth article of the treaty left intact previous treaties and legislation. By reaffirming "all obligations arising out of treaty stipulations or acts of legislation with regard to the Choctaw and Chickasaw Nations, entered into prior to the late rebellion, and in force at that time," the federal government thus left open the path to pursue the Net Proceeds Case. The Treaty of 1866 set the conditions for social and political change the Choctaws and Chickasaws would inevitably have to deal with.

CHAPTER 7

STRINGS OF LITTLE HOUSES

I have ridden on those railroads east of the Mississippi. They have little houses on wheels—whole strings of them. One string can carry several hundred people. These little houses can be shut up and the doors locked. If we allow the railroads to come, the men will give a picnic some time by the side of the iron road and will invite all the fullbloods to attend. They will get the men to play ball off a piece. Then they will get our women to go into the little houses on wheels and will lock them up and run off with them into Texas or Missouri. Then what will we do for women?[1]

The strings of little houses is a powerful metaphor for the impact of railroads on the Choctaw Nation. The little houses did indeed come down the iron road, full of white men. Some men did take Choctaw women away, not by locking them in the little houses but by marrying them and thus gaining the privileges of Choctaw citizenship. Through marriage they gained access to the resources of the Nation in order to promote industry and exploit the value of Indian land.[2] Other white men worked their way into the territory as laborers on the railroads, and many rode in as entrepreneurs to start new businesses that would benefit the railroads and the rapidly growing commercial markets in Texas, Kansas, and Missouri. Their presence posed a real threat to the Choctaw government, which had no legal jurisdiction over them. As Coleman Cole, the governor of the Choctaw Nation in 1874, complained, "For God sake, when we bought this country, we did not buy white man with it."[3] The Choctaw Nation was facing significant pressure for change, and during the 1870s it gathered its political resources to resist.

The railroad was the key to American industrial development and wealth in the mid-nineteenth century. The Choctaws were not averse to railroads. They had given a virtual blanket grant of right of way to railroads in the Treaty of 1855, but after the Civil War they had reason to be concerned about the implications of that decision.[4] It was apparent that the expansion of railroads was intimately related to the federal government's intention to create a new state out of Indian Territory.

Indian Territory in the early 1850s ostensibly covered the entire Midwest, but the federal government easily forced land cession treaties in 1854 with the tribes in what became the new states of Kansas and Nebraska. It had become perfectly apparent by 1855 that the integrity of the much-diminished Indian Territory was under attack. The treaty of that year laid out a plan for dividing land into individual holdings if the Choctaws and Chickasaws would agree. The issue divided the Nation politically in the Constitution of 1857. George Harkins described how "some want the country surveyed & divided, & some want freesoilism established." Harkins would have supported a territorial government were it not for his fear that it would become another Kansas-Nebraska situation with regard to slavery.[5]

The national issues of free soil, popular sovereignty, and slavery could not be contained. The outbreak of the Civil War did not entirely end the westward march of the railroads, but it slowed it.[6] In the post–Civil War era, however, railroad-building boomed as a key element in the national program of Reconstruction that would knit the American nation together both politically and physically. Railroads would overcome the economic division between the agrarian South and the industrial North by providing the means to redistribute the resources of the nation.[7]

Congress fostered the boom by subsidizing railroads with grants of major swaths of public lands for right of way. Railroads depended for their capital on the sale of public lands and Indian lands as the government could clear Indian titles. The government's financing scheme for expanding railroads was a double-edged sword, however. By developing new markets for agricultural goods, the government gave hope to farmers that they could succeed in raising crops on the Great Plains. But granting large tracts of public land to the railroads for resale raised the possibility that land speculators would drive the price of land out of reach of the yeoman farmer.[8] Indian Territory land was still under Indian control, and how it would play into the great American scheme of railroad-building was still an unknown factor in the post–Civil War period.

Thus railroads emerged once again as a major issue confronting the Choctaws. The main question was not whether railroads were desirable but who would control them. The Treaty of 1866 limited right of way through Choctaw and Chickasaw lands to one east-west route and one north-south route. It guaranteed that the nations would be compensated for any property taken or destroyed because of the railroads and that railroad employees would be subject to U.S. laws governing intercourse with the tribes. It also, however, opened a wedge for the sale of Indian land to the railroads. Indian Territory was not public land that Congress could grant to the railroads at will. It was private land held by the tribes in fee simple title, but article six of the treaty provided that the tribes could buy stock in the railroads that they could pay for with their land, "unoccupied lands for a space of six miles on each side of said road or roads, at a price per acre to be agreed upon between said Choctaw and Chickasaw Nations and the said company or companies, subject to the approval of the president of the United States."[9] The stock option was yet another example of the way in which Indian land was being converted into money value. The tribes could use land to buy stock and collect their dividends, but their lands would pass into the hands of the railroads. As soon as a railroad company had completed a twenty-mile section of track and built stations, it could get a patent to all land within six miles on either side of the track. The treaty offered a back-door way to the sectionizing of land that was such a political issue within the nations.[10]

Even as the treaties with the Five Tribes in Indian Territory were being negotiated and signed, Congress was putting into place the great east-west transcontinental railroad. On July 27, 1866, Congress authorized the incorporation of the Atlantic and Pacific Railroad and granted it alternate sections of public land along its proposed route. The route roughly followed the 35th parallel, beginning in Missouri and cutting southwestward through the Indian Territory and the New Mexico and Arizona territories to California.[11] The east and west coasts would be linked in a great commercial network. Most significantly for the Choctaws, the government agreed to "extinguish, as rapidly as may be consistent with public policy and the welfare of the Indians, and only by their voluntary cession, the Indian title to all lands falling under the operation of this act and acquired in the donation to the road named in the act."[12]

The other major link in a national railroad system was between the North and the South, a railroad that would connect the rich state of Texas, with its cotton and cattle and its ports on the Gulf Coast, to the commercial centers of Kansas City, St. Louis, and Chicago. That link also had to pass through the Indian Territory. The rush to Texas put three railroads in competition for the single right of way that was guaranteed by the Treaty of 1866. Three lines, the Kansas and Neosho Valley Railroad,[13] the southern branch of the Union Pacific Railroad Company,[14] and the Leavenworth, Lawrence, and Fort Gibson Railroad Company were all authorized to build southward through Kansas. The one that reached the border of Indian Territory first would get the right of way.[15]

The prize in the race was rich. Each railroad was subsidized with a grant of ten alternate sections of public land per mile on each side of the road through the state of Kansas, to be sold by the state for the benefit of the road, and by an outright grant of a right of way of 100 feet on each side of the line through the public lands of Kansas. It also received land for stations, workshops, depots, and other buildings necessary for the operation of the line. The successful line would be guaranteed a right of way through Indian Territory and a grant of alternate sections of land through the territory, but only "whenever the Indian title shall be extinguished by treaty or otherwise."[16] The integrity of Indian Territory was a major obstacle to railroad expansion. The right of way was guaranteed, but the land grants that would subsidize the building of the railroads depended upon the tribes' giving up title to their lands. And that action would destroy their governments and national identities.

In its rush to promote railroad-building, Congress authorized companies to negotiate directly with tribes for right of way, giving up its fiduciary responsibility to protect tribal rights.[17] The "but only" clause in the congressional legislation made it obvious to Choctaw leaders that the federal government was bent on pursuing its policy of extinguishing national titles that allotted Indian land to individuals and making Indian Territory a part of the United States. The promise of land grants gave a powerful impetus for railroad companies to pressure Congress to extinguish Indian title without tribal consent, and federal agents recommended liberal grants of land to railroads as a means of economic development.[18] Choctaw treaties had guaranteed that Choctaws would have title to their lands as long as they lived upon them as a nation. Allotment would destroy the national title, which would thus destroy the land base and the political identity of the tribe, and the railroads could collect their congressional land grants. The protest of the General Council of the Indian Territory in 1870 against "the sale or grant of any lands directly or contingent upon the extinguishment of the Indian title"[19] was very feeble against the collective weight of the Congress of the United States and the great railroad companies it had authorized in the late 1860s.

As the federal government subsidized rail lines through Kansas, the Choctaw Nation decided to get into the railroad-building business on its own. As a sovereign government, the council could seize the initiative to promote the railroad under its own control. Allen Wright, who was elected principal chief of the Choctaw Nation in 1866, saw railroads as a sign of progress and also as a financial resource for the support of Choctaw schools.[20] In October 1869, Wright submitted to the General Council a proposal by the Thirty-Fifth Parallel Railroad Company, of the state of Arkansas, to build the east-west route provided for in the Treaty of 1866.[21] At a special session in April of 1870, the council granted charters to two railroads, the Thirty-Fifth Parallel and the Central Choctaw and Chickasaw Rail Road.[22]

The prospect of railroads and land grants did not sit well with members of the Nation. Although the charters were approved, Wright's support of railroads precipitated his political downfall. His reputation was already damaged by his part in the financial dealings of the Choctaw delegates with Cooper, Latrobe, and Cochrane around the negotiations of the Treaty of 1866, and he lost the 1870 election to William Bryant. There was also a significant turnover in the membership of the General Council in that year. As E. S. Mitchell wrote to Pitchlynn, "The people want a change. They want men that will not give their land away to railroads. . . . All the rail road men are laid in the shade for the present and there is no telling what the next council will do."[23] What the next council did was call for a review of the railroad charters, and when it was revealed that the Chickasaws had raised a protest against the Choctaw action and the secretary of the interior refused to approve the charters, the council repealed the action approving the incorporation of the two lines.[24]

Tribal concerns with control over railroad-building collided head on with the hardening attitude of the Office of Indian Affairs against tribal self-government. Ely S. Parker, commissioner of Indian affairs and himself a member of the Seneca tribe, declared that "the Indian tribes of the United States are not sovereign nations, capable of making treaties, as none of them have an organized government of such inherent strength as would secure a faithful obedience of its people in the observance of compacts of this character." He declared that "the only title the law concedes to them to the lands they occupy or claim is a mere possessory one." He argued that because the government made treaties with them for land cessions, "they have become falsely impressed with the notion of national independence." Parker advocated an end to the treaty-making process, saying that the federal government should "cease the cruel farce of thus dealing with its helpless and ignorant wards."[25] Responding to his rhetoric, the U.S. Congress put a rider on the Indian Appropriation Act for 1871 that effectively ended its practice of making treaties with Indian tribes. The rider did not abrogate previous treaties, but it marked a growing disdain for the notion of treaty rights for American Indians.[26]

As Congress became more aggressive in its domination of tribes, the Choctaw General Council issued a formal protest to the president of the United States and the secretary of the interior against the prospect of railroad-building and the investment of tribal funds in railroad bonds.[27] Such investments would deprive the Choctaws of control of their funds and force them to rely on taxation to support their government. In its role as guardian for its "helpless and ignorant wards," the federal government had a fiduciary responsibility for their assets, which were generally invested in U.S. or state bonds. Given the political climate, it was a real possibility that Choctaw funds would indeed end up supporting railroads. The Choctaws were politically astute enough to send copies of their protest to the *Fort Smith Herald* and *Sherman Courier* in order to reach a public audience.[28]

By 1870, the battle lines between the tribes of Indian Territory and Congress were being drawn. Peter Pitchlynn protested to Congress against two pending bills, one to adopt a modified form of the Okmulgee Constitution as a territorial government for Indian Territory and the other to incorporate two railroad lines to build a single line through Indian Territory to the Gulf.[29] Citing Choctaw treaty rights and using the Net Proceeds Case and the unresolved issue of the Choctaw-Arkansas border as examples of unfulfilled treaty obligations, Pitchlynn criticized the language in the territorial bill that extended the powers of the General Council of Indian Territory to include jurisdiction over the creation of corporations for construction of internal improvements. He argued that through this change, "the whole country may be sold out or given away to foreign adventurers and financial rogues." In addition, Pitchlynn protested that the railroad bill did not include the guarantees of Indian land rights contained in the Treaty of 1866. On the contrary, it implied that Indian land rights would be extinguished and that Indian land would become part of the public domain of the United States. He closed the document with a ringing appeal to Congress "to protect its loyal and obedient people against the rapacity and craft of those who desire and hunger by crooked means and seemingly just legislation, to possess themselves of their lands, to invade their country like locusts, and to devour their substance."[30]

C. J. Hillyer, a lawyer for the Atlantic and Pacific Railroad, pressed for federal status for Indian Territory. In a pamphlet widely circulated to congressmen, he lamented that Indian Territory was "substantially undeveloped" and that federal policy kept it "practically a wilderness" for the indefinite future. There was no commercial industry in Indian Territory that would make it profitable for the railroads to do business there. Indeed, Hillyer declared, "We might as well, for all business purposes, build a road for three hundred miles through a tunnel or a desert, as through the fertile Indian country in its present condition."[31]

Where Peter Pitchlynn argued that the United States had to keep its treaty obligations to the tribes, Hillyer declared that Indians had no "*property* right. . . . It is a *public political* right, belonging to the tribe in its *national* capacity," and he argued that congressional action ending treaty-making "*destroys the political existence of the tribe.*" He declared triumphantly that "the restless advance of an industrial civilization has reached these bounds [of reservations], has recognized in them an obstacle to its progress, and in obedience to a law which knows no exception, has removed them from its path."[32]

The rhetoric of Pitchlynn's remonstrance and Hillyer's pamphlet brought into sharp focus the major issues that confronted the Choctaws and other tribes of the Indian Territory. Hillyer was a spokesman for the doctrine of manifest destiny and the inexorable force of industrialized society. Pitchlynn relied on the rhetoric of treaty obligations and the failure of the U.S. government to honor them. Hillyer explicitly denied treaty rights as a historical artifact that was irrelevant in the current time, while Pitchlynn spoke as the representative of a self-governing nation. Hillyer argued for the power of Congress to legislate the fate of dependent peoples by extending its jurisdiction over them, while Pitchlynn argued for the customs and culture embodied in the Indian land base. Hillyer held up the specter of a monopoly that deprived hard-working citizens and private industry of rights to land, while Pitchlynn argued for the right of the Choctaw Nation to protect its land.

While the debate over treaty rights and progress went on, both in public statements and in the halls of Congress, another kind of contest was being waged in the field, one marked by suspense and chicanery, high drama, and extraordinarily high stakes. The race to build a railroad to the border of the Indian Territory was on, and the prize was the land grants that could be claimed as soon as the Indian title to the land was cleared and the Indian Territory became public domain. The Leavenworth, Lawrence, and Fort Gibson Railroad Company dropped out fairly early, having been merged into the

Kansas and Neosho system controlled by New York entrepreneur James Joy, and the Kansas and Neosho took its place in the race. The southern branch of the Union Pacific went bankrupt in 1870 and was reorganized as the Missouri, Kansas and Texas Railroad (MK&T).[33] The two lines frantically laid track toward the southern border of Kansas. George S. Stevens, general manager of the MK&T (popularly known as the Katy), was a master at the cutthroat competition that was the hallmark of the railroad industry in the United States. He essentially stole the race when he employed Robert Greenwell, an adopted member of the Quapaw tribe, as a special agent. Greenwell, in the guise of a Quapaw, intercepted the surveying party for the Kansas and Neosho and pointed them toward the southern Kansas boundary line established in 1837. That line, however, had been altered by the Kansas-Nebraska Act, and the actual boundary lay several miles to the south along the 37th parallel.[34]

The race was also marked by violence. As the lines neared the border, a gang of Kansas and Neosho workers attacked an MK&T work party at Chetopa, Kansas, precipitating what was called the Battle of Chetopa on May 28, 1870. It ended quickly as the MK&T men beat off their attackers. The Katy's last few miles of line were laid almost literally on the bare earth of the great Texas Road, worn hard and flat by the hooves of countless cattle driven north to market, and on June 6, a tiny Grant 4-0-0 wood-burning locomotive chugged triumphantly over the line into Indian Territory.[35]

Theoretically, at least, the Kansas and Neosho had actually won the race since its line reached the Kansas border south of Baxter Springs on April 30, 1870, and awaited only the approval of the secretary of the interior to enter Indian Territory, but because of Greenwell's misdirection, its point of entry was in the reservation of the Quapaw Nation, which had never given assent to a railroad right of way. It also lay on a branch of the Neosho River, not in the river valley itself, as specified by its authorizing legislation. The Kansas and Neosho was disqualified on these two counts, and the victorious MK&T forged onward through the Cherokee and Creek nations toward its first major objective in the Choctaw Nation, the emerging village of McAlester, which was in the heart of the rich coalfields that were waiting to be exploited.[36]

If the Katy expected a quick reward in the form of extinguishment of Indian title and bestowal of the promised land grants, it was greatly disappointed. Not only did the Choctaws show no inclination to give up title to their lands, they also strongly protested the government's implied promise to the MK&T. That promise indicated the government's goal of destroying the identity of the Indian tribes as "organized political communities" in order to assert the "inchoate titles" of the railroads to Indian land. The General Council issued a strong memorial to Congress to protest its actions, asking "Can a great, intelligent, and Christian nation afford to enact so great an injustice?"[37] First in Congress, then in the U.S. Court of Claims[38] and then in the Supreme Court[39] the Nation steadfastly protested against the authorized land grant to the MK&T, thus adding that case to its file of litigation and ultimately thwarting the railroad's attempt to collect its reward.[40]

The Nation also exercised its control over the resources of Choctaw land that it needed for its building—stone for roadbeds and timber for railroad ties. In 1872, the council passed a law making it illegal for Choctaw citizens to sell timber, rock, and stone coal to railroads or to ship these things out of the Nation.[41] The very fact that Choctaws were selling these things to the railroad, however, marked the emergence of a growing sense of economic self-interest in the Nation, a self-interest that Coleman Cole and the General Council were bent on controlling. The General Council appointed a national agent to make contracts with individual suppliers and collective contracts with the railroad. Individuals who engaged in illegal sales of stone and timber were subject to a $1000 fine. By 1880 the council was also legislating standard prices for stone and timber and collecting royalties on them.[42] If the council could not block the railroad, it could take maximum advantage of its presence by regulating its supply of materials. It could both promote individual enterprise by its citizens and control it at the national level.

In 1873, however, the Katy came to a screeching halt, stopped not by Choctaw resistance but by the collapse of the American economy in the financial panic of that year. The overextension of bond issues for railroads toppled the investment banking firm of Jay Cooke, which closed its doors on September 18, 1873. The failure shook the confidence of investors, and railroads found themselves without the funds to continue building. Numerous railroads went into bankruptcy, and financiers such as Jay Gould were able to pick up bargains (including the MK&T), consolidate lines, and create monopolies. By the late 1870s, Gould effectively controlled the only railroad route into Texas.[43]

The depression that followed the collapse affected the Indian Territory, as it did the entire country. The MK&T had completed its line through Indian Territory and on into Texas but found very little to ship from the territory. Its directors debated whether to give up its claim to the land grant (3,100,000 acres) and instead press Congress to open Indian Territory to settlement.[44] The Choctaw Nation was also making demands on the railroad for judgments for damages to property and for loss of livestock killed or injured by passing trains.[45] By 1876, the General Council, citing "the most exorbitant rates of freight and passenger fare" on the MK&T, passed an act levying a 1.5 percent tax on railroad property.[46] And by 1881 the Nation had launched a suit for damages against the MK&T in the U.S. Court, Western District of Arkansas and appointed Allen Wright to represent it.[47]

As the nation and the railroads recovered from the depression, competition for lucrative markets intensified. Texas was one of the most attractive, but Indian Territory still stood in the way, and the Katy had the north-south route guaranteed by the Treaty of 1866. New rail lines could be had only by negotiations with the tribes, and the Choctaw constitution had provision for "internal improvements" under which it could invoke power over the development of railroads.[48] This time, a railroad would be a matter of tribal choice, not tribal obligation, although the tribe's action was still subject to approval by the secretary of the interior.

When the St. Louis and San Francisco Railroad (SL&SF) determined to break Jay Gould's stranglehold on the Texas market, it had to deal directly with the Choctaw government. However, the SL&SF had a competitor that originated in Texas, the Chicago, Texas and Mexican Central (CT&MC). In October 1881, the general manager of the CT&MC contacted the secretary of the interior to initiate negotiations with the Choctaws for a north-south right of way across

Choctaw Territory. The secretary wrote to the president, citing "the material interests of the people of the United States as well as the prosperity of the Indians" as reasons for promoting the building of the proposed road.[49] In the Nation itself, however, opinion about railroads was deeply divided. Although the General Council had twice defeated proposed rights of way for the SL&SF, in the 1880 election two political parties formed around the issue and eleven counties elected men who favored the railroad, while only five counties elected those who opposed it.[50]

The negotiations for a right of way degenerated into a struggle for control between a minor federal clerk; the Choctaw General Council, whose members were confused by the whole proceedings; and the railroad representatives who desperately wanted to build their lines across Indian Territory. The clerk was Uri J. Baxter, appointed by the secretary of the interior to present the CT&MC claim to the council. Baxter's role was problematic because the secretary of the interior had agreed to send an agent to present a private company's claim to an Indian tribe. The tribal delegates assumed that they had the power to negotiate directly with the representatives of the competing companies who were present and that the final agreement would be automatically approved by the secretary and the president of the United States. Baxter's presence, however, made it appear that the federal government favored the CT&MC case.[51] His actions caused confusion as well. He addressed Chief J. F. McCurtain as "governor," as if the Nation were in actuality a federal territory. He presented a printed copy of a committee recommendation to the General Council that differed from the manuscript copy drawn up by the committee the council had appointed to study the proposals. When J. P. Folsom and Allen Wright objected to a vote on the printed version, Baxter told the council members that they had to take a vote: "He then got up and told us it was no use talking that way, that we must come to a vote that he had not time to stay there." Baxter made a motion to adopt the preamble to the report, which he had no right to do since he was not a member of the committee. He ignored Folsom's objections to the fact that the proposed bill gave jurisdiction to the U.S. federal court in Fort Smith in disputes between tribal members and the railroad. Folsom felt that it was within the council's power to "control the whole thing" and that if lawsuits arose between the Choctaws and the Railroad, "why[,] let it be decided by our courts by our laws." This suggestion, however, "did not seem to settle well with the Secretary of the Interior's representative."[52] Baxter also signed the final agreement "on the part of the United States," thus implying that the government had an ownership stake in the railroad.[53] That a law clerk from the secretary of the interior's office bullied the General Council and signed a significant document on the federal government's behalf says something about the arrogance of the government in its dealings with Indian nations.

The final agreement was not Baxter's work, however, and the process by which it was reached revealed the deep divisions within the Nation over the issue of railroad expansion. The General Council finally resolved the issue itself by negotiating with the CT&MC for joint use of any line to be constructed. When the CT&MC withdrew its proposal, the council voted on the matter of approving the charter with the SL&SF.[54] The vote in the House was six in favor and five against. In the Senate it was nine in favor and eight against, at which point B. F. Smallwood, speaker of the House, cast his vote against the bill and declared it defeated.[55] The problem was that Smallwood had voted as a member of the House but declared the defeat in his role as speaker, whose vote was authorized to break a tie. A tie vote was unprecedented, but the Choctaw attorney general ruled that Smallwood had clearly voted twice, which was illegal.[56] Chief McCurtain finally affirmed council approval of the bill, albeit by a two-vote margin, and submitted it to Congress for final ratification.

A delegation of Choctaws, including Smallwood, J. F. Folsom, and Isham Walker appeared in Washington to block the ratification.[57] The Choctaws certainly had a vested interest in railroads. The schools and the capital building were in disrepair, and the Nation desperately needed money to construct new facilities. The railroad would make possible the development of the coal mines and the rich timber resources of the Nation. It would also create competition for Jay Gould and the MK&T. Gould had evidently influenced the Choctaw council in its previous resistance to the SL&SF right of way,[58] and the Choctaw delegation now appearing before Congress had evidently been funded for their trip by a vague "Mr. Fisher," most likely Daniel

Fisher, a Choctaw-Chickasaw man who was one of Gould's agents.[59] It would certainly be in Gould's interest to block the construction of any other railroads in the Choctaw Nation. The Chickasaw Nation also objected vigorously to the Choctaw council's action on the ground that the land of the two nations was held in common but that the Choctaw council had not consulted the Chickasaw Nation in the matter, thus excluding the Chickasaws from both the negotiations over the right of way and any possible financial benefit.[60]

The rivalries between the railroads and the dispute between the Chickasaws and Choctaws paled as Senator Samuel Bell Maxey of Texas took on Gould's monopoly with legislation in the form of Senate Bill No. 60. He wanted to break Gould by extending the federal power of eminent domain over Indian Territory, an action that would destroy the integrity of tribal territories and seriously undermine the power of tribal governments. "Are the rights of the Indians more sacred than are those of white people?" Maxey asked on the floor of the Senate. "Your land, or my land, or the land of any of our constituents, can be condemned for the use of railroads by virtue of the right of eminent domain residing in the Government and in that way subjected to the public convenience." Indian rights were not "sacred," Maxey argued, and Indian lands should "be subjected to the same burden borne by the lands of everybody else in this country." Maxey asked whether Indian rights should be permitted to stand between "one great State in this Union" (i.e., Texas) and "all progress." With a rhetorical flourish, he demanded, "Shall they be permitted to erect a Chinese wall beyond which the commerce of this country shall not be allowed to pass?"[61]

Maxey's political goal was to break the MK&T monopoly on the Texas market. He asserted the right of eminent domain as a way to break the power of the Indian nations in Indian Territory to resist. Ultimately, he failed on the first count when Gould acquired control of the St. Louis and San Francisco on January 27, 1882, but he succeeded on the second when Senate Bill No. 60 was passed by Congress and was signed into law on April 13, 1882. Although it would not accomplish what Maxey originally intended, it gave Congress the right of eminent domain over Indian Territory, thereby stripping the tribes of any authority in granting right of way to railroads.[62]

The new law led to a rush of bills to grant right of way to railroad lines through Indian Territory, but most did not pass. Many were inspired by speculators who hoped to secure right of way but who had no intention of building. They intended to sell their rights to legitimate developers who wanted to avoid the delay and uncertainty of the legislative process. The proposed branch of the St. Louis and San Francisco that was the cause of the whole fiasco was not built until 1886. The Choctaw Nation tried to exercise what little control it could over railroad expansion by requiring that no railroad could be built to a pinery or coal mine without a permit from the tribal government.[63]

The strings of little houses began to encroach on Choctaw territory during the late 1880s. The white men did indeed come, some to marry Choctaw women and introduce a new kind of entrepreneurship into the Nation, based on the exploitation of coal and grazing lands and town sites that sprang up around railroad stops. The railroads had also set the precedent for Indian Territory as public domain subject to the sovereignty of the U.S. government, and they brought with them white men who fully supported the idea that the communal lands of the Choctaws should give way to the private property that would make individuals rich.

CHAPTER 8

IRON HORSES AND CHOCTAW MAIDENS

In late December 1888, the Bachelor's Club of Muskogee, Indian Territory, held its regular meeting to celebrate the joys of bachelorhood and resolve that they "travel in pairs and never allow one of our number to be inveigled into a corner by a marriageable maiden." With tongue firmly in cheek, the group also voted to thank "Grandma Dawes" (Senator Henry L. Dawes of Massachusetts) for his "heroic stand" to protect innocent white bachelors from succumbing to the wiles of the "dusky maidens of the forest" and marrying into a tribe (which would give them an equal right to their wives' land and cattle). The Bachelors noted, however, the civilizing influence of mixed Indian-white marriages upon Indian tribes and criticized Dawes's "unholy and short sighted bill" that would "discourage civilization by blood relationship." They called on the "dusky maidens" to resist Dawes's congressional resolution as an insult to their freedom of choice.[1]

The not-so-subtle satire in the newspaper report had serious undertones. If intermarriage was a way to implement the federal policy of civilizing Indians, it was also a way to wealth for white men, who could gain tribal citizenship and privileges, including access to and control over the resources of the Indian Territory. The bachelors of Muskogee drew the line at the altar, unless the woman standing on the line was Seminole, Creek, Cherokee, Choctaw, or Chickasaw. If the bachelors saw an advantage in marriage to the dusky maidens, the Choctaw Nation confronted a major challenge to its sovereignty—how to regulate the behavior of its non-Indian population.

The marriages of three Choctaw women who were members of politically powerful families to white men and their subsequent business dealings demonstrate how intermarriage and white entrepreneurship fostered the coal and railroad industries in the Choctaw Nation and with them the spirit of private enterprise and individual profit that characterized American society in general in the latter part of the nineteenth century and influenced many Choctaws. The marriages of these "dusky maidens" fostered powerful forces of economic change in the Choctaw Nation.

In August 1872, James Jackson McAlester married Rebecca Burney, a Choctaw citizen and sister of Benjamin Crooks Burney, who would be chief of the Chickasaw Nation from 1878 to 1880.[2] McAlester, a native of Arkansas and a Confederate war veteran, had acquired a map from a government surveyor showing extensive coal deposits in Indian Territory and moved to the Choctaw Nation in 1866.[3] He began his career in Indian Territory as a clerk in a general merchandise store owned by Reynolds & Hannaford at Bucklucksy, which was near the intersection of the Texas and California Roads and the coal outcropping shown on his map.[4] His success in managing that store enabled him to buy Reynolds out, and the firm became McAlester and Hannaford. When McAlester learned of the impending entry of railroads into the Choctaw Nation, he dug a wagonload of coal from an outcropping and drove it to the headquarters of the MK&T in Parsons, Kansas. Subsequently, when the MK&T plotted its route across Indian Territory, the settlement at McAlester's store became its first major stop in the Choctaw Nation, and the town there assumed his name.[5] His marriage to Rebecca Burney was what gave him the rights of citizenship in the Nation, including the constitutional right to mine coal.

McAlester was generally recognized as the founder of the coalmining industry in the Choctaw Nation, and he held controlling interests in the Osage Coal and Mining Company, which was in turn controlled by the MK&T. By the late 1880s, McAlester was an extremely wealthy man. In 1911, he was elected lieutenant governor of the new state of Oklahoma.[6]

The second marriage took place sometime before 1875 between Anna Guy, sister of William Guy, who would become chief of the Chickasaw Nation from 1886 to 1888, and Robert L. Ream, Jr., an engineer and son of a former U.S. surveyor general for Kansas Territory. Both Anna and Robert showed strong entrepreneurial spirits. Robert established a wagon road and toll bridge across Rock Creek in Tobucksey County in the Choctaw Nation, but the MK&T built its line over his road and blocked his bridge. He thereupon filed a claim for damages against the railroad for loss of tolls.[7] The Reams also attempted to establish claims on coal lands owned by other people. In 1875, Anna had a house built on land where two Choctaw citizens, Daniel M. Hailey and John Dawson, were operating a coal mine. The house had a notice posted that the land belonged to Eastman Lewis. Despite her obviously illegal actions, Hailey and Dawson relinquished their claims to her.

The silent partner in this complicated legal maneuvering was G. S. Willifred, the white superintendent of Osage Coal Mines, who furnished the $15 for the building materials for the house whose existence gave Mrs. Ream her claim on Hailey and Dawson. With all the conveyances in place and the land consolidated, Willifred sold the mine in 1876 to agents of the Texas Central Railroad Company, who in turn sold it to the Osage Coal and Mining Company. Since the Choctaw constitution declared coal mines private property, they thus passed out of the hands of Choctaw citizens and into the hands of white entrepreneurs.[8] Anna Ream's coal claims were the entering wedge in a process by which the federal government worked to impose its jurisdiction in Indian Territory. The chief means of achieving this goal was corporations controlled by non-Indians that attempted to do business with and assert their rights with respect to Choctaws who controlled resources.

The third marriage took place between Fritz Sittel and Melvina Pitchlynn on September 3, 1883. Fritz was the son of Edward Sittel, a German immigrant to Indian Territory who was a buffalo hunter for the MK&T, and his wife, Lena. Melvina was the daughter of William G. Pitchlynn, county clerk of Tobucksey County, and the niece of Peter Perkins Pitchlynn. The couple was married at the Elk House Hotel in McAlester, which had been established by the parents of the groom. The marriage gave Fritz control over land south of McAlester, which he leased to the Choctaw Coal and Railway Company, for which he worked as agent in procuring supplies for the railroad crews. In 1890, he established the Choctaw Trading Company with $10,000 in capital and his father as a partner. He bought ties for the railroad, and in exchange for his business, his suppliers agreed to buy all their merchandise at the Sittels' store.[9]

In 1885, Fritz Sittel met Edwin D. Chaddick, a newspaper reporter from Minneapolis who was on a turkey-hunting trip and who had ridden the MK&T into McAlester. Sittel pointed out the rich coal deposits in the area to him. Chaddick was intrigued, and he went to Philadelphia where he interested the Lehigh Valley Railroad in his idea to build a railroad to export the coal to U.S. markets. The company sent a mining engineer to investigate the prospects for coal-mining. In 1888, Congress authorized the construction of the Choctaw Coal & Railway Co. (CC&RC), and Chaddick became its manager. The CC&RC established it headquarters at South McAlester, a new town established where the line crossed the MK&T, and Sittel was its contractor for ties and timber.[10] The expansion was not as grand as Chaddick's original vision of a transcontinental line from Memphis to Albuquerque where it would connect with the Atchison, Topeka and Santa Fe Railroad. The railroad's charter extended only from the eastern border of Indian Territory to Fort Reno 216 miles to the west, and the CC&RC went into receivership in 1891. It reorganized as the Choctaw, Oklahoma & Gulf Railroad in 1894 and ultimately came under the control of the Chicago, Rock Island and Pacific Railroad in 1903.[11]

The railroad boom of the post–Civil War era brought new economic opportunities and greater mobility to Americans in general. When the MK&T entered the Cherokee Nation in 1870, the towns of Vinita and Muskogee sprang up virtually overnight, and the town of McAlester in the Choctaw Nation burgeoned when the railroad reached the settlement around James McAlester's store in 1872. The railroad brought an influx of white men as workers on the railroads, as entrepreneurs anxious to profit from a growing trade in goods and services of various kinds, and, all too often, as individuals who merely sought freedom from the law in frontier communities.

Treaties and U.S. Indian policy, embodied in the trade and intercourse acts of the early nineteenth century, guaranteed tribes protection against white "intruders" and established the principle that the U.S. government had jurisdiction over its citizens and the Choctaws and Chickasaws had jurisdiction over their members. The United States regulated the activities of its citizens who traded with Indians through licenses. The 1855 treaty established the power of the Choctaws and Chickasaws to grant permits to individuals to reside in their lands without becoming citizens or members.[12] The nations were becoming dependent upon the technical and mechanical skills of white men to develop their economic resources and provide the services of a "civilized" society. However, the legal status of noncitizen permit-holders was problematic.

The Choctaw General Council had consistently regulated the access of non-Indians to its territory. In 1836, it had passed a law permitting Choctaw citizens to employ whites. In 1856, it had exercised its regulatory power under the 1855 treaty by authorizing district chiefs to levy a "moderate tax" on permit-holders. In 1867, it had passed a law that levied a 1.5-cent ad valorem tax on the inventory of traders and laid a $25 yearly tax and $2 permit fee on members of various other professions such as mechanics, carpenters, and blacksmiths.[13] The council also restricted citizens from leasing land to noncitizens for grazing and timber-cutting, although the practice evidently continued under the sanction of Chief William Bryant (1870–1874).[14] The growing influence of white men in the Nation, however, led the General Council to reconsider its action. Although "the more intelligent among the Choctaws" who employed or depended upon white traders, farmers, and mechanics opposed the action, the council repealed the permit law in April 1870, and permit-holders faced expulsion from the Nation at the end of the year.[15] The repeal left white tradesmen, leaseholders, and craftsmen, a significant economic element in the Nation, in a state of uncertainty.

Although the council had passed the law, it did not move to implement it, and it finally extended existing permits and made the permit law more stringent in 1875. Traders had to post a bond of $1,000 for a permit. The tax on inventory was raised to 2 percent. Carpenters, wagon makers, blacksmiths, wheelwrights, millwrights, tailors, shoemakers, millers, machinists, sawyers, tanners, clerks, renters, doctors, and editors, "or any other such like mechanic or artisan or professional character," paid $25 for a permit and had to post a $500 bond. Laborers had to post a $100 bond and pay $6 for a permit. All permit-seekers had to present the signatures of twenty or more "respectable citizens" who would certify "the moral character and industrious and temperate habits of the applicant" and attest that he was "not a gambler." Yearly permits were issued in October and November.[16]

By 1876, the population of the Choctaw agency had grown to an estimated 16,000 persons, including 11,000 mixed-bloods, 200 white employees, and 4,800 other whites. All the Indians wore "citizen's dress" and lived in houses, obvious signs of civilization.[17] But the Choctaw government had little control over the non-Indian population within its boundaries. It could not bring non-Indians into its courts, and its only recourse was to require permits and call upon the U.S. agent to remove "intruders" who did not acquire them.

Moreover, Choctaws themselves were becoming imbued with the spirit of self-interest, and the Choctaw council sought to regulate that as well. The MK&T needed stone and timber for bridges and milling ties, and some enterprising Choctaw citizens had signed contracts with railroad companies to provide those things, thereby using communally held resources for private profit. In November 1871, the Choctaw council took matters into its hands by appointing a national agent to negotiate contracts with Choctaw citizens for timber and stone and then make contracts with outside entities and collect royalties on the materials sold. Existing private contracts were nullified, and anyone who sold stone and timber would be considered a "transgressor" and be subject to a fine of $1,000 plus the cost of his prosecution.[18] However, the act was ruled unconstitutional by the Choctaw Supreme Court on the ground that the Chickasaw council had not been consulted about or approved such an act. A second attempt to establish a national agent in 1873 was also ruled unconstitutional.[19]

Railroad officials were, of course, strongly opposed to regulation by the Choctaw council. Robert S. Stevens, general manager of the MK&T, described the tax on laborers as a form of "blackmail."[20] The council's prohibition of private contracts went against "the habits of civilization." He felt that the Department of the Interior should not prohibit individual Choctaws from "trading and trafficking" and that the Choctaw Nation sought to suppress private enterprise for the benefit of the national government.[21] That conflict between tribal sovereignty and self-interest created a dilemma for federal policy-makers committed to promoting civilization and lay at the heart of the political struggles facing the Nation.

A growing reaction in the Nation against private entrepreneur-ship and non-Indian influence led to the election of Coleman Cole as chief in 1874. Politically, Cole's election represented the influence of the full-blood element of the tribe, the Buzzard Party,[22] and his poli-cies represented a significant shift from the more laissez-faire atti-tude of Chief Bryant. Cole declared adamantly that he would not issue permits to white people: "When we bought this land or soil from the United States Government, we never bought the white peo-ple with it."[23] He also made the Net Proceeds claim a key political issue in his administration because he was one of the dispossessed claimants under the fourteenth article.[24]

At Cole's urging, the General Council tightened the intermarriage law. Declaring that "the Choctaw Nation is being filled up with white persons of worthless character by so called marriages to the great injury of the Choctaw people," the law stated that white men had to obtain a license to marry from a circuit clerk or Choctaw judge. To qualify, they had to present to the clerk or judge a certifi-cate of good moral character signed by at least ten respectable Choctaw citizens by blood who had known the man for at least twelve months, pay a $20 fee, and swear an oath to "honor, defend, and submit to the Constitution and laws of the Choctaw Nation." Although the bill specified men who married Choctaw women, it implicitly included women who married into the Nation.[25]

Cole's reelection in 1876 indicated general support for his policies. In his second term, he challenged the burgeoning coal industry and moved to restrict the actions of Choctaw citizens who were profiting from it. In 1877, the General Council passed a law that prohibited Choctaw citizens from leasing lands to noncitizens. The punishment for infractions was a fine of not less than $250 or more than $1,000.[26] A more drastic act required noncitizens who were not employed by citizens to sell their improvements to citizens by January 31, 1878, or be removed from the Nation by the U.S. Indian agent.[27]

The General Council also passed resolutions declaring timber, stone, and minerals to be "the property of the Choctaw and Chickasaw people, and subject to the control of the National Councils" and requesting Cole to ask the secretary of the interior to prevent any further working of coal mines and manufacture of timber within the Nation until the Choctaw and Chickasaw legislatures could agree upon a joint law to appoint an agent to collect royalties on coal production.[28] The latter law was an attempt to nationalize the proceeds of the coal industry, although coal mines were still private property under the Choctaw constitution.

Although Cole made a valiant and concerted effort to control the spirit of individualism and the growing sense of private property that had begun to pervade some of the nation's citizens, it was too strong for many to resist. At the same time, the federal government thwarted the Nation's attempts to control its white inhabitants. On August 27, 1877, the secretary of the interior disapproved the Nation's permit law.[29] Cole strongly questioned the secretary's authority, but there was no clear-cut precedent to give the Nation the right to regulate the behavior of noncitizen permit-holders.

Cole's efforts to gain control of the coal industry brought him in direct conflict with James McAlester and Robert Ream, who, along with Tandy Walker and William Pusley, attempted to establish a coal mine near McAlester in 1875. McAlester and Ream sent a wagonload of coal to Parsons, Kansas, a railhead for the MK&T line, and Cole, invoking an 1839 law making sale of any land of the Nation an offense punishable by death, ordered their arrest. They escaped from the lighthorseman sent to apprehend them and fled the Choctaw Nation on a railroad handcar.[30]

The white population in McAlester strongly criticized Cole's actions in ordering the arrests. The editor of the *Star Vindicator* declared that Cole's "common sense must be sacrificed, as no sane man with pure motives would have done as he has done."[31] The General Council attempted to impeach him. Although the attempt failed, it demonstrated the depth of feeling around the right of private entrepreneurship.[32]

Cole responded to the impeachment charges with a pointed message to the General Council, saying that he had visited the Mushulatubbee District (where McAlester was located) and that "there seems to be an abiding and growing disposition there to ignore the holding of our lands in common and to regard it rather individualized." He demanded that "the practice . . . of leasing lands, laying off town lots, surveying land, marking trees or laying off boundary lines" should be stopped at once.[33]

In 1878, Cole's constitutionally prescribed two terms of office ended. When he sought reelection in 1880, he was defeated by Jackson McCurtain and thereafter retired from political life.[34] His two terms in office coincided with a time of significant economic change in the Nation, and he fought a valiant fight against encroaching outside influences. But change was inevitable.

Under Cole's successor, Isaac Garvin, the General Council continued to try to regulate non-Indian activities in the Nation. In 1880, it passed an act prohibiting noncitizens from engaging in the stock business.[35] It also prohibited Choctaw citizens from cutting and shipping prairie or wild grass out of the Nation.[36] The Office of Indian Affairs was flooded with letters of protest concerning the permit laws, but in 1881 the attorney general of the United States sustained the Choctaw government's right to pass permit laws and levy taxes and fees on noncitizens.[37]

At this point, we can revisit the three couples whose marriages began this chapter. J. J. McAlester's coal mines prospered. In 1884, he bought a coal claim from Ena ho ka tubbee,[38] and despite his brush with the Choctaw lighthorse, he went on to a political career in the nation. He served as a marshal for the U.S. court from 1893 to 1897, was elected to the Oklahoma Corporation Commission at the time of statehood in 1907, and served a term as Oklahoma lieutenant governor beginning in January 1911. He died on September 22, 1922.

The career of Fritz Sittel demonstrates that the spirit of entrepreneurship was taking deep root in Choctaw soil. His mercantile business profited from his role as a buyer of coal and ties for the railroads. Together with Robert J. Ward, G. M. Bond, J. M. Grady, and James F. Freeney, he incorporated the Tobucksey Mining Company in April 1889, although the company was dissolved in 1893. He branched out into cattle-ranching on a small scale. He ultimately was employed by the Chicago, Rock Island and Pacific Railroad, which became a major player in the economic development of the state of Oklahoma. He and Melvina Sittel had seven children— Edward; William B.; Myrtle Lottie; Josie; Fritz, Jr.; Farris G.; and Melvin Cornish—who were enrolled as citizens of the Choctaw Nation under the Dawes Commission in 1903.[39]

The claims of Anna and Robert Ream to coal mines would have powerful significance for the future of Choctaw sovereignty since it focused attention on the issue of legal jurisdiction in the Choctaw Nation. After the Osage Coal and Railroad Company bought the coal mines in which Anna Ream claimed a share, it shut down the mines and dismantled the buildings. The company's actions may well have been a response to the Choctaw council's resolution in 1875 that all timber, stone, and coal were the property of the Choctaw Nation, but whatever the reason, the mining operation was suspended for five years. In 1880, a new claim was made by William Chunn's widow, who had married again to James A. Hill, a white man. Mrs. Hill entered an agreement with William Pusley and D. M. Hailey to make a new coal claim on pasture land on Chunn's (now Mrs. Hill's) farm.

When Mrs. Ream learned of the new claim, she and her husband filed suit in the Choctaw circuit court in Tobucksey County asserting that she still had an undivided half-interest in the mine now operated on Mrs. Hill's property and was entitled to half of the royalties from the coal. Mrs. Hill, Pusley, and Hailey argued that the sale of the consolidated claim by Willifred in 1876 terminated all original claims, that the suspension of previous mining operations caused the coal to revert to the Choctaw and Chickasaw nations, and that their mine was a wholly new one on which Mrs. Ream had no claim. The circuit court found in favor of Mrs. Ream, but the decision was not officially recorded because the judge was related to Mrs. Ream. Green McCurtain, Choctaw national treasurer and "a party in interest" (although he was not named as a defendant), then took the case to the Choctaw Supreme Court, which reversed the circuit court's decision on the grounds that the abandonment of the mines caused them to revert to the Choctaw and Chickasaw nations, nullifying Mrs. Ream's claim. Mrs. Ream and her husband then filed a motion to have the circuit court judgment officially filed and to set aside the Supreme Court judgment on the grounds that the Supreme Court had no jurisdiction because there had been no judgment to be appealed.

Amid this complicated legal maneuvering, Anna Ream also went outside the Nation to direct her appeal to the commissioner of Indian affairs. That action had profound significance for the Choctaw court system because it focused attention on its operation. The commissioner ordered an investigation and report on Anna Ream's case from the local Indian agent, John Q. Tufts. Based on Tufts's report, the secretary of the interior took jurisdiction over the case and upheld Mrs. Ream's claims.[40]

Did the secretary of the interior have the power to decide a case between Choctaw citizens being argued in Choctaw courts? That was the critical question. The Choctaw leadership argued strongly that he did not because the Treaty of 1855 explicitly reserved jurisdiction over Choctaw citizens to the Choctaw government. The interior secretary argued that he did have jurisdiction because Hailey, Pusley, and Mrs. Hill had a contract with a private non-Indian run corporation, the Atoka Coal and Mining Company, and the circuit court's decision in Mrs. Ream's favor effectively nullified that contract.

The secretary's argument hinged on two factors. The first was the failure of the Choctaw circuit court to file the judgment it had handed down in Mrs. Ream's favor. That failure cast doubt on the functioning of the Choctaw court system. According to John Tufts's report, the Choctaw courts were "alleged to have been irregular, unjust, contrary to the law of the nation, and subversive of the recognized practice of judicial tribunals."[41] The second factor was that contracts with outside companies were involved, and an opinion of the U.S. attorney general gave the secretary the right to intervene in matters of "foreign judgments."[42]

In essence, the Ream case breached the wall of treaty rights the Choctaw government had actively maintained around itself. It gave the secretary of the interior cause to uphold a decision of a Choctaw circuit court that, because of a procedural failure that might have been rectified internally, had not been fully appealed. Because the case involved coal mines operated by non-Indians under leases with

Indians, the secretary justified his intervention with an attorney general's opinion regarding foreign judgments. Anna Ream's case highlighted the significant issue of who had jurisdiction over non-Indians in Indian Territory.

In 1900, Rev. W. H. Bullard, of Rosh, Alabama, wrote to Green McCurtain, then chief of the Choctaw Nation:

> I understand that your tribe offered an inducement in money and land to good moral white men that would marry your young maidens. If this be true, write me at once and I will come. I also will furnish all references you ask as to honesty and sobriety and morality. Me being a minister of the Gospel of Christ, I can do this.[43]

Choctaw lands and money were still making Choctaw maidens powerfully attractive to acquisitive white men as the century turned. It was also clear by the early 1890s that intermarriage had done much to change the complexion of the Choctaw Nation, both physically and politically. U.S. Indian Agent Dew Wisdom reported to the commissioner of Indian affairs in 1893 that

> the Indians who inhabit the Territory are civilized and have adopted many of the customs and ways of their white brethren. They wear "store clothes," attend places of religious worship, and by intermarriage the old type of the aboriginal Indian is fast disappearing among the living. A genuine full-blood Indian will soon be a curiosity in the Indian Territory, and will be looked on as a relic of an extinct species."[44]

As the "species" verged on disappearance, however, the Choctaw Nation was waging a tremendous struggle to maintain its political identity. As the Nation had assumed the trappings of "civilization," including notions of private property and economic entrepreneurship, the federal government was preparing to submerge that identity completely into American society.

The growing white population constituted a threat to the Choctaw Nation both because of the new value systems white men brought into Indian Territory and because these men did not have any political rights in the government of the lands in which they lived, although they were subject to tribal regulation. The U.S. government expressed great concern for the well-being of its citizens. Henry Dawes was convinced that the situation of the whites in Indian Territory was the fault of the Indians. They had allowed intermarriage and they had hired white workers in large numbers. In the treaties, the federal government had pledged to preserve the Indians in their own way of life by removing them from contact with white society. If the government had failed to preserve the Indians entirely from white intrusion, the Indians had failed to exclude whites and had indeed invited them into their territory. White intermarried citizens had gained control of Indian resources and monopolized them for their own benefit, depriving other citizens of their just share of tribal holdings. White settlers had built stores, hotels, homes, even whole towns on land to which they could gain no title. White capitalists had invested in railroads and coal mines that could not be torn down.[45]

Intermarriage between Indian women and white men contributed to both economic development and political decline in the Choctaw Nation. White men brought new knowledge and skills to exploit the resources of their land more effectively, and Choctaws learned the value of individual enterprise from them. This individualism and entrepreneurial spirit challenged the political strength of the Choctaw government and the idea of holding land in common, the essential attribute of its sovereignty. The iron horses of the railroads did not necessarily carry Indian women away; rather, they introduced ideas and practices that significantly undermined the sovereignty of the Nation.

Choctaw Lighthorsemen, 1893. Antlers, Indian Territory. Courtesy Leon Chase Phillips Collection, Western History Collections, University of Oklahoma Libraries.

Enrollment of citizens of Choctaw Nation, 1899. Courtesy Leon Chase Phillips Collection, Western History Collections, University of Oklahoma Libraries.

Senate of the last Choctaw Council, ca. 1905. Courtesy Green McCurtain Collection, Western History Collections, University of Oklahoma Libraries.

Choctaws and Chickasaws registering for their government allotments of land, ca. 1900. Courtesy Warren P. Chaney Photograph Collection, Western History Collections, University of Oklahoma Libraries.

Gilbert Webster Thompson family, Cornish, Indian Territory, ca. 1905. Author's collection.

Susie Thompson (on wagon wheel), ca. 1915. Author's collection.

Peter Pitchlynn. Courtesy Division of
Manuscripts, Western History
Collections, University of Oklahoma
Libraries.

Gilbert Dukes. Courtesy Herbert
Otho Boggs Collection, Western
History Collections, University of
Oklahoma Libraries.

Green McCurtain.
Courtesy Green McCurtain Collection,
Western History Collections,
University of Oklahoma Libraries.

Choctaw Council House, Tuskahoma, Oklahoma, 1909. Courtesy Western History Collections, University of Oklahoma Libraries.

CHAPTER 9

THE NET PROCEEDS CASE

If you were to tell a man who was not acquainted with the way you did things here, that for forty-four years the authorized and legal representatives of a weak and humble people had beset the Congress of the United States for simple justice, and session after session and year after year had been spurned with contempt from the doors of Congress, he would reply that the reason why a lobby existed, if any did exist, was because the honorable gentlemen who composed Congress were unwilling to do justice.[1]

Congressman Isaac Parker (R-Missouri) summed up succinctly the history of the Net Proceeds Case. The "lobby" in question was the accumulation of lawyers and other agents Choctaw leaders enlisted in the struggle to wrest payment for their land from an increasingly reluctant Congress. The Treaty of 1866 had reaffirmed their existing treaty rights, primarily the Net Proceeds claim, and it also provided the basis for a new claim, the treaty annuities the U.S. government had withheld during the Civil War because of the tribe's allegiance to the South. The Net Proceeds Case demonstrates how Choctaw claims were being transformed into money value as the Choctaw Nation hired lawyers and lobbyists on contingency fees to press the claims. The case became a defining factor of the Choctaws' relationship with the U.S. government after the Civil War.[2]

The financial futures of at least two lawyers, John Latrobe and John Cochrane, rested on the actions of Congress, and Douglas

Cooper, Peter Pitchlynn, and members of the treaty delegation also had financial interests in the claims. In the Net Proceeds Case, there were two payments at stake. One was the $1.8 million award made by the Senate in 1859 and the other was the $250,000 in bonds that were part of the $500,000 appropriated by Congress in 1861.

Before anything could be done about the $250,000 in bonds that Congress had approved, the Choctaw Nation had to account for the $250,000 in cash it had been paid. Cooper had drawn over $134,000 of that amount ostensibly to buy corn for starving Choctaws, but the vast majority of it went for other purposes, including, seemingly, Cooper's private gain. Nevertheless, the treaty delegates, without any substantiating evidence from Cooper as to how the money was spent, signed a statement on May 4, 1866, asking the U.S. treasury to credit the money to the Choctaw treasury and clear Cooper's obligation as U.S. agent to account for its use.[3] In effect, the delegates removed Cooper's liability for the corn money as part of the deal with Latrobe's contract.

In 1868, national attorney Sampson Folsom challenged the validity of the delegates' action, saying that after an investigation of the matter at the direction of the General Council, it had been repudiated.[4] In a rather abrupt about face, however, he withdrew his objections on August 8, 1868, on the grounds that he had been "mistaken as to the most material facts connected with said settlement."[5] He saw the threat to the larger claim that his objections raised.

The Net Proceeds claim still had to be pursued in the U.S. Congress. The crucial question was who would represent the claims. Pitchlynn's involvement in contracts with Pike, Cochrane, and Latrobe to represent the Net Proceeds claim raised suspicions concerning the financial dealings of the "Old Delegation," and there was some question as to whether the General Council had ever approved a financial contract with that group. Allen Wright, who was elected chief of the Nation in 1866, was precluded from serving on any new delegation appointed, but he held the power of appointment and he was a political foe of Pitchlynn's.[6] Pitchlynn hired E. S. Mitchell for a fee of $10,000 to assure that he would be appointed as a delegate once again.[7] And probably through Mitchell's lobbying efforts, the "Old Delegation," Pitchlynn, Israel Folsom, and Peter Folsom, who had replaced the deceased Dixon Lewis, was reappointed by Allen Wright on December 14, 1867, to go to Washington to pursue Choctaw claims.[8]

The General Council ratified the 1866 treaty in October 1867 and, by affirming the actions of the treaty delegation in negotiating it, implicitly if not explicitly also approved the contract with Latrobe.[9] The contract issue was significantly complicated, however, by the death of John Cochrane on October 21, 1866. His passing both shifted the makeup of the group that came to be called in some quarters "the lobby" and ultimately threatened the future of the Net Proceeds claim. The subsequent history of the claim became positively Byzantine.

Cochrane, knowing that he was dying, had salvaged what he could of his contract with the Choctaws by instructing the executor of his estate, John D. McPherson, to negotiate the sale of his financial interest in the contract. The value of that interest was contingent on the amount of money the holder of the contract, whoever that would be, could recover for the Choctaw Nation. In November Thomas A. Scott, vice president of the Pennsylvania Central Railroad, purchased Cochrane's interest for $150,000, in the hope that the amount rewarded to the Choctaws for the Net Proceeds would return a contingency fee much greater than that amount. Scott paid $75,000 in cash as an advance, and McPherson contracted with Jeremiah Black, a respected Washington jurist and former attorney general during the administration of President James Buchanan, to take over the Net Proceeds Case. The Net Proceeds claim thus became a matter of speculative interest for Scott,[10] and Black and his partner, Ward D. Lamon, also claimed an equal share of the value of the final judgment.[11]

At that point, Latrobe came forward to claim $50,000 for his share of Cochrane's contract, although their agreement had not been made in writing. The new contract with Black effectively cut Latrobe out of the picture, but it was certainly in Douglas Cooper's interest to keep him in it. Latrobe, fighting to keep control of the Cochrane contract in the face of its sale to Scott, Black, and Lamon, called for help upon Cooper, whose former role as U. S. agent for the Choctaws and Chickasaws gave him extensive Washington connections. Cooper in turn contracted with John Davis of Indiana, the son-in-law of Sampson Folsom, and Perry Fuller, a Kansas merchant and land speculator who had also been an Indian agent, to convince the Choctaw council to reinstate Latrobe's initial 1866 contract with the Choctaw delegation. Fuller and Davis, in turn, were agents for a prosperous merchant and supplier to the U.S. government, Charles Stettauer.[12] It is likely that Fuller's dealings as a land speculator in Kansas were known to members of Congress since he had purchased large tracts of the Osage land cession of 1854. It is also likely that Fuller's work in the Choctaw Nation around the claims issue cast suspicion on the whole process.[13]

In the meantime, Pitchlynn tried to persuade Albert Pike to rejoin the legal team, but Pike feared his southern sympathies would undermine the case.[14] Since Black was a staunch Union man, Pitchlynn ultimately accepted his representation and supported his efforts.[15] But the "complications" and "chronic controversy" surrounding the contract frustrated Black, who had largely abandoned the Net Proceeds claim by 1870.[16] Faced with Black's neglect, Pitchlynn and Peter Folsom, "in despair," negotiated a contract with Henry McKee and James Blunt, a former Confederate general, in July 1870 to take the Net Proceeds Case for a 30 percent contingency fee.[17]

The situation by 1870 was thus that Thomas Scott and Jeremiah Black had largely given up their interests in the Cochrane contract, while Ward Lamon and John Latrobe continued to contend for theirs, with the support of Douglas Cooper. Henry McKee and James Blunt, supported by Peter Pitchlynn and Israel and Peter Folsom, also held a new contract under essentially the same terms as the Cochrane contract.[18] Against this confused backdrop of competing interests, Pitchlynn and the rest of the delegation pursued the Net Proceeds claim.

The prospects for the claim had seemed bright after the war, but the maneuvering of financial interests cast a cloud over it. The Senate judgment of 1859 still stood, and Israel Folsom disparaged the comments of "intriguing" and "medling" men who accused the "Old Delegation" of having sold out the claim for their own interests. He assured the Choctaw General Council that the case was now in "as good a shape as it has ever been."[19] Despite Folsom's optimism, when the matter of the payment of the $250,000 in bonds came before the Thirty-Ninth Congress in February 1867, it met with less-than-favorable responses. The House refused to insert it into the

Indian appropriation bill. Although some congressmen argued that Congress ought to keep its treaty agreements with Indians, the Choctaws had allied themselves with the Confederacy, and Senator William Stewart (R-Nevada) declared that "they have no claim upon us, equitable or otherwise. They have been rebels, and they have cost us a great deal of money in that way." The senators knew that the Choctaw delegation was in Washington anxiously awaiting the outcome of the debate, but Senator Charles Buckalew (D-Pennsylvania) observed that the only justification for a payment appeared to be their "considerable expense" and "necessitous circumstances."[20] In the end, Congress rejected the amendment for the $250,000 in bonds, leaving the waiting delegates disappointed once more.

The Fortieth Congress held renewed promise that the entire payment would be made. The secretary of the interior issued a favorable letter to the House committees on appropriations and the Senate Committee on Finance.[21] The House Committee on Indian Affairs made a favorable report on a bill to pay the award as adjusted by the Senate, less the $500,000 payment approved in 1859 (i.e., $1,832,460).[22] In the eyes of a lawyer with a 30 percent contingency fee, the claim was worth about $550,000.

The bill for payment was proposed as an amendment to the Indian Appropriation Act of 1868, but the size of the award and the complexity of the issues involved made the House reluctant to attach it to the appropriation bill, and the lobbying efforts of the Choctaw delegation aroused suspicion in Congress. The frantic efforts of Pitchlynn and Cooper to protect the claim were undermining its viability. Representative Elihu Washburne (Republican-Illinois) was suspicious that "this money is not to go to the Indians, but to an Indian 'ring' of which Perry Fuller is one of the chief managers." He opposed any bill that might give money to a "rotten Indian ring," which he believed was in collusion with the Indian department, "one of the rottenest departments of the Government."[23] Representative William Kelley (R-Pennsylvania) recalled that in the former Congress, "it required a good deal of vigilance for gentlemen upon this floor to resist the influence of the lobby or ring that was here about this very payment." Representative Reader Clarke (R-Ohio) proposed an amendment that explicitly prohibited payments to any "assignees" or purchasers of Choctaw claims, venturing that "there are men now within the sound of my voice waiting with anxious expectation for the result of our action on this section, knowing that the very moment we are seduced into the trap they have set for us they become millionaires."[24]

The Choctaw claims were highly visible before Congress but in a very negative way. Rather than confront the issue head on, however, Congress referred the matter back to the committees on Indian affairs of the two houses for further study.[25] When the bill for the payment was introduced in the third session of the Fortieth Congress, the reaction was the same. Representative William Scofield (R-Pennsylvania) railed that it was twenty-five years after the sale of their lands before "they employed some gentlemen in Washington, whose business it is to hang around these Halls and make something for themselves by getting something for the Indians, and agreed to give those claim agents one quarter of what they could get from Congress."[26] Although a payment had seemed assured in early 1868, it died with the end of the Fortieth Congress.

The failure of the effort in the spring of 1869 drove Pitchlynn and Folsom to ally themselves with Douglas Cooper and his Washington connections. They and Samuel Garland signed a contract with Cooper on March 24, 1869, to represent the claim in the Forty-First Congress.[27] The issue of who represented the case became even more complicated when on October 1, 1869, Albert Pike, who had not been active in the case since 1861, suddenly reappeared and declared that he was still the attorney for the Choctaw Nation. He had unexpectedly come into possession of a copy of the 1855 Cochrane contract to which he had assented and was appalled to learn that his contract had been annulled. Cochrane had informed him only that his own name was substituted for Pike's and that the contingency fee had been raised to 30 percent. Pike had given his written assent to the contract without actually reading the document, a rather unlawyerly thing to do.[28] But it was too late for Pike, and despite his continued importuning, Pitchlynn declined to support the reinstatement of his contract. He was now working actively with Cooper and Latrobe.

Pitchlynn pressed the claim in the first session of the Forty-First Congress with a memorial (written by Latrobe). It was referred to the

Senate Committee on Indian Affairs, which affirmed the previous Senate award but recommended that the matter be referred to the Committee on the Judiciary for resolution of "questions of law and equity."[29] In other words, the Senate punted once again. Pitchlynn promptly sent the judiciary committee a letter outlining the nature of the claim and the reason for the delay in action,[30] but the judiciary committee did not issue a report. The possibility of payment reached the floor of the Senate in the form of an amendment to the Indian Appropriation Act offered by Senator Benjamin Rice (R-Arkansas) in June 1870. The Senate was unwilling to act without the judicial committee report, and Rice withdrew his motion.[31] He reintroduced it as an amendment to the civil appropriation bill, but the Senate rejected it with the same concerns for the size of the award, the wartime loyalty of the Choctaws, and the role of lobbyists and claims agents.[32]

Pitchlynn was becoming very frustrated with government bureaucracy, and he changed his strategy. Since much of the Senate debate had centered on the size of the award, he decided to pursue the $250,000 in bonds that was still due to the Nation under the Senate appropriation of 1861. In March 1870, he made an agreement with George W. Wright, a Republican and former member of Congress from California, to secure the release of the bonds. Pitchlynn promised all of the interest paid on the bonds or 25 percent of the principal, whichever was larger, as a contingent fee.[33] Pitchlynn's new strategy marked a growing rift between him and Douglas Cooper over the direction of the Net Proceeds Case, as did the contract that he and Folsom signed with McKee and Blunt.

The divisions within the Choctaw "lobby" were evident when the third session of the Forty-First Congress received two memorials on behalf of the Choctaw Nation, one from Latrobe and one from Pitchlynn. Latrobe, writing "in behalf of the Choctaw Nation of Indians," requested the payment of the whole award, arguing that "technical equity, as well as common honesty" required that it should be paid with interest.[34] Less than a month later, the Senate received Pitchlynn's memorial requesting the $250,000 in bonds, which he described as "no longer a claim; it is a debt . . . due under treaty stipulations; a debt of a peculiar and sacred obligation."[35] Congressional sentiment was favorable to the award. The U.S. attorney general issued an

opinion that the Treaty of 1866 was constitutional in its acknowledg-
ment of treaty rights that existed before that time.[36] And the Senate
agreed to the issue of the bonds.[37] Congress authorized their appropriation on March 3, 1871.[38]

But the bonds were not immediately released. The Choctaw
Nation had to pass an act requesting them and designating the
appropriate tribal officials to receive them. On March 18, 1872, the
Choctaw General Council passed a lengthy resolution in which it
repudiated Latrobe's contract, authorized the conversion of the
$250,000 in bonds to cash, and authorized Pitchlynn and Folsom, the
two remaining members of the original delegation, to sign all necessary releases and conveyances for the bonds and collect the interest
on them to pay for their own expenses in prosecuting the claims. The
$250,000 would be put in trust for the payment of individual claims
under the Treaty of Dancing Rabbit Creek.[39]

But the Nation still did not get its money. The Net Proceeds claim
took another bizarre twist when the secretary of the treasury received
reports that it was invalid because of the resolution of the Choctaw
General Council in 1852 that accepted the payment of $872,000 as "a
final release" of fourteenth article claims.[40] The department's solicitor
recommended against the award.[41]

If the Nation had indeed already accepted payment for its claims
under the Treaty of Dancing Rabbit Creek, there was no reason for
the Senate to have made the award that it did in 1859. The Senate had
not known about the document in question when it made the award
because it had been filed in the Department of the Treasury rather
than in the Department of the Interior. That it had been "found" was
the result of collusion among the secretary of the treasury, a Washington claim agent named Nathaniel Paige, and an unemployed
former government bureaucrat, Edward B. Grayson. If Congress
suspected the Choctaws of political chicanery, the executive branch
of the federal government was fully willing to practice it as well. In
a written but unsigned agreement between the treasury secretary
and Paige, dated March 30, 1872, an unnamed individual agreed to
give information about the fraudulent nature of "a certain claim . . .
pending in the Treasury Department . . . amounting to the sum of
between three and four hundred thousand dollars," and the secre-

tary agreed to pay 20 percent of the claim, or up to $30,000, to Paige and the unnamed informant for the information.[42]

The "unnamed informant," Grayson, was a longtime employee of the Office of Indian Affairs. He had located individual land claims among the Choctaws as early as 1830 and had been hired by John T. Cochrane to gather information with regard to the Net Proceeds Case. He tried to get his own 1 percent of the Net Proceeds from Cochrane, and when Cochrane refused, he threatened "the Choctaw delegate" (presumably Pitchlynn) that he would work to defeat the claim if his demands were not met. Grayson maintained that the 1855 treaty was "inspired by Cochrane," that lawyers had "foisted themselves" upon the claim, and that they would get the lion's share of the money if the award was made.[43]

Caught in his conspiracy, the secretary of the treasury deferred to the Senate to make a full investigation of the matter,[44] while the secretary of the interior asked John H. P. Shanks, chair of the House Committee on Indian Affairs, to introduce a bill to prevent delivery of the bonds on the ground that the claim was not valid.[45] Once again, Pitchlynn and his colleagues were frustrated as the executive branch dodged responsibility by sending the issue back to Congress. In the Nation, frustrated Choctaws questioned why the council had delayed and why the money they had been expecting for so long was not immediately forthcoming.

In the Nation, the prospect of money payments and individual gain was increasingly important, and it led to widespread suspicion that Pitchlynn and Folsom were involved in some scheme to defraud it.[46] The suspicion was also widespread in Congress, and it followed on more general concerns about corruption and fraud in the administration of the Office of Indian Affairs. William Walsh, director of the newly established Indian Rights Association, accused Commissioner of Indian Affairs Ely S. Parker of mismanagement.[47] American capitalism had found an arena for profit in supplying Indian reservations, but the abuses of the system soon became apparent.[48] It seemed that Indians were easy pickings for shady lawyers and corrupt merchants.

Concerns in Congress led Representative John Shanks to launch an investigation of the Choctaw claims.[49] Even as Shanks was compiling his report, Pitchlynn continued to send memorials to Congress. In

1872, he explicitly redefined the relationship between the Choctaw Nation and the United states as "that of debtor and creditor, not that of sovereign and subject, or guardian and ward." He demanded not only a final judgment on the Net Proceeds but also the interest on it since the initial Senate award. As he pointed out, "Moneys in judgment always bear interest."[50] The Senate Committee on Indian Affairs reaffirmed the Senate's 1859 award and recommended to the full Senate that the Choctaws receive their payment of $250,000 in bonds.[51]

The award became the center of controversy again when Shanks issued his report, which was almost 800 pages long, at the very end of the legislative session in 1873, without time for final congressional approval. Indeed, there were charges that Shanks had written the entire report himself.[52] It constituted a vituperative attack on Douglas Cooper and the Choctaw "lobby."[53] Shanks accused Cooper of being "both the *serpent and the brains*" of a cadre of lawyers seeking to defraud the Choctaws."[54]

Even before Shanks's report became public, the tone of congressional debate on the floor of the House shifted dramatically under the weight of the revelations about the Choctaw release. Congressman Aaron Sargent (R-California) went so far as to characterize the Net Proceeds claim as "a fraud *ab initio.*"[55] There was a general feeling that if the money was awarded, the bulk of it would go to lawyers and claims agents rather than to the Nation and to the individual claimants it was the Nation's responsibility to pay. The damage was done, and Congress suspended previous payments until it could take further action.[56]

The Shanks report ripped apart the Choctaw lobby. It led to an open break between Cooper and Pitchlynn. Cooper charged that Pitchlynn was "a mere tool in the hands of the unscrupulous ring who use his name to re-affirm and reiterate what has been time and again proved to be false."[57] Pitchlynn wrote of Cooper's attempts to have Latrobe confirmed as the Choctaw attorney, "Can anything exceed the villainy here developed? And yet this is but a fair sample of all the doing of this corrupt 'ring.'"[58]

The question becomes Which faction was the ring? Pitchlynn was certainly aware of the share the Choctaw delegates claimed in

Latrobe's contract, and although he had not been able to participate in the contract since he was not a delegate, he certainly had a share in the Cochrane contract on the Net Proceeds Case. Latrobe defended himself with a public statement to the Choctaw and Chickasaw people disclaiming any prior knowledge of the financial arrangements—that is, the $100,000 advance—with regard to his contract. He said that he had been offered the advance by Pitchlynn at the time of the contract negotiations.[59] And Albert Pike, although he had turned down Pitchlynn's previous overtures to him to take on the case, now emerged to defend his right to the fee from John Cochrane's original contract.[60] Given Pike's history with the Choctaws and his performance in the Civil War, it is hard to know what to make of his assertions.

The Choctaw lobby disintegrated into charges and countercharges. Pitchlynn had relied heavily on Pike and Cochrane to get the initial bond payment. Cooper had set up the Latrobe contract, which involved Cochrane. Cochrane's inconvenient death led to the sale of the contract to Black, and the Latrobe-Cooper-Fuller "lobby" soured Black and Congress on the claim. Pike's anguished appeals for reinstatement only deepened the contention over control of the case.[61]

The scandal also cast doubt on the power of the Choctaw delegates as an autonomous arm of the Choctaw government. Had the General Council indeed approved the Cochrane contract? Although by implication the council's approval of the Treaty of 1866 had ratified all the delegates' actions, including the contract, the Shanks report raised questions, and Chief William Bryant denied any record of the Latrobe contract, although Allen Wright, chief at time the treaty was submitted for ratification, declared that it had been approved.[62] As a consequence of the legislation and the general scandal that developed around the Choctaw claims, the General Council acted to repeal all contracts, thus leaving all the competing factions, including the ever-hopeful Pike, out in the cold.[63]

Pitchlynn was undaunted. He laid yet more memorials before yet another Congress, the forty-third, in January 1874.[64] Although the House Committee on Indian Affairs reported favorably on the award, recommending the payment of bonds in the amount of

$2,731,247,[65] the attention of Congress was now focused on threat of the "lobby." In addition, the Choctaw delegation's autonomy was undercut when Congress required the General Council to designate an official to receive the funds.[66] It also required the secretary of the treasury to determine the exact amounts due to individual Choctaws so it could establish a fund for "educational and other purposes" with the excess of the judgment.[67] Because of the scandal surrounding the Net Proceeds claim, Congress asserted increasing control over its distribution, and, having banished the dreaded "lobby," it was willing to return to the merit of the claim.

The Forty-Third Congress took up the matter yet again. If 5 percent interest from the date of the original award was added, the amount at stake had increased to $2,981,247. Congress was willing to restore the original amount determined by the secretary of the interior in 1859 and to include interest. It was also willing to consider the payment as a separate bill rather than as simply an amendment to the Indian appropriation bill. An issue as large and complex as the Net Proceeds claim certainly deserved consideration in its own right.[68] The debate, however, revived fear of "the lobby" amid charges that land speculators had secured all the Choctaw claims and would get the money instead of the Indians. The economic health of the Nation was also an issue after the Panic of 1873, and the House voted 136 to 89 (64 not voting) against the Choctaw payment.[69]

In despair, Pitchlynn addressed an exhaustive history of the whole case to the committees on Indian affairs of the House and Senate and vehemently denied the existence of "THE LOBBY."[70] If Congress would not approve the Net Proceeds claim, he would seek justice in the federal courts, he wrote.[71]

The seeming failure of the Net Proceeds Case and the influx of non-Indians into the territory with the railroads caused politics in the Nation to take a decidedly conservative turn, and in 1874, Coleman Cole, a full-blood, was elected chief. Cole had two main political agendas—the regulation of non-Indians in the Choctaw Nation and the distribution of the Net Proceeds. He had a very personal stake in the Net Proceeds claim because he was one of the original fourteenth article claimants whom William Ward had not registered.

Cole blamed the Choctaw delegation for the delay in receipt of the Net Proceeds payment and mounted an aggressive campaign of his own for the claim.[72] He revived the Choctaw court of claims with the intention of distributing the payment through the Nation rather than through the delegates.[73] He persuaded the General Council to send its own memorial to the U.S. government requesting the payment with 5 percent interest.[74]

He also distrusted Peter Pitchlynn, declaring that "if Pitchlynn's party is allowed control of that money, the rightful owners will never get one cent,"[75] and attempted to oust him as delegate.[76] It is difficult to say whether Cole's letters and memorials influenced Congress, but on May 15, 1876, the House Committee on Indian Affairs conceded the binding force of the award and concluded that it should be paid. The amount, however, was still unresolved between the House and Senate, and the House recommended that the case be referred to the U.S. Court of Claims.[77]

The Choctaw Nation thus became an active litigant in its case against the U.S. government. Although the move can be seen as yet another congressional delaying tactic, the recommendation gave the Choctaw Nation the possibility of a new venue for its claims. In 1881, after a series of bills, Congress finally granted the U.S. Court of Claims jurisdiction over the Net Proceeds claim, and the Choctaws thus became the first Indian Nation to have its case adjudicated by that court.[78]

Peter Pitchlynn did not live to see the outcome of the case and collect his fee. He died in Washington on February 17, 1881, worn out by the long struggle he had waged.[79] The Choctaw Nation noted his passing in a resolution that acknowledged his contribution "to the forming and perfecting the form of the Choctaw government." It appropriated $1,268 for his medical and burial expenses in 1883.[80]

The Choctaws entered the U.S. court system in a new relationship with the U.S. government in a number of important ways. When the Nation sued the United States, it became subject to the rules of U.S. courts and their judgments. It gave up a part of its sovereignty in an attempt to gain justice from the U.S. government.[81] The congressional act set aside the original Senate award and allowed the court of claims "to review the entire question of difference de novo." The court was not to be estopped by the previous award by the Senate. In other words, the Choctaws were back to the beginning.[82]

The Net Proceeds Case and the Choctaw Nation were not operating under a totally new set of rules. The court of claims accepted the spirit of liberal interpretation of the language in the eighteenth article of the Treaty of Dancing Rabbit Creek but said that it could not "enlarge the jurisdiction of this court." It rejected the key argument of the Choctaw Nation, the special treaty relationship between tribes and the U.S. government, asserting that its jurisdiction covered only contracts. It also rejected a key point of Pitchlynn's argument, that the claim under the fourteenth article was a national rather than an individual one. The court decided that the infamous release by the General Council in 1852 accepting a payment from the federal government in settlement of its claims covered only fourteenth article claimants who had actually been registered by William Ward. Pitchlynn had based his case on the many claims that had been rejected, but the court declared that the Choctaw Nation had not taken any action with regard to those claims and that only the protests of individual claimants in Mississippi led to the subsequent investigations.[83]

The court of claims decision in the case rejected the notion of treaty rights in favor of individual contractual rights. It awarded the Choctaws $408,120 for claims by individuals, rejecting the notion that the Choctaws had any claims as a nation to the Net Proceeds.[84] Both sides immediately appealed the case to the Supreme Court— the federal government to block the court's judgment and the Choctaw General Council to reassert its claim to the original Senate judgment. The Supreme Court accepted the Senate award of 1859 as evidence of the legitimacy of the Choctaw claims, reversed the decision of the court of claims, and restored the whole judgment of $2,981,247. It also affirmed the sum of $59,449 for unpaid annuities and $68,102 for the 161,000 acres on the eastern boundary.[85] The long, hard struggle had been won, although most of its key players had succumbed in the battle. But the victory was bittersweet for the Nation.

On June 29, 1888, Congress appropriated $2,858,798 for the final payment of the Choctaw claims.[86] Almost immediately afterward, the lawyers descended. Ward H. Lamon and Chauncy F. Black, survivors of the firm of Jeremiah Black, filed a restraining order against Henry E. McKee in order to collect their fees under the Cochrane contract, but McKee collected $783,768 from the federal treasury and promptly vanished.[87]

In the Choctaw Nation, a generation had passed since the events that precipitated the net proceeds claim. The Choctaws and their heirs were finally receiving their money, "about $600,000 or $700,000." At least $100,000 of that amount had already ended up in the hands of lawyers.[88] The distribution also led to major scandals in the Choctaw Nation because rolls were changed arbitrarily. Haggling continued in the courts over various claims to part of the proceeds.[89] Groups of attorneys disagreed over their fees for working on the case, delegates on the Net Proceeds Commission for the Choctaws debated the amounts owed them, and the heirs of Pitchlynn and Samuel Garland took their cases to the U.S. Court of Claims.[90]

The Net Proceeds Case laid the basis for the Choctaws' emergent political identity during the latter half of the nineteenth century. Through it they established their presence in the halls of Congress and, ultimately, in the U.S. Courts. It also established their status as adversaries rather than wards of the U.S. government. Their reliance on lawyers and lobbyists involved them in legal scandals that slowed the progress of the case, but, ironically, the longer the case went on, the longer the Choctaws remained a thorn in the side of Congress.

Ward Lamon, one of the lawyers involved in the claim, testified before a congressional committee concerning the lobbyists that "the woods were full of them. Nearly everybody you would meet had something to say about the Choctaw claims." Members of Congress "got out of temper with being annoyed by every Tom, Dick, and Harry representing the Choctaw claim until it became odious to them."[91]

When the Choctaws finally gained access to the U.S. Court of Claims in 1881, they were no longer wards but litigants. The Net Proceeds Case demonstrates the complexity of the relationship between the Choctaw Nation and the U.S. government. For more than thirty years, the government passed the claim back and forth between the executive branch and Congress, and finally to the federal courts. The

Nation's delegations worked in the halls of Congress to promote its interests, and the Choctaw government added its own voice in memorials. The Nation relied upon legal council and lobbyists to present its case. In the end, it was the sheer persistence and litigiousness of the Choctaws that gained what Peter Pitchlynn had originally wanted—a sense of justice for the Nation.

CHAPTER 10

SELFISHNESS AND CIVILIZATION

On a fall day in 1885, in the elegant Lake Mohonk House resort in upstate New York, Senator Henry L. Dawes (R-Massachusetts) waxed eloquent about his experience in Indian Territory on his summer vacation. He had visited in the Cherokee Nation, where "the head chief told us that there was not a family in that whole Nation that had not a home of its own. There was not a pauper in that Nation, and the Nation did not owe a dollar. It built its own capitol . . . and it built its schools and its hospitals." The picture was not all rosy, however. Dawes continued, "The defect of the system was apparent. They have got as far as they can go, because they own their land in common. . . . There is no enterprise to make your home any better than that of your neighbors." He concluded with the ringing declaration that "there is no selfishness, which is at the bottom of civilization."[1]

Thus did Dawes characterize the underlying cause of the "Indian problem." Indians were not selfish. They owned their land in common and there was no competitive spirit. Certainly in this respect Indians were not civilized. Dawes's comment echoed the general American ethos of the early nineteenth century, which equated private ownership of land and civilization. It glorified equal opportunity and the ideal of the self-sufficient yeoman farmer, but by the late nineteenth century that ideal was fast being overwhelmed by the growth of an increasingly industrialized and capitalist society. Financial upheavals and the expansion of railroads made the life of the yeoman farmer far from ideal. It is a telling comment on federal policy that the Dawes Act imposed an essentially obsolete idea on American Indians.[2] Perhaps it was to the general state of affairs that Commissioner of Indian Affairs T. J. Morgan referred in his report in 1889, where he wrote that Indians needed to "conform their mode of living substantially to our civilization." He went on to declare that "this civilization may not be the best possible, but it is the best the Indians can get. They can not escape it, and must either conform to it or be crushed by it."[3] The commissioner's statements reflect both federal policy and the cutthroat capitalist ethics of the late nineteenth century.

Dawes tried to enforce selfishness on Indians through the General Allotment Act passed by Congress in 1887.[4] The idea of dividing Indian lands into private holdings was certainly not new. Proposals to allot Indian land and extend a territorial government over the Indian Territory had been floated in Congress since the 1850s during the debate over the Kansas-Nebraska Act, and "sectionizing" had emerged as a potentially divisive issue in the Choctaw Nation during the constitutional crisis of 1858–1860. Dawes's act finally gave the federal government the tool it needed to impose allotment on Indian nations.

Progressive politicians opposed economic concentrations and monopolies and espoused the very Protestant notion that economic success was linked to character.[5] In one respect, Dawes acted on that notion. Giving Indians the opportunity to gain financial success as individual farmers would allow them to prove themselves as full members of American society. If they failed, others with more character could take their land. White advocates of the new policy pointed out that allotment would give Indians access to the federal courts for protection of their rights. As Lyman Abbott said, "The Indian is no longer to be cared for by the executive department of the government; he is coming under the general protection under which we all live, namely, the protection of the courts."[6] The Choctaw Nation was well aware of the torturous process of federal courts.

A more subtle issue was the growing class distinctions within the Nation. The notion of communal property did not prevent individuals from monopolizing large portions of land. As the editor of the *Caddo Banner* observed, "The intelligent Choctaws are gobbling up all the best lands, and the uneducated class is being left without anything."[7] The existence of rich Indians who controlled large amounts of property confirmed that Dawes's ideal of selfishness was indeed alive and well in Indian Territory, but it worked against his other ideal of the self-sufficient yeoman farmer.[8]

The Choctaws viewed allotment as a threat for two reasons. For one thing, it contradicted the deeply held cultural value of communal land-holding. Although Choctaws had strongly developed notions of personal property and individual use of the communal lands, these were rights of occupancy and use rather than the right to buy or sell. The second reason was that treaties guaranteed land to the Nation as a self-governing entity. Allotment would break up the national land base and destroy the integrity of the national government. Choctaws could point to the congressional land grant to the Missouri, Kansas and Texas Railroad once Indian title was extinguished. They had consistently challenged the legality of the grant to the MK&T, and they argued that the dissolution of their tribal land base would allow the railroad to claim some 3 million acres of their land.[9]

The General Allotment Act specifically excluded the Five Tribes in Indian Territory. One reason was because they held their land under fee simple title from the federal government. In that respect, the Nation was a land owner in a way that Congress could recognize and had to respect. Another was that it was to the advantage of white cattlemen who held large leases on tribal lands of the Five Tribes, particularly in the Cherokee Nation, to maintain the communal land-holding pattern, and some of them influenced the legislation.[10]

The Dawes Act provided for the distribution of reservation lands in 160-acre plots to heads of households, 80 acres to each single person over 18 and orphan under 18, and 40 acres to single persons under 18, the land to be held in trust for a period of 25 years. Allottees became citizens of the United States. The excess reservation land not allotted to Indians would be bought by the government for sale to homesteaders, and the funds from the sale would be used for the "education and civilization" of the tribes.[11]

In his message to Congress in 1901, President Theodore Roosevelt triumphantly described the Dawes Act as "a mighty pulverizing

Indian Territory in 1889. (Adapted from Goins and Goble, *Historical Atlas of Oklahoma*, 4th ed.)

engine to break up the tribal mass." It is interesting to note that the same Congress that passed the Dawes Act also passed a number of bills granting various railroad companies rights of way across Indian lands.[12] The "selfish interests" of private enterprise were served by allotment, and railroad lobbyists undoubtedly had some influence in the passage of the act.[13] Lyman Abbott, a stalwart of the Lake Mohonk Conference, put a more benevolent face on the situation. "The railroad, with all its corruptions, is a Christianizing power, and will do more to teach the people punctuality than schoolmaster or preacher can."[14]

Although the Five Tribes escaped the General Allotment Act, the existence of the Indian Territory as an imperium in imperio was a cause for great concern among both Indian reformers and government officials. Reports of corruption in their tribal governments and general lawlessness in the territory were widespread in the national press. And the growing white population in the territory had no political rights under the Choctaw government. Dawes felt that their children could not attend Choctaw schools and remained uneducated. The sanctity of private property rights for American citizens in Indian Territory could be secured only if the nations would accept allotment. Laws and courts had to prevail over all people, Indians and whites alike. As Dawes himself said, "This condition of things is as certain to pass away as that the sun will rise tomorrow morning. The only question is how shall it pass away?"[15]

And so it was that on March 3, 1893, Congress created the Commission to the Five Tribes, whose charge was to go to the Indian Territory and negotiate with the Five Tribes "to enable the ultimate creation of a State or States of the Union which shall embrace the lands within said Indian Territory."[16] Dawes was clear in his own mind, however, that if the Indians would not accept allotment willingly, the situation would lead to "some violent war of race or in blood" or Congress would impose it upon them.[17] Dawes was the logical choice to head the commission. The other members appointed were Meredith Kidd of Indiana and Archibald McKennon of Arkansas. The commissioner of Indian affairs prepared instructions to the committee, pointing out the delicacy of its task and, because its purpose was to negotiate rather than dictate, leaving the commissioners a good deal of latitude.[18] The Dawes Commission began its work with a brief organizational meeting in Washington on December 8, 1893, and then took the train to Muskogee in Indian Territory. They set up their office there in January 1884, but in March they moved their headquarters to McAlester, a more central location in the territory.[19]

Despite some reasonable arguments in favor of allotment, the majority of Choctaw people remained obdurate in its resistance. In 1870, by an overwhelming majority, the Nation's voters had rejected the plan of surveying and allotment proposed in the Treaty of 1866, and in 1890, Chief Wilson Jones had proclaimed to the General Council his opposition to "sectionizing our country."[20] When the commission appeared in 1894, Jones called on Choctaw citizens to hold county meetings to consider allotment.[21] The Dawes Commission and the Choctaw council met for the first time at Tushkahoma on January 25, 1894. The commissioners also attended an international council of tribes in the Indian Territory. During the course of the meeting, some of the Indian delegates received telegrams from Washington, D.C., saying that Congress would not force allotment on the tribes without their consent. Bolstered by this "treaty guarantee," the council passed a resolution opposing allotment and urging the individual tribes to do likewise. The telegrams discouraged the tribes' willingness to negotiate, and Dawes was convinced that the international council's resistance was also a result of its being controlled by tribal officials and large land-holders."[22]

The Choctaw council told the commissioners bluntly that it would not "agree or consent to any proposition looking to a change of their present system of holding their land in common or any change in their present tribal government whatever."[23] Nevertheless, the Dawes Commission presented the council with a list of propositions on April 23, 1894. The gist of the propositions was that all lands owned by the Choctaws and Chickasaws would be divided among the citizens of those nations, except for town sites along the railroads and coal and minerals, which would be sold and the proceeds divided per capita. All outstanding claims of the nations against the government would be settled (this proposition opened the door for ongoing litigation over the Leased District). Tribal governments would be continued until final distribution of tribal land, money, and resources was complete, and when the Choctaws and Chickasaws would agree, a territorial government would be extended over their lands and those of the other Five Tribes who agreed.[24]

The commission's propositions made the federal government's position plain, and they inspired a kind of cat-and-mouse game between the commissioners and the Choctaws. A contingent of Choctaws met with the commissioners at their offices in Muskogee and asked them to hold meetings with citizens at various points throughout the Nation. At those meetings, the Dawes commissioners were accompanied by a commission of three Choctaws appointed by the council. These men were fluent in Choctaw and English so they could act as interpreters, but they had also been instructed to discourage people from accepting the commission's propositions. Although the Choctaw Council had the commission's propositions before it at its October session, it adjourned without taking any action on them, and Dawes had had no response from the council.[25]

The commission found other respondents who were more than willing to give evidence for charges of inequity within the Choctaw and Chickasaw nations. Black freedmen were vocal in their complaints. Although the Choctaws had adopted freedmen as tribal members in 1883, their rights were limited. The Chickasaws had never adopted their freedmen. The Choctaw freedmen had not received the forty acres apiece that they had been promised under the Treaty of 1866. There was only one school in the Nation for their children, and they had been excluded from the Leased District payment. When they tried to meet with the commission, they were threatened with death by a "prominent Indian citizen."[26] The commission found a powerful issue in the rights of the freedmen.

The Nation was also dealing with the issue of its jurisdiction over non-Indians. When mine owners tried to lower wages, about 2,000 miners went on strike on April 1, 1894.[27] Almost all of the miners were foreign born and working under tribal permits. If they were not working they could be classified as intruders, and Chief Wilson Jones asked U. S. Agent Dew Wisdom to remove about 200 of them from the Nation. The council questioned Jones's authority to call Wisdom and U.S. forces into the Nation. In the end, only forty-three men were removed and the labor unrest died down, but the situation focused attention on the problematic relations between the Choctaw Nation and the U.S. government over jurisdictional issues and the control of "intruders" in the Choctaw Nation.[28]

Dissatisfied freedmen, striking miners, disgruntled Buzzards, poor uneducated white children—all conspired to present a picture of general social disorder in the Choctaw Nation. Although the General Council kept its distance from the Dawes Commission, stories of government corruption in the white-controlled newspapers and complaints heard in the field surely influenced the members of the Dawes Commission against the tribal government.[29]

The commission renewed its attempt to negotiate in the spring of 1895. The invitation came this time directly from the president of the United States, Grover Cleveland. He was, he said, anxious to reach an agreement that would give the tribes "all your just rights and promote your highest welfare" and would "contribute to the best interests of the whole country." The nations were conspicuously silent. Dawes sent a second letter on May 18, and finally Choctaw chief Jefferson Gardner responded, on May 27, saying that the Choctaw people, rather than he as chief, had to consent to any negotiations. He invited the commissioners to a meeting of the Choctaw Board of Education at Tuskahoma on July 8. Dawes assured Gardner that the commission respected Choctaw treaty rights and wanted "neither their lands or any other rights they enjoy under their treaties." But he insisted that "some change in the present condition of affairs is necessary for the good of your people" and that the commission was there to help the Choctaws "make that change yourself."[30]

The issue of allotment led to new political alignments in the Nation. On July 10, a group of pro-allotment Choctaws gathered in Hartshorn and called on the General Council to establish a commission to meet with the Dawes Commission.[31] The moving force in the meeting was Green McCurtain, son of a former chief of the Nation, brother of another, and national treasurer.[32] McCurtain argued that "if we take this question up of our own free will then we will have the authority to dictate terms to the U.S. government."[33] For McCurtain, the issue was not whether allotment would take place but on whose terms.

In October 1895, the General Council finally agreed to send representatives to meet with the Dawes Commission.[34] On October 28, Olosachubbee, president of the newly appointed negotiating committee, notified the Dawes Commission that the committee was willing to meet the following day at the capitol. The commission's original propositions were on the table.[35] The meeting produced no results, and the council declared that the commission's overall proposal "does not meet with the approval . . . or the consent of the Choctaw and Chickasaw people at large."[36] The council also considered a bill that would certainly have discouraged approval or consent by making it a crime for any citizen "to attempt to overthrow the Choctaw government by exciting or subverting the minds of the people against the Choctaw form of government" or to "hold or attempt to hold Choctaw land in severalty" or "to convey any part or parcel of Choctaw land to a non-citizen or citizens, or . . . into the hands of a foreign power." The bill passed in the Choctaw Senate. It failed in the House, but only by one vote. The closeness of the vote indicates the division of sentiment over allotment.[37]

Henry Dawes was becoming frustrated in his attempts to convince the nations in Indian Territory that allotment was in their own best interest. He was increasingly convinced that the government needed to take the initiative to enforce allotment. Although the nations had been "wisely given every opportunity and tendered every possible assistance to make this change for themselves," they had "persistently refused and insist upon being left to continue present conditions." There was "no alternative left to the United States but to assume the responsibility for future conditions in their Territory." The federal government had created tribal governments and they depended upon its authority. They were "wholly corrupt, irresponsible and unworthy to be longer trusted with the care and control of the money and other property of Indian citizens, much less their lives, which they scarcely pretend to protect." Dawes declared that Congress should extend territorial government and legal jurisdiction over the Indian Territory immediately.[38]

Allotment was now the most pressing political issue in the Nation. Green McCurtain recognized allotment as a foregone conclusion but asserted the Nation's power to dictate its terms, and he consolidated his power base by forming a new political party at a meeting in Tuskahoma on January 23, 1896. The Tuskahoma Party promptly nominated him for chief in the upcoming election.[39] The campaign of 1896 became essentially a referendum on allotment. Both the National and Progressive parties opposed it, but in the three-way race, they split the vote and McCurtain was elected.[40]

McCurtain now staked the political future of the Choctaw Nation on its ability to preserve its political power under an allotment agreement with the U.S. government. He assured the General Council that "if we allot our lands the U.S. government will permit us to retain our present form of government until such time as we think necessary to prepare our people to cope with their white brothers in the struggle for existence."[41] Change was inevitable, but the Choctaw government could control its progress.

The U.S. Congress, however, gave the Dawes Commission two powerful new weapons against the tribes in 1896—the power to control tribal membership and the federal mandate to establish a government for the Indian Territory that would "rectify the many inequalities and discriminations now existing" and "afford needful protection to the lives and property of all citizens and residents thereof."[42] Congress authorized the commission to compile final rolls of all citizens of the Five Tribes in preparation for the distribution of land. The tribal rolls were accepted as definitive, although the commission had to ask repeatedly before the Choctaw Nation handed over a copy of its 1896 census. Because of the arbitrary power sometimes exercised in the past by General Councils, the tribal rolls were the subject of charges of bribery and corruption, but they represented the tribal membership for the Dawes Commission's purposes.[43]

The General Council finally appointed its commissioners—Green McCurtain, J. S. Standley, N. B. Ainsworth, Ben Hampton, Wesley Anderson, Amos Henry, D. C. Garland, and A. S. Williams. They insisted on meeting at Fort Smith, Arkansas, ostensibly because it was neutral territory but quite possibly because its members feared reprisals from anti-allotment partisans in the Nation. The Dawes commissioners moved themselves, lock, stock, and voluminous enrollment records to Fort Smith for the meeting on November 16.[44]

The Dawes Commission's basic negotiating points were that all communal property and resources should be divided on an equal basis among tribal members, that land should be set aside for towns, and that U.S. courts should take over legal jurisdiction in Indian Territory. The Dawes Commission would oversee the settlement of outstanding Choctaw claims and the Choctaw government would continue to exist until all property was distributed.[45]

The Choctaw commissioners laid out their position. They agreed to the equitable distribution of property but insisted that freedmen could not be included. They agreed to the establishment of towns, but they flatly refused the extension of U.S. courts over their territory. They insisted that the Dawes Commission be the final arbiter of outstanding claim—the final payment for the Leased District and damages for railroad rights of way. They added other demands— that the president of the United States would continue to approve Choctaw legislation directly, that they would be compensated for loss of land to railroads, that individual lands could not be sold or taxed, that the 98th meridian (the western boundary of Choctaw and Chickasaw lands) would be surveyed, and that lands still set aside in Mississippi for Choctaw orphans in the Treaty of 1830 should be sold for the benefit of the Nation.[46]

The issues were complex, pitting the federal policy of assimilation against Choctaw demands for recognition of their rights. But finally, after what Dawes characterized as "long, arduous negotiations," a draft agreement was reached on December 18, 1896. The Choctaw delegates announced that they needed to take it back to the Nation for discussion, but Dawes suspected that they were merely using a ploy to avoid signing. He was relieved when the delegation sent word for him to meet them in Muskogee for the signing. His account of the event is melodramatic.

> We sat round a table in a large room lighted by electricity, and just as we were ready to put our names to it something happened to the machinery, and the electric lights went out and left us in utter darkness. I thought the end had come. I thought these Indians would certainly say that this was an omen and a warning, and leave the room. But we got kerosene lamps, and I was exceedingly gratified to find them still sitting there, and

we gathered round the table again, and, to my surprise, the incident had had no effect upon these men, and they put their names beside ours to that first instrument.[47]

To Henry Dawes, the Choctaw Nation was both a foreign and exotic tribe of superstitious men who needed to be assimilated into American society by the power of private property. In some respects, Dawes's belief in that power was as strong as the beliefs he attributed to the Choctaw delegates.

The Choctaws were not the only players in the drama, however. The Chickasaws also had to agree since the land was owned in common. Their delegates had appeared but had withdrawn from the discussion, saying that they were not empowered by the Chickasaw legislature to negotiate a binding agreement. Indeed, the Choctaws and Chickasaws disagreed strongly on the issue of allotment. On the same day that the Choctaw commissioners signed the agreement with the Dawes Commission, the Chickasaw legislature passed a resolution opposing it.[48] But it was obvious that allotment was inevitable, and the Chickasaw council finally appointed a commission with authority to negotiate. The final agreement was signed at Atoka on April 23, 1897.[49]

The Atoka Agreement laid out the plan for allotment, and it demonstrated once again how the value of land was being translated into money. The land of the nations would be distributed on the basis of equal monetary value among all the citizens of the Choctaw and Chickasaw nations except the freedmen. Each man, woman, and child would receive a fair share of the tribal estate. (The agreement made no special provision for dealing with children as land-owners, a situation that would have significant consequences in the future.) Federal surveyors would determine the value of the land based on its use. Market value (land near towns, coal mines, and railroads was generally of significantly higher value than rural land) would not enter into the equation. From his or her allotment, each citizen was to select a homestead of 160 acres. The homestead was inalienable and untaxable for a period of twenty-one years from its issue. The remainder of the allotment could be sold, one-fourth in the first year, one-fourth in the third year, and the remainder after five years. The agreement thus provided Choctaws with a source of capital—their surplus lands—that they could sell to finance the development of their homesteads.

Land containing coal, asphalt, and other minerals was retained as tribal property to be used for the benefit of all citizens. Town sites were to be surveyed, platted, and sold and the proceeds to be distributed on a per capita basis to Choctaw citizens. The Dawes Commission agreed to protect Choctaw claims, to survey railroad rights of way, to survey the 98th meridian, and to sell the orphan lands in Mississippi. The commission refused, however, to resolve the Leased District issue. It chose to refer the matter to the U.S. Court of Claims rather than to Congress.

The Choctaw delegates lost their major battle regarding federal jurisdiction. They agreed to extend the power of the federal courts over the Choctaw and Chickasaw nations in a wide range of matters where non-Indians were involved, thus effectively dismantling the Choctaw court system. And finally, the Atoka Agreement set the date for the final termination of the Choctaw government: March 4, 1906.[50]

The agreement was a political compromise that satisfied neither side. Green McCurtain was forced to admit the defeat of his political strategy to dictate terms to the commissioners. The terms of the Atoka Agreement were "repugnant to our feelings and against our wishes," but it was clear that the federal government was "much more powerful than we are" and that it could "enforce these demands should we refuse to accede to them." The Choctaw Nation could no longer depend on its treaties. It was overwhelmed by the white population in the Nation over which it had no control, and "our government has outlived its time."[51] Henry Dawes, on his part, conceded that the agreement did not "in all respects embody those features which the commission desired," but "they were the best obtainable."[52] On this unsatisfactory note, the stage was set for allotment.

The Choctaw elections for General Council in 1897 became a referendum for the Atoka Agreement. A new political party, the Union Party, formed to oppose allotment, but the Tuskahoma Party carried the election, and the Choctaw council ratified the Atoka Agreement on November 4, 1897.[53] On June 30, 1898, the U.S. Congress ratified it as part of the euphemistically entitled "Act for the Protection of the

People of the Indian Territory," more commonly known as the Curtis Act.[54] It required that the Choctaws and Chickasaws approve the Atoka Agreement at a general election before it could take effect. Green McCurtain, fighting a rearguard action, lobbied vigorously for its approval, arguing that the agreement would still allow the Nation to regulate the activities of non-Indians in its territory through fees and taxes.[55]

On August 28, 1898, Choctaw voters ratified the Atoka Agreement by a vote of 2,164 to 1,366.[56] Tribal members were now subject to U.S. courts in a number of significant ways, but tribal councils could still make laws that did not conflict with U.S. laws and the Constitution, and the secretary of the interior had upheld the right of the tribes to tax non-Indians.[57] Green McCurtain had made the Nation's last stand against the U.S. government, and he had lost the war. The Choctaw Nation was forced to accept the jurisdiction of U.S. courts over its citizens in their dealings with U.S. citizens. It agreed to the final determination of its citizenship by the Dawes Commission. It essentially agreed to its own dissolution.

The allotment of tribal land and resources proved to be an extraordinarily complex and litigious process. The failure of the General Allotment Act and the Atoka Agreement to end tribal identity was a general failing of the U.S. government's Indian policy. It assumed an ending point at which Indians would simply cease to exist as Indians. Once the final list was made, land ownership would make them like all American citizens, and the nations of Indian Territory would cease to exist. Congress set deadlines and the Choctaw Nation challenged them. Choctaws continued to be born and to die while the enrollment process dragged on. And there were still Choctaws living in Mississippi. The U.S. government soon discovered that termination of the identity of the Choctaw Nation could not be accomplished solely by congressional fiat.

CHAPTER 11

THE LEASED DISTRICT CLAIM

The Choctaw Nation became a landlord with the Treaty of 1855, and landlord-tenant relationships often become contentious. The agreement of the Choctaw and Chickasaw nations to lease its western lands beyond the 98th meridian became a legal issue between the tribes and the U.S. government. In 1855, the nations could capitalize on the desire of the federal government to find land on which to settle Indians who had been displaced by treaties in 1854 that made way for the establishment of Kansas Territory. The Choctaws and Chickasaws had land the U.S. government needed. By 1866, however, the Choctaw and Chickasaw nations, having fought on the wrong side in the Civil War, had virtually no bargaining power with regard to land. The lease of 1855 became a cession in the Treaty of 1866. With the General Allotment Act of 1887, Congress had a way of opening former Indian land to white settlement, and when that happened, the Choctaws argued, the 1855 treaty was broken and Choctaws and Chickasaws, as joint owners, had to be compensated for the whole value of the land. The Choctaw Nation thus had yet another claim based on the abrogation of treaty rights to complicate the final settlement of its affairs with the U.S. government.

The Leased District claim was the kind of legal issue that refused to die even after the ostensible dissolution of the Choctaw tribal government in 1906, and into the 1930s it kept the Choctaw Nation alive as a legal entity if not a viable government. Its history parallels in some ways that of the Net Proceeds Case—both were claims based in the interpretation of treaty language that bounced between Congress and the courts over a long period of time. Following as it did upon the distribution of the judgment in the Net Proceeds Case, it compounded the effects of the conversion of land into money on Choctaw society.

The Leased District Case stemmed, as did so much of Choctaw legal action, from the vagueness of treaty language, in this case going back to the Choctaw Treaty of Doaks Stand in 1820. In that treaty, the Choctaws exchanged the bulk of their eastern lands for land west of the Mississippi. The treaty defined the western boundary of the new Choctaw lands as beginning at the headwaters of the Canadian River, a point that had not yet been clearly demarcated in 1820 by exploration and survey but was located somewhere beyond the 100th meridian. In 1819, the United States signed a treaty with the Spanish government setting the 100th meridian as the boundary between U.S. and Spanish territory. That treaty conflicted with the Treaty of Doaks Stand, leaving the western boundary of Choctaw Territory uncertain. The federal government attempted to solve the problem in the Treaty of Dancing Rabbit Creek by defining the Choctaws' western lands as running "to the source of the Canadian fork; *if in the limits of the United States, or to those limits*" [emphasis added].[1]

In the 1855 treaty, the problem of the western boundary was ostensibly settled when the Choctaws and Chickasaws agreed to relinquish all claims to lands beyond the 100th meridian and to lease their lands between the 98th and 100th meridians to the U.S. government for the settlement of the Wichita "and certain other tribes or bands of Indians." In exchange, the tribes received a payment of $800,000.[2] The treaty did not, however, specify how much of the payment was for the cession of the lands beyond the 100th meridian (approximately 6 million acres) and how much was for the lease of the land between the 98th and 100th meridians (approximately 7.7 million acres). In essence, the 1855 treaty gave the federal government the right to approximately 13 million acres for $800,000, but the uncertainty of the terms of the payment would continue to haunt the U.S. government for years to come.[3]

The land beyond the 98th parallel proved virtually worthless to the Choctaws and Chickasaws. The Kiowas and Comanches raided it on a regular basis and there was no water. The federal government, however, found it the ideal place to establish reservations for western tribes it hoped to turn into farmers (an untenable proposition given the lack of water).[4] The lease arrangement in the 1855 treaty seemed to benefit both parties, and after 1859, Wichitas, Kiowas, and Cheyennes were settled in the Leased District. After the Civil War, the federal government saw it as a place to settle the Choctaw and Chickasaw freedmen if the nations would not adopt them. In the language of the 1866 treaty, the "lease" became a cession, and the Choctaw and Chickasaw nations received a payment of $300,000 for approximately 13 million acres of land.[5] Although the Five Tribes were spared the effect of Henry Dawes's allotment act in 1887, the tribes who had been settled in the Leased District were subject to it. The Jerome Commission, which was appointed by the U.S. Congress to negotiate allotment agreements with the western tribes in Indian Territory, negotiated the distribution of their lands beginning in 1890. The Wichitas and Cheyennes agreed to accept allotment, and a vast area of the Leased District was opened to purchase by non-Indians.[6]

The 1866 treaty had specifically prohibited white persons from going into Choctaw and Chickasaw territory except for railroad employees, travelers passing through, and white mechanics, teachers, and so forth employed in the nations.[7] But the federal government was intent on extinguishing title to as much Indian land as it could. By its postwar treaties with the Creeks, Seminoles, and Cherokees, it had acquired their western lands, supposedly for the settlement of Indian tribes, but when it did not assign any tribes to the area, white men clamored for it and Congress opened it to white settlement.[8] In the great land run of 1889, some 50,000 settlers and speculators surged into the unassigned lands, creating the area that would become Oklahoma Territory.[9] The wedge had been driven, and the nations were left to salvage what they could of their territory.

For the Choctaw Nation, the Dawes Act held out the threat of the dismantling of the Leased District, and the General Council appointed a delegation to go to Washington to negotiate what they saw as a just payment for the land.[10] It gave them a contingent fee of 25 percent of what they could recover.[11] A federal commission, however, rejected the delegation's arguments. It asserted that the Choctaws had ceded the land outright, had accepted payment, and had no further rights.[12] The council launched an immediate memorial to Congress complaining that its claim was being dismissed by the government.[13]

The crux of the Leased District case was the interpretation of the single word "cede" in the 1866 treaty. The Nation argued that the treaty delegation had understood the word to mean a conveyance in trust for the purpose of settling Indian tribes; they were allowing the government to use the land it held in trust for the purposes specified in the Treaty of 1855 and the Choctaws still owned the land. If the land was used for other purposes, the treaty was broken and the Choctaws should receive full payment for it, an estimated sum of $2,991,450. The Choctaw delegation used its lobbying power to persuade Senator James Jones of Arkansas to attach a rider to the Indian Appropriation Act for 1891 for payment for 2,393,160 acres of land sold to non-Indians after the allotment of the Cheyenne and Arapahoe reservation, and the act passed the House.[14]

In the Choctaw Nation, the Leased District payment represented a major political victory in the struggle for treaty rights. It also became the political prize in the 1892 election campaign for chief of the Nation. The party in power would have control over the distribution of these funds. But the prize was not yet in hand. Although the appropriation had been made, it would not be delivered until representatives "duly selected and authorized by the Choctaw Nation" signed conveyances of title to the U.S. government. Moreover, disturbing charges of fraud, chicanery, and the influence of lawyers began to emerge. Once again, individual interest seemed to overcome tribal interests.

The situation became more complicated in 1892 when Robert Ward, one of the Choctaw delegates, charged that he had been approached by George Thibeau, a citizen of Paris, Texas, who told him that certain members of the General Council objected to Ward's appointment but offered to fix matters if Ward would pay certain Choctaw senators sums of money ranging from $2,500 to $15,000. Ward agreed to the payments, which he considered blackmail. His affidavit was obviously intended to discredit certain senators while protecting his own interest in the 25 percent fee.[15] Thibeau, as it turned out, was associated with John Sypher, the Washington attorney the Choctaw delegation had hired to help them in their lobbying efforts.[16] Thibeau had a 10 percent commission from Sypher that was worth $224,000 if he could collect the Leased District claim from Congress. Choctaw chief Wilson Jones; councilman Thomas Ainsworth, and national treasurer Green McCurtain assured President Harrison that the judgment money would not be put to "improper or illegal uses,"[17] but Robert Owen, federal agent for the Indian Territory and himself a Cherokee, charged that Ainsworth and McCurtain were trying to seize control of the judgment money for themselves rather than for the Nation and that Jones was "very weak, and absolutely under the[ir] control."[18] It appeared that a new "lobby" was forming around the Leased District claim.

The damage to the Nation's credibility was done, and President Harrison and Secretary of the Interior John Noble refused to issue the appropriate conveyances for the sale and final payment. Indeed, Harrison informed Congress that he would have vetoed the appropriation if it had come to him as a separate bill, but because it was part of the Indian appropriation bill he chose not to hold it up. The Sypher contract convinced him that if the federal government had a responsibility to tribes as wards, "Congress should protect them from such extortionate exactions."[19] Harrison was also firmly convinced that the term "cede" in the 1866 treaty and the payments that the Choctaws had received in 1855 and 1866 were adequate to obtain clear title for the federal government.

The General Council responded forcefully with a memorial to Congress that pointed out that the Senate Committee on Indian Affairs had studied the matter thoroughly, upheld the Choctaw argument concerning their title to the lands, and recommended that the payment be made.[20] There was really nothing that Harrison could do since he had not vetoed the appropriation law, however much he might object after the fact. In June 1893, the treasury finally released nearly $3,000,000 to the Choctaw national treasurer to be distributed on a per capita basis among the tribal members.

Although the award represented a political victory for the Nation, the prospect of distributing it created political havoc. Whoever controlled the government would control the distribution of the payment, well over $2,000,000 even after the delegates collected their

25 percent contingency fee and $25,000 for necessary expenses. Although the money was not yet in hand as the election campaign began, the prospect of distributing it created high expectations and tensions throughout the Nation. The council established a payment roll that excluded white intermarried citizens and freedmen.[21] Control of the roll already constituted significant political power.

The national election in August 1892 brought the political crisis of the Nation to a head. The campaign pitted the incumbent Wilson Jones, the candidate of the Progressive Party (designated by its opponents as the Eagles), against national secretary Jacob Battiest Jackson, who represented the National Party (designated by its opponents as the Buzzards). When the General Council met to confirm the election results, it appeared that Jones had won by a comfortable margin, but charges of fraud immediately surfaced, including allegations that noncitizens had tampered with the votes.[22]

A virtual civil war over the contested election broke out on September 11. A party of nationals killed four Progressive Party officeholders near Wilburton and then moved on to McAlester in search of other Progressives. But was it murder or self-defense in the context of a civil war? Were tensions so high that political differences would lead to bloodshed? That question ultimately colored the whole political situation in the Nation. As the Progressives approached, citizens in McAlester sent a frantic telegram to U.S. agent Leo Bennett in Muskogee (some 150 miles away) asking him to come to the capital at Tuskahoma. Bennett immediately telegraphed the chief of the Indian police instructing him to handle the situation, but the chief insisted that Bennett come at once. When Bennett arrived in Tuskahoma that evening, he learned that the killers were camped about two miles west of McAlester. Bennett went on to South McAlester, where about fifty of Jones's heavily armed supporters had occupied the U.S. courthouse. He negotiated a precarious agreement between Jones and his followers and the National Party group. The Nationals agreed to surrender the killers within twenty-four hours and both groups agreed to disarm.

Although Bennett thought he had resolved the conflict, the agreement fell apart when some of Jones's supporters told him that the men who were surrendering were not the actual killers. About 100 armed Progressives joined the men in the courthouse in McAlester. The following day, some of them rode out toward the National camp. An all-out confrontation seemed inevitable until Bennett's twenty Indian policemen drew their guns to protect their prisoners and the Progressives backed down. Confronting some 200 armed men, Bennett read them a federal law passed in 1888 that prohibited interfering with an officer of the United States in carrying out his duties and threatened them with the power of the U.S. courts. Rather remarkably in what had seemed like a totally lawless situation, he was able to prevent an all-out shooting match. The sheriff of Gaines County arrived the next day to collect the accused.

The continuing threat of violence required Bennett's presence at the Choctaw council meeting on October 3 when the votes would be counted and the winner of the election formally declared. He feared that "unless whichever side is defeated will accept such defeat," there would be further deaths and "acts of violence."[23] Bennett did not want any further responsibility in what was clearly an internal Choctaw dispute. Nevertheless, he called in U.S. troops to supervise the final counting of the ballots.[24] Chief Jones questioned Bennett's jurisdiction in the matter even though he had been called on by members of the Nation to intervene.[25] The Nation remained under a virtual state of martial law until October 28, when the federal troops were withdrawn.

The election of 1892 and its aftermath demonstrates the extent to which partisan politics brought the Choctaw Nation to a state of political paralysis in the early 1890s at exactly the time when charges of lawlessness and corruption in tribal governments reinforced the determination of the U.S. Congress to move to allotment and the imposition of a territorial government on Indian Territory. The Leased District payment was a major factor in the bitterness of the dispute between the Progressives and the Nationals.

The violence in Indian Territory attracted national media attention. The "election war" was widely reported, and the political turmoil further undermined the standing of the Nation's claim to the Leased District. Congresswoman Alice Robertson, a member of the Creek Nation, declared that "the appropriation would never have been made but for the untiring efforts of those who were interested in dividing the twenty-five per cent. Lawyer's fees involved." Congresswoman Robertson was not above mixing her metaphors to make her point. The "great windfall" meant that "every politician in the Choctaw nation wants a finger in the pie." She believed that the "Indians have been paid money they would have been far better off without." She urged the Lake Mohonk Conference to support the extension of federal legal jurisdiction over Indian Territory, the allotment of its land, U.S. citizenship for tribal members, and statehood for the territory.[26]

The Choctaw council was, however, determined to collect what it felt was due to it, and it had learned that lawyer's fees were a necessary part of doing business in Washington. As J. S. Standley said poignantly in response to Harrison's opposition to the Leased District judgment, "The Choctaws have always had peculiar difficulty in collecting anything from the United States."[27] In the minds of council members, without the fees, delegates could not hire the legal assistance they needed or spend the amount of time and effort they had to expend in Washington to lobby for the tribe's claims. A 25 percent fee was not an unreasonable payment for the recovery of what the tribe considered to be the fair value of its lands.[28] Unfortunately, the system of contingent fees led both federal officials and friends of the Indians to conclude that self-interest was overtaking tribal interests. Charges of bribery and corruption were common. John Ward's exposé of his payments to Choctaw senators provided evidence, and Senator Dawes asserted that "boodle is said to work marvelously in their legislation; and their judiciary. . . . You cannot get a measure through without proper fructifying influences."[29] It appeared that selfishness was indeed rampant in Indian Territory.

The election of 1892, with its attendant violence, raised serious issues with regard to the whole judicial system of the Choctaw Nation. Could the Choctaw courts maintain order in the extraordinary circumstances of the time? It appeared that they could not. Quiet prevailed in the Nation until the early spring of 1893 when further violence, the so-called Antlers War erupted. In December 1892, Chief Jones ordered the Choctaw lighthorsemen to arrest Willis Jones in connection with the murders of the Progressive Party members in Wilburton, but as Jones was being taken to jail in February of 1893, he was rescued by Albert Jackson, a National Party member, and spirited away to the home of V. M. Locke, an intermarried white man. Chief Jones formed a militia and ordered the arrest of Jones and all of his rescuers. Jones and Jackson and about 100 armed men were holed up in Locke's home. As the militia approached Locke's house, gunfire broke out, and in the ensuing battle the sheriff of Kiamichi County and three of Locke's men were wounded.[30] Locke summed up the situation succinctly. The killers should not be punished. "It was like all political feuds—the quickest man comes out on top. . . . A certain element was planning to exterminate them, but they happened to get there first."[31] For Locke, the Antlers War was a matter of self-defense, and Leo Bennett basically agreed with him. He characterized the national militia as "a drunken, irresponsible, and uncontrollable mob" banded together to intimidate political opponents.[32] In the face of murder as political expedience and mob violence as law, Bennett invoked martial law in the Choctaw Nation on April 11, 1893. The situation was ominous for the future of Choctaw sovereignty.

The National Party members accused of murder were not tried until June 1893. Of the sixteen defendants, nine were convicted and sentenced to be shot. But the secretary of the interior intervened with Chief Jones to commute the sentences.[33] The special agent who oversaw martial law concluded that the condemned "are not criminals in the ordinary acceptation of the term" and that Jones showed "a spirit of revenge" against the Locke faction. Prominent citizens of the Nation also sent the secretary letters protesting the executions.[34] He threatened to intervene if the Nation carried out its judgments. Jones to ask the Choctaw court to suspend their sentences and give the defendants a temporary "respite,"[35] but he declared that the federal government had "usurped entirely" the power of the Choctaw nation."[36]

In the end, eight of the nine convicted men were allowed to go free and emigrate to the Chickasaw Nation. Only Silan Lewis, a 54-year-old full-blood, was executed for the crime, and he died in true Choctaw fashion, living free until he appeared voluntarily at the time scheduled for his death in November 1894.[37] Lewis's execution seems anticlimactic after the high drama of political warfare, but the election dispute and its aftermath demonstrate the political stresses in the Nation that were undermining its political autonomy. Four men had been killed in the name of politics and the Choctaw court had convicted nine men of the crime. The federal government had imposed martial law in Indian Territory and pressured the Choctaw Nation to lift their sentences. In the end, Silan Lewis was executed for a murder he probably did commit, whether in self-defense or not, but the episodes of the election war and the Antlers War left the Choctaw Nation almost mortally wounded.

The Leased District claim was not dead, however. The payment in 1893 was based on the sale of the residue of lands after the allotment of the Cheyenne and Arapaho reservation, and Congress resolved that it would not in any way commit the government to further payment to the Choctaws and Chickasaws for any "alleged interest" in the remaining Leased District lands.[38] The Choctaws refused to give up. In 1895, Congress ratified the allotment of the Wichita reservation, and once again the Choctaw and Chickasaw nations claimed the proceeds of the sale of the surplus land. Congress referred the claim to the U.S. Court of Claims.[39] The Leased District claim thus followed the same path as the Net Proceeds Case. Congress was not willing to consider it on the intrinsic merit of the federal obligation to provide justice to the nations. Instead, the claim became a matter of legal interpretation under U.S. law.

The Leased District case was filed in the U.S. Court of Claims in 1895. The nations' attorneys pursued the legal interpretation of the term "cede," arguing that it did not "*per se* transfer, or divest, private property in lands embraced in the cession." The term had to be read in the context of the treaty and the circumstances of its signing.[40] The language of the 1855 and 1866 treaties made it clear that the Choctaws and Chickasaws believed that they had "leased" and then "ceded" the western lands beyond 98th parallel for settlement of "wild" Indians only, not for the settlement of whites.[41] The U.S. government disagreed, claiming that the Choctaws had given up all rights to the land and that it could do with it what it wanted.

The Leased District claim became a condition of the Atoka Agreement in 1897, which pointed out that the U.S. Senate should make a final settlement based on treaty rights, but Congress had modified the agreement without the consent of the Choctaw and Chickasaw delegates and left the matter with the court of claims.[42] The court of claims decided in favor of the Choctaws. It agreed that the intent of the cession was to provide permanent homes for various Indians and that when that purpose no longer held, the land would revert to the government as the trustee for the Choctaws and Chickasaws.[43] The federal government and the Wichita and Affiliated Tribes immediately appealed the case to the U.S. Supreme Court. The Supreme Court interpreted the term "cede" to mean exactly what it said, a complete cession of all rights to the land. It did not, however, reject the tribes' monetary claims. These, it said, were a matter of federal policy, not legal right. It was for Congress to decide upon the merits of the Choctaws' claims.[44] The Supreme Court handed the issue back to Congress.

The decision marked a growing divide between the U.S. courts and the U.S. Congress with regard to American Indian tribes in the late nineteenth century. After 1871, Congress rejected the idea of making treaties with Indian tribes. The federal government dealt with tribes through executive orders and special legislation, and by the late 1800s the Supreme Court largely deferred to the power of Congress to make decisions with regard to Indian tribes.[45] So the Choctaws took their case back to Congress. They argued that the Leased District had been treated as trust land for the settlement of Indians from the Treaty of 1855 onward. Why, in 1892, would Congress suddenly reject that understanding?[46] Congress did not respond to the Choctaw memorial, but the Leased District issue was still not dead. It would surface again as one of the persistent issues that gave the Choctaw Nation a continuing legal and political identity that transcended its ostensible dissolution by the U.S. Congress.

CHAPTER 12

THE ISSUE OF CITIZENSHIP

The Choctaw Nation of Oklahoma shall consist of all Choctaw Indians by blood whose names appear on the final rolls of the Choctaw Nation approved pursuant to Section 2 of the Act of April 26, 1906.[1]

The final rolls of the Choctaw Nation determine the origin of the approximately 165,000 members of the Choctaw Nation of Oklahoma in 2004. People seeking to establish some claim to Indian identity regularly consult the final rolls established by the Dawes Commission to the Cherokee, Choctaw, Chickasaw, Creek, and Seminole tribes in Indian Territory. The history of those rolls may, however, surprise the casual seeker of Choctaw identity.

In the late 1800s, the U.S. government was trying to make Indians disappear into American society, while the Choctaw Nation continued to demand its rights under treaties. The legal imposition of allotment on the Five Tribes marked the federal government's final step in converting communal land into individual interests in the name of civilization and assimilation. Per capita payments of the Net Proceeds and Leased District payments also distributed tribal resources on an individual basis. With the allotment process, Choctaw identity became explicitly equated with land and money, and the Choctaw national government fought for its very survival in the face of this fact. The crucial question in the struggle was Who was a Choctaw? The political question was Who determined who was a Choctaw? Congress gave that power to the Dawes Commission and the federal courts in 1896, and after that the question of identity became a matter of politics as the Choctaw Nation fought for control in the U.S. courts.

The heart of the matter lay in citizenship. Determining citizenship is a basic function of the exercise of sovereignty for any government, but with the allotment policy in Indian Territory, it became a highly contentious issue whose results are still felt in the Five Tribes in Oklahoma. The Choctaw Nation had consistently exercised its power to determine its citizenship. It had also acted fairly regularly to admit Choctaws who continued to emigrate from Mississippi.[2] It had regulated the citizenship of white men who married white women. It had mandated periodic censuses of the Nation's citizens.[3] It had established a commission to determine which Choctaw citizens were eligible for the Net Proceeds payment.[4] With the Leased District payment, control of citizenship had become a politically volatile issue. But throughout its history, the Nation had controlled access to citizenship.

The Dawes Commission changed all that. When it asked for the rolls of the Five Tribes, the tribes resisted. The balance of power hovered for a moment, but ultimately the U.S. Congress gave the Dawes Commission the authority to determine tribal citizenship in 1896.[5] That power was not absolute, however. Citizenship depended not on blood alone, as Henry Dawes noted in 1897, but on "the constitution, laws and usages" of the nations the commission had to respect in making its determinations."[6] The commission's decisions could also be appealed to the federal courts, both by rejected claimants and by the tribes.[7]

If citizenship was ultimately to be decided by the U.S. courts, the Choctaw General Council prepared for the battle by hiring lawyers, the firm of Stuart, Gordon, and Hailey, to represent its appeals of the Dawes Commission decisions.[8] The federal court judges who heard the appeals did not agree on their criteria for enrollment. One required only proof of Indian blood, while another required residency in the Choctaw Nation. Both relied on "masters in chancery" (special judges who assisted the court) to review the cases and make recommendations. The courts would also accept new evidence. Claimants thus had a new playing field.

Ultimately, the federal court decisions added 2,154 names to the Choctaw rolls during the period 1897 to 1900.[9] The "court citizens" were potential claimants to an allotment of tribal land, but were they indeed Choctaws? Green McCurtain declared rather melodramatically that "the fraud and perjury" in the claims brought before the Dawes Commission were "without parallel in the history of the world."[10] The Choctaws, with the other four Civilized Tribes, challenged the constitutionality of the whole enrollment process before the U.S. Supreme Court, but that court upheld Congress's right to legislate tribal affairs.[11]

Despite the court's decision, the Choctaw General Council and Chief McCurtain were determined to continue their legal attack on the court citizens. They called on a formidable array of lawyers to do so. One was J. R. McMurray, a lawyer from Texas who had recently settled in McAlester. His subsequent career in representing Choctaw claims shows how litigiousness became a way of life for the Choctaw government as it struggled to preserve its existence. The cases he conducted both as a member of the firm of Mansfield, McMurray, and Cornesh before its dissolution in 1907 and as an independent practitioner thereafter reveal the complex issues raised by the allotment process itself and by the communally held resources of the tribe.

Chief Green McCurtain hired McMurray's firm in 1899, along with several other firms, to defend the Nation against the court citizens. The secretary of the interior refused to approve the contract because he felt that the 9 percent contingency fee in it was too high. In order to get around the secretary, the Choctaw council passed a law increasing the governor's contingency fund for operating the government, and McCurtain's successor Gilbert Dukes argued that lawyers were a necessary expense for governmental operations.[12] Dukes finalized the contract in 1900, providing an annual fee of $5,000 for salary and expenses for services to the Nation and a percentage of the value of the Choctaw land the firm could protect from claimants. In plain terms, the more court citizens a lawyer could keep off the rolls, the greater was his pay.[13] The council considered the contract with McMurray binding despite the secretary's failure to approve it and renewed it in 1901, again without the secretary's approval.[14]

The legal strategy McMurray came up with was simple but effective. The Choctaws and Chickasaws owned the land in common, but almost all the court citizens had applied for enrollment in one tribe without notifying the other tribe, thus denying it a right to intervene to defend its interest in the property.[15] The court citizens could be challenged on this legal technicality. The ensuing legal battles over who was or was not a citizen of the Choctaw nation pitted the Nation against the U.S. government, and the Choctaws used the forums of the federal courts and Congress to attempt to control Choctaw identity.[16] Their only remaining political bargaining chip was the desire of Congress to settle the issue of allotment and the dissolution of the tribes once and for all, and the Choctaw Nation extracted what few concessions it could using this issue as leverage.

The issue of the court citizens was one complication of the enrollment process. The other was the status of the Mississippi Choctaws. The Dawes Commission was pushed into the legal morass of treaty language that had entangled Choctaw affairs since the Treaty of Dancing Rabbit Creek. It had been given control of the citizenship rolls so it could distribute land to tribal citizens, but final distribution depended upon final rolls, which could not be completed until all citizens were identified. The fourteenth article of the Treaty of Dancing Rabbit Creek was one of the major issues in the Net Proceeds Case. Not only did the article give land rights to Choctaws who chose to stay in Mississippi but it also guaranteed that they would retain "the privilege of a Choctaw citizen."[17] But what did that privilege entail? Did it include an allotment and per capita payments? Or had those who remained behind already received their share of the tribal estate in the land to which they were entitled (but which virtually none received) in Mississippi? The Dawes Commission had to resolve those issues.[18]

The Choctaws in Mississippi who could claim the privilege of citizenship were mainly full-bloods who lived as sharecroppers or in small communities centered on Christian mission churches. They spoke Choctaw almost exclusively, were largely uneducated, and lived in poverty. Their situation was anomalous in the South—they were neither black nor white. They both shunned white society because of their treatment at the hands of white land speculators and settlers in the postremoval period and were shunned by southern society because of their color.[19]

Mississippi Choctaws as individuals or in family groups had migrated back and forth to Indian Territory throughout the postremoval period. When the Net Proceeds judgment in 1889 made it possible for the Nation to settle their claims, the General Council encouraged them to move west.[20] When Congress refused the Nation's request for funds to pay for their emigration, the council appropriated some $1,800 of its own money for that purpose in 1891, but only 181 Choctaws out of the approximately 3,000 remaining in Mississippi moved to the Nation and were granted citizenship.[21]

If the prospect of citizenship was not particularly attractive to the Mississippi Choctaws, it was of keen interest to lawyers who saw the prospect of profit in the land that was associated with citizenship in the allotment process. Prominent Cherokee Robert L. Owen and his law partner Charles Winton sought to take advantage of the situation. Winton went to Mississippi to make contracts with Choctaws to represent their rights to citizenship before the Dawes Commission in return for a fee of 50 percent of the value of land they would receive as citizens. He ultimately signed approximately 1,000 contracts with potential Mississippi Choctaw claimants. By the time the Owen-Winton partnership got into full operation, however, the Dawes Commission's deadline to file applications for citizenship had passed.[22]

The first case Owen and Winton brought to the Dawes Commission was that of Jack Amos and his extended family, some 300 people. The commission ruled against Amos on the ground that he did not live in the Choctaw Nation, and his appeal to the federal court failed.[23] Thwarted in the courts, Winton took the case to Congress, arguing that Mississippi Choctaws did not have to reside in the Nation to establish their claims. Although it may have been true that Choctaws in Mississippi had remained there because of a deep and abiding attachment to their homeland, it was also the case that they were too poor to afford to move to Indian Territory. If they had to do so in order to claim land, they would be dispossessed once again, de facto if not de jure. Although Owen enlisted the political support of Congressman John Sharp Williams of Mississippi, in whose district most of the Choctaws lived, Congress simply referred the issue back to the Dawes Commission.[24]

The commission held to its former position that to be eligible for enrollment, Mississippi Choctaws would have to move to the Choctaw nation and live there for three years before they could be eligible for allotments. Taking a very American view of citizenship, the commissioners argued that privileges went along with responsibilities, which included participating in the governance of the Nation, something the Mississippi Choctaws could not do if they remained in their homes.[25] The Curtis Act left the matter hanging, stating merely that "nothing contained in this act shall be so construed as to militate against any rights or privileges which the Mississippi Choctaws may have under the laws of or the treaties with the United States."[26]

The Dawes Commission sent one of its members to enroll the Mississippi Choctaws in 1899 and prepared a list of 1,923 names, but it was rejected by the secretary of the interior.[27] The commission made a second attempt in 1900. Its sessions in Mississippi produced a total of 4,715 individuals as possible enrollees and a final list of 2,335 actually eligible for enrollment.[28] But what to do about their claims? Henry Dawes agonized over the issue. How could the commission make a final roll until the Mississippi Choctaw claims had been settled?[29] Meanwhile, Charles Winton petitioned Congress again to allow the Mississippi Choctaws to received land in Indian Territory without moving there, but Congress instead passed a law making residence mandatory. However, the law gave Mississippi Choctaws the right to move to the territory any time up to the closing of the rolls.[30]

This congressional act opened the "Mississippi loophole."[31] It cut off applications from individuals not on a tribal roll, but it allowed Mississippi Choctaws to enroll until the rolls closed.[32] That act opened the possibility that anyone who had been denied by the Dawes Commission and the federal courts could now appeal as a Mississippi Choctaw. Therein lay the legal conundrum. The rolls could not close until the claims of the Mississippi Choctaws could be finally determined, but since claims could be made until the rolls closed, there could be no final determination. As long as it was possible for new claimants to come forth, the final distribution of tribal property could not be fairly assured. And in the meantime, the flood of ostensible Mississippi Choctaw claimants continued.

From July 1 to November 30, 1900, the Dawes Commission accepted applications at its headquarters in Muskogee.[33] "Day after day and week after week crowds of people showing absolutely no trace of Indian blood, whites and negroes of all ages and conditions, were making applications under a vague idea of their rights."[34]

Lawyers advertised in papers throughout the Southeast that they would represent Choctaw claimants for a nominal fee. Faced with the prospect of continuing claims, Congress finally set the application deadline for Mississippi Choctaws at March 25, 1903. At that point, an astounding 24,634 people had applied for enrollment, and Dawes noted that in almost every case there was a contract with a lawyer to represent the claimant.[35] Following the legal principle that claimants had to have tried to establish claims under the fourteenth article, the commissioners identified 2,534 individuals as eligible for allotments, although ultimately only 1,643 were enrolled.[36]

The prospect of the legal challenge to the court citizens and the Mississippi loophole promised to drag the process on indefinitely. The Dawes Commission ultimately had to deal with over 75,000 applications for membership among the Five Tribes of Indian Territory, almost 26,000 of them from Choctaw and Chickasaw claimants alone. At this point, it was becoming obvious that the Atoka Agreement was an unworkable document. If all Choctaw land was to be distributed evenly, all Choctaws had to be identified and placed on the rolls, and allotment could not be completed until the rolls closed. Choctaws had the unfortunate habit of dying and being born while the enrollment process was going on, which complicated the finalizing of the rolls. It appeared indeed that it might never be possible to close the rolls as long as the equitable distribution of the Nation's resources was the criterion the Dawes Commission had to meet.

The Choctaws attempted to solve the problem by asking Congress to set a final date for the closing of the rolls. As long as enrollment offered lawyers the prospect of financial reward, they would oppose final closure. In December 1899, representatives of the Choctaw and Chickasaw nations negotiated an agreement with the Dawes Commission to close the rolls as of October 31 of that year, but Congress failed to ratify that agreement.[37] It was not until 1902 that the nations were finally able to reach a satisfactory modification of the Atoka Agreement, known as the Supplementary Agreement.[38] It set a limit of 320 acres for each allotment, preserving the 160-acre homestead. The U.S. government would sell the excess land beyond the homestead at public auction and the U.S. government would distribute the proceeds on a per capita basis to tribal members. The Supplementary Agreement thus shifted responsibility for disposing of surplus land from individual tribal members to the government, although individuals could sell the surplus themselves if they wished. The coal and asphalt deposits were to be sold by the government within two years from the ratification of the agreement and the proceeds divided on a per capita basis.

In the critical matter of citizenship, the federal government agreed to create the Choctaw and Chickasaw citizenship court, which would have until December 31, 1903, to rehear the cases decided by the U.S. courts in 1896 as well as applications from newly intermarried white citizens and applications for newborn children for a period of 90 days from the ratification of the agreement. All cases before the citizenship court were to be considered de novo, which meant that new evidence could be submitted. Its judgments were to be final.

The agreement also closed the Mississippi loophole. Charles Winton had lobbied hard in Congress to preserve his interests in the Mississippi Choctaw claims, and he largely shaped the resolution of that issue.[39] Mississippi Choctaws had six months from the ratification of the agreement to apply to the Dawes Commission for enrollment and they had to establish residence in the Choctaw Nation within six months thereafter. Because the circumstances of their ancestors' claims to land under the fourteenth article of the Treaty of Dancing Rabbit Creek were now more than seventy years old and the documentary evidence was scant, the agreement essentially created a set of legal conditions and assumptions to govern their identification. Full-bloods were assumed to be descended from Choctaws who had attempted to lay claims under the fourteenth article and were thus eligible for enrollment, and full or mixed-bloods who had actually acquired a title under the fourteenth article were also eligible. If others could prove that they or their ancestors had rights to claims under the fourteenth article, they could submit such evidence.[40] Once more, the law rather than custom served to define Choctaw identity.[41]

With the 1902 agreement, the stage was set for the final legal determination of Choctaw citizenship and the final dissolution of its land base.

The firm of Mansfield, McMurray, and Cornesh represented the Choctaw Nation before the citizenship court. The men stood to make a considerable amount of money since each potential claim was valued at $4,800 and the contract gave them a 9.5 percent contingency fee on the total value of the claims they could discredit.[42] They dug deep and uncovered much in the way of contradictory and fraudulent evidence. In one instance, the maker of an affidavit swore that he knew the applicant's grandparents in Indian Territory, while the applicant himself swore that his grandparents had died in Mississippi and never removed to Indian Territory.[43] By December 10, 1904, the citizenship court had heard 259 appeals involving 3,520 individuals, had admitted only 161 claimants, and had denied 2,792 others.[44]

The court did allow certain legal precedents established by the federal courts to stand in the matter of intermarried white citizens. Mary Martin, whose mother was an intermarried Chickasaw and her father an intermarried Choctaw, was enrolled. It was thus possible for an individual with no Choctaw blood to be born into tribal citizenship.[45]

One of the final acts the Choctaw and Chickasaw citizenship court did was to settle the final fee of Mansfield, McMurray, and Cornesh. Green McCurtain had estimated that their services would save the Nation some $12,222,000, a relatively accurate estimate when all was said and done.[46] The court granted them $750,000. Although the sum was less than the 9.5 percent contingency fee, it was a very significant amount of money, and it aroused considerable controversy both within the Nation and in the halls of Congress.[47]

During this period of ongoing negotiations about the final enrollment and the vociferous protests of the Choctaws and Chickasaws over the court citizens, J. F. McMurray, according to his own testimony, was virtually running the Choctaw government on behalf of the firm of Mansfield, McMurray, and Cornesh. He later declared that he was "willing to take the responsibility of half the Choctaw and Chickasaws peoples' doings during these years . . . . There was hardly a bill affecting their general affairs that was passed that we did not O.K. And there never was a bill suggested by us that was not passed."[48]

Lawyers and litigation colored the very fabric of Choctaw government in this critical period. McMurray took credit for crafting the 1902 Supplementary Agreement that resolved the allotment logjam and getting it passed in Congress. By setting a fixed number of acres for allotments, it provided the basis for an equitable distribution of Choctaw land. By establishing the citizenship court, it allowed McMurray to deny enrollment to almost 2,800 claimants, a number of whom had already taken allotments, established homes, and even buried their dead in Indian Territory.[49] By setting a final deadline for the enrollment of Mississippi Choctaws, it allowed the closure of their claims, and in 1903, Congress appropriated $20,000 to move them to Indian Territory. A special train from Meridian carried 290 Choctaws to the territory to take up their new homes and responsibilities as citizens of the Choctaw Nation. Winton, with other contracts in his pocket, moved about 200 more at his own expense.[50]

The final issue that seemed to be resolved in the Supplementary Agreement was the disposition of the coal and asphalt deposits. The 1897 Atoka Agreement had reserved them as communal resources that would support the Nation's schools. In 1899, however, the secretary of the interior decided to take control of the Nation's schools and to appoint his own superintendent. The issue of school support suddenly became moot.[51]

The Supplementary Agreement precipitated a political crisis in the Choctaw Nation. A decade after the conflict in 1892, the election of 1902 became a referendum on the issue of allotment embodied in the new agreement. It pitted Gilbert Dukes and Thomas Hunter as anti-allotment candidates against Green McCurtain, who had made allotment his major political issue.[52] Dukes had been elected as Green McCurtain's hand-picked successor as the candidate of the Tuskahoma Party in the election of 1900.[53] But he split with McCurtain over the provisions in the Supplementary Agreement that withheld the coal and asphalt deposits from allotment and mandated their sale at

Political Districts of Indian Territory, 1907. (Adapted from Goins and Goble, *Historical Atlas of Oklahoma*, 4th ed.)

public auction. Dukes argued that an auction would favor existing leaseholders and that the coal and asphalt should be sold at a preset price in order to benefit the Nation.[54]

The political split threatened to derail the whole Supplementary Agreement. McCurtain would not support Dukes for a second term as chief and ran as the Tuskahoma Party candidate himself. Dukes's election had also been challenged by a group of about 200 full-bloods in Gaines County who met in January 1901 and passed a resolution deposing Dukes and electing Daniel Bell as chief. The threat of an uprising by a full-blood faction in the Nation revealed political strains.[55]

McCurtain made the Supplementary Agreement the key issue in his campaign. He argued that it would actually give citizens more land (320 acres) than they would get under the Atoka Agreement (312 acres). His political opponents argued that an equitable distribution under the Atoka Agreement would amount to 512 acres, but that figure did not deduct lands reserved for townsites, coal and asphalt, and freedmen.[56] McCurtain felt that by setting a concrete figure on the amount of land to be allotted to each individual, the Supplementary Agreement would solve the problem of equitable distribution of the tribal estate. The provision for the sale of the coal and asphalt would solve the problems of the title to the lands overlaying those resources. All the surface land as well as the proceeds of the underlying resources could be distributed, and McCurtain promised that the agreement would guarantee "a perfect title to your allotment.[57]

McCurtain seemed to have won the election in August 1902, and the Supplementary Agreement was approved by a vote of 2,140 to 704 in a special election on September 25 of that year.[58] McCurtain's campaign in favor of the agreement had succeeded, as, apparently, had his campaign for election to the office of chief. But as in the election of 1892, there were charges of fraudulent voting and ballot-tampering in the 1902 election. The major site of resistance to McCurtain's election was the Apukshunnubbee District, and Dukes challenged the poll books there. McCurtain and his supporters threatened to ignore the Apukshunnubbee vote altogether in the ballot count.

When the General Council convened to confirm the election on October 6, chaos ensued.[59] McCurtain supporters organized a senate, while Hunter supporters organized a house. When U.S. agent Blair Shoenfelt and U.S. marshal Benjamin F. Hackett declared the council meeting suspended, McCurtain's men occupied the capitol building, and Dukes sent the Nation's lighthorsemen to drive them out. The McCurtain men then proceeded to hold sessions on the lawn and in the neighboring Gilbert Thompson hotel, and on two successive days, a throng of McCurtain supporters rushed the capitol in an attempt to gain entrance. Shoenfelt was helpless in the situation. Dukes and Marshall Hackett refused to force the factions to put down their weapons. Confronted with what appeared to be a conspiracy by Dukes and Hackett to maintain control of the capitol, Shoenfelt sent a request for federal troops to handle the situation. A contingent arrived to disarm the lighthorsemen and the electoral process proceeded. The Choctaw Supreme Court judges counted the ballots and declared that McCurtain had been elected by 689 votes.

The election was far from final. Dukes refused to accept the council's decision. He issued a proclamation that McCurtain had not been legally elected and that he (Dukes) would continue as chief until a legal successor was chosen.[60] The situation became even more tense when, in the interval between the attack on the capitol and the arrival of federal troops, Thomas Hunter, who had won in one precinct, claimed to have taken the oath as principal chief of the Choctaw Nation and demanded that Shoenfelt recognize him as chief.[61]

For a brief moment, the Choctaw Nation had three ostensible chiefs, Dukes, McCurtain, and Hunter; a partial legislature meeting on the lawn; and a capitol under virtual martial law. Only Shoenfelt's ability to maintain his composure and the arrival of federal troops defused the potential for bloodshed. The episode was a final convulsion of the political process in the Nation, which had been so weakened by the encroachment of white settlers, entrepreneurs, federal officials, and the ideals of white reformers that it could no longer sustain itself. Shoenfelt characterized Indian politicians as "partisans of the worst stripe," and indeed partisan politics and political self-interest had become the dominant factors in Choctaw government.

Green McCurtain was finally confirmed as chief, and Shoenfelt concluded that Choctaw citizens felt that his election "was to the best interests of the Choctaw people, as he is progressive and liberal in his ideas and is in harmony with the views of the Department in settling up the affairs of the Indians in the Indian Territory in accordance with recent Congressional acts."[62] It behooved the Nation only to await its final demise.

In the face of pressure for statehood and the slow pace of allotment in the Choctaw and Chickasaw nations, Congress finally acted to close the rolls and bring the affairs of the Five Tribes to a close. An act passed on April 26, 1906 set the final deadline for applications for citizenship as December 1, 1905, except for those of minor children living on March 4, 1906 whose parents were enrolled, and set the final date for closing of the rolls as March 4, 1907. It also provided, among numerous other details, that Charles Winton's estate could sue the Mississippi Choctaws for services rendered in their removal.[63] Although Winton had not lived to see the profits of his contracting and legislative efforts, he continued to exert a vicarious influence on Choctaw affairs in the courts.

In 1901, Chief Gilbert Dukes declared that the citizenship court's actions involved "not only vast property interests, but the purity and integrity of our citizenship," and that "every sentiment of patriotism and national pride is aroused to a continued, united and mighty effort to bring the Government of the United States to a realization of the magnitude of the wrong that threatens us, and the cruel injustice of it all."[64]

Given the amount of fraud, charges of corruption and bribery, and imposition of legality on the whole concept of Choctaw citizenship, it is hard to say that the final rolls of the Dawes Commission represented in any way the "purity and integrity" of Choctaw citizenship. They had rather subjected the tribe to an extraordinary legal process that subverted its basic sovereign right to determine its own membership. The disputed election of 1902 was symptomatic of the divisions the allotment process had created within the Nation. The Choctaw council seemed unable to govern the Nation effectively, and the federal government saw the situation as reason to dissolve it.

CHAPTER 13

A FAMILY HISTORY

While political factionalism and the allotment of Choctaw land proceeded, daily life went on for citizens within the Nation. The history
of one Choctaw family in this crucial period demonstrates the
effects of political and economic change on ordinary people in an
extraordinary period. Gilbert Webster Thompson and his family are
typical of a certain class in Choctaw society in the late nineteenth
and early twentieth centuries, a relatively prosperous although certainly not wealthy family and one interested in the politics of the
Nation. Thompson was a close friend, business partner, and political associate of Gilbert Dukes, principal chief from 1900 to 1902. In
1937 he was interviewed in Tuskahoma (the old capital of the
Choctaw Nation) as part of a Works Progress Administration project for the Oklahoma Historical Society.[1] (Collecting the life histo-
ries of the Indian and white settlers in the state became a source of
gainful employment in Oklahoma in the wake of the Great Depression of the 1930s.) Although certainly civilized and acculturated by
the standards of American society, Thompson declared at the end of
his interview with the field worker, "I am a Choctaw Indian; all of
my folks were Choctaws and I was reared among them and have
lived with them all my life and I guess I will live among them until
I die."[2] He thus affirmed an enduring sense of Choctaw identity in
the face of cultural, historical, and political change. Gilbert Webster
Thompson was my great-grandfather, and his daughter Susie was
my grandmother. Like him, she grew up speaking the Choctaw lan-

guage, but as her husband was white, she did not pass the language on to her son, my father. But she also considered herself Choctaw and passed that sense of heritage and history on to her son and daughter.

Thompson was born on September 15, 1848, near the village of Whitesboro on the Kiamichi River about fifteen miles north of the present town of Talihina. The area was thinly populated with Choctaws and richly populated with wild game—deer, wild turkeys, and bears—and the Kiamichi had abundant fish, which young Gilbert caught with a bow and arrows. There were no white people at all. The Thompson family farm was small like those of most other Choctaws. "They had farms just big enough to raise corn for their bread." His mother ground the corn in a mortar made of a section of log about three feet high with a hole burned in one end. Young Gilbert spent hours sitting on the floor seeding cotton so his mother could spin it into yarn for socks and gloves.

His parents, Garrett and Belinda Thompson, were born in Mississippi and made the trek to the Indian Territory with the Choctaw Nation in the early 1830s. Young Gilbert heard from his father about the rigors of the march. "He said that lots of the Choctaws died on the road by freezing and lots died by sickness. They did not have clothes to keep them warm, and they did not have bedding to keep them warm at night when they camped out." Garrett Thompson, although he moved with the Choctaws, might have been Creek. A note on the Dawes rolls indicates that he was listed on the Creek roll, and family history reports that he had been a resident of the old Sasakwa Town, a Creek settlement. His Choctaw citizenship is verified by his listing on the census roll in Wade County in the Apukshunnubbee District of the Choctaw Nation in 1861 (1867?).[3] These stories of his origins indicate the fluid nature of national identity in the Indian Territory in the early nineteenth century.

Garrett Thompson served in the Confederate Army but Gilbert was too young, so he stayed behind to tend the family farm.[4] After the war, in 1868, Gilbert Thompson married Isabel Anderson, daughter of Dixon Anderson, a prominent member of the Choctaw Nation. The Anderson family evidently had some French heritage. Of the seven children born to the couple, three died in infancy. Those who lived to adulthood were Josephine, born in 1873; Ellis, born in 1876; Harris, born in 1878; and Susie Ellen, born in 1886.[5]

Gilbert Webster Thompson and his family lived through a time of crucial changes in the Choctaw Nation. He served in the tribal courts during the period when they were coming under attack for corruption and incompetence but when they also represented the maturation of the government of the Choctaw Nation. His children Ellis and Susie benefited from the Nation's commitment to education. His daughters Josephine and Susie married non-Indian men. He was a minor entrepreneur, holding part interest in the development of a toll road on Sugar Loaf Mountain.[6] In return for the privilege of collecting 50 cents for the passage of a four-horse or four-ox wagon, 25 cents for a two-horse wagon, 10 cents for a one-horse wagon, 10 cents for a man on horseback, and one cent for each head of stock, Thompson and his partners were required to grade the road, remove rocks, and maintain it in good condition. Thompson also briefly had an interest in a coal mine in Skullyville County in 1891.[7] He thus participated actively in the benefits that post–Civil War economic development brought to the Choctaw Nation. He, his wife, and his children received allotments when the Choctaw Nation's lands were distributed, and they continued to live within the historical boundaries of the Nation through the early twentieth century.

Thompson was educated in Arkansas, although he could not remember where the school was. He was bilingual and literate in both Choctaw and English.[8] In 1881, at the age of 33, he was elected the judge of Skullyville County, in the very northeastern corner of the Mushulatubbee District, near its border with the Cherokee Nation. He served in that capacity until 1884.[9] Sometime after that, he moved his family to Tuskahoma in Wade County in the Apukshunnubbee District. There, he was appointed captain of a militia troop called out by Wilson Jones to quell the faction headed by Victor Locke during the bitter political battle over the election of 1892. Thompson, with about fifty men, engaged in a shootout with the men barricaded in Locke's house during the Antlers War. As he described the aftermath, "The house was shot all to pieces. I do not think that there was any place in that house that didn't have a hole through it and the men we wanted were not there." After intervention by U.S. Indian agent Leo Bennett and a company of federal troops, Jones finally told Thompson to disband his men. "This," Jones said, "is our own affair but the United States Government has stepped in and sent those soldiers down here to stop us and I guess it would be nothing but right to give in and let the thing go and forget about it."[10]

In addition to his service in the militia, Thompson was also in charge of maintaining the capitol building at Tuskahoma.[11] Perhaps because of his civic-mindedness or his service with the militia (or both), he was elected judge of Wade County in 1894, a post that by his account he held for eight years, although his name appears in the county records only from 1894 to 1896.

Thompson's children benefited from the Choctaw Nation's commitment to education. His son Ellis was among the select group of twenty young men and women that the General Council sent each year to be educated "in the states." In 1895, Ellis was a student at Drury College in Springfield, Missouri. Thompson's daughter Susie was probably a student at one of the Nation's day schools, and she also attended Tuskahoma Female Academy, one of two new boarding schools built in the Choctaw Nation in 1892.[12] His daughter Josephine, like the daughters of many leading Choctaw citizens of the time, married a white man, William Isherwood, on November 10, 1893. Isherwood was born in Virginia[13] and came to Indian Territory to escape the consequences of some crime he had committed in the east. In that regard his situation was similar to that of other whites who realized that it was difficult for the long arm of the law to stretch into Indian Territory. He built up a successful dry goods business in Talihina, and he eventually served as the recording secretary of the House of Representatives in the Choctaw government.[14] Susie Ellen also married a white man, Hardin Milam Kidwell, who established himself as a cattleman on her allotment lands in the Chickasaw Nation.

The Apukshunnubbee District where Thompson and his family lived was a fairly immoral place in the eyes of the Choctaw and Chickasaw Baptist Association, which considered it a fertile field for missionary activity. For undetermined reasons, the association could not succeed in establishing a church in "that same old destitute region Apack sho nubbie District."[15] One church functioned fitfully beginning in 1893, but by 1895 the situation had not improved. "The

Chickasaw Nation, the almost dead and dying condition of our Choctaw churches, the great Apuckshonubbee District, all furnish many fields among the Indians."[16] For the Baptists, at least, Christianity had not had the effect missionaries had hoped for.

Although the Atoka Agreement extended U.S. criminal and civil jurisdiction over all crimes involving Indians and non-Indians, the Nation still retained jurisdiction over its citizens in its own courts. In 1900, Thompson was appointed the judge of the Apukshunnubbee (second) judicial district. Whether his presence on the bench made the district a more moral place is questionable, but the cases that he tried from December 1901 to December 1902 give some idea of the crimes most often committed in the county. These include seven cases of petit larceny, six cases of introducing liquor into the Nation, five cases of adultery, two cases of violating the permit law, and one case each of grand larceny, polygamy, and libel and slander.[17] Stealing cattle, fornicating, and bootlegging appear to be the primary pastimes of the criminal class of the Apukshunnubbee District. To help him in his work, Thompson saw that his son Ellis was appointed as a deputy sheriff in Wade County in 1901. The young man moved into the position of county clerk and treasurer the following year, thus fulfilling an important function for those educated "in the states"—service to the Nation.[18]

Thompson also invested in the coal-mining industry in partnership with Gilbert W. Dukes, and his politics, like those of Dukes, were associated with the Progressive Party. It is unclear what role he may have played in the hotly disputed (and last) popular election for the chieftainship in 1902, but a crucial meeting between the McCurtain and Hunter factions took place at the Gilbert Thompson Hotel, a boarding house his wife Isabelle Thompson ran to serve the members of the Choctaw General Council when the legislature was in session.[19] He shared in the per capita distribution of the Leased District claim, $103 in 1893, the instance for the political warfare of that time.[20]

When allotment finally became a fact in the Choctaw Nation, the Thompson family was enrolled by the Dawes Commission on January 16, 1903, and received its allotments in October and November of 1905. William Isherwood, his wife Josephine, and their three children, Lillie, Pearl and Frank, received theirs in February 1906. As was often the case, the surplus lands were allotted at a distance from the homestead. Thompson's daughter Susie had land in the Chickasaw Nation, an area that had always been cattle country.[21] Susie married Hardin Milam Kidwell, a white man, in 1910. He was a cattleman who came to his profession through family connections. His father, Hardin McClain Kidwell, was a land broker, cattle buyer, and speculator and was a manager of the Evans-Snider-Buel Livestock Commission in Fort Worth, Texas.[22] The elder Kidwell was evidently an admired and respected man. His obituary in the *Ringling Eagle* in August of 1921 proclaimed "A mighty oak has fallen. A noted cattleman has passed away." His son, my paternal grandfather, was not particularly successful in business. He staked his fortunes on what was the most important economic activity in the Choctaw and Chickasaw nations, the cattle trade.

Although Gilbert Webster Thompson lived in Tuskahoma until his death, Susie Thompson Kidwell and her husband settled near the new community of Ringling in the old Chickasaw Nation. The town was named after John North Ringling, the circus entrepreneur, who was interested in developing "Grahamite," a form of asphalt, and investing in a railroad route between Ardmore and Dallas. When oil was discovered near Healdton, Ringling's attention was diverted from asphalt, the railroad stopped, and the town of Ringling was born.[23]

On March 28, 1918, Susie Kidwell gave birth to her son Hardin Milton in the new town just three months after her mother, Isabelle, had died. Although Hardin Milam sometimes made money in the cattle business, he as often lost it. He too speculated in land, selling parts of his wife's allotment and buying other acreage for grazing land. When he could not make a go of the cattle business, his father set him and his sister up in a mercantile business. The business did not succeed because they didn't collect the money owed to them fast enough to enable them to renew the inventory. There was probably truth to my father's assertion that the only reason his father married my grandmother was for her land, because the couple separated when my father was in his early teens. My grandmother moved to the northeastern part of the state to be near her daughter Amelia and her family, who lived in Ochelata, and she supported herself and her son by running a restaurant in the nearby town of Ramona.

Her brothers were dead by the early 1930s. Ellis Thompson, evidently developing a weakness for the alcohol whose importation into the Nation was such a problem, died on August 7, 1930. Harris Thompson had met an untimely and rather mysterious death on July 8, 1908, when he was ambushed and shot to death. It may have been over a woman, since he and an infant child are buried in a small cemetery near Cornish, Oklahoma, but perhaps not. Statehood had obviously not made Choctaw country a completely safe place to live.

Gilbert Webster Thompson and his son Ellis were prominent members of the Republican Party in the Choctaw Nation, and he served in the Nation's court system. He was also a prominent Mason, a status he shared with many of the leading men of the Nation.[24] The Masonic order drew white and Indian leaders together, both socially and politically, creating that artificial fraternity that operated in some ways as earlier familial and kinship ties had done to promote political leadership in the old Choctaw Nation.[25]

The marriages of his daughters Josephine and Susie to non-Indian men and their enterprises of their husbands indicate the changes that had been taking place in the Choctaw Nation since the 1870s. Non-Indian men married Indian women, perhaps for love but also perhaps for the economic benefits they could gain from the exploitation of Indian land and the market economy in the Nation. Gilbert Thompson received his share of the Nation's resources in the form of per capita distributions beginning in about 1910 or 1912. The largest sum he remembered was about $300. But he also recalled in 1937 that "it has been a long time since we have had any more payments. The timber land was all sold and the surface land was sold but the coal had not been sold yet but it seems that we will not be able to sell the coal now at any price."[26] Indeed, when he died on November 30, 1941, the Choctaw coal had still not been sold. He did not live to receive the per capita payment of the proceeds of the sale of that last Choctaw resource. Like so many other Choctaws, he never shared in the final distribution of the tribal estate that the federal government had forced upon the Nation. But what was important to him to the end of his life was the fact that "I am a Choctaw Indian."

CHAPTER 14

OKLAHOMA!

The new state of Oklahoma was admitted to the Union on November 16, 1907. During the inaugural ceremony for the first governor, Charles N. Haskell, a symbolic marriage was performed on the steps of the new state capitol for Miss Indian Territory and Mr. Oklahoma Territory. The bride, a tastefully dressed young Cherokee woman, and the groom, who wore a business suit, were united in wedlock by a minister wielding the power of Congress. The part of the bride was taken by Anna Trainor Bennett, a renowned territory beauty who was the wife of the publisher of the *Muskogee Phoenix* and former Indian agent Leo Bennett, and the groom was C. C. Jones, representative from Oklahoma County. The bride was "given" in marriage by William A. Durant, sergeant at arms during the constitutional convention of 1906, who would later serve as the appointed chief of the Choctaw Nation.[1]

Metaphorically, the marriage was a shotgun wedding. Miss Indian Territory had tried to say no. She was joined to the overweening Oklahoma Territory not of her own free will but by the partisan politics of the Republican Party. The differences between the bride and groom seemed to pose major difficulties for the marriage, and the debate over their union was a vigorous one, both at the local level and in the halls of Congress. The groom came from farming people. Ironically, it was Oklahoma Territory, not Indian Territory, that had become the nation of small yeoman farmers Henry Dawes had envisioned in his allotment act. The bride's folks were primarily landlords and commercial entrepreneurs—Indians who mostly leased their newly allotted land to white tenants for farming or white ranchers for cattle-grazing. The reserved coal, asphalt, oil, and timber lands set aside by the Atoka and Supplementary agreements created islands of commercial development in a sea of cows, cotton, and corn.[2]

The groom's antecedents were largely northerners. Many came from Kansas and Nebraska, riding the railroads that linked Oklahoma Territory with the north, although there were some southerners from Arkansas and Texas.[3] The bride was a true southern belle, not only in her Indian ancestry but in the predominance of Texans and Arkansans in her background. The southern influence was particularly strong in the Choctaw Nation because of its proximity to those two states.

The difference in their regional backgrounds was most obvious in the politics of the couple. The groom was a Republican and the bride was a Democrat—certainly a major impediment to marital bliss and one that caused the groom particularly some qualms about the marriage.[4] Would the bride be acceptable to this political family? The bride's experience with Republicans, going back to the Civil War, had been unfortunate. In the Choctaw Nation, Republican administrations had held up the payment of the Net Proceeds funds, and it was only under Grover Cleveland's Democratic administration that the Nation had finally received them.

Finally, the groom drank, while the bride was a teetotaler. In fact, the groom was notorious for his free use of alcoholic beverages. The bride not only did not imbibe but objected violently to those who did and to those who served alcoholic beverages to the public. This objection was one of her oldest and most deeply held beliefs and one in which she was supported by the Women's Christian Temperance Union, the Indian Rights Association, and the Congress of the United States.[5] Once the couple was married, the bride would have no control whatsoever over the serving of strong drink to her citizens.

The bride would, however, bring to the marriage a significant dowry, and her suitor realized its economic importance. Her total resources were estimated at "$400,000,000 in taxable property . . . railroad properties . . . worth $50,000,000 . . . farm products not less than $175,000,000." She had "20,000,000 acres of land, worth, on an average, $10 per acre."[6] A significant portion of her wealth was in the coal, asphalt, and timber lands of the Choctaw Nation. An estimate in 1909 put the value of the coal at over $12,000,000 and the timber at $1,800,000.[7]

The bride and groom were both very small in comparison with surrounding states—Oklahoma Territory had only 38,830 square miles and Indian Territory 31,000 square miles. Together, however, they would have a land area close to the average of the states west of the Mississippi that had been admitted to the Union.[8] According to Congressman Thomas Doyle,

> The splendid natural resources of Indian Territory need the aid of Oklahoma in their development. What Oklahoma lacks in order to become an industrially and productively powerful and prosperous State is entirely made up and supplied by the Indian Territory. By combining the two we get in wealth and resources a perfect State—Agriculture, stock raising, lumbering and mining—all that is needed for the development of an ideal commonwealth.[9]

The Bride, though relatively wealthy, was also largely nontaxable. The Curtis Act and the Supplementary Agreement had both preserved the restrictions on the allotted lands of the Five Tribes. The general rule was that Indian title on homesteads was restricted for a period of twenty-one years from the date of the patent, while the rest of the land was alienable in set proportions after one, two, and five years. The two acts also provided that the land would not be subject to taxes while still in the possession of the original owner. As long as almost the entire eastern half of the new state was not contributing to the tax base, citizens in the western half had to bear the burden of paying for the government, of which Indians were reaping the benefit.[10]

Green McCurtain, chief of the Choctaw Nation, was one of the primary leaders of the opposition to the union of Indian Territory and Oklahoma Territory (single statehood). Having failed to preserve the Choctaw national government in negotiations with the Dawes Commission, he made the preservation of Indian Territory as a separate state his next political agenda. The basis for his argument was treaty rights. The Treaty of Dancing Rabbit Creek had guaranteed that the Choctaw Nation would never be subsumed into any territory or state of the United States, but Congress was now threatening to take that very action.

McCurtain tried to rally the Five Tribes by calling for an intertribal meeting at Eufaula in 1902, but the Chickasaws and Seminoles did not attend, although Palmer Mosely, chief of the Chickasaws, sent McCurtain a letter supporting the sentiment against single statehood. McCurtain was convinced, however, that the Chickasaws did not support his position.[11] He called a second meeting at Eufaula on May 21, 1903,[12] where a resolution was passed calling for a separate state whose constitution would prohibit alcohol. The delegates proposed to put the question of separate statehood to a vote of tribal citizens. McCurtain invited the support of white residents of the Indian Territory for the idea, which is rather ironic because the overwhelming preponderance of white residents in the territory was one of the leading arguments for the extension of U.S. jurisdiction and the dissolution of tribal governments. It had proved impossible for Indian leaders to maintain control in their own territories, but McCurtain actively promoted the idea of control of a new state by a unified Indian government.[13]

Although the Okmulgee Constitution of 1870 had failed, the Kinta Separate Statehood Club waxed eloquent in favor of a single government: "The Indian people belonging to the five tribes which had regular systems of government before the foot of the pale-face had trod the fair soil of this continent desire not that their ancient governments shall come to an abrupt end, but that they shall continue, united into one fair commonwealth."[14] The separate statehood movement was a final attempt to protect the sovereignty of Indian people. Although the individual tribal governments would pass out of existence, an Indian state would give assurance that Indian people collectively would still exercise self-rule as a state.[15]

If the Indian Territory was to have any hope of separate statehood, it had to have some form of organized government to propose. As it was, Oklahoma Territory had its Organic Act of 1890, which had created it as a territory of the United States, but Indian Territory, with the pending dissolution of the tribal governments, was subject to the laws of Arkansas and the whims of Congress. McCurtain and W. C. Rogers, chief of the Cherokee Nation, called a meeting of tribal delegates in Muskogee on August 21, 1905, to establish a government.[16] The Chickasaws were not enthusiastic. Despite Mosely's earlier letter of support, he did not join in the call for the convention, nor did he put his name on the supplement to the call that spelled out the process of selecting delegates.[17]

A constitution for Indian Territory was hammered out in the Hinton Theater in Muskogee during the heat of the summer of 1905. The new Sequoyah Constitution was formulated under the watchful eye of numbers of ladies of Muskogee, who observed the proceedings from the gallery of the building. After a month of debate and deliberation, the constitution was ratified by thirty-five delegates on September 8, 1905. It was put to a vote of tribal citizens on November 7, and on November 18 the election board certified its passage by a vote of 56,279 to 9,072.[18]

The Sequoyah Constitution reflected the values that had shaped the separate governments of the Five Tribes, values that had informed the Choctaw Constitution of 1860. It began with a Bill of Rights, of which section one declared that "all political power is vested in and derived from the people; is founded upon their will, and is instituted for the good of the whole."[19] The Sequoyah Constitution established a bicameral legislature and provided checks and balances among the legislative, executive, and judiciary branches of the government. The document was strongly populist in its leanings, showing a basic distrust of centralized authority and putting its trust in the people.[20] It was an extremely long and detailed document, even defining the boundaries of the counties that would constitute the state of Sequoyah. It demonstrated how fully the Five Tribes had assimilated the structures of American government in an attempt to preserve their own autonomy.

The Sequoyah Constitution, like the Okmulgee Constitution before it, was doomed to fail as a governing document for the Indian Territory. Like the Okmulgee Constitution, it did not receive unanimous tribal support. Although representatives from the Chickasaw and Creek nations ratified the document when it was submitted to the popular vote, support in the Chickasaw Nation was lukewarm at best, and the Creek legislature had specifically voted against any form of statehood before finally agreeing to participate in the constitutional process.[21] Even if the Sequoyah Constitution had had full tribal support, it would never have been approved because President Theodore Roosevelt had already decided that Oklahoma Territory and Indian Territory should be joined into a single new state.

The Sequoyah Constitution was submitted to Congress, where it shared the session with five bills proposing single statehood for Oklahoma and Indian Territory and one that proposed the merger of the Choctaw and Chickasaw districts with the state of Arkansas, a plan that Green McCurtain had supported if he could not achieve separate statehood for Indian Territory.[22] Although two bills were introduced in Congress to admit the state of Sequoyah, they languished in committee while the House and Senate discussed an omnibus bill linking the fates of Indian Territory to that of Oklahoma, New Mexico, and Arizona territories. The Sequoyah Constitution never reached the floor of Congress. After a series of proposals and counterproposals, the two houses finally agreed on a bill that would admit Oklahoma and Indian territories as one state and New Mexico and Arizona as another if their citizens would agree separately to the plan.[23] President Roosevelt signed the bill on June 16, 1906, paving the way for Oklahoma statehood by authorizing a constitutional convention.

The men who wrote the constitution for the new state drew heavily on the experience of delegates to the Sequoyah Convention, and indeed many of them had served as delegates to that convention. Oklahoma's constitution was closely modeled on the Sequoyah document, down to its concern for prohibition.[24] Although Green McCurtain and the Choctaw Nation lost the battle for the sovereign autonomy of Indian Territory, Indian leaders as individuals helped shape the future of the new state.

It is hard to imagine two more unlikely candidates for marriage that Miss Indian Territory and Mr. Oklahoma Territory, but when Theodore Roosevelt himself declared that the couple should be joined, the match was consummated. Roosevelt's main motivation was the fear that Indian Territory as a separate state would bring two more Democratic Senators to Congress to undermine the Republican

Party.[25] Under Roosevelt's aegis, the hard-working groom and the well-endowed bride became the state of Oklahoma, proving the truth of the saying that politics makes strange bedfellows.

The issue of taxation continued to trouble the marriage. The pressure in the new state was strong to compel Indians to pay their share of the cost of state government.[26] In 1908, the U.S. Congress passed a law lifting the restrictions on all lands, including homesteads, of intermarried whites, freedmen, and mixed-bloods with less than one-half degree of blood (including minors). It preserved the restriction on homesteads of mixed-bloods of one-half to three-quarters degree of blood (including minors) but allowed them to sell excess lands at will. Only full-blooded Indians remained fully restricted on all their lands. By making Indian land private land held in fee simple, the act opened it to potential sale. The act also gave the secretary of the interior complete discretionary power to remove restrictions from any Indians he judged competent to handle their own affairs, but restricted Indians were still considered federal wards rather than U.S. citizens.[27] It removed all restrictions from the lands of deceased Indians, which meant that full-blood heirs lost any protection for their patents. In the Choctaw Nation the law affected 1,636 individuals of one-half to three-quarter degree of blood and 9,563 individuals of less than half or white blood, in addition to 5,994 freedmen.[28] The act of 1908 reified the distinction between mixed-bloods and full-bloods that had been a part of Choctaw society throughout the eighteenth and nineteenth centuries. Now that distinction had significant economic ramifications. The rhetoric of the act stressed the need of Indians to be able to sell their land to raise capital to improve their homesteads and become self-sufficient citizens of the state. But its immediate impact was to make over 8 million acres of Indian land subject to taxation and/or sale.

Taxation was also a major issue in the new state. The Oklahoma congressional delegation had lobbied vigorously in Congress to get restrictions on Indian allotments lifted.[29] Its members argued that the tax-exempt status of Indian land was a barrier to economic development in the state. Not only did the 1908 act put Indian allottees of less than one-half degree of blood at the mercy of probate courts, legal guardians, and attorneys in the state of Oklahoma, with a resulting national scandal, but the state also began planning to tax Indian lands.[30]

J. F. McMurray wanted to fight the state's plans, but his partners Mansfield and Cornish feared the backlash from the state government that was sure to occur, and the firm was formally dissolved in 1908.[31] McMurray took on the case alone. He sent out agents to solicit individual contracts from Choctaws whose lands were subject to taxation. For $10 each, they could be guaranteed that McMurray would "take charge of and prosecute all matters relative to the resistance of the payment of taxes on our lands held by the original allottees."[32]

With 8,000 contracts in his pocket, McMurray filed the case of *Choate v. Trapp* in the state court, which sought to block the assessment of lands for tax purposes. George W. Choate, a Creek allottee, was the named plaintiff against M. F. Trapp, who was secretary of the Oklahoma State Board of Equalization. McMurray's motion for an injunction against the assessments was denied. He immediately appealed to the state Supreme Court, which ruled that Congress had plenary power over Indians and that the exemption from taxation was not part of a contract guaranteed by the federal government but "a mere gratuity which could be withdrawn at will." McMurray then appealed to the U.S. Supreme Court, which decided that the tax exemption "was a vested property right which could not be abrogated by statute." The Curtis Act had implied a contract between the government and Indians who gave up their claims in communal property in exchange for individual allotments, and that contract could not be violated by subsequent congressional action, such as the act of 1908. The court thus extended constitutional protection over Choctaws' exemption from taxation.[33]

The court's decision was a victory for McMurray and the Choctaw Nation, but it also marked how completely Choctaw identity had become associated with private property. McMurray stepped into the legal vacuum created by the destruction of tribal governments to create a class action suit based on the former status of those governments' members as tribal citizens. His legal victory protected Choctaw lands from approximately $30,000,000 in taxes, thus depriving the state of Oklahoma of the income.

Although tax exemption was protected, the act of 1908 had disastrous consequences for "minors and incompetents" (restricted landholders). It shifted jurisdiction over their affairs from federal courts to the probate courts of the state of Oklahoma. The end result was a frenzy of land-buying, the enrichment of people who were appointed by Oklahoma judges as guardians for Indians, and the impoverishment of many Indians.[34] The probate situation was complicated because so many of the allottees were minors. It was an unprecedented situation to have so much land in the names of children, who were particularly vulnerable to exploitation.[35]

Reports of fraud and corruption in the McCurtain County probate court reached such a point that in 1912 state and federal officials and tribal leaders called for an investigation of the situation. Kate Barnard, commissioner of charities and corrections for the state of Oklahoma and a tireless crusader for children's rights, revealed that over 4,000 acres of the land of Indian minors had been sold for over $72,000. As a result, the probate judge resigned and was subsequently indicted for his part in the sales and Barnard was able to have the sales rescinded and the land and money recovered.[36]

By 1923, the situation of Indian guardianships in Oklahoma had reached the proportions of a national scandal. The discovery of the great oilfields of east central Oklahoma made some allottees wealthy, and the national press seized on stories of oil-rich Indians taken into guardianship and stripped of their money by unscrupulous guardians.[37] The Indian Rights Association published a report, *Oklahoma's Poor Rich Indians*, that made Ledcie Stechi, a seven-year-old Choctaw orphan, a virtual poster child for its charges of graft and corruption. Ledcie lived with her grandmother in a shack near Smithville in McCurtain County in southern Oklahoma. Her uncle was her guardian, but when oil was discovered on twenty acres of land she had inherited from her mother, she was promptly taken in hand by the owner of the First National Bank of Idabel, who assumed guardianship and hired a lawyer to assist in managing Ledcie's rather considerable assets. From 1921 to 1923, however, the girl and her grandmother continued to live in the shack and to subsist on the $15 monthly allowance granted by the guardian. In 1922, the guardian attempted to sell part of her property, which had been

appraised at $90,000, for $2,000. It seemed a common practice in
such transactions for the seller and buyer to collude to share in the
value of the property when it passed out of the hands of the Indian.
In this case, however, the sale was blocked. Ledcie and her grandmother were brought to Idabel in 1923, where Ledcie, who was
filthy, vermin ridden, and emaciated, was given medical care and
then placed as a student at Wheelock Academy. Her guardian, however, took her out of the school within twenty-four hours, and she
disappeared. On August 14, 1923, her grandmother received word of
her death, a totally unexpected blow. At the funeral, grafters sent
flowers for the grave of the little girl who, in the dramatic words of
the report, "had known only thorns." When the grandmother, suspicious because of the blackened appearance of the corpse, decided
that the child had been poisoned, the guardian instructed an immediate burial. The grieving grandmother, now heir to her grand-
daughter's wealth, had a guardian appointed for her by the court,
and as the report concluded, on an even more melodramatic note,
"She, too, will go the way of her grandchild, as sheep for slaughter
by ravenous wolves in men's forms, unless the good people of
America intervene immediately by remedial Congressional action.
Such action is the duty of all loyal Americans for the protection of
America's wards.[38]"

Subsequent congressional investigation revealed that Ledcie
Stechi's estate, which was valued at from $125,000 to perhaps as
much as $500,000, became involved in a contest between lawyers
seeking contingency fees of 50 percent to represent the claims of the
girl's grandmother and half-sister.[39]

Ledcie Stechi became a symbol of the accusations of the Indian
Rights Association against greedy whites—guardians, lawyers, and
probate court judges—who were determined to strip the Indians of
the Five Tribes of all their resources, but the abuses were real
enough. If, as Thomas Doyle maintained, Indian Territory needed
Oklahoma Territory to develop her resources, the union of the territories might be considered more of a rape than a marriage.

CHAPTER 15

AFTER STATEHOOD

Although the Indian tribes in Oklahoma largely disappear from history books after 1907, the legal and political reality was that their affairs were far from resolved. The Choctaws still had unallotted land, coal, asphalt (an inconsequential resource by 1906), and timber. The Leased District claim was still outstanding. And many individuals still clamored for enrollment as Mississippi Choctaws despite the closing of the rolls. The claims and suits resulting from attempts to settle these issues kept the Choctaws in Congress and in the courts as a political lobby, even though the nation no longer was a fully functional sovereign government. Individual interests transcended communal identity, but communal interests kept Choctaw legal identity alive. Government bureaucracy and policy changes caused delays in carrying out the terms of agreements, human greed kept the question of enrollment before Congress, and the prospect of ultimate justice for the Choctaw in the Leased District Case kept hope alive in the minds of some prominent leaders.

In the Supplementary Agreement of 1902, the federal government had promised to sell Choctaw coal and asphalt resources at public auction and divide the profits among Choctaw enrollees on a per capita basis. In 1904, however, the secretary of the interior changed the method of sale from public auction to sealed bid and withheld all leased land from sale. He then rejected all the bids on the grounds that they were too low.[1] Green McCurtain and Douglas Johnson, the chiefs of the Choctaw and Chickasaw nations, hired J. F. McMurray's law firm to force the sale of the resources, but the president refused to authorize the contract.[2] Unable to represent the Choctaws as a nation, McMurray sent his own agents out in the fall of 1908 to make contracts with individual Choctaws. He would represent their rights to their share of the communal resources for a fee of 10 percent of the proceeds he could recover.[3]

In the early twentieth century, however, the discovery of oil in the great Glen Pool in 1904 and the Cushing Pool in 1913 undercut the price of coal, and what had been the source of Choctaw wealth in the 1870s became a virtually worthless resource. In 1906, the secretary suspended coal sales altogether until existing mining leases expired.[4] The vagaries of the coal market made it increasingly obvious that continued leasing rather than outright sale was the only way to get any monetary benefit from the coal.

McMurray's contracts to represent the coal sale raised the suspicion of Congress, which sent a special committee to investigate the situation.[5] The Winton-Owen contracts with Mississippi Choctaws in the citizenship issue had put Congress on alert to the activities of lawyers, and it forced McMurray to drop his individual contracts. In 1910, the Choctaw General Council demanded that the U.S. government buy the surface land and coal (now appraised at approximately $19,000,000) for the sum of $60,000,000.[6] Choctaw claims would not go away. Commissioner of Indian Affairs Francis Leupp opposed the sale. He did not trust the General Council and instead proposed putting the coal, asphalt, and any oil resources of the tribe into a private joint stock company that would protect the individual shareholders "from their own improvidence" and "the company as a whole from a careless directorate." Congress failed, however, to act on his recommendation.[7]

In 1912, the Department of the Interior offered the surface rights to the lands at public sale but reserved the mineral rights to the tribes.[8] The sale produced a modest trickle of income. In 1914, the outbreak of the First World War gave Choctaw coal value as a national resource that had to be protected. Choctaw chief Victor M. Locke observed pointedly that the U.S. government had promised to sell the coal fourteen years previously and that about one-third of the original allottees had died without getting their share of this

resource.[9] In 1918, after the war, the interior department tried unsuccessfully to sell the coal. It tried again in 1921, but prices remained
low, and less than 65,000 acres had been sold by 1938.[10]

The paper value of Choctaw resources was no help to the many
Choctaws, who, having lost their land to "grafters" or taxes, lived in
remote, sparsely furnished log cabins.[11] Their conditions were much
as they been before European contact, but now they were impover-
ished in a money economy instead of being self-sufficient hunters
and farmers. As the Oklahoma oil boom continued in the 1920s and
1930s, the market value of the coal continued to decline. The
Choctaws and Chickasaws were saddled with mineral resources
they could not get rid of at any price. In 1930, Congress authorized
fifteen-year extensions of existing leases on Choctaw coal as the
only viable way to generate any income for the tribe.[12] By the early
1930s, the Choctaw and Chickasaw nations were "still the unwilling
owners of 381,077.05 acres of unsold coal and asphalt valued at
$10,088,649.57."[13] The existence of these resources committed the
government to an ongoing relationship with some semblance of the
Choctaw Nation.

The Choctaw government resorted to the U.S. courts in 1940,
when it filed suit in the U.S. Court of Claims to recover more than $2
million the government had expended from its trust funds for
expenses involved in carrying out the provisions of the Atoka Agreement. The claim included $68,165 for expenses incurred in the
process of trying to sell the coal and asphalt lands and deposits. With
interest, the claim amounted to over $4 million, but the court denied
it. It asserted that the Supplementary Agreement of 1902 did not
exempt the tribe from government charges and that all the charges
were legitimately used for the well-being of the Choctaws.[14]

With the outbreak of the Second World War, however, Choctaw
coal once again surfaced as a national resource. In 1942, Harold
Ickes, secretary of the interior, proposed to lease the Choctaw coal
for use in coke plants to be built in Houston, Texas, as part of the war
effort, and William Zimmerman, commissioner of Indian affairs, was
definitely in favor of leasing. The coal was a potential source of a per
capita payment if it was sold, but the government once again failed
to carry out its agreement with the Choctaws. Many were anxious

for the money. Elmer Thomas, chair of the Senate Committee on Indian Affairs, received a number of letters from Choctaws opposing the leasing idea. Kathleen Hunter wrote, "I am a widow and have three children to support and need my proportionate share of these properties now." Walter Colbert wrote asking for a per capita payment.[15] A telling exchange occurred during the course of the federal hearings on the leasing plan. Senator William Langer (R-North Dakota), a committee member, asked Elmer Thomas, the chair, "Should not the Government keep its promises, Senator?" to which Thomas replied, "Well, that is not debatable. It should, of course, but then it hasn't, it isn't, and it won't."[16]

Ultimately, the government conceded that purchase was more practical than leasing. In 1944, Congress authorized and appropriated $8,500,000 to buy the Choctaw coal and asphalt, and in 1948 the final contract for sale was ratified by Congress.[17] The final per capita distribution of the money took place between 1949 and 1952. As with the case of the Net Proceeds, the failure of the federal government to fulfill the terms of its agreement with the Choctaws deprived a generation of claimants of their share in the tribal estate. At the same time, the promise of a payment kept the hopes of a new generation of Choctaws alive and perpetuated its awareness of its Choctaw identity.

The Nation's timber resources were subject to the same manipulation by the federal government. When the Choctaws arrived in Indian Territory, the pine and hardwood forests of their new lands, particularly those of the Apukshunnubbee District in the far southeast, were rich hunting areas that attracted Choctaw families. As life in the Nation changed, the district remained the stronghold of Choctaw full-bloods who lived primarily by hunting and remained politically conservative. As the timber became increasingly valuable for building materials, it became a source of individual profit. But it was still the communal property of the Nation.[18]

Timber was peculiarly susceptible to theft since what went on in the woods was largely invisible to the casual observer, and throughout the late 1800s Indian agents regularly reported depredations on Indian timber by non-Indian thieves. Federal law prohibited the taking of timber belonging to the United States, but attempts to extend that law to protect Indian lands failed in Congress. Timber thieves could be expelled as intruders, and they were, but as soon as they were driven out they generally returned.[19]

Rather like the failure of Congress to regulate buffalo hunting on the Plains, the failure to extend the protection of law to Indian forest lands contributed to the exploitation of an Indian resource.[20] There were over 1 million acres of commercially valuable pine timber in the Choctaw Nation. The Dawes Commission wanted to withhold it from allotment to protect it from speculators, but the secretary of the interior directed that it be allotted on April 25, 1904. Henry Dawes reported that "in almost every case of an allotment of pine timber land the selection has been made by full-blood Indians, at the instigation of some speculator."[21] It seemed that the timber would be cut by lumber companies and speculators and the allottees would be left with worthless land.[22]

Green McCurtain denounced the secretary's directive as a violation of the Atoka Agreement, arguing that timber and stone were an essential part of the land.[23] The 1906 act wrapping up the affairs of the Five Tribes recognized the value of the timber and set aside the sections of land that constituted the main forest areas in the Choctaw Nation for sale at public auction or by sealed bid.[24] The final sale of the reserved timber finally took place in the 1920s, and it was the basis for the lumber industry that still dominates the forests of the Choctaw Nation in the early twenty-first century and that provided much of the economic base for Choctaw men as wage laborers throughout the twentieth century.[25] The ultimate economic benefit of the timber went to non-Indians, not to the Choctaws.

The case of the Mississippi Choctaws refused to die when the rolls of the Five Tribes were closed. If the power of Congress was indeed plenary over Indian Tribes, there was still the possibility that claimants might share in the estimated $30,000,000 in unallotted land and tribal resources that remained. Reopening the rolls of the tribes was the political goal of Representative Pat Harrison of Mississippi, who was elected to Congress in 1910. Harrison spent eight years in the House fighting the distribution of per capita payments to the Choctaws and Chickasaws and arguing for the enrollment of Mississippi Choctaw claimants.[26]

Although Congress was suspicious of claims for Choctaw citizenship that were represented by lawyers on contingency fees, lawyers in the early twentieth century found many people who were easily convinced that they had Choctaw blood, and Harrison had a political constituency in Mississippi before whom he could demand justice for supposed Mississippi Choctaws. Luke Ward Conerly, an elderly Choctaw who practiced law in Gulfport, Mississippi, headed an organization called the Gulfport Council of Mississippi Choctaws. He was also an agent for the St. Louis law firm of Cantwell and Crews, soliciting contracts for the firm to represent claimants for enrollment as Mississippi Choctaws.[27] Cantwell, in turn, contacted Pat Harrison to get the Choctaw rolls reopened so his clients could get land. It appeared that once again lawyers rather than legitimate Choctaw claimants would benefit from the distribution of Choctaw land.

Harrison introduced a bill to reopen the Choctaw rolls, allow the secretary of the interior to make contracts with lawyers to represent the cases, and guarantee a payment of $2,080 to each successful claimant.[28] He maintained that Choctaws who remained in Mississippi retained the rights of Choctaw citizens and did not have to move to Indian Territory to claim their rights to Choctaw lands. Harrison had no interest in Choctaw claims per se. He was a Mississippi politician bent on making a name for himself. It was clear that for him issues of Choctaw identity and land claims were strictly political, and he used highly romanticized rhetoric to make his case.

> And to-day, even though Pushmataha has long since gone to the happy hunting ground, his spirit still lives and animates the breasts of the scattered remnant of his race in the land of his nativity, and, methinks, if he were present to-day he would appeal to his white father in yonder White House, to his brethren in Oklahoma, to his white friends in this Chamber, and say "Give to the Mississippi Choctaws the rights guaranteed to them under the fourteenth article of the treaty of 1830." [applause][29]

Harrison, with unconscious irony, summed up the essence of Choctaw political identity in the poststatehood era—a continued appeal to treaty rights in the halls of Congress, before the executive branch, and in the courts. The appeal may have been rhetorical, but the stakes were very real. Significant sums of money depended upon the actions of Congress and the courts, and the people who stood to benefit the most were often white lawyers rather than identifiable Choctaws.

The nature of the Mississippi Choctaw claims was particularly problematic because there were certainly full-bloods in Mississippi with very valid claims who had not come forth to the Dawes Commission because of their (justifiable) fear that its work would simply mean that they would lose their homes once again. The full-blood Mississippi Choctaws who remained in that state after the 1903 removal suffered from health problems, lack of educational opportunities, and the economic hardships of tenant farmers.[30]

There were also, however, many gullible souls who believed the story of Mr. A. P. Powell, another of Cantwell and Crews's agents, that he had a book that would allow him to trace a person's ancestry and show whether they were descended from someone on the original 1831 roll of the Choctaws in Mississippi. It was obvious that Powell was simply interested in getting as many contracts as he could, usually at a contingency fee of 25 to 35 percent. When Cantwell fired Powell for his questionable practices, Powell went on representing himself as an agent for William B. Matthews, an attorney in Washington, D.C., and collecting contracts, charging a fee of $1.25 to $2.50 for his expenses. Other individuals representing Cantwell and Crews and Luke Conerly charged as much as $7.50 to execute a contract. Cantwell and Crews were confident enough in the prospect of the reopening of the rolls that they solicited investors to create the Texas-Oklahoma Investment Company, which was capitalized at $100,000. With 9,558 contracts valued at approximately $2,080, they could expect approximately $19,000,000 worth of property for their clients, of which they would collect about 30 percent.[31]

Despite an exposé of these highly questionable practices, Representative Harrison continued his determined effort to reopen the rolls. Although his original bill was favorably reported by the Committee on Indian Affairs,[32] Congress did not consider it. Patrick Hurley, the Choctaw tribal attorney, submitted a lengthy and detailed report to Secretary of the Interior Cato Sells arguing vigorously against the reopening of the rolls.[33] Hurley's arguments prevailed, and Congress appointed a subcommittee of the Committee on Indian Affairs to investigate the situation. Harrison did succeed, however, in getting an appropriation for a $100 per capita payment removed from the Indian Appropriation Bill in March of 1913 on the grounds that no distribution of funds should be made until the rights of the Mississippi Choctaws were settled. Any distribution, he argued, would ultimately diminish the amount that they would receive when they were enrolled.[34]

Hurley took his campaign against Harrison's legislation to the Lake Mohonk Conference in October of 1913. He blamed the government's failure to liquidate the coal, asphalt, and timber resources of the tribe and sell the remaining unallotted land for keeping alive the hopes of claimants for enrollment. Each claim, he said, was worth $5,000 to $8,000, and lawyers now represented as many as 50,000 potential claimants for Choctaw land. Congress had not reopened the rolls, but it had not distributed the proceeds of the sale of Choctaw lands either.[35] The per capita payments that enrolled tribal members had been led to expect as a result of the Supplementary Agreement were being held hostage by lawyers and legislators who were acting variously out of self-interest or some vague idea that Indians had been wronged or that the federal government had failed to live up to its obligations under treaties. Hurley's arguments point to significant reasons why the Choctaw Nation persisted as a political entity.

Although Harrison was pursing his own political agenda to bring financial benefits to Mississippi citizens, his efforts inspired a political agenda for Choctaws in Oklahoma. When Harrison proposed laws to reopen the rolls in 1913 and 1914, spurred on by members of the Choctaw Council of Alabama, Louisiana, and Mississippi, a group newly constituted in Oklahoma, the General Convention of Choctaws, mounted its own campaign against reopening the rolls.[36] Meeting at McAlester on October 28, 1914, it adopted a series of resolutions and elected W. A. Durant and D. C. McCurtain (son of Green McCurtain) as delegates to Washington to protect tribal interests.[37] As long as there were tribal resources at issue, there was cause for Choctaws to unite, even for the ultimate sake of self-interest regarding the distribution of those resources.

In an attempt to settle the issue once and for all, Robert Owen, Cherokee citizen and Oklahoma senator, negotiated the addition of 318 people to the final Dawes rolls.[38] Owen's act left open the possibility of still further congressional action, and Harrison declared his continued opposition to per capita payments for the Choctaws until the Mississippi Choctaw claimants could be heard.[39]

Harrison's final bill received a negative report from the House Committee on Indian Affairs. It would "completely upset and undo 11 years of careful, painstaking work" by the interior department to settle the affairs of the Five Tribes.[40] It would "turn the wheels of progress backwards for more than 20 years," and, according to President William Taft, it would "open up a Pandora's box of troubles, which the life of the present generation might never see closed."[41] Since a generation of Choctaws had not seen the money that had been promised them in the Supplementary Agreement, there was a certain irony in Taft's expression of concern.

Harrison's bill died in the House, but in the Senate, Robert LaFollette, a very liberal politician from Wisconsin, proposed an amendment to reopen consideration of some 10,000 cases involving all five tribal rolls that were filed and acted on in haste in the weeks immediately before the closing of the rolls on March 4, 1907. He argued that these cases had not received the full attention that earlier cases had and that the claimants had not received proper consideration. Once again, Choctaw claims were kept alive by the U.S. political process. LaFollette's amendment failed, despite a seven-hour filibuster by a senator from North Dakota who favored reopening the rolls, and the proposed per capita payment died with the bill.[42]

In 1915, Harrison's last attempt to reopen the rolls and block a per capita payment failed. The Oklahoma congressional delegation stood firmly behind the payment, in part because the distribution of Choctaw and Chickasaw funds would benefit the Oklahoma economy as Indians spent the money.[43] Harrison did not achieve his political ends, but the Mississippi Choctaw issue drew out the process of enrollment in a legal entanglement that lasted until 1916. Sporadic attempts to get special legislation or judicial entitlements continued through the late 1920s.[44] The whole situation points up the clash of reformist efforts to right wrongs done to American Indians in the past and the acquisitive and individualistic nature of a segment of American society. Liberal congressmen supported what they saw as efforts to assure that all Choctaws who had been guaranteed land by federal treaty would receive it. Claimants responding to lawyers' advertisements of possible wealth through litigation represented the acquisitive nature of American society.

In the end, the government recognized the rights of the Mississippi Choctaws when it appropriated $75,000 to establish an agency in 1918 and began purchasing land to create a reservation for them.[45] In 1924, the U.S. Supreme Court made a final decision in a case that had begun in 1896 when Charles Winton made a contract with Jack Amos to represent his claim. Amos was ultimately enrolled, but Winton never received payment for his services. The court decided that Winton had not advanced Amos's cause, and the claim of Winton's heirs was dismissed.[46] Yet another protracted set of legal battles finally ground to a close.

The Leased District claim held out the promise of financial gain for Choctaws even after the ostensible dissolution of the Nation. In 1911, Patrick Hurley, the newly appointed Choctaw national attorney, revived the claim. His legal tactic was to get it referred to the U.S. Court of Claims for final adjudication. Although Congress had not responded to the last Choctaw memorial on the issue in 1901, the claim was still very real. Its existence, however, caused new political fractures in the Nation.

Patrick Hurley pursued the claim, but so did a group calling itself the Choctaw-Chickasaw Treaty Rights Association. The genius behind the association was J. F. McMurray, the omnipresent legal mind in Choctaw affairs in the late nineteenth century. McMurray sent a memorial to Congress concerning the claim, and the Choctaw-Chickasaw Treaty Rights Association sent three delegates to Washington.[47] The Leased District claim became a contest between the vestiges of the Choctaw government and the seasoned lobbyist. McMurray insisted that Hurley cooperate with him in representing the claim, but Hurley refused to do so. He feared that McMurray's past contracts with the Choctaw Nation and a congressional investigation of his actions (in 1910) made him suspect in the eyes of Congress. Although Hurley and George D. Rodgers, attorney for the

Chickasaw Nation, were prepared to represent the claim, the treaty rights association did not give up the fight easily. McMurray did not intend to be ousted. When Hurley appeared at an association meeting in McMurray's hotel room in Oklahoma City, he was pointedly told to leave.

The contest heated up when Congress received two memorials regarding the claim, one signed by McMurray and Douglas Johnson, the Chickasaw governor, and the other signed by Hurley and Victor Locke, the Choctaw chief.[48] The two memorials showed how political forces were dividing the Nation. They were very similar, which seemed to support the claim, but the fact that they emanated from two sources represented growing conflicts within and between the Choctaw and Chickasaw nations.[49]

In Congress, the Committee on Indian Affairs reported favorably on two bills referring the claim to the U.S. Court of Claims but both failed, and the Leased District claim appeared to be dead.[50] Its brief resurgence, however, had focused media attention on the contention between McMurray and Hurley and the power that McMurray still wielded among members of the Choctaw Nation who saw litigation as a means of financial reward. Hurley suggested, but had no proof, that members of the Choctaw-Chickasaw Treaty Rights Association had a financial interest in the payments McMurray claimed for his services.[51]

The claim was obviously a highly political issue in the Choctaw Nation, and in 1924, Charles D. Carter (D-Oklahoma) finally achieved Hurley's original objective by getting a bill passed in Congress that referred the Leased District claim to the U.S. Court of Claims.[52] He also proposed a House resolution that called for a seven-member committee to investigate the claim.[53] Carter was defeated for reelection in 1926, but his successor, Wilburn Cartwright, was persuaded to carry on the fight. In 1931, Cartwright resurrected the Leased District claim with two bills that allowed the Choctaw government to hire lawyers with contingency fees and bring the case to trial in federal court.[54] Cartwright also pushed a bill through Congress referring the claim to the court of claims for a fact-finding review to determine its total money value.[55] But the country was in the midst of a major depression, and President Herbert Hoover

vetoed the referral, citing it as a dangerous precedent for the renego-
tiation of treaties. It was not the time to raise the potentially costly
issue of unfulfilled Indian claims.[56]

In January of 1939, the court of claims issued its findings under
Hurley's original submission in 1911. It denied the Choctaws and
Chickasaws any "legal or equitable rights" to the Leased District and
reduced their arguments for treaty rights to "a request for a gift,
grant, or bounty."[57] In essence, the court dumped the case back into
the lap of Congress. So back to Congress the Choctaws went. In 1940,
the U.S. Senate considered a bill with the recommendation that
$8,095,763 be appropriated to pay for the Leased District, but again
Congress did not act.[58]

The long and torturous saga of the Leased District Case illustrates
the shifting relationship between the Choctaw government and the
U.S. government in the first half of the twentieth century. The power
of Congress over the Indians in the United States increased as a
result of certain key Supreme Court decisions in the late 1800s and
1900s (U.S. v. Kagama; Lone Wolf v. Hitchcock), and in the early twentieth century, the federal courts began to defer to Congress by consid-
ering Indian claims as merely matters of federal policy rather than
matters of legal right. After 1906, the Indians of the Five Tribes had
federally appointed chiefs rather than formal governments and
allotment had destroyed their land base. The secretary of the interior
had virtually complete authority over their affairs. Although the
Choctaws managed to get the Leased District claim into the U.S.
Court of Claims, that court declared the claim a matter of policy
rather than a legal right under treaty. By 1940, however, legislative
persistence paid off with favorable recommendations by Congress
that somewhat over $8,000,000 be paid to the Choctaws for their for-
mer lands. It is one thing to propose legislation, however, and quite
another to pass it, and by the late 1940s the Choctaws had still not
received a payment for the Leased District.

The period after statehood was a time of struggle between the
state of Oklahoma, which wanted to gain control over all land
(including Indian land) in the state, and the Choctaw government,
which wanted a fair settlement of its remaining claims and the distribution of its remaining resources. Political struggles had revealed

the extent to which self-interest and material resources had eroded a sense of tribal cultural identity. Per capita payments of the Net Proceeds money and the Leased District judgment had indeed converted the value of Choctaw land to money. In the case of the Net Proceeds, the eastern lands in question may still have been within the immediate memory of older people, but as the last generations of original immigrants died, the memory was less clear and had become embedded in stories passed down from parents to children about the rigors of the migration. In the case of the Leased District, the remoteness and aridness of the land and the fact that it was the range of the Comanche, Kiowas, and Wichitas meant that it was not useful to the Choctaws or the Chickasaws, and the claim for payment became a matter of principle based on treaty rights and fair payment for what the United States had guaranteed to the Choctaws in exchange for their eastern lands. After statehood, what remained of the Choctaw government was left to fight a rearguard action to assure that each individual received the full value of what the federal government had guaranteed to him or her.

CHAPTER 16

TERMINATING THE CHOCTAWS

The Choctaw Nation, some 20,000 people in central Mississippi in the late eighteenth century, had endured the impact of Andrew Jackson's Indian removal policy in 1831–1832, the allotment of its tribal land base in what is now the state of Oklahoma in 1898, and the dissolution of its tribal government with Oklahoma statehood in 1907. After 1907, it existed politically only as a shadow government to oversee the final disposition of the remaining unallotted land and coal and asphalt deposits that remained in tribal holdings. Choctaw families and communities persisted, however. In small rural enclaves, often clustered around a Christian church, they could raise some crops and some cattle. Christianity was a pervasive influence in Choctaw life. It was also a last bastion of Choctaw language, since many young people were not learning Choctaw in their own homes. In churches, hymns, preaching, and scripture-reading used the Choctaw language.[1]

However, Choctaw families could no longer be totally self-sufficient. They were now dependent on a market economy. Their major cash crops were cotton and corn, and the average annual income for families growing cotton in the late 1930s was $54.40, and $20.10 for those growing corn.[2] Since the surplus lands of most full-blood families were generally far to the west in the rich farming and grazing lands of the Chickasaw Nation, many Choctaws lived primarily off rental income. By the early 1950s, their lifestyles appeared to one historian to be "a picture of appalling social and economic degradation," but they actually represented a largely culturally intact full-blood lifestyle that was being judged against the standards of 1950s American society.[3]

The full-blood Choctaws in the mountains clung to community and language and so became a kind of backwash in the wave of post–Second World War American prosperity. For example, a sheep-raising project the Bureau of Indian Affairs devised for the Choctaws remained marginal in the nation's economy. The bureau designed the project to produce income; women would weave cloth out of the wool and the men could sell the excess wool. The project proved to be an opportunity for social activity among women, but it did not develop into an economically viable cooperative enterprise.[4]

The mixed-blood element of the Choctaw population lived in the area around Durant, where they raised peanuts, cotton, and feed crops. Choctaw homesteads in this area were, for the most part, poorly suited for agriculture. Communities continued a loosely knit structure of government in the form of councils in each Oklahoma county within the boundaries of the old Choctaw Nation.[5]

It is unlikely that most Choctaws in the 1950s were aware of the establishment of the Indian court of claims in 1946. Its creation, however, gave the Choctaw tribe a new legal venue for its claims. It had gained access to the U.S. Court of Claims in 1881 with the Net Proceeds Case, and it had taken the Leased District claim to that court.[6] The Indian Claims Commission offered a new venue because its decisions were to be based on matters of fact as well as of law, thus opening the door to the doctrine of liberal interpretation that was unique to Indian treaty litigation. However, it was also Congress's way of settling Indian claims with payments that would finally allow it to terminate its relationship with Indian tribes.[7]

After 1946, the Nation had two sources of income, one real and one potential. The first was the congressional appropriation for the sale of the coal and asphalt resources. Although the bill for sale of the resources authorized a payment of $8.5 million, the initial payment authorized by Congress was only $1.5 million, and Senator Elmer Thomas of Oklahoma had to wage a determined fight for the full amount.[8] The second potential source was the Indian Claims Commission, where past unsuccessful claims could be reheard. Interest in the distribution of that income brought forth a surge of requests for individual payments, the dreaded per-cap that would destroy any sense of communal interest.

Thomas received a steady stream of letters inquiring about the progress of legislation concerning the sale of the coal and asphalt.[9] "I ask you to do your duty and cause them to pay the full amount we have waited for settlement 47 years," said one letter-writer.[10] Many Choctaws had given up the idea of a tribal government. Kathleen Hunter, a Choctaw living in Oklahoma City, wrote, "It was provided long ago that the tribal estate be wound up, and the residue of properties be converted into cash and paid out to the individual allottees. . . . We want the tribal government dissolved and such waste discontinued." And Victor Locke, former appointed chief, declared that "the Choctaw people regard the continuation of the tribal government as a useless ornament, costly to these Indian people and the sooner disposed of by the Government the better will be the outcome from a financial standpoint to all concerned."[11] To what extent Locke spoke for Choctaw people generally is questionable, but his and Mrs. Hunter's views reflect a distinct sense of individualism and a basic distrust of any organized tribal government.

The $8.5 million plus the more than $1 million in the Choctaw trust fund would amount to a per capita payment of approximately $330 to each tribal member.[12] It was not until 1948, however, that Congress finally approved the contract for the final sale at the $8.5 million figure. The final per capita payment for the coal and asphalt sale was made in a period from 1949 to 1952.[13]

In 1948, Harry Belvin was appointed the chief of the Choctaw tribe.[14] In 1951 he took a claim of $753,609 to the Indian Claims Commission. The amount represented administrative costs charged against the funds from the sale of their assets. Among the expenses was a claim of $38,416 for expenses incurred with the sale of the coal and asphalt. However, the case had already been rejected by the U.S. Court of Claims, and the Choctaws' lawyers had no new evidence to present to the Indian Claims Commission.[15]

For individual Choctaws, the failure of the tribe's suits against the government were largely unnoticed as they collected their per capita payments from the coal sale. Most either saw no need for a tribal government or viewed it as a needless expense. Belvin had begun to establish a form of government in a democratically elected tribal council and Choctaw councils in each of ten counties in southeastern Oklahoma, and he had plans for a constitution to reestablish a functioning tribal government.[16] Belvin maintained that the Bureau of Indian Affairs recognized his tribal council and sought its sanction for its recommendations, but ultimately the area director of the Bureau of Indian Affairs opposed his efforts as well.[17]

Belvin's relationship with Paul Fickinger, the area director for the Muskogee Area Office, was both ideologically and personally antagonistic. Belvin accused Fickinger of being "very dilatory in pursuing his duty" with regard to sale of the Choctaw resources; Fickinger had not gotten a final appraisal of the remaining Choctaw resources so they could be offered for sale.[18] Belvin turned away from the Bureau of Indian Affairs and toward Congress to restructure the relationship of the Choctaws to the federal government. He appealed to Representative Carl Albert for a bill that would terminate bureau authority over the Choctaws. He looked to Albert to give him a new form of Choctaw government based on the remaining communal resources. He expected that individual Choctaws would still be eligible for various federal services. Although the coal and asphalt assets of the tribe had been sold to the government, the reservation of mineral rights on the remaining unallotted lands resulted from his feeling that "one never knows where oil might be found in Oklahoma."[19] Belvin's political strategy fit into federal policy in the 1950s, which was to terminate relationships between the U.S. government and Indian tribes.[20] Carl Albert accepted Belvin's proposition and sponsored a bill to amend the 1906 act; its intention was to hasten the disposition of tribal resources and place the approximately 7,000 acres of unsold Choctaw land into a private trust fund in order to terminate federal supervision over the Choctaws.[21]

Albert reassured his Choctaw constituents that "this was not a general termination bill."[22] It would apply only to the remaining Choctaw assets—the Choctaws' three-quarter interest in 7,731 acres of unallotted tribal land and 8,610 acres purchased for and held in trust by the federal government and half of the mineral rights in these lands. The lands and reserved mineral rights would be placed in a corporation to be organized under state law. The proceeds of the sale of this land, together with the approximately $433,000 in the tribal trust account, would be distributed in a per capita payment to the living tribal members on the Dawes rolls and their heirs.[23] The majority of tribal members who expressed any opinion on the matter were interested in distribution of funds on an individual basis; that is, per capita payments.[24] The transition from tribal to individual identity for Choctaws seemed to be virtually complete. Although Albert's bill reaffirmed the existence of a tribal entity, it was now based on a vestige of original tribal communal land-holding, and it was a political entity with decision-making powers over limited communal assets rather than a governing body over a group of people.[25]

The termination act proved, however, to be a replay of the Atoka Agreement of 1897 and its supplement in 1902. Then, the government had committed itself to the sale of Choctaw resources and distribution of the income, leading to dissolution of the tribal government. This time, the plan failed because of circumstances arising from the 1902 agreement. It proved almost impossible for the federal government to identify and locate the heirs of the original allottees and to clear title to land for the sale of the mineral reserves beneath them.

More important, the Bureau of Indian Affairs, contrary to Albert's assurances and Belvin's understanding, interpreted the act as a complete termination of the federal relationship, including access to Bureau of Indian Affairs services. The 1959 act lifted the terms of the Oklahoma Indian Welfare Act and the Indian Reorganization Act. Choctaws were no longer eligible for loans from the Bureau of Indian Affairs.[26] Suddenly, termination was not a move toward political freedom but a threat to Choctaw access to economic resources.[27]

Belvin's attempt to terminate the Choctaws came during a time of rising political consciousness among American Indians throughout the United States. In 1961, a number of American Indian scholars and community leaders and a group of anthropologists and social scientists gathered in Chicago to discuss the status of Indians and draw up a declaration calling for reforms in the administration of Indian affairs.[28] In the turmoil of the civil rights movement and growing opposition to the Vietnam War, a new sense of Indian nationalism began to emerge. It expressed itself in the sense that grassroots people were capable of effecting change in American government and their own communities through organized political action. Robert K. Thomas, a Cherokee anthropologist, offered the concept of Indian reservations and communities as "internal colonies" of the U.S. government. His writings helped fuel the new sense of Indian nationalism based on liberation from oppressive colonial policies that had kept American Indians in a state of submission and allowed the exploitation of their land and resources.[29]

In Oklahoma, this Indian political awareness was embodied in a new organization, Oklahomans for Indian Opportunity (OIO), which capitalized on President Lyndon Johnson's War on Poverty. A key component of Johnson's antipoverty policy was the Office of Economic Opportunity (OEO), which had a commitment to grassroots political activism to solve problems of poverty at the community level.

One of the major supporters of Johnson's policies was Senator Fred Harris of Oklahoma, who was elected in 1964. Harris, son of a sharecropper, was born and raised in Walters, Oklahoma. His wife, LaDonna, was also born and raised in Walters by her Comanche grandparents. She supported her husband through law school, campaigned with him as he ran for the Senate, and used his office to advance their mutual commitment to promoting access of American Indians in Oklahoma to the economic advantages of American society. In 1965, the couple decided that the best means of access was through the programs of the Office of Economic Opportunity, Johnson's mechanism for fighting his War on Poverty. Convinced that the Bureau of Indian Affairs was not helping Indians, they used the resources of Senator Harris's Washington office and Mrs. Harris's position as a member of the Executive Board of the Southwest Center for Human Relations at the University of Oklahoma to convene a conference on the university campus.[30]

Federal programs administered by the Bureau of Indian Affairs were aimed primarily at reservation communities, and the unique status of Oklahoma tribes who did not have extensive land bases meant that they were not served by many of these programs. Also, the historic division between the Five Tribes in the eastern part of the state and the tribes in the western part who had been settled there in the latter part of the nineteenth century meant that there was no real basis for unified action among Oklahoma Indians.[31] Nevertheless, over 500 people gathered in Norman on August 14, 1965, and became the initial membership of the new organization. Among them was Harry J. W. Belvin, who was elected to a five-year term on the board of directors.[32] Other representatives included the area directors of the Anadarko and Muskogee area offices of the Bureau of Indian Affairs.

Although the Harrises used the OEO as their primary funding source, they saw the political advantages of cooperating with the Bureau of Indian Affairs. Not only would a working relationship help them create a broad-based organization but it would also enable them to put pressure on the agency to carry out its responsibilities to Indians in areas such as housing and education. The OIO also put a significant emphasis on youth programs, sponsoring community youth councils and statewide meetings that brought high school and college students together to hear speakers, hold elections, and in general practice public speaking and political action skills.

The Harrises were a high-profile Washington political couple, both because of their youth, attractiveness, and vocal stand on Indian issues and because of their outspoken criticism of the Vietnam War and their support of Johnson's controversial antipoverty programs. LaDonna Harris became the first wife of a politician to appear before a congressional committee when she testified against the abolition of the Office of Economic Opportunity.[33] Suddenly, LaDonna and Fred Harris, rather than the tribal chairmen of the state, seemed to be the main spokespeople for Indian issues in Oklahoma, and inevitable tensions arose within the multifaceted leadership of the OIO.[34] Iola Hayden, a Comanche tribal member and distant relative of LaDonna Harris, had become executive director of the organization in 1965, and she had some association with Robert K. Thomas, the Cherokee anthropologist whose work with a Cherokee literacy project in Eastern Oklahoma had stirred up community opinions against the tribal government. Thomas's writings and growing reputation as an Indian activist threatened the status quo in

Indian relationships with the federal government. Some Indian people viewed the OIO as too "radical" for its own good and not respon-
sive to direct community needs.[35]

In 1969, the OIO received a grant from the OEO through its research
division for a rural poverty demonstration project. In the Choctaw
area, it established community groups to buy groceries in bulk for discounted prices and a feeder pig cooperative. The OIO used federal
funds to encourage a sense of community activism at the time that
Harry J. W. Belvin and many Choctaws were committed to the dissolution of the bulk of the tribal estate and distribution of tribal assets on
a per capita basis. It gave Choctaw communities new resources not
tied to the Bureau of Indian Affairs. The OIO and the Bureau of Indian
Affairs were now in competition for the attention and allegiance of
Indian people, although OIO director Iola Hayden denied that there
was competition, "because we do not have that kind of money."[36]
Although Belvin, as Choctaw chief, served as a member of the Board
of Directors of the OIO, he soon realized that the organization threatened his own political agenda. The OIO was having its own problems.
LaDonna Harris left the organization to concentrate her energy in
Washington. Belvin chaired a special personnel committee of the OIO
board to investigate charges that Iola Taylor's alienation of staff members led to significant staff turnover and that she had ignored applications from community groups for funding.[37] Belvin declared that the
investigation proved that the OIO "was shot through and through
with politics, favoritism, prejudice, and mismanagement," but it was
also clear that the activities of the OIO to develop community groups
and promote Choctaw identity contradicted Belvin's vision of the
Choctaw Nation as a simple corporate entity.

The activities of the OIO challenged Belvin's authority by creating community-level political activities, such as buying clubs that
brought community members together to place bulk orders with
grocers to get discount prices. The OIO's educational activities
with Indian students smacked of "militancy," a term that became
shorthand for overt challenge to the American government, a
stance that was anathema to Choctaws who had grown up in the
assimilation eras of the late nineteenth and early twentieth centuries.[38] It was the OIO's independence that irked Belvin the most.

He wrote a vituperative letter to OEO official William Bowman accusing OIO officials of overstepping their bounds. Belvin's greatest concern was that the OIO's program might be "designed to foster confusion among the people, to teach prejudice and hate, to fight the Government and its agencies, and the Tribal leadership."[39] Belvin, having found that his attempt at self-determination through termination would not have the desired effects, was now trying to maintain a good relationship with the Bureau of Indian Affairs. This strategy was more likely to succeed than his earlier goal; Virgil Harrington, an Oklahoma Choctaw, had been appointed area director for the eastern area office in Muskogee in 1965.[40]

Belvin was also under attack by members of his own council. Delos Wade asked pointed questions about the chief's salary and the tribe's landholdings and accused Belvin of withholding information from tribal members, whereupon Belvin accused him of "disloyalty" and fired him from the council.[41] The termination issue was costing him political capital, and a group of Choctaws, the Oklahoma City Council of Choctaws, under the leadership of Charles Brown, who identified himself as a full-blood, published a mimeographed newsletter that became the medium for vigorous attacks on Belvin, the expense of maintaining a government, and the fact of a federally appointed chief.[42]

The exchange provided a basis for a new Choctaw political identity, one especially important in light of President Richard Nixon's repudiation of the termination policy of the 1950s and Oklahoma senator Henry Bellmon's legislation giving the Five Tribes in Oklahoma the power to select their own leaders.

By 1967, Belvin was asking Oklahoma congressman Ed Edmondson to sponsor legislation to repeal the termination legislation. The act was unworkable because heirs of original allottees could not be identified, and unless it was possible to establish a corporation by August 25, 1968, Choctaw mineral rights would be forfeited to owners of surface rights and unclaimed funds would revert to the U.S. treasury. It was also possible to dispose of tribal property under the terms of the original 1906 act. Also, Belvin wrote, "Repeal of the Act would be in accord with the majority opinions expressed in the 1966 and 1967 opinion polls."[43]

Opinion was building against the termination act. At a meeting at Camp Israel Folsom, near Bethel, on July 5, 1969, one speaker raised the issue of treaty rights, charging that past treaties between the Choctaw tribe and the federal government would have no effect because the Choctaw tribe would no longer exist in a legal sense.[44] Belvin defended the act, provided it was significantly modified.

Although the original act had been set to expire in 1962 and had been twice amended to remain in effect to allow sufficient time for the sale of assets, the cumbersome processes of government had not effected the liquidation of Choctaw assets, and the termination act had cut Choctaws off from government services. Belvin again sought to redefine the Choctaw relationship with the U.S. government through the legislative process. He proposed to Oklahoma senator Mike Monroney that the 1959 act be amended to protect Choctaw tribal property but also that the office of principal chief and the tribe's tax exemption be continued.[45]

However, Congress proceeded with the complete repeal of the termination legislation. The proposed sale of assets had created an administrative nightmare. Heirs of deceased allottees often proved difficult to find, which contributed to the problems of clearing title to land. Many Choctaws had expressed their desire to keep their tribal government. Individual Choctaws could obtain federal services only if the tribe was recognized by the federal government, and the termination legislation had to be repealed for services to continue, a policy that would lead to what the U.S. Congress referred to as "the economic betterment of the tribe."[46]

Senator Fred Harris of Oklahoma also supported the repeal legislation. He noted that the 1959 act as amended would terminate the tribe as of August 25, 1970. His argument was premised on humanitarian grounds and a sense of the importance of tribal identity. He declared that " we now know that the actual results of termination are contrary to the well-being of the American Indian. The end of Federal assistance to the tribal entity destroys the Indian community and the Indian's sense of dignity."[47] Carl Albert in his testimony before the House Committee on Interior and Insular Affairs expressed a contrary opinion of the significance of the termination act, an economic one: "The Act will, when it becomes effective, terminate the eligibility of individual Choctaw members for certain federal services now provided Indians because of their status as Indians."[48]

The fallout of the proposed termination legislation for many individual Choctaws was a rise of political activism in the Choctaw Nation. The urban population in Oklahoma City was an important source of the activism. As early as the 1930s, a number of Choctaws had moved from their rural homes to the major urban area in the state of Oklahoma. An organization that formed there adopted the name of the Oklahoma City Council of Choctaws. By 1970 it was publishing a mimeographed newsletter, *Hello Choctaw*. Charles E. Brown, a full-blood, was president. The newsletter portrayed itself as the voice of the "Average Choctaw." It became a way to question Belvin's actions: "For over 20 years . . . the Government has been appointing a 'leader' for the Choctaw tribe. . . . For over 20 years the AVERAGE CHOCTAW has not known the NAMES of the people who actually got the money that was taken out of the AVERAGE CHOCTAW'S tribal funds. . . . For over 20 years the AVERAGE CHOCTAW has not known for sure how many thousands of dollars were taken out of his tribal funds in 'annual budgets'. . . . For over 20 years the AVERAGE CHOCTAW has not known how much of his tribal land was sold or how much it was sold for. Government 'appointed' people had the power to sell the AVERAGE CHOCTAW'S TRIBAL LANDS without the AVERAGE CHOCTAW even knowing his lands were being sold or how much they were being sold for." The organization issued a challenge to Choctaws throughout the state to "organize YOUR OWN TRIBAL GROUP IN YOUR OWN COMMUNITY."[49]

At issue in this new political climate was the ability of the Choctaws to exercise their sovereignty through a popularly elected government. In the 1940s, tribal members had demanded per capita payments and the complete dissolution of the tribal government. In 1959, the termination act eliminated the popular election of tribal chiefs. Belvin, as the appointed chief, could retain control over the political affairs of the Nation. By the early 1970s, however, an undated issue of *Indian Affairs* reported that "the Choctaws believe if they can get rid of this rubber-stamp official they can voluntarily elect a chief of their own." The power of the Bureau of Indian Affairs to appoint the tribal chief was a major infringement on the identity of the Choctaws as a self-governing people, and the newsletter urged Choctaws to organize their own clubs.[50] The Oklahoma City Council saw itself as a leader in initiating a tribal organization and allowing members to elect their own leader.[51]

This commitment to election was the major statement of a resurgent sense of tribal self-government for the Choctaws. In the political foment in the Choctaw Nation, a new statement for tribal identity emerged in a constitution drafted by a young Choctaw man, Mike Charleston. The initial paragraph is an eloquent statement of the hopes of a new generation of Choctaw leaders:

> The purpose of the Constitution of the Choctaw Nation is to provide unity and direction of efforts for the re-establishment of a traditional Choctaw Trial Government. The constitution is the basis of a tribal government responsible to all of the Choctaw people and representative of their desires, interests, and needs; and it provides the structure and method necessary for the operation of the government. The writing and distribution of this constitution is intended to act as a catalyst for the development of an acceptable tribal government resulting from the cooperation and actions of a great many Choctaw people.[52]

Charleston's constitution was an eloquent statement for a generation of Choctaws who grew up in a period of a federal policy of assimilation and who still retained a commitment to Choctaw tribal identity. Although financial advantage in the form of per capita payments drew many Choctaws away from tribal identity, in the 1970s the core of that that tribal identity persisted, changed by political forces but still embedded in the lives of Choctaw communities in the old Choctaw territory and in the idealism of a younger generation.

The Choctaw Nation had entered a market economy in the period after the Civil War, and as a result had seen the distribution of tribal resources in per capita payments and the transition of Choctaw identity to individualism. The communal land-holding pattern had been destroyed, but a cultural sense of community had remained, and economic poverty in the American sense represented a continuation of traditional Choctaw community ways of life. Political sovereignty and self-government emerged out of a conflict between the Bureau of Indian Affairs and its appointed leaders of the Nation and an emerging political activism based both in rural community-based community activity and an urban population that, although ostensibly acculturated, was vocal in its search for Choctaw self-government through popular elections.

Epilogue

The Choctaw Nation in 2006 had approximately 175,000 enrolled members. The vast majority lived in states other than Oklahoma. The Choctaw population of the ten-county service area of the Nation in southeastern Oklahoma was about 29,000. The area encompasses only a small portion of the approximately 13 million acres originally granted to the Choctaw Nation in the Treaty of Doaks Stand in 1820.[1] The majority of the land was held by non-Indian owners; approximately 136,000 acres was owned by individual Choctaws in trust status, while the Nation owned approximately 20,000 acres under various provisions of federal law.[2]

The Nation's budget in 2005 was approximately $300,000,000. Its various business enterprises included a manufacturing plant that fabricated parts for the U.S. aerospace industry, a personnel management office that received contracts from the federal government to manage personnel services for military bases around the world, resort facilities on Lake Eufaula in southeastern Oklahoma, horse racing tracks in Pocola and Sallisaw, and casinos in Hugo and Durant that drew large crowds across the Red River from Texas.

In many respects, the Choctaw Nation at the beginning of the twenty-first century is much like a large multinational corporation devoted to making a profit. It is also, however, a sovereign government, and in this regard it operates in a manner unique to modern Indian nations—it both provides its citizens with services and runs businesses to generate income. In American society, taxes provide the basis for government social services while private business generates the profits upon which taxes are based. Many Indian nations provide health, education, and welfare services; police protection; and housing, mostly funded through the Bureau of Indian Affairs and other federal agencies. They also run businesses that are exempt from federal and state taxation as a function of tribal sovereignty. That exemption promotes the profitability of national business enterprises, thus allowing them to generate their own income base to provide services to individual members. There is no division of public sector and private sector economies as in American society.

Many Indian nations and tribes still rely on direct services from or contractual agreements with the Bureau of Indian Affairs to handle social services. The Choctaw Nation prides itself on the economic self-sufficiency it has achieved. Its hospital in Talihina, for instance, was built entirely with funds raised from its businesses. The Nation has also used its funds to promote Choctaw cultural identity. Preservation of the language is a significant concern, and the Nation has turned to a very modern technology, the Internet, to offer language classes to its far-flung constituency. Head Start classes include language instruction for tiny Choctaws. An annual cultural festival at Fort Towson features Choctaw songs and dances. The old capitol building in Tuskahoma has been maintained as a museum, a continuing symbol of national identity, and the focal point of the annual Choctaw Labor Day celebration, where big-name country and western music acts coexist comfortably with open-air Christian services where hymns are sung in the Choctaw language. The annual Choctaw Veterans' Day celebration honors the members of the Nation who fought in American wars, particularly the Choctaw code talkers, whose service in the First World War is a special point of pride.

The Choctaw Nation is governed under a constitution formally adopted in 1983. It replaced the constitution, so painfully achieved, that had been in place since 1860. In some respects it followed the general outlines of the 1860 constitution. The Nation is composed of twelve districts, each with a representative, while the 1860 constitution had only four districts. The executive, legislative, and judicial branches remain, but the militia has disappeared.

The 1860 constitution was notable for its attention to individual rights. Its first article was a Bill of Rights that contained seventeen sections. The 1983 constitution introduced a Bill of Rights in Article IV, and it included only five sections covering freedom of speech, assembly, and religion and protection of private property. The 1860 constitution reflected the philosophical concerns of balancing individual and national interests in a painful period of adjustment to the larger forces of sectional interest in American society. The 1983 constitution is a very efficient document that spells out procedures for the conduct of a modern, self-governing Indian nation.

A critical issue for contemporary Indian nations is the matter of citizenship. Who is a Choctaw in contemporary society under this modern government? The 1983 constitution's second article establishes an explicit criterion for citizenship—descent from a person originally enrolled by the Dawes Commission. Blood is thus the primary factor in Choctaw identity, although the complicated history of the enrollment process raises many questions about who was or was not enrolled. The 1860 constitution had no criteria for Choctaw citizenship, although the Choctaw Council had passed laws regulating intermarriage between Choctaw citizens and white men. In 1860, the Nation was its own entity, and it had no need to define its members. In 1983, citizenship was a critical issue because of the vagaries of federal legislation.

The requirement of blood descent raises an important and complicated political issue for the Nation: the status of contemporary descendents of Choctaw freedmen who were adopted by the Nation in 1883 and listed on a separate roll by the Dawes Commission. The 1983 constitution effectively disenfranchises them as members of the Nation. After the Civil War, freedmen and freedwomen intermarried with Choctaw citizens and produced mixed-blood descendents. Others of the Five Tribes, the Seminoles and the Cherokees, confronted or contemplated the prospect of extended litigation over freedmen's rights. Although Choctaw freedmen did not initiate any legal action, the rights of those individuals to participate in Choctaw identity and political process in contemporary Choctaw society potentially raises as many issues as did the status of white permit-holders in the nineteenth century.

Litigation remained a hallmark of the Choctaw Nation in the late twentieth and early twenty-first century. The Arkansas River bed was the point of contention. It was defined in treaties as the eastern boundary of the western lands of the Cherokee, Choctaw, and Chickasaw nations, but it was a movable boundary. Its vagaries and meanderings over time created extensive areas of dry land that vastly complicated the lines drawn in treaties. That land contained the economically important resources of natural gas deposits and potential valuable mineral deposits, which the state of Oklahoma considered its property. The use of the land by private land owners thus constituted mismanagement by the federal government of Indian lands. The Choctaws, Cherokees, and Chickasaws asserted their treaty rights to the lands when the Choctaw Nation initiated a suit against the Cherokee Nation to test tribal rights in 1969. In 1970, the U.S. Supreme Court ruled in favor of the Nation, thereby affirming the rights of the Choctaws, Chickasaws, and Cherokees to the riverbed but ruling that they had no claim for damages caused by the federal government's use of the river for navigation.3 The tribes took their case to the U.S. Court of Claims in 1987, where the case was still pending in 2002, when the Congress of the United States finally agreed to pay the Cherokee, Choctaw, and Chickasaw nations $40 million as a final settlement for their claims. The legislation forestalled the prospect of extended and expensive litigation.[4]

The Choctaw and Chickasaw nations also have water rights in the Kiamichi River basin in southeastern Oklahoma that are potentially very valuable for economic development. Those rights are based on the treaties of Doaks Stand and Dancing Rabbit Creek and are sustained by precedents in federal court decisions that when the federal government provided land to Indians, it assured that they would have water to make the land productive. In Oklahoma, state interest in regulating water set up a potential conflict situation when the North Texas Water Administration approached the Oklahoma Water Resources Board with an offer to buy water from the Kiamichi watershed. Rather than enter extended litigation to protect their rights, the Choctaw and Chickasaw nations negotiated a compact in 2001 with the state of Oklahoma to administer water. Although the state legislature refused to approve the proposed sale of water rights to north

Texas, the compact provides a basis for future management of water resources.[5]

In 2004, the Choctaw Nation was a highly visible political force in Oklahoma with its push for a state referendum that would legalize high-stakes gaming under the provisions of the Indian Gaming Regulatory Act of 1988. Tribal casinos would make it possible for the Nation to provide a wide range of social services to its citizens, and the negotiated agreement between the Nation and the state of Oklahoma would give the state a percentage of tribal gaming revenues. The referendum was part of a larger state initiative to promote a state lottery that would provide funding for public schools. Many non-Indian voters in the state, however, saw the issue as both a moral one against gambling and a statement that Indians should not have special privileges over other citizens of the state. The victory of the referendum gave the Choctaw Nation a new political status both at the federal level and in its relationship with the state of Oklahoma.

Over the 150 years from 1855 to 2005, the Choctaw Nation has changed and adapted. From a self-governing tribe that spoke its own language, pursued its own customs, and operated under its own constitution and laws to a virtually powerless entity maintained by the federal government to oversee the final disposition of land and resources to a modern Nation operating businesses and providing services to a geographically far-flung population, the Choctaw Tribe/Nation has been the source of identity for generations of Choctaws.

Choctaw identity is not a monolithic thing. It has different meanings for different people. It may be cultural (retention of language and customs or residence on Choctaw land) or political (based primarily on enrollment in the tribe based on biological descent) or some combination of the two. It may derive from family traditions and a sense of the history of the Nation. It may serve as justification for access to social services. If Choctaws derive some aspect of their identity from association with the tribe, the contemporary reality of the Choctaw Nation is in the collective identity of its citizens and in its unique relationship with the U.S. government based on its treaties. In the twenty-first century it is also based in its relationship to the government of the state of Oklahoma based on legal agreements and compacts. The Choctaw Nation has sustained its legal and political identity through defense of its treaty rights. The continuous nature of its relationship with the U.S. government, despite the attempt of the government to diminish or end it, was explicitly acknowledged in the legislation settling the Arkansas River bed claims. The Choctaw Nation has survived the vagaries of federal policy, and some of its members have preserved the language, customs, and land that were the core of its identity in 1855. Its adaptability has and will sustain it in the future.

NOTES

INTRODUCTION

1. Journal of the Mission at Mayhew, August 8, 1822, Series 18.3.2, Vol. 1, Folder 86, Papers of the American Board of Commissioners for Foreign Missions, Houghton Library, Harvard University (hereafter cited as ABCFM Papers).

2. *The Missionary Herald* 29, no. 1 (January 1823): 9–10. The American Board established its first mission in the Choctaw Nation in 1818.

3. American Board of Commissioners for Foreign Missions, *Report of the American Board of Commissioners for Foreign Missions, Compiled from Documents Laid before the Board, at the Seventeenth Annual Meeting, Which Was Held in Middletown (Conn.), Sept. 14 and 15, 1826* (Boston: Crocker and Brewster, 1826), Appendix IV. The Choctaw council referred to was held on August 5, 1826; see Kingsbury to the Office of the Board, Mayhew, January 28, 1829, Folder 35, ABCFM Papers.

4. Charles J. Kappler, *Indian Affairs: Laws and Treaties*, 5 vols. (Washington, D.C.: Government Printing Office, 1904–1941), 2:190–195.

5. Jill Nordgren, *The Cherokee Cases: Two Landmark Federal Decision in the Fight for Sovereignty* (Norman: University of Oklahoma Press, 2004).

6. Oklahoma Indian Affairs Commission, *Oklahoma Indian Nations Information Handbook* (Oklahoma City: Oklahoma Indian Affairs Commission, 2002), 13.

7. C. B. Clark, *Lone Wolf v. Hitchcock* (Lincoln: University of Nebraska Press, 1994).

8. In their work on Choctaw history in the colonial period, James Carson and Gregory O'Brien stress the ability of the Choctaws to negotiate with Europeans from a position of power. Donna Akers, whose book covers primarily the American period, argues for the recovery of a Choctaw voice that was suppressed but not destroyed by colonial contact. Michelene Pesantubbee, in her work on Choctaw women, asserts that the Choctaw view of women's roles were never recognized by Europeans who described Choctaw cultural practices. See James Taylor Carson, *Searching for the Bright Path: The Mississippi Choctaws from Prehistory to Removal* (Lincoln: University of Nebraska Press, 1999); Gregory O'Brien, *Choctaws in a Revolutionary Age, 1750–1830*

(Lincoln: University of Nebraska Press, 2002); Donna Akers, *Living in the Land of Death: The Choctaw Nation, 1830–1860* (East Lansing: Michigan State University Press, 2004); and Michelene E. Pesantubbee, *Choctaw Women in a Chaotic World: The Clash of Cultures in the Colonial Southeast* (Albuquerque: University of New Mexico, 2005).

9. Harvey Daniel Rosenthal, "Their Day in Court: A History of the Indian Claims Commission" (Ph.D. diss., Kent State University, 1976), 22–23.

CHAPTER 1

1. *Journal of Proceedings, Treaty of Dancing Rabbit Creek, Documents Concerning the Negotiation of Ratified Indian Treaties, 1801–1869*, Microfilm Series T494, Reel 2, National Archives and Records Administration, Washington, D.C. The Choctaws had previously ceded land through the treaties of Hopewell (1786), Fort Adams (1803), Hoe Buckintoopa (1803), Mount Dexter (1805), St. Stephens (1816), and Doaks Stand (1820); see Charles J. Kappler, *Indian Affairs: Laws and Treaties*, 5 vols. (Washington, D.C.: Government Printing Office, 1904–1941), 2:11–14, 56–58, 63–64, 69–70, 87–88, 137, and 191–195.

2. Cyrus Kingsbury to Jeremiah Evarts, Mayhew, May 13, 1829, Vol. 3, Folder 39, ABCFM Papers.

3. Fee simple is a legal concept embodying the idea of private property, but in this case the western land was owned communally by the Choctaw Nation. This tension between the idea of private property and the practice of holding property communally has continued throughout the Nation's history.

4. Richard White, *Roots of Dependency; Subsistence, Environment, and Social Change among the Choctaws, Pawnees and Navajos* (Lincoln: University of Nebraska Press, 1983), 96–146. White analyzes changes in Choctaw society from the perspective of world systems economic analysis. His account of social change in the Choctaw Nation in the early nineteenth century is a good overview of a crucial period in Choctaw history.

5. Thomas Jefferson to William Henry Harrison, February 27, 1803, in Thomas Jefferson, *The Writings of Thomas Jefferson*, edited by Andrew A. Lipscomb (Washington, D.C.: Thomas Jefferson Memorial Association of the United States, 1905), 10:369–371.

6. Kappler, *Indian Affairs: Laws and Treaties*, 2:311; John Stuart, *A Sketch of the Cherokee and Choctaw Indians* (Little Rock, Ark.: Woodruff and Pew, 1837), 26–27.

7. John Edwards, "The Choctaw Indians in the Middle of the Nineteenth Century," *Chronicles of Oklahoma* 10, no. 3 (1932): 404.

8. The 1834 constitution, the earliest such document known to have been executed in what is now Oklahoma, is unpublished; see Lester Hargrett, *A Bibliography of the Constitutions and Laws of the American Indians* (Cambridge: Harvard University Press, 1947), 56.

9. Arminta Scott Spalding, "Cyrus Kingsbury: Missionary to the Choctaws" (Ph.D. diss., University of Oklahoma, 1974).

10. W. David Baird, "Cyrus Byington and the Presbyterian Choctaw Mission," in *Churchmen and the Western Indians, 1820–1920*, edited by Clyde A. Milner II and Floyd A. O'Neil (Norman: University of Oklahoma Press, 1985), 22.

11. John Edwards, "What Hath God Wrought," 39–40, unpublished manuscript, Bancroft Library, University of California, Berkeley; American Board of Commissioners for Foreign Missions, *Report of the American Board of Commissioners for Foreign Missions, Presented at the Forty-fifth Annual Meeting, Held in Hartford, Connecticut, September 12–15, 1854* (Boston: T. R. Marvin, 1854), 163. The heads of the stations were Cyrus Byington (Stockbridge), Elias L. Boing (Yazoo Creek), John Edwards (Wheelock), Cyrus Kingsbury (Pine Ridge), Ebenezer Hotchkin (Good Water), Oliver P. Stark (Good Land), Abraham G. Lansing (Bennington), Charles C. Copeland (Mount Pleasant), and Simon L. Hobbs (Lenox). Pliny Fisk was the native preacher at the outstation at Mount Zion and Jonathan E. Dwight was the native preacher at Bok Chito.

12. Edwards, "The Choctaw Indians," 414.

13. Stuart, *A Sketch of the Cherokee and Choctaw Indians*, 30; Edwards, "The Choctaw Indians," 413; Ethan Allen Hitchcock, *A Traveler in Indian Territory: The Journal of Ethan Allen Hitchcock*, edited by Grant Foreman (1930; reprint, Norman: University of Oklahoma Press, 1996), 210–211; Henry C. Benson, *Life among the Choctaw Indians, and Sketches of the South-west* (Cincinnati, Ohio: Published by L. Swormstedt and A. Poe for the Methodist Episcopal Church, 1860; reprint, New York: Johnson Reprint Corporation, 1970), 33.

14. Balduin Möllhausen, *Diary of a Journey from the Mississippi to the Coasts of the Pacific with a United States Government Expedition* (London: Longman, Brown, Green, Longmans, & Roberts, 1858), 1:25; Grant Foreman, *Marcy and the Gold Seekers: The Journal of Captain R. B. Marcy, with an Account of the Gold Rush over the Southern Route* (Norman: University of Oklahoma Press, 1939), 193.

15. Möllhausen, *Diary of a Journey from the Mississippi to the Coasts of the Pacific*, 1:44.

16. Edwards, "The Choctaw Indians," 411.

17. Choctaw Nation, *Constitution and Laws of the Choctaw Nation: Together with the Treaties of 1855, 1865 and 1866* (New York: Wm. P. Lyon & Son, 1869), 70–71.

18. Grant Foreman, "The California Overland Mail Route through Oklahoma," *Chronicles of Oklahoma* 9, no. 3 (September 1931): 306.

19. U.S. Department of the Interior, Office of Indian Affairs, *Annual Report of the Commissioner of Indian Affairs to the Secretary of the Interior for the Year 1855* (Washington, D.C.: A. O. P. Nicholson, 1856), 157–159; American Board of Commissioners for Foreign Missions, *Report of the American Board of Commissioners for Foreign Missions, Presented at the Forty-eighth Annual Meeting, Held in Providence, Rhode Island, September 8–11, 1857* (Boston: T. R. Marvin & Son, 1857), 147.

20. Benson, *Life among the Choctaw Indians*, 97.

21. Arthur H. De Rosier, Jr., "Pioneers with Conflicting Ideals: Christianity and Slavery in the Choctaw Nation," *Journal of Mississippi History* 21, no. 3 (July 1959): 174–189.

22. John E. Semmes, *John H. B. Latrobe and His Times, 1803–1891* (Baltimore, Md.: Norman, Remington Co., 1917), 532.

23. Stuart, *A Sketch of the Cherokee and Choctaw Indians,* 30.

24. Horatio Cushman, son of Calvin Cushman, a missionary of the American Board of Commissioner for Foreign Missions, grew up among the Choctaws and gives probably the most comprehensive account of the genealogy of these families, although his account is not completely reliable. See H. B. Cushman, *History of the Choctaw, Chickasaw, and Natchez Indians* (1899; reprint, Norman: University of Oklahoma Press, 1999), 102, 235–238, 262–264, 328, 330–331.

25. Kappler, *Indian Affairs: Laws and Treaties,* 2:486–488.

26. John R. Swanton, *Source Material for the Social and Ceremonial Life of the Choctaw Indians,* Smithsonian Institution Bureau of American Ethnology Bulletin 103 (Washington, D.C.: Smithsonian Institution, 1932), 12–13.

27. Chickasaw treaties were the Treaty of Hopewell (1786), Treaty of Chickasaw Bluffs (1801), Treaty at the Chickasaw Council House (1816), Treaty near Old Town (1818), and the Treaty of Franklin (1830); see Kappler, *Indian Affairs: Laws and Treaties,* 2:14–16, 55–60, 135–137, 174–177, 1035–1040.

28. Choctaw Nation, *Constitution and Laws of the Choctaw Nation* (Park Hill, Cherokee Nation: John Candy, 1840).

29. Charles Lanman, "Peter Pitchlynn, Chief of the Choctaws," *Atlantic Monthly,* April 1870, 491.

30. Choctaw Nation, *Constitution and Laws of the Choctaw Nation: Together with the Treaties of 1837, 1855, 1865, and 1866* (Dallas, Tex.: John F. Worley, 1894; reprint, Wilmington, Del.: Scholarly Resources, Inc., 1973), 78–79. The new constitution was ratified on November 10, 1842.

31. "An Act of the Choctaw General Council," November 29, 1842, Folder 1, #5, Cyrus Kingsbury Collection, Western History Collections, University of Oklahoma, Norman, Oklahoma (hereafter Kingsbury Collection).

32. Ibid.

33. Israel Folsom to Peter Pitchlynn, n.d., Box 1, Folder 76, Peter Perkins Pitchlynn Collection, Western History Collections, University of Oklahoma, Norman, Oklahoma (hereafter Pitchlynn Collection).

34. Folder 1, #5, Kingsbury Collection; W. David Baird, *Peter Pitchlynn: Chief of the Choctaws* (Norman: University of Oklahoma Press, 1972), 25.

35. The fact that the Choctaws and the other four southeastern tribes that had been moved west had title in fee simple is a significant distinction between them and Indians who ceded their lands to the U.S. government and lived in areas reserved by the government for their special use.

36. Foreman, *Marcy and the Gold Seekers,* 193.

37. See, for example, *Chahta yakni ikastitushvn micha I nan vlhpisa Tokosowil ak o atobe* [Doaksville, 1852] and *Chahta okla i nanalhpisa nanapisa affami 1876 micha 1877, Aiena nanalhpisa tok oke* (Atoka, Chahta yakni: W. J. Hemby, holisso ai ikbe, [1878]). They also published "a respectable paper" in Choctaw and English at Doaksville; see Foreman, *Marcy and the Gold Seekers,* 193.

38. Virginia R. Allen, "Medical Practices and Health in the Choctaw Nation," *Chronicles of Oklahoma* 48 (Spring 1970): 69; Foreman, *Marcy and the Gold Seekers*, 193.

39. "An Act Allowing the Choctaws to Intermarry Without Any Regard to Distinction as to Iksa," approved October 6, 1836, in Choctaw Nation, *Constitution and Laws of the Choctaw Nation: Together with the Treaties of 1855, 1865 and 1866* (New York: Wm. P. Lyon & Son, Printers and Publishers, 1869), 71.

40. Choctaw Nation, *Constitution and Laws of the Choctaw Nation* (Park Hill: Cherokee Nation, John Candy, Printer, 1840), 22.

41. Edwards, "The Choctaw Indians," 410.

42. Möllhausen, *Diary of a Journey from the Mississippi to the Coasts of the Pacific*, 1:25, 36–38.

43. Ibid., 36–38; Benson, *Life among the Choctaw Indians*, 43.

44. Cushman, *History of the Choctaw, Chickasaw, and Natchez Indians*, 167–169.

45. Edwards, "The Choctaw Indians," 418–419.

46. Möllhausen, *Diary of a Journey from the Mississippi to the Coasts of the Pacific*, 1:47–48; George Catlin, *Letters and Notes on the Manners, Customs, and Condition of the North American Indians . . . Written during Eight Years' Travel amongst the Wildest Tribes of Indians in North America. In 1832, 33, 34, 35, 36, 37, 38, and 39*, 2 vols. (London: Tosswill and Myers, 1841; reprint, Mineola, N.Y.: Dover Publications, 1973), 2:123–126.

47. Benson, *Life among the Choctaw Indians*, 51, 47.

48. Edwards, "The Choctaw Indians," 397–398.

49. Choctaw Nation, *Constitution and Laws of the Choctaw Nation . . . 1866* (1894), 151.

50. Edwards, "The Choctaw Indians," 399, 403. The Sixtowns people had always been recognized by other Choctaws as having their own distinctive culture and were considered the most culturally conservative group in the Nation.

51. Ibid., 408–409; Stuart, *A Sketch of the Cherokee and Choctaw Indians*, 30.

52. Allen, "Medical Practices and Health in the Choctaw Nation," 65, 72.

53. Edwards, "The Choctaw Indians," 415–416.

54. "An Act Making the Killing a Person for a Witch a Capital Offence," approved November 6, 1834, in *Constitution and Laws . . . 1866* (1869), 69; Edwards, "What Hath God Wrought," 42.

55. American Board of Commissioners for Foreign Missions, *Report of the American Board of Commissioners for Foreign Missions . . . 1857*, 167.

56. Edwards, "What Hath God Wrought," 42.

57. Benson, *Life among the Choctaw Indians*, 28; Rufus Anderson, *Memorial Volume of the First Fifty Years of the American Board of Commissioners for Foreign Missions*, 5th ed. (Boston: Published by the Board, 1862), 259.

CHAPTER 2

1. *Papers Relating to the Claims of the Choctaw Nation against the United States arising under the Treaty of 1830* (Washington, D.C.: A. O. P. Nicholson, 1855), 16.

2. Charles J. Kappler, *Indian Affairs: Laws and Treaties*, 5 vols. (Washington, D.C.: Government Printing Office, 1904–1941), 2:314.

3. Peter was the son of John Pitchlynn, an Englishman who became the interpreter for the Nation in the early 1800s and who married Sophia Folsom, daughter of Nathaniel Folsom, a white trader who married two Choctaw women and became the progenitor of a large mixed-blood family. The younger Pitchlynn, after a brief stint at the University of Nashville, a stay at the Choctaw Academy in Kentucky, and an unsuccessful quest for financial success in American society, returned to the Choctaw Nation and gave up his political career. When Forbis LeFlore and Thompson McKenney negotiated the payment to the tribe in 1852 and received 5 percent of the award for their services, Pitchlynn saw the prospect of getting in on a monetary windfall by reviving claims for other sums of money. See W. David Baird, *Peter Pitchlynn: Chief of the Choctaws* (Norman: University of Oklahoma Press, 1972), 95–97. See Kappler, *Indian Affairs: Laws and Treaties*, 2:313.

4. The fourteenth article provided for individual land claims and the nineteenth article provided that Choctaws who cultivated land in Mississippi would be compensated after removal at the rate of 50 cents an acre; Kappler, *Indian Affairs: Laws and Treaties*, 2:313–315.

5. The Treaty of Dancing Rabbit Creek was signed on September 27, 1830, but was not ratified by the U.S. Senate until February 21, 1831, making the deadline for registration August 24, 1831. Ward's instructions to begin the registration did not reach him until June 1831, giving claimants less than two months to file their claims.

6. *Land Claims &c. under the 14th Article*, 24th Cong., 1st sess., May 11, 1836, H. Rep. 663, 18–20, 41–47; Kappler, *Indian Affairs: Laws and Treaties*, 2:310, 313; *The Choctaw Nation of Indians vs. the United States*, 21 Ct. Cl. 135.

7. *Land Claims &c. under the 14th Article*, 41–43; *Memorial of the Choctaw Indians of the State of Mississippi, to the Congress of the United States, by Andrew Hays, Agent*, 24th Cong., 1st sess., February 1, 1836, H. Doc. 119.

8. *Memorial of the Choctaw Indians of the State of Mississippi*, 3.

9. *Message from the President of the United States in Compliance with a Resolution of the Senate of the 13th October, 1837, in Relation to the Adjustment of Claims to Reservations under the 14th Article of the Treaty of 1830, with the Choctaw* Indians, 25th Cong., 2nd sess., December 19, 1837, S. Doc. 25, 4–5; *Indian Appropriation Act*, 5 Stat. 180 (March 3, 1837).

10. Mary Elizabeth Young, *Redskins, Ruffleshirts, and Rednecks: Indian Allotments in Alabama and Mississippi 1830–1860* (Norman: University of Oklahoma Press, 1961).

11. *Reservations of Land under Fourteenth Article of Treaty of 1830 with the Choctaw Indians*, 25th Cong., 3rd sess., February 22, 1839, H. Doc. 294, 2.

12. *In Relation to the Location of Reservations Under the Choctaw Treaty of the 27th of September, 1830*, 23rd Cong., 1st sess., April 11, 1834, Public Lands No. 1230, in *American State Papers: Documents, Legislative and Executive of the Congress of the United States*, series 2, *Indian Affairs* (Washington, D.C.: Gales and Seaton, 1832–1861), 2:1–3; *Claims to Reservations under the Treaty with the Choctaw Indians. An Act to Emend an Act*

Entitled "An Act for the Appointment of Commissioners to Adjust the Claims to Reserva-
tions of Land under the Fourteenth Article of the Treaty of Eighteen Hundred and Thirty,
with the Choctaw Indians," 5 Stat. 211 (February 22, 1838); *Pre-emption Rights to Settlers*
on the Public Lands. An Act Supplemental to the Act Entitled "An Act to Grant Pre-emption
Rights to the Settlers on the Public Lands," Approved June Twenty-second, Eighteen Hundred
and Thirty-eight," 5 Stat. 382 (June 1, 1840); *Claims under the Treaty of Dancing Rabbit*
Creek. An Act to Provide for the Satisfaction of Claims Arising under the Fourteenth and
Nineteenth Articles of the Treaty of Dancing Rabbit Creek, Concluded in September, One
Thousand Eight Hundred and Thirty, 5 Stat. 513, 517 (August 23, 1842).

13. T. Hartley Crawford to J. C. Spencer, Secretary of War, March 7, 1843, in *Message from the President of the United States Transmitting the Correspondence in Relation to the Proceedings and Conduct of the Choctaw Commission, under the Treaty of Dancing Rabbit Creek,* 28th Cong., 1st sess., S. Doc. 168, January 30, 1844, 6–7.

14. Baird, *Peter Pitchlynn,* 95.

15. "An Act Ratifying an Act of Congress of the United States, Appropriating Money to Pay Claimants, under the 14th Article of the Treaty of 1930," approved November 10, 1852, in *Acts and Resolutions of the General Council of the Choctaw Nation, from 1852 to 1857, Both Inclusive* (Fort Smith, Ark.: Josephus Dotson, Printer for the Nation, 1858), 38.

16. Kappler, *Indian Affairs: Laws and Treaties,* 652–653; *Papers Relating to the Claims of the Choctaw Nation,* 33–36.

17. Arrell M. Gibson, *The Chickasaws* (Norman: University of Oklahoma Press, 1971), 218–220.

18. Choctaw Nation, *Constitution and Laws of the Choctaw Nation: Together with the Treaties of 1855, 1865 and 1866* (New York: Wm. P. Lyon & Son, 1869), 123–125.

19. *Acts and Resolutions of the General Council of the Choctaw Nation . . . 1857,* 54–55.

20. Baird, *Peter Pitchlynn,* 97.

21. Walter Lee Brown, *A Life of Albert Pike* (Fayetteville: University of Arkansas Press, 1997), 300–305. On August 12, 1856, Harkins wrote to Peter Pitchlynn, "I concluded it was best for us to have an extra council and call on the government for the 250 thousand dollars—The longer government has Indian monies in her hands the more difficult it is to get at it. The council agreed to make an annuity of the 150 thousand, the 100 thousand to go to her attornies—also the 25 thousand of interest money if sent out to same. The Council showed every disposition to do Justice to her attornies." Harkins knew that Manypenny would block the payment if he knew that attorneys would be involved: "It is truly a hard case that we should have such a master as Manypenny is." Box 2, Folder 87, Pitchlynn Collection.

22. Copy of contract between John T. Cochrane and Peter Pitchlynn, Samuel Garland, Israel Folsom, and Dickson Lewis, February 13, 1855 (signed by Cochrane February 14, 1855), Folder 939, Peter Pitchlynn Papers, Gilcrease Museum, Tulsa, Oklahoma (hereafter Pitchlynn Papers); Baird, *Peter Pitchlynn,* 102–103.

23. Albert Pike, *Letter of Albert Pike to the Choctaw People* (Washington, D.C.: Cunningham & McIntosh, Printers, 1872), 72.

24. *Papers Respecting the Rights and Interests of the Choctaw Nation, and Their Relations with the United States, the Chickasaws and Other Indian Tribes* (Washington, D.C.: Geo. S. Gideon, 1855), 5.

25. Ibid., 11–12.

26. P. P. Pitchlynn, Israel Folsom, Samuel Garland, and Dickson W. Lewis to Hon. G. W. Manypenny, Washington City, April 5, 1854; R. McClelland to Commissioner of Indian Affairs, April 15, 1854; Geo. W. Manypenny to Douglas H. Cooper, April 20, 1854, all in *Papers Respecting the Rights and Interests of the Choctaw Nation*, 13–17, 18.

27. Geo. W. Manypenny to Douglas H. Cooper, May 1, 1954, in *Papers Respecting the Rights and Interests of the Choctaw Nation*, 18.

28. George McClelland to Charles Mix, June 20, 1854, in *Papers Respecting the Rights and Interests of the Choctaw Nation*, 37.

2. Asa Whitney, *A Project for a Railroad to the Pacific* (New York: George W. Wood, 1849), 13.

30. Frank H. Hodder, "The Genesis of the Kansas-Nebraska Act," in *Proceedings of the State Historical Society of Wisconsin for 1912* (Madison: State Historical Society of Wisconsin, 1913), 70–71.

31. *An Act Making Appropriations for the Support of the Army, for the Year Ending the Thirtieth of June, in the Year Eighteen Hundred and Fifty-four*, 10 Stat. 219 (March 3, 1853).

32. Amiel Weeks Whipple, Thomas Ewbank, and Prof. Wm. W. Turner, *Report upon the Indian Tribes: Explorations and Surveys for a Railroad Route from the Mississippi River to the Pacific Ocean* (Washington, D.C.: n.p., 1854).

33. *Congressional Globe*, 32nd Cong., 2nd sess., February 10, 1853, 560.

34. Hodder, "The Genesis of the Kansas-Nebraska Act," 78, 82; *An Act Making Appropriations for the Support of the Army, for the Year Ending the Thirtieth of June, in the Year Eighteen Hundred and Fifty-four*, 238–239.

35. H. Craig Miner and William E. Unrau, *The End of Indian Kansas: A Study of Cultural Revolution, 1854–1871* (Lawrence: Regents Press of Kansas, 1978).

36. P. P. Pitchlynn, Israel Folsom, Saml. Garland, and Dickson W. Lewis to Genl. D. H. Cooper, Washington City, April 10, 1855, Microfilm Series M234, Reel 174, Frames 49–51, Record Group 75, Records of the Bureau of Indian Affairs, Microfilm Series M234, Register of Letters Received by the Office of Indian Affairs, 1824–1880, National Archives and Records Administration, Washington, D.C. (hereafter Office of Indian Affairs, Letters Received).

37. P. P. Pitchlynn, Samuel Garland, and Dickson W. Lewis to Charles C. Mix, July 11, 1854, in *Papers Respecting the Rights and Interests of the Choctaw Nation*, 41.

38. D. H. Cooper to Gentlemen (Pitchlynn, Garland, Dixon Lewis), Choctaw Agency, January 21, 1852, Box 2, Folder 27, Pitchlynn Collection. The letter is marked "Private and Confidential."

39. P. P. Pitchlynn, Samuel Folsom, Samuel Garland, and Dickson Lewis to Geo. W. Manypenny, June 14, 1855, in *Papers Respecting the Rights and Interests of the Choctaw Nation*, 74–83.

40. P. P. Pitchlynn, Samuel Folsom, Samuel Garland, and Dickson W. Lewis to General D. H. Cooper, Washington, April 24, 1855, Reel 174, Frames 65–71, Office of Indian Affairs, Letters Received.

41. R. McClelland to Charles E. Mix, Acting Commissioner of Indian Affairs, June 20, 1854, in *Papers Respecting the Rights and Interests of the Choctaw Nation*, 37.

42. P. P. Pitchlynn, Samuel Garland, and Dickson W. Lewis to Charles C. Mix, July 11, 1854, in *Papers Respecting the Rights and Interests of the Choctaw Nation*, 37–42.

43. Gibson, *The Chickasaws*, 219.

44. Kappler, *Indian Affairs: Laws and Treaties*, 2:706.

45. Baird, *Peter Pitchlynn*, 105–106; Douglas Cooper to Charles E. Mix, Acting Commissioner of Indian Affairs, Fort Towson, August 10, 1855, Reel 174, Office of Indian Affairs, Letters Received.

46. Kappler, *Indian Affairs: Laws and Treaties*, 2:706–707.

47. Ibid., 706.

48. Ibid., 707–709.

49. Ibid., 710.

50. Francis Paul Prucha, *The Great Father: The United States Government and American Indians*, 2 vols. (Lincoln: University of Nebraska Press, 1984). The Indian Trade and Intercourse Acts, which were passed between 1790 and 1834, defined the Indian policy of the United States. They regulated the activities of U.S. traders and established principles of jurisdiction for the punishment of crimes.

51. Baird, *Peter Pitchlynn*, 53; John Bartlett Meserve, "Chief George Hudson and Chief Samuel Garland," *Chronicles of Oklahoma* 20, no. 1 (March 1942): 14.

52. Kappler, *Indian Affairs: Laws and Treaties*, 2:710.

53. Ibid., 212.

54. Charles Mix, Department of the Interior, Office of Indian Affairs, to A. H. Jones and H. M. C. Brown, January 8, 1858, Folder 1451, Pitchlynn Papers.

55. For quotations from communication from Choctaw delegates of May 15, 1854, see ibid.

56. Tandy Walker, Choctaw Agency, to Peter Pitchlynn, Washington City, February 15, 1858, Folder 1479, Pitchlynn Papers.

57. A. H. Jones, Fort Smith, to Col. Peter Pitchlynn, June 5, 1858, Folder 1553, Pitchlynn Papers; Charles E. Mix to Majors A. H. Jones and H. W. C. Brown, January 8, 1858 (Frames 237–241) and Brown and Jones to Chas. E. Mix, Fort Smith, January 21, 1858 (Frames 246–249), both in Reel 175, Office of Indian Affairs, Letters Received.

58. Israel Folsom to the Choctaw Council, Cottage Hill, C.N., October 14, 1867, Reel 177, Frames 19–22, Office of Indian Affairs, Letters Received.

CHAPTER 3

1. The incident was not immediately reported to the American Board of Commissioners for Foreign Missions and it did not reach public attention until a year later; see William G. McLoughlin, "The Choctaw Slave Burning: A Crisis in Mission

Work among the Indians," *Journal of the West* 13, no. 1 (1974): 113–125; Charles K. Whipple, *The Relation of the A.B.C.F.M. to Slavery* (Boston: R. F. Wallcut, 1871).

2. Rufus Anderson, *Memorial Volume of the First Fifty Years of the American Board of Commissioners for Foreign Missions*, 5th ed. (Boston: Published by the Board, 1862), 259.

3. Stanley Elkins, *Slavery: A Problem in American Institutional and Intellectual Life*, 2nd ed. (Chicago: The University of Chicago Press, 1968), 61.

4. Cyrus Kingsbury to David Greene, May 31, 1845, Box 3, Folder 9, #4, Kingsbury Collection.

5. Arthur H. DeRosier, Jr., "Pioneers with Conflicting Ideals: Christianity and Slavery in the Choctaw Nation," *Journal of Mississippi History* 21, no. 3 (July 1959): 174–189.

6. George Harkins to Peter Pitchlynn, August 12, 1856, Box 2, Folder 87, Pitchlynn Collection.

7. Kingsbury to Greene, May 31, 1845.

8. Ibid.

9. Choctaw Nation, *Constitution and Laws of the Choctaw Nation* (Park Hill, Cherokee Nation: John Candy, 1840), 11, 19.

10. Cyrus Kingsbury, Pine Ridge, C.N., to David Greene, Mission House, Boston, November 22, 1839, Box 1, Folder 2, #1, Kingsbury Collection.

11. The issue of slavery caused deep divisions within the Presbyterian Church, which split into two factions in 1837–1838; see George M. Marsden, *The Evangelical Mind and the New School Presbyterian Experience: A Case Study of Thought and Theology in Nineteenth-Century America* (New Haven, Conn.: Yale University Press, 1970).

12. C. Kingsbury, Alfred Wright, Cyrus Byington, E. Hotchkins, C. C. Copeland, David Breed, H. H. Copeland, and D. H. Winship to the Prudential Committee, Norwalk, C.N., March 31, 1848, Box 3, Folder 8, #53, Kingsbury Collection.

13. American Board of Commissioners for Foreign Missions, *Report of the Committee on Anti-Slavery Memorials, September, 1845, with a Historical Statement of Previous Proceedings* (Boston: T. R. Marvin, 1845), 4–5; American Board of Commissioners for Foreign Missions, *Report of the American Board of Commissioners for Foreign Missions, Presented at the Forty-fifth Annual Meeting, Held in Hartford, Connecticut, September 12–15, 1854* (Boston: T. R. Marvin, 1854), 165.

14. Cyrus Kingsbury, on Behalf of the Brethren of the Choctaw Mission, to S. B. Treat, Stockbridge, April 14, 1849, Box 2, Folder 5, #41, Kingsbury Collection. The Prudential Committee was the administrative branch of the American Board.

15. S. B. Treat to the Choctaw Mission, Missionary House, Boston, June 22, 1848, Folder 693, Pitchlynn Papers; American Board of Commissioners for Foreign Missions, *Report of the American Board of Commissioners for Foreign Missions. . . Thirty-ninth Annual Meeting*, 102–110.

16. American Board of Commissioners for Foreign Missions, *Report of the American Board of Commissioners for Foreign Missions, Presented at the Thirty-ninth Annual Meeting, Held in Boston, Massachusetts, Sept. 12–15, 1848* (Boston: T. R. Marvin, 1848), 80, 81–92.

17. Cyrus Kingsbury on behalf of the Brethren of the Choctaw Mission to S. B. Treat, Stockbridge, April 14, 1849, Box 2, Folder 5, #41, Kingsbury Collection.

18. Cyrus Kingsbury to David Green, December 27, 1844, Box 1, Folder 3, #3, Kingsbury Collection.

19. Cyrus Kingsbury to William Slocomb, August 8, 1848, Box 3, Folder 9, #7, Kingsbury Collection.

20. Israel Folsom to Cyrus Kingsbury, Fort Washita, May 1, 1848, Box 3, Folder 9, #6, Kingsbury Collection.

21. Cyrus Kingsbury to S. B. Treat, July 19, 1858; Kingsbury to Treat, October 18, 1858, Box 2, Folder 5, #25 and #26, respectively, Kingsbury Collection.

22. Cyrus Kingsbury and Cyrus Byington to Committee on Missions, December 14, 1853, Box 3, Folder 9, #12, Kingsbury Collection; Report of Committee in Case of Rev. William Hotchkins, October 11, 1853, signed by C. Kingsbury, Joseph Dukes, Abraham G. Lansing, J. Folsom, and N. Cochnauer, Box 3, Folder 9, #52, Kingsbury Collection.

23. Kingsbury to William Slocomb, August 8, 1848, Box 3, Folder 9, #7, Kingsbury Collection.

24. American Board of Commissioners for Foreign Missions, *Report of the American Board of Commissioners for Foreign Missions . . . Forty-fifth Annual Meeting*, 165.

25. Cyrus Kingsbury and Cyrus Byington to S. B. Treat, December 27, 1853, Box 2, Folder 5, #39, Kingsbury Collection.

26. Robert Jones to Peter Pitchlynn, July 21, 1854, Box 2, Folder 45, Pitchlynn Collection.

27. George W. Harkins to Peter Pitchlynn, October 19, 1855, Box 2, Folder 65, Pitchlynn Collection.

28. *Acts and Resolutions of the General Council of the Choctaw Nation, from 1852 to 1857, Both Inclusive* (Fort Smith, Ark.: Josephus Dotson, Printer for the Nation, 1858), 63; American Board of Commissioners for Foreign Missions, *Report of the American Board of Commissioners for Foreign Missions . . . Thirty-ninth Annual Meeting*, 165.

29. Cyrus Kingsbury to S. B. Treat, February 1, 1854; Kingsbury to Treat, February 21, 1854, Box 2, Folder 5, #37 and #38, respectively, Kingsbury Collection.

30. Cyrus Kingsbury to S. B. Treat, August 14, 1854, Box 2, Folder 5, #34, Kingsbury Collection.

31. George W. Wood, *Report of Mr. Wood's Visit to the Choctaw and Cherokee Missions, 1855* (Boston: T. R. Marvin, 1855), 4.

32. Treat to the Choctaw Mission, October 5, 1858, Folder 8, #56, Kingsbury Collection.

33. Wood, *Report of Mr. Wood's Visit*, 9–10.

34. Ibid., 10.

35. Ibid., 13.

36. Cyrus Kingsbury, Cyrus Byington, Ebenezer Hotchkin, and O. P. Stark to S. B. Treat, November 13, 1855, Box 2, Folder 5, #31, Kingsbury Collection.

37. American Board of Commissioners for Foreign Missions, *Report of the American Board of Commissioners for Foreign Missions, Presented at the Forty-seventh Annual Meeting, Held in Newark, New Jersey, October 28–31, 1856 with the Minutes of the Special Meeting Held at Albany, New York, March 4–6, 1856* (Boston: T. R. Marvin, 1856), 195.

38. Cyrus Kingsbury, Cyrus Byington, Ebenezer Hotchkin, and Oliver P. Stark, Bennington, to S. B. Treat, April 15, 1856, Box 2, Folder 5, #30, Kingsbury Collection.

39. Cyrus Kingsbury, Cyrus Byington, Ebenezer Hotchkin, Oliver P. Stark, C. C. Copeland, and John Edwards to S. B. Treat, Lenox, September 6, 1856, Box 2, Folder 5, #28, Kingsbury Collection.

40. S. B. Treat to the Choctaw Mission, Mission House, Boston, October 5, 1858, Box 1, Folder 8, #56, Kingsbury Collection.

41. Cyrus Kingsbury to S. B. Treat, Yakni Okchaya, December 24, 1858, Box 2, Folder 5, #23, Kingsbury Collection.

42. McLoughlin, "The Choctaw Slave Burning," 113–114.

43. Robert W. Nail, George Folsom, and Kennedy McCurtain, Choctaw Nation, to S. B. Treat, Mission House, Boston, December 6, 1858, Box 2, Folder 5, #24, Kingsbury Collection.

44. Joseph P. Folsom, Bennington, Blue County, to Rev. Selah B. Treat, April 7, 1859, Box 2, Folder 5, #17, Kingsbury Collection.

45. To the Choctaw Mission, from Missionary House, Boston, July 27, 1859, Box 1, Folder 1, #13, Kingsbury Collection.

46. Baird, "Cyrus Byington," 33.

47. *Missionary Herald* 44 (October 1848): 352–363.

48. William Slocomb, Marietta, to Cyrus Kingsbury, July 14, 1848; Kingsbury to William Slocomb, August 8, 1848; both in Box 3, Folder 9, #7, Kingsbury Collection.

CHAPTER 4

1. Sampson Folsom to Peter Pitchlynn, December 9, 1857, Box 3, Folder 2, Pitchlynn Collection.

2. John R. Swanton, *Source Material for the Social and Ceremonial Life of the Choctaw Indians*, Smithsonian Institution Bureau of American Ethnology Bulletin 103 (Washington, D.C.: Smithsonian Institution, 1932), 56.

3. Patricia Galloway, *Choctaw Genesis* (Lincoln: University of Nebraska Press, 1995); Swanton, *Source Material*; Charles J. Kappler, *Indian Affairs: Laws and Treaties*, 5 vols. (Washington, D.C.: Government Printing Office, 1904–1941), 2:57, 64, 70, 138, 194.

4. Angie Debo, *The Rise and Fall of the Choctaw Republic* (Norman: University of Oklahoma Press, 1934), 50–52.

5. David Folsom was the son of Nathaniel Folsom, a white North Carolina–born trader who had entered Choctaw Country in the late 1770s, and one of his two Choctaw wives; see H. B. Cushman, *History of the Choctaw, Chickasaw and Natchez Indians*, edited by Angie Debo (New York: Russell & Russell, 1962), 328.

6. Debo, *Rise and Fall*, 52–53.

7. The 1834 constitution was never published. Hargrett describes it as "the earliest constitutional instrument known to have been executed within the borders of the present state of Oklahoma"; Lester Hargrett, *A Bibliography of the Constitutions and Laws of the American Indians* (Cambridge: Harvard University Press, 1947), 55.

8. Cushman, *History of the Choctaw, Chickasaw and Natchez Indians* (1962), 88–89.

9. In 1832, the Chickasaws effectively sold their eastern territory to the United States for a cash payment with which they could buy a new homeland, but the land in the Indian Territory had all been assigned to other tribes. After searching unsuccessfully for a new territory, they finally negotiated an agreement in 1837 to lease the western lands of the Choctaw Nation for $530,000, $500,000 of which was to create a trust fund that would pay annual interest to the Choctaws. Kappler, *Indian Affairs: Laws and Treaties*, 2:486–487; Arrell M. Gibson, *The Chickasaws* (Norman: University of Oklahoma Press, 1971), 162.

10. Choctaw Nation, *Constitution and Laws of the Choctaw Nation* (Park Hill, Cherokee Nation: John Candy, 1840), 4.

11. Ibid., 7. Nunihwayah was about a mile and a half west of Tuskahoma; see Hargrett, *A Bibliography of the Constitutions and Laws of the American Indians*, 56.

12. Choctaw Nation, *The Constitution and Laws of the Choctaw Nation* (Park Hill, Cherokee Nation: Edwin Archer, 1847).

13. Sec. 15, in Choctaw Nation, *The Constitution and Laws of the Choctaw Nation* (Doaksville, 1852).

14. *Acts and Resolutions of the General Council of the Choctaw Nation at the Called Sessions Thereof, Held in April and June 1858, and the Regular Session Held in October, 1858* (Fort Smith, Ark.: Josephus Dotson, 1859), 55–56.

15. Douglas H. Cooper, Fort Towson, to Hon. Charles W. Dean, Superintendent of Indian Affairs, Fort Smith, August 28, 1855, in U.S. Department of the Interior, Office of Indian Affairs, *Annual Report of the Commissioner of Indian Affairs to the Secretary of the Interior for the Year 1855* (Washington, D.C.: A. O. P. Nicholson, 1856), 151–154.

16. T. J. Pitchlynn to Peter Pitchlynn, March 30, 1851, Box 2, Folder 19, Pitchlynn Collection.

17. Grant Foreman, "A Journal Kept by Douglas Cooper of an Expedition by a Company of Chickasaws in Quest of Comanche Indians," *Chronicles of Oklahoma* 5, no. 4 (December 1927): 383.

18. T. J. Pitchlynn to Peter Pitchlynn, March 30, 1851.

19. Leonidas Pitchlynn to Peter Pitchlynn, January 12, 1855, Box 2, Folder 59, Pitchlynn Collection.

20. *Acts and Resolutions of the General Council of the Choctaw Nation . . . 1858*, 102.

21. "An Act Regarding Persons Dying Intestate or Without a Will" (approved October 10, 1847); "An Act Regarding Appointment of Guardians for Orphans" (approved October 10, 1847); "An Act Allowing Guardians to Sell Property of the Wards" (approved October 12, 1848); "Probate Responsibility Resides with County Judges" (approved October 30, 1860), all in Choctaw Nation, *Constitution and Laws of the Choctaw Nation: Together with the Treaties of 1855, 1865 and 1866* (New York: Wm. P. Lyon & Son, 1869), 99, 94–95, 101, 280.

22. Tandy Walker to George Harkins, September 15, 1857, Box 1, Folder 1, Folder 9, Kingsbury Collection.

23. George Harkins to Peter Pitchlynn, Doaksville, February 10, 1860, Box 3, Folder 58, Pitchlynn Collection.

24. Israel Folsom to Peter Pitchlynn, March 19, 1860, Box 3, Folder 64, Pitchlynn Collection; Douglas Cooper to Commissioner of Indian Affairs Greenwood, April 2, 1860, Reel 176, Frames 82–83, Office of Indian Affairs, Letters Received; Basil LeFlore to General D. H. Cooper, Doaksville, March 28, 1860, Reel 176, Frames 84–85, Office of Indian Affairs, Letters Received; Tandy Walker to Peter Pitchlynn, Skullyville, March 18, 1860, Box 3, Folder 63, Pitchlynn Collection; Cooper to A. B. Greenwood, March 31, 1860, Reel 176, Frame 71, Office of Indian Affairs, Letters Received.

25. W. Dean to Manypenny, Fort Smith, January 5, 1857, Reel 175, Frame 48, Office of Indian Affairs, Letters Received.

26. Folsom to Pitchlynn, December 9, 1857.

27. Lycurgus Pitchlynn to Peter Pitchlynn, last day of winter [1858], Box 3, Folder 6, Pitchlynn Collection.

28. Lycurgus Pitchlynn to Peter Pitchlynn, March 22, 1858, Box 3, Folder 18, Pitchlynn Collection.

29. Cooper to Elias Rector, October 14, 1858, in U.S. Department of the Interior, Office of Indian Affairs, *Annual Report of the Commissioner of Indian Affairs to the Secretary of the Interior for the Year 1858* (Washington, D.C.: William A. Harris, 1858), 156.

30. Hargrett uses these terms with respect to the 1860 constitution; see *A Bibliography of the Constitutions and Laws of the American Indians*, 56.

31. George W. Harkins, Chief of Apuckshanubbee District, to Tandy Walker, August 14, 1857, Box 1, Folder 1, Folder 9, Kingsbury Collection.

32. George Harkins to Peter Pitchlynn, April 19, 1858, Box 3, Folder 21, Pitchlynn Collection.

33. Walker to Harkins, September 15, 1857.

34. Cyrus Kingsbury to S. B. Treat, Pine Ridge, March 1, 1858, Box 2, Folder 5, #27, Kingsbury Collection.

35. Joseph Dukes to Peter Pitchlynn, Norwalk, March 5, 1858, Box 3, Folder 16, Pitchlynn Collection.

36. Cyrus Kingsbury to S. B. Treat, March 1, 1858; Douglas Cooper, Skullyville, to Elias Rector, Fort Smith, September 15, 1857, in U.S. Department of the Interior, Office of Indian Affairs, *Annual Report of the Commissioner of Indian Affairs to the Secretary of the Interior for the Year 1856* (Washington, D.C.: A. O. P. Nicholson, 1857), 231.

37. Folsom to Pitchlynn, December 9, 1857.

38. Tandy Walker to Peter Pitchlynn, [March 1858], Box 3, Folder 19, Pitchlynn Collection.

39. George Harkins to Sampson Folsom, Doaksville, August 3, 1858, Reel 175, Office of Indian Affairs, Letters Received.

40. Sampson Folsom to Peter Pitchlynn, December 1, 1857, Box 3, Folder 1, Pitchlynn Collection.

41. Hargrett, *A Bibliography of the Constitutions and Laws of the American Indians*, 59–60; Peter Pitchlynn to Israel Folsom, Washington City, February 15, 1858, Box 3, Folder 14, Pitchlynn Collection.

42. Sampson Folsom to Peter Pitchlynn, December 1, 1857, Box 3, Folder 1, Pitchlynn Collection.

44. George W. Harkins to Peter Pitchlynn, November 15, 1857, Box 2, Folder 107, Pitchlynn Collection.

45. Douglas Cooper to Charles E. Mix, [Choctaw] Agency, August 13, 1858, Reel 175, Frame 314, Office of Indian Affairs, Letters Received.

46. Tandy Walker to Peter Pitchlynn, [March, 1858], Box 3, Folder 19, Pitchlynn Collection; Dukes to Pitchlynn, March 5, 1858; Lycurgus Pitchlynn to Peter Pitchlynn, March 22, 1858.

47. Cyrus Kingsbury to S. B. Treat, October 18, 1858, Box 2, Folder 5, #25, Kingsbury Collection.

48. Joseph Dukes to Peter Pitchlynn, May 21, 1858, Box 3, Folder 24, Pitchlynn Collection; Sampson Folsom to Peter Pitchlynn, May 19, 1858, Box 3, Folder 23, Pitchlynn Collection; Cyrus Kingsbury to S. B. Treat, May 31, 1858, Box 2, Folder 5, #49, Kingsbury Collection.

49. Harkins to Folsom, August 3, 1858.

50. Cyrus Kingsbury to S. B. Treat, July 19, 1858, Box 2, Folder 5, #26, Kingsbury Collection; Peter Pitchlynn and Peter Folsom to Charles E. Mix, Washington, September 3, 1858, Reel 175, Frames 296–302, Office of Indian Affairs, Letters Received.

51. Folsom to Pitchlynn, December 9, 1857.

52. George Hudson to Peter Pitchlynn, Eagle Co., February 23, 1858, Box 3, Folder 15, Pitchlynn Collection.

53. Lycurgus Pitchlynn to Peter Pitchlynn, last day of March 1858, Box 3, Folder 20, Pitchlynn Collection.

54. Dukes to Pitchlynn, March 5, 1858.

55. Cooper to Charles E. Mix, Scullyville, August 13, 1858, Reel 175, Frame 314, Office of Indian Affairs, Letters Received.

56. Acts and Resolutions of the General Council of the Choctaw Nation . . . 1858, 33.

57. Pitchlynn to Mix, September 3, 1858.

58. Elias Rector, Superintendent of Indian Affairs, Southern Superintendency, to Charles E. Mix, October 22, 1858, Roll 175, Frames 337–343, Office of Indian Affairs, Letters Received.

59. Elias Rector to Charles E. Mix, October 26, 1858, in Report of the Commissioner of Indian Affairs . . . 1858, 130.

60. Acts and Resolutions of the General Council of the Choctaw Nation, for the Year 1859 (Fort Smith, Ark.: Printed at the Times Office for Campbell LeFlore, 1860), 45.

61. Ibid., 62.

62. Tandy Walker, Acting Governor of the Choctaw Nation, to General Douglas H. Cooper, Boggy Depot, October 27, 1858, Reel 175, Frames 351–352, Office of Indian Affairs, Letters Received.

63. Acts and Resolutions of the General Council of the Choctaw Nation . . . 1859, 63–64.

64. Folsom to Peter Pitchlynn, May 19, 1858.

65. Rector to Mix, October 22, 1858.

66. Kingsbury to Treat, March 1, 1858.

67. Lycurgus Pitchlynn to Peter Pitchlynn, June 2, 1858, Box 3, Folder 26, Pitchlynn Collection.

69. *Acts and Resolutions of the General Council of the Choctaw Nation . . . 1859*, 45.

CHAPTER 5

1. William H. Seward, "Speech at Chicago, October 3, 1860," in *Senator Seward's Western Tour* (n.p., [1860]), available at Newberry Library, Chicago, Illinois.

2. Charles J. Kappler, *Indian Affairs: Laws and Treaties*, 5 vols. (Washington, D.C.: Government Printing Office, 1904–1941), 2:710.

3. Tandy Walker to George Harkins, September 15, 1857, Box 1, Folder 1, #9, Kingsbury Collection.

4. Lary C. Rampp and Donald L. Rampp, *The Civil War in the Indian Territory* (Austin, Tex.: Presidial Press, 1975), 3–5.

5. Ibid., 3.

6. *An Act Making Appropriations for the Current and Contingent Expenses of the Indian Department and for Carrying Out Treaty Stipulations with Various Indian Tribes for the Year Ending June Thirtieth, 1863*, 12 Stat. 528 (July 5, 1862).

7. Peter Pitchlynn, undated speech, Folder 1899, Pitchlynn Papers.

8. Peter Folsom to Peter Pitchlynn, January 19, 1861, Box 3, Folder 93, Pitchlynn Collection.

9. Rampp and Rampp, *The Civil War in the Indian Territory*, 29.

10. Abel disputes the idea that Indians harbored memories of southern injustice, maintaining that "strangely enough none of the tribes seems to have charged the gross injustice of the thirties exclusively to the account of the South. On the contrary, they one and all charged it against the federal government"; see Annie Heloise Abel, *The American Indian as Slaveholder and Secessionist; an Omitted Chapter in the Diplomatic History of the Southern Confederacy* (Cleveland, Ohio: Arthur H. Clark Company, 1915), 72.

11. U.S. Department of the Interior, Office of Indian Affairs, *Annual Report of the Commissioner of Indian Affairs to the Secretary of the Interior for the Year 1861* (Washington, D.C.: Government Printing Office, 1861), 3–4.

12. Walter Lee Brown, *A Life of Albert Pike* (Fayetteville: University of Arkansas Press, 1997), 353.

13. Albert Pike, *Message of the President, and Report of Albert Pike, Commissioner of the Confederate States to the Indian Nations West of Arkansas, of the Results of His Mission* (Richmond, [Va.]: Enquirer Book and Job Press, Tyler, Wise, Allegre & Smith, 1861), 33.

14. Cooper owned a plantation, Mon Clova, and about 100 slaves in Wilkinson County, Mississippi; see Muriel H. Wright, "General Douglas H. Cooper, C.S.A.," *Chronicles of Oklahoma* 32, no. 2 (Summer 1954): 144–145; and U.S. Department of the Interior, Office of Indian Affairs, *Annual Report of the Commissioner of Indian Affairs to the Secretary of the Interior for the Year 1855* (Washington, D.C.: A. O. P. Nicholson, 1856), 148.

15. L. P. Walker, Secretary of War, to Major Douglas H. Cooper, Choctaw Nation, War Department, C. S. Army, Montgomery, May 13, 1861, in Robert N. Scott, H. M. Lazelle, George B. Davis, Leslie J. Perry, Joseph W. Kirkley, Fred C. Ainsworth, John S. Moodey, and Calvin D. Cowles, *The War of the Rebellion: A Compilation of the Official Records of the Union and Confederate Armies* (Washington, D.C.: Government Printing Office, 1880–1901), series 1, vol. 3, 574–575 (hereafter cited as *War of the Rebellion*).

16. For Cooper's commission to raise a regiment, see L. P. Walker to Douglas Cooper, May 13, 1861, in *War of the Rebellion*, series 1, vol. 3, 574–575; Abel, *American Indian as Slaveholder and Secessionist*, 207.

17. Abel, *American Indian as Slaveholder and Secessionist*, 211.

18. Pike, *Message of the President, and Report of Albert Pike*, 12.

19. Cyrus Kingsbury to S. B. Treat, October 18, 1858, Box 2, Folder 5, #25, Kingsbury Collection; George Harkins to Peter Pitchlynn, Doaksville, February 10, 1860, Box 3, Folder 58, Pitchlynn Collection.

20. Brown, *A Life of Albert Pike*, 359.

21. "Articles of Confederation Entered into by the Creeks, Choctaws, Chickasaws, and Seminoles at North Fork, 1861 (July 1, 1861)," Folder 1904, Pitchlynn Papers.

22. Article XLIV, Treaty with the Choctaw and Chickasaw, July 12, 1861, in Vine Deloria, Jr., and Raymond Demallie, *Documents of American Indian Diplomacy* (Norman: University of Oklahoma Press, 1999), 1:612.

23. Ibid., 603–618; Brown, *A Life of Albert Pike*, 359, 362–663.

24. Rampp and Rampp, *The Civil War in the Indian Territory*, 7–8; *Congressional Globe*, 37th Cong., 2nd sess., February 14, 1862, 815.

25. Jno. Withers, Assistant Adjutant-General Richmond, Virginia, November 22, 1861, Special Orders, No. 234, in *War of the Rebellion*, series 1, vol. 8, 690; Albert Pike to Hon. R. W. Johnson, Little Rock, May 11, 1861, in *War of the Rebellion*, series 1, vol. 3, 572–574.

26. General Orders No. 1., Hdqrs. Trans-Miss. Dist. Dept. No. 2, Little Rock, Ark., January 29, 1862, in *War of the Rebellion*, series 1, vol. 8, 745–746.

27. Brown, *A Life of Albert Pike*, 384.

28. Report of Col. John B. Clark, Jr., Commanding, Third Division, Missouri State Guard, Camp Near White River, Ark., March 11, 1862, in *War of the Rebellion*, series 1, vol. 8, 318–320; Samuel R. Curtis to Captain, Cross Timber, Ark., April 1, 1862, in *War of the Rebellion*, series 1, vol. 8, 115–204; Annie Heloise Abel, *The American Indian as Participant in the Civil War* (Cleveland, Ohio: Arthur H. Clark Company, 1919), 26–29.

29. Report of Brig. Gen. Albert Pike, C.S. Army, Commanding, Department of Indian Territory, Dwight Mission, Cherokee Nation, Ind. T., March 14, 1862, in *War of the Rebellion*, series 1, vol. 8, 286–292; Abel, *American Indian as Participant*, 28–29.

30. Report of Brig. Gen. Albert Pike, 289; Abel, *American Indian as Participant*, 32–33.

31. Rampp and Rampp, *The Civil War in the Indian Territory*, 9.

32. Albert Pike to Sir, Fort McCulloch, May 4, 1862, in *War of the Rebellion*, series 1, vol. 13, 822.

33. Sampson Folsom to Peter Pitchlynn, June 19, 1862, Box 3, Folder 103, Pitchlynn Collection.

34. Brown, *A Life of Albert Pike*, 396–419; Abel, *American Indian as Participant*, 31, 191.

35. Albert Pike to [Unknown], Hdqrs. Department of Indian Territory, Fort McCulloch, May 4, 1862, in *War of the Rebellion*, series 1, vol. 13, 819–823; Brown, *A Life of Albert Pike*, 403–404.

36. Brown, *A Life of Albert Pike*, 407–408; Albert Pike to Major-General Hindman, Commanding Trans-Mississippi District, Headquarters, Department of Indian Territory, Fort McCulloch, Indian Territory, July 15, 1862, in *War of the Rebellion*, series 1, vol. 13, 857–858.

37. Brown, *A Life of Albert Pike*, 408–409; Abel, *American Indian as Participant*, 159; Albert Pike to President Davis, Fort Washita, Indian Territory, July 21, 1862, in *War of the Rebellion*, series 1, vol. 8, 869–871; Albert Pike to the Chiefs and People of the Cherokees, Creeks, Seminoles, Chickasaws, and Choctaws, July 31, 1862, in *War of the Rebellion*, series 1, vol. 12, 869–871.

38. Douglas H. Cooper, Colonel, Commanding, to Major General T. C. Hindman, Headquarters of Indian Department, Cantonment Davis, August 7, 1862, in *War of the Rebellion*, series 1, vol. 13, 977.

39. Albert Pike to Peter Pitchlynn, Washington, Arkansas, May 13, 1864, Box 4, Folder 10, Pitchlynn Collection.

40. Report of Colonel Douglas H. Cooper, C. S. Army, Commanding Division, Headquarters Field Division, Camp Coffee, Missouri, October 2, 1862, in *War of the Rebellion*, series 1, vol. 13, 297–298; Abel, *American Indian as Participant*, 194–195.

41. Abel, *American Indian as Participant*, 197–198; Reports of Brigadier General Douglas H. Cooper, C. S. Army, Commanding Brigade, including Operations since September 30, Headquarters, First Brigade, Cantonment Davis, Cherokee Nation, October 25, 1862, in *War of the Rebellion*, series 1, vol. 13, 331–332.

42. Brown, *A Life of Albert Pike*, 411.

43. Albert Pike to Lieut. Col. S. S. Anderson, Headquarters Department of Indian Territory, Fort Washita, Ind. Ter., October 26, 1862, in *War of the Rebellion*, series 1, vol. 13, 903–905.

44. Brown, *A Life of Albert Pike*, 410–411.

45. Abel, *American Indian as Participant*, 218.

46. Ibid., 337–351, quote on 351.

47. Maxey, Headquarters District of Indian Territory in the Field, C. N. June 25, 1864, in *War of the Rebellion*, series 1, vol. 34, part 4, 694–695.

48. Abel, *American Indian as Participant*, 265.

49. Peter Pitchlynn to Sam[pson Folsom], November 20, 1863, Box 4, Folder 5, Pitchlynn Collection.

50. Rampp and Rampp, *The Civil War in the Indian Territory*, 19.

51. Report of John A. Foreman, Third Indian Home Guards, Fort Blunt, July 5, 1863, in *War of the Rebellion,* series 1, vol. 22, 382; Abel, *American Indian as Participant,* 285–286.

52. Rampp and Rampp, *The Civil War in the Indian Territory*, 21–23.

53. Ibid., 23; Abel, *American Indian as Participant,* 290.

54. Abel, *American Indian as Participant,* 290.

55. Rampp and Rampp, *The Civil War in the Indian Territory*, 71–72.

56. Abel, *Indian as Participant,* 328.

57. Rampp and Rampp, *The Civil War in the Indian Territory*, 71–72; Abel, *American Indian as Participant,* 326.

58. Rampp and Rampp, *The Civil War in the Indian Territory*, 110–114; Abel, *American Indian as Participant,* 332–333.

59. Special Orders, No. 45, Headquarters, Trans-Mississippi Department, February 21, 1865, in *War of the Rebellion,* series 1, vol. 48, part 1, 1396.

60. Stand Watie, Principal Chief of the Cherokees, to His Excellency the Governor of the Choctaw and Chickasaw Nations, Executive Office, Cherokee Nation, August 9, 1863, in *War of the Rebellion,* series 1, vol. 22, part 2, 1106–1107; Reports of Colonel William A. Phillips, Third Indian Home Guard, Commanding Indian Brigade, Little Rivertown, Near Old Fort Arbuckle, Creek Nation, February 16, 1864, in *War of the Rebellion,* series 1, vol. 34, part 1, 106–108.

61. Brad R. Clampitt, "'An Indian Shall Not Spill an Indian's Blood': The Confederate-Indian Conference at Camp Mapoleon, 1865," *Chronicles of Oklahoma* 83, no. 1 (Spring 2005): 34–53; "Compact Made and Entered into between the Confederate Indian Tribes and the Prairie Tribe of Indians, Made at Camp Napoleon on Washita River, May 26, 1865," Folder 2051, Pitchlynn Papers.

62. Annie Heloise Abel, *The American Indian under Reconstruction* (Cleveland, Ohio: Arthur H. Clark Company, 1925), 154–155.

63. Compact Made and Entered into between the Confederate Indian Tribes and the Prairie Tribes of Indians, Made at Camp Napoleon on Washita River, May 26, 1865, in *War of the Rebellion,* series 1, vol. 48, part 2, 1103–1104.

64. James Veatch to Brevet Lieutenant Colonel J. Schuyler Crosby, Headquarters Northern Division of Louisiana, Shreveport, Louisiana, July 20, 1865, in *War of the Rebellion,* series 1, vol. 48, part 2, 195–197.

65. William T. Stephens to Peter Pitchlynn, June 27, 1865, Box 4, Folder 28, Pitchlynn Papers.

66. Report of Isaac Coleman, U. S. Agent to Elijah Sells, September 19, 1865, Fort Smith, in U.S. Department of the Interior, Office of Indian Affairs, *Annual Report of the Commissioner of Indian Affairs to the Secretary of the Interior for the Year 1865* (Washington, D.C.: Government Printing Office, 1865), 280.

67. Report of Brigadier General William Steele, C. S. Army, of Operations in the Indian Territory in 1863, in *War of the Rebellion,* series 1, vol. 22, 34.

68. William Steele to Brigadier General W. R. Boggs, Bonham, Texas, September

21, 1863, in *War of the Rebellion*, series 1, vol. 22, part 2, 1024; Abel, *Indian under Reconstruction*, 250.

69. Pitchlynn to [Folsom], November 20, 1863.

70. Abel, *Indian under Reconstruction*, 73–79.

71. U.S. Department of the Interior, Office of Indian Affairs, *Annual Report of the Commissioner of Indian Affairs . . . 1865*, 32–33.

72. Ibid., iii.

73. Peter Pitchlynn to E. Kirby Smith, May 17, 1865, Box 4, Folder 19, Pitchlynn Collection.

CHAPTER 6

1. *Congressional Globe*, 33rd Cong., 1st sess. February 23, 1854, 29.

2. Harlan's bill (S. 459) was introduced in the Senate by James Doolittle on February 20, 1865; see *Congressional Globe*, 38th cong., 2nd sess., February 23, 1865, 1021–1024.

3. *Congressional Globe*, 38th Cong., 2nd sess., March 2, 1865, 1302–1305.

4. Annie Heloise Abel, *The American Indian under Reconstruction* (Cleveland, Ohio: The Arthur H. Clark Company, 1925), 219–227.

5. The commissioners were Commissioner of Indian Affairs D. N. Cooley; Elijah Sells; Thomas Wister, a member of the Society of Friends; Brigadier General W. S. Harney; and Colonel Ely S. Parker, the Seneca Indian who would become commissioner of Indian affairs under President Ulysses S. Grant; *Congressional Globe*, 38th cong., 2nd sess., February 23, 1865, 1021–1024.

6. Peter Pitchlynn to Cyrus Bussey, August 9, 1865, Box 4, Folder 35, Pitchlynn Collection; Cyrus Bussey to Peter Pitchlynn, August 25, 1865, Box 4, Folder 39, Pitchlynn Collection; U.S. Department of the Interior, Office of Indian Affairs, *Annual Report of the Commissioner of Indian Affairs to the Secretary of the Interior for the Year 1865* (Washington, D.C.: Government Printing Office, 1865), 34.

7. Choctaws were represented at the commissioner's meeting by A. J. Stanton, Jeremiah Ward, William Patton, and Robert Patton; U.S. Department of the Interior, Office of Indian Affairs, *Annual Report of the Commissioner of Indian Affairs . . . 1865*, 310. The Loyal Choctaws had established a constitution at New Hope on March 14, 1864, and elected Edward Perkins, a white man married to a Choctaw woman, as their delegate to Washington, D.C.; see William T. Stephens to Peter Pitchlynn, June 27, 1865, Box 4, Folder 28, Pitchlynn Collection; Edward P. Perkins, Delegate from Choctaw Nation, to W. P. Dole, April 1864, Reel 176, Office of Indian Affairs, Letters Received.

8. *Annual Report of the Commissioner for Indian Affairs . . . 1865*, 310; A. J. Stanton, Fort Smith, to Peter Pitchlynn, June 29, 1865, Box 4, Folder 29, Pitchlynn Collection.

9. *Annual Report of the Commissioner for Indian Affairs . . . 1865*, 310.

10. Ibid., 318.

11. Ibid., 514; Kappler, *Indian Affairs: Laws and Treaties*, 2:1050–1051.

12. *Annual Report of the Commissioner for Indian Affairs . . . 1865*, 517.

13. Ibid., 349.

14. Ibid., 529–531.

15. Ibid, 532–537; Kappler, *Indian Affairs: Laws and Treaties*, 2:1052.

16. *Reply of Peter P. Pitchlynn, Choctaw Delegate, to a Libellous Pamphlet Published by Douglas H. Cooper* (Washington, D.C., 1873), 11–12.

17. Winchester Colbert, Edmund Pickens, Holmes Colbert, Colbert Carter, and Robert H. Love were the Chickasaw commissioners; Kappler, *Indian Affairs: Laws and Treaties*, 2:931.

18. John H. B. Latrobe, "An Address to the Choctaw and Chickasaw Nations, in Regard to Matters Connected with the Treaty of 1866," Ayer Collection, Newberry Library, Chicago, Illinois, 23 (hereafter Ayer Collection). Page was later defrocked for drinking; see Hargrett, *A Bibliography of the Constitutions and Laws of the American Indians*, 65–66.

19. W. David Baird, *Peter Pitchlynn: Chief of the Choctaws* (Norman: University of Oklahoma Press, 1972), 146.

20. John E. Semmes, *John H. B. Latrobe and His Times, 1803–1891* (Baltimore, Md.: The Norman, Remington Co., 1917), 535–537; Muriel H. Wright, "General Douglas H. Cooper, C.S.A.," *Chronicles of Oklahoma* 32, no. 2 (Summer 1954): 144; Baird, *Peter Pitchlynn*, 151.

21. Baird, *Peter Pitchlynn*, 151; Memorandum signed by Allen Wright, John Page, Alfred Wade, James Riles, Choctaw delegates, Washington, D. C., May 16, 1866, concerning hiring of Hon. L. H. B. Latrobe of Baltimore, Maryland, Folder 2120, Pitchlynn Papers.

22. Latrobe, *An Address to the Choctaw and Chickasaw Nations*, 10.

23. Baird, *Peter Pitchlynn*, 151–154.

24. Latrobe, *An Address to the Choctaw and Chickasaw Nations*, 9; Semmes, *John H. B. Latrobe and His Times*, 544–545.

25. Charles J. Kappler, *Indian Affairs: Laws and Treaties*, 5 vols. (Washington, D.C.: Government Printing Office, 1904–1941), 2:931.

26. Ibid., 929.

27. Ibid., 919.

28. Daniel F. Littlefield, Jr., *The Chickasaw Freedmen: A People without a Country* (Westport, Connecticut: Greenwood Press, 1980).

29. Kappler, *Indian Affairs: Laws and Treaties*, 2:928.

30. Ibid., 2:921.

31. Ibid., 2:921–923.

32. *A Bill to Provide for the Consolidation of the Indian Tribes, and to Establish Civil Government in the Indian Territory*, 38th Cong., 2nd sess., February 20, 1865, S. 459.

33. Roy Gittinger, *The Formation of the State of Oklahoma, 1803–1906* (Berkeley: University of California Press, 1917), 33; James B. Wright, *Allen Wright, Minister of the Gospel: Scholar, Translator, Lexicographer, Educator, Principal Chief (Governor) Choctaw Nation and Gentleman* (McAlester, Okla.: [Democrat Print.], 1961), 4. It is interesting

to note that Wright originally proposed the name for the western lands that the Choctaws ceded for the settlement of the so-called wild Indians; see pages 84–85. The fact that Van Horn's bill was favorably reported to the floor by the Committee on Indian Affairs of the House meant that the threat of congressional action was becoming more serious, but the bill was called from the floor into the Committee on Territories, from whence it did not emerge again.

34. "Journal of the General Council of the Indian Territory," *The Chronicles of Oklahoma* 3, no. 1 (March 1925): 35–36, 42.

35. The council convened on December 6, 1870. The Choctaw delegation included Campbell LeFlore, John McKinney, William Fry, Ma-ha-tubbee, Alexander R. Durant, James Thompson, Joseph P. Folsom, and Alfred Wright. The Chickasaws were represented by Charles P. H. Percy, Joseph James, and Hopiah-Tubbee; see "Journal of the Adjourned Session of First General Council of the Indian Territory," *Chronicles of Oklahoma* 3, no. 2 (June 1925): 121.

36. "Journal of the Adjourned Session," 125–126. Two members of the Choctaw delegation, Joseph Folsom and Campbell LeFlore, sat on the committee. The General Council adopted its formal statement on December 20 by a vote of 52 to 3 (134–135).

37. "Okmulgee Constitution," *Chronicles of Oklahoma* 3, no. 3 (September 1925): 220–221.

38. Ibid., 218–229.

39. Curtis L. Nolen, "The Okmulgee Constitution: A Step towards Indian Self-Determination," *Chronicles of Oklahoma* 58 (Fall 1980): 274; "A Proposed Resolution for the Ratification of the Okmulgee Constitution, Adopted December 20, 1870" (approved October 24m 1871), Box 2, Folder 12, Choctaw Nation Collection, Western History Collections, University of Oklahoma, Norman, Oklahoma.

40. Nolen, "The Okmulgee Constitution," 275–279.

CHAPTER 7

1. James D. Morrison, "The Union Pacific, Southern Branch," *Chronicles of Oklahoma* 14, no. 2 (June 1936): 176.

2. White men could circumvent the permit laws by marrying into the Nation. The Choctaws had since 1840 accepted marriage between white men and Indian women as a way of granting men the rights and privileges of citizenship, although it also prevented a man from disposing of his wife's property without her consent and stripped him of tribal membership if he left her. A law in 1849 was intended primarily to compel cohabiting couples to marry legally, but it was also a way to prevent any white man who was "under a bad character" from marrying into the Nation. See "An Act in Relation to White Men Marrying in the Nation &c. Oct. 1840," in Choctaw Nation, *Constitution and Laws of the Choctaw Nation: Together with the Treaties of 1855, 1865 and 1866* (New York: Wm. P. Lyon & Son, 1869), 106.

3. "Protest of Coleman Cole," *Indian Journal*, Eufaula, February 6, 1878, Coleman Cole Collection, Western History Collections (hereafter Cole Collection).

4. On November 7, 1854, the General Council passed a "Resolution in Relation to the Territorial Bill and Railroads" and appointed a committee to study the issues and make recommendations. See *Acts and Resolutions of the General Council of the Choctaw Nation, from 1852 to 1857, Both Inclusive* (Fort Smith, Ark.: Josephus Dotson, Printer for the Nation, 1858), 71.

5. George Harkins to Peter Pitchlynn, November 29, 1857, Box 2, Folder 110, Pitchlynn Collection.

6. The federal government took over construction of the southwest branch of the Union Pacific railroad in 1862 in order to use it for troop transport. The railroad was a tenuous tie that held the state of Missouri to the Union, but the volatile political atmosphere in the state, one of four slaveholding states that remained in the Union, kept the trains under attack by guerilla forces; H. Craig Miner, *The St. Louis–San Francisco Transcontinental Railroad: The Thirty-fifth Parallel Project, 1853–1890* (Lawrence: University Press of Kansas, 1972), 31–35.

7. Eric Foner, *Reconstruction: America's Unfinished Revolution, 1863–1877* (New York: Harper & Row, 1988), 210–211.

8. *An Act Granting Lands to Aid in the Construction of a Railroad and Telegraph Line from the States of Missouri and Arkansas to the Pacific Ocean*, 14 Stat. 292 (July 27, 1866).

9. Charles J. Kappler, *Indian Affairs: Laws and Treaties*, 5 vols. (Washington, D.C.: Government Printing Office, 1904–1941), 2:920–921.

10. H. Craig Miner, *The Corporation and the Indian* (Columbia: University of Missouri Press, 1976), 6–7.

11. H. Craig Miner, "The Struggle for an East-West Railway into the Indian Territory, 1870–1882," *Chronicles of Oklahoma* 47 (Spring 1969): 565.

12. *An Act Granting Lands to Aid in the Construction of a Railroad and Telegraph Line from the States of Missouri and Arkansas to the Pacific Ocean.*

13. *An Act Granting Land to Kansas to Aid in the Construction of the Kansas and Neosho Valley Railroad and Its Extension to Red River*, 14 Stat. 236 (July 25, 1866).

14. On July 27, Congress authorized a similar grant of public lands to Kansas to support the construction of a southern branch of the Union Pacific Railway and Telegraph from Fort Riley, Kansas, to Fort Smith, Arkansas; see *Lands to Kansas. An Act Granting Lands to the State of Kansas to Aid in the Construction of a Southern Branch of Union Pacific Railway and Telegraph from Fort Riley, Kansas, to Fort Smith, Arkansas* 14 Stat. 289 (July 26, 1866).

15. *An Act Granting Land to Kansas to Aid in the Construction of the Kansas and Neosho Valley Railroad and Its Extension to Red River.*

16. Ibid.

17. *The Congressional Globe*, 39th Cong., 1st sess., June 22, 1866, 3334–3336.

18. George Sanborn to James Harlan, Fort Smith, January 27, 1866, in U.S. Department of the Interior, Office of Indian Affairs, *Annual Report of the Commissioner of*

Indian Affairs to the Secretary of the Interior for the Year 1866 (Washington, D.C.: Government Printing Office, 1866), 286.

19. "Journal of the General Council of the Indian Territory," *Chronicles of Oklahoma* 3, no. 1 (March 1925): 42.

20. U.S. Congress, Senate Committee on Railroads, *Railroad through Indian Territory: Proceedings before the Committee on Railroads of the United States Senate Relative to the Bill (S. No. 60) "Ratifying the Act of the General Council of the Choctaw Nations of Indians Granting to the Saint Louis and San Francisco Railway Company Right of Way for a Railroad and Telegraph Line through the Nation"* (Washington, D.C., 1882), 28.

21. Untitled resolution beginning "Whereas the Thirty-fifth Parallel Railroad Company . . . ," Box 1, Folder 7, Choctaw Nation Collection.

22. "Resolution Authorizing the National Secretary, to Have the Charters of the Thirty-fifth Parralell [sic] and the Central Choctaw and Chickasaw Rail Road Companies Translated into the Choctaw Language, Approved April 8, 1870," Box 2, Folder 14, Choctaw Nation Collection.

23. E. S. Mitchell to Peter P. Pitchlynn, Boggy Depot, August 14, 1870, Folder 2342, Pitchlynn Papers.

24. "An Act to Repeal an Act Entitled "An Act to Incorporate the Choctaw and Chickasaw Central Rail Road Company Approved April 8, 1870, as Well as to Repeal an Act Entitled 'An Act to Incorporate the Choctaw and Chickasaw Thirty Fifth Paralel [sic] Rail Road Company Approved April 8th A.D. 1870,'" approved October 21, 1870, Box 2, Folder 24, Choctaw Nation Papers; "An Act to Repeal an Act Entitled 'An Act to Incorporate the Choctaw and Chickasaw Central Rail Road Company Approved April 8 1870, as Well as to Repeal and Act Entitled An Act to Incorporate the Choctaw and Chickasaw Thirty-fifth Paralel [sic] Rail Road Company Approved April 8t A.D. 1870,'" Box 2, Folder 27, Choctaw Nation Papers; J. D. Cox to Commissioner of Indian Affairs, Washington, July 29, 1870, Reel 179 Frame 92, Office of Indian Affairs, Letters Received; J. D. Cox to D. H. Barnes, Genl. Ag. C&C 35th Par. R.R. Co., Washington, July 29th 1870, Reel 179 Frame 101, Office of Indian Affairs, Letters Received; W. T. Otto to Commissioner of Indian Affairs, Washington, November 3, 1870, Reel 179, Frame 108, Office of Indian Affairs, Letters Received; William Bryant to Hon. J. D. Cox, Executive Offices, Chahta Tamaha, Choctaw Nation, October 21, 1870, Reel 179, Frame 112, Office of Indian Affairs, Letters Received.

25. E. S. Parker to Hon. J. D. Cox, Washington City, D.C., December 23, 1869, in U.S. Department of the Interior, Office of Indian Affairs, *Annual Report of the Commissioner of Indian Affairs to the Secretary of the Interior for the Fiscal Year 1869* (Washington, D.C.: Government Printing Office, 1870), 6.

26. "Provided, That hereafter no Indian nation or tribe within the territory of the United States shall be acknowledged or recognized as an independent nation, tribe, or power with whom the United States may contract by treaty"; *Indian Appropriation Act*, 16 U.S. 566 (March 3, 1871).

27. Indian funds were largely invested in state bonds, which might in turn be serviced by railroad bonds. See Miner, *The Corporation and the Indian*, 9.

28. "Resolution of the Choctaw General Council, Approved October 30, 1869," Box 1, Folder 30, Choctaw Nation Collection.

29. Peter Pitchlynn, *Report of P. P. Pitchlynn, Choctaw Delegate, to His Excellency the Principal Chief and General Council of the Choctaw Nation, with Appendix Containing Correspondence on the Survey of the Chickasaw District, and Letter Addressed to the Secretary of the Interior Requesting a Survey of the Eastern Boundary Line of the Choctaw Nation* (Washington, D.C.: Cunningham & McIntosh, Printers, 1870), 3–4, 10.

30. The Kansas, Indian Territory, and Gulf Railway Company was later allowed to merge with the Missouri River, Fort Scott and Gulf, and Leavenworth, Lawrence and Galveston Railroad companies; see Peter P. Pitchlynn, *Remonstrance, Appeal, and Solemn Protest of the Choctaw Nation Addressed to the Congress of the United States* [Washington, D.C., 1870], 1–3, 19–20.

31. C. J. Hillyer, *Atlantic and Pacific Railroad and the Indian Territory* [Washington, D.C.: Gibson Bros., 1871], 5–6.

32. Ibid., 25–28, 40.

33. V. V. Masterson, *The Katy Railroad and the Last Frontier* (Norman: University of Oklahoma Press, 1952), 19–20.

34. Ibid., 33–34.

35. Ibid., 70–71.

36. James D. Morrison, "The Union Pacific, Southern Branch," *Chronicles of Oklahoma* 14, no. 2 (June 1936): 180–181; Masterson, *The Katy Railroad and the Last Frontier*, 161–162.

37. "A Resolution Endorsing the Report of the Committee on Memorial and Accompanying Memorial of the General Council of the Indian Territory to the President and Congress of the United States and for Other Purposes, Approved October 27, 1875," Box 7, Folder 5, Choctaw Nation Collection.

38. *Missouri, Kansas & Texas Railway Co. v. the United States*, 47 Ct. Cl. 59 (1882).

39. *Missouri, K. & T. Ry. Co. v. U.S.*, 235 U.S. 37 (November 9, 1914).

40. "A Resolution Expressing the Sense of the Choctaw Nation in Reference to the Rights of the M. K. & T. Ry. in Her Borders, Approved November 3, 1885, Edmund McCurtain, Prin. Chief," Box 17, Folder 39, Choctaw Nation Collection.

41. "An Act Entitled 'An Act Prohibiting the Sale and Shipment of Timber, Rock and Stone Coal by Any Citizen or Resident of the Choctaw Nation, Approved October 24, 1873,'" Box 5, Folder 8, Choctaw Nation Collection.

42. "An Act Entitled 'An Act Providing Protection for Timber and Stone in the Choctaw Nation and for Other Purposes, [1871],'" Box 2, Folder 26, Choctaw Nation Collection; "An Act to Provide for the Collection of Royalty in the Choctaw Nation, Approved November 5, 1880," Box 12, Folder 28, Choctaw Nation Collection; Angie Debo, *The Rise and Fall of the Choctaw Republic* (Norman: University of Oklahoma Press, 1934), 134–135.

43. Walter T. K. Nugent, *Money and American Society, 1865–1880* (New York: The Free Press, 1968), 176–177; Miner, *St. Louis–San Francisco Transcontinental Railroad,* 88–89, 127; Masterson, *The Katy Railroad and the Last Frontier,* 204–205.

44. Masterson, *The Katy Railroad and the Last Frontier,* 205.

45. "A Resolution Authorizing the National Agent to Settle All Unsettled Business in Regard to Rail Road Ties and Other Timber, and Stone Used in Constructing and Repairing the M. K. & T. Rail Road within the Limits of the Choctaw Nation, Approved October 24, 1873," Box 4, Folder 13, Choctaw Nation Collection.

46. "An Act Entitled 'An Act Levying a Tax upon Railroad and Other Kinds of Property within the Limits of the Choctaw Nation, Approved March 9, 1876,'" in *Laws of the Choctaw Nation Passed at the Choctaw Councils of 1876 and 1877* (Atoka, Choctaw Nation: W. J. Hemby, Printer, 1878), 13–15.

47. "A Resolution Authorizing the Principal Chief to Appoint One Competent Person to Proceed with the Prosecution of the Claim of the Choctaw Nation against the Missouri, Kansas and Texas Railway, Approved October 20, 1881," in *General and Special Laws of the Choctaw Nation Passed at the Regular Session of the General Council Convened at Chahta Tamaha, Oct. 3rd and Adjourned Nov. 12th, 1881* (Denison, Tex.: Murray & Dearing, 1881), 7.

48. Section 11 of the Constitution of 1860 gave the General Council the power "to pass such laws and measures as they shall deem expedient for the General good of the Choctaw People." This provision implicitly sanctioned the council's approval of railroad contracts.

49. Dwight K. Tripp, Washington, D.C., to Secretary of the Interior, September 20, 1881; 4; S. J. Smallwood to the President, Washington, D.C., October 6, 1881, 3; Dwight K. Tripp, Washington, D.C., September 20, 1881 to Secretary of the Interior, 4; S. J. Smallwood to the President, Washington, D.C., October 6, 1881, all in *Message from the President of the United States Transmitting a Communication from the Secretary of the Interior, with Accompanying Papers, in Reference to the Bill of Choctaw Council, Approved November 10, 1881, Granting a Right of Way through the Choctaw Nation to the Saint Louis and San Francisco Railway Company, &c. January 9, 1882,* 47th Cong., 1st sess., December 15, 1881, S. Exec. Doc. 44.

50. U.S. Congress, Senate Committee on Railroads, *Railroad through Indian Territory,* 16.

51. *Message from the President . . . Granting a Right of Way through the Choctaw Nation,* 6, 10, 14, 20.

52. U.S. Congress, Senate Committee on Railroads, *Railroad through Indian Territory,* 33; "Message from the President," 12–14.

53. "Testimony of Peter Folsom before a U.S. Government Committee," Carton 75, #19743, Frames 344, 348, 350–351, Choctaw Nation Papers, Oklahoma Historical Society, Oklahoma City, Oklahoma.

54. "An Act to Grant Right-of-Way through the Choctaw Nation to the St. Louis and San Francisco Railway Company, Approved November 10, 1881," in *General and Special Laws of the Choctaw Nation Passed at the Regular Session of the General Council*

Convened at Chahta Tamaha, Oct. 3rd and Adjourned Nov. 12th, 1881 (Denison, Tex.: Murray & Dearing, 1881), 31–34.

55. *Message from the President . . . Granting a Right of Way through the Choctaw Nation*, 2, 19; Miner, *Saint Louis–San Francisco Transcontinental Railroad*, 126–127.

56. *Message from the President . . . Granting a Right of Way through the Choctaw Nation*, 15.

57. Miner, *St. Louis–San Francisco Transcontinental Railroad*, 127–128; U.S. Congress, Senate Committee on Railroads, *Railroad through Indian Territory*, 1.

58. U.S. Congress, Senate Committee on Railroads, *Railroad through Indian Territory*, 26.

59. Miner, *St. Louis–San Francisco Transcontinental Railroad*, 129.

60. *Message from the President . . . Granting a Right of Way through the Choctaw Nation*, 2–3.

61. "Statement by Samuel Bell Maxey," *Congressional Record*, 47th Cong., 1st sess., December 5, 1881–February 9, 1882, vol. 13, pt. 1, 502–505.

62. Miner, *St. Louis–San Francisco Transcontinental Railroad*, 132–134; *Congressional Record*, 47th Cong., 1st sess., April 13, 1882, vol. 13, part 3, 2857.

63. "An Act to Prevent the Building of Railroads and Railroad Branches, without Authority from the General Council, Approved October 22, 1883," in *Laws of the Choctaw Nation Passed at the Choctaw Council at the Regular Session of 1883* (Sedalia, Mo.: Democrat Steam Printing House and Book Bindery, 1883).

CHAPTER 8

1. "Meeting of the Bachelor's Club," *Muskogee Weekly Phoenix*, December 23, 1888, 1. The bill in question became law as 25 Stat. 392 on August 9, 1888. Members of the Five Tribes were exempt from it, presumably because they had their own laws regulating intermarriage. The act provided that no white man who married an Indian woman was entitled to her property and an Indian woman who married a white man became a citizen of the United States.

2. John Bartlett Meserve, "Governor Benjamin Franklin Overton and Governor Benjamin Crooks Burney," *Chronicles of Oklahoma* 16, no. 2 (June 1938): 229.

3. Paul Nesbitt, "J. J. McAlester," *Chronicles of Oklahoma* 11, no. 2 (June 1933): 760.

4. Nesbit, "J. J. McAlester," 760; I. C. Gunning, *When Coal Was King: Coal Mining Industry in the Choctaw Nation* (n.p.: Eastern Oklahoma Historical Society, 1975), 7.

5. V. V. Masterson, *The Katy Railroad and the Last Frontier* (Norman: University of Oklahoma Press, 1952), 161–162; Nesbitt, "J. J. McAlester," 761.

6. Gunning, *When Coal Was King*, 13; David Bowden, "Choctaw Toll Roads and Railroads," *Chronicles of Oklahoma* 44 (Winter 1996–1997): 389; Angie Debo, *The Rise and Fall of the Choctaw Republic* (Norman: University of Oklahoma Press, 1934), 120.

7. Ream claimed $25 a day for tolls lost since October 1, 1873; see H. B. Henton, Sect. MK&T, New York, to E. P. Smith, June 28, 1872, Reel 180, Frame 546, Office of Indian Affairs, Letters Received, and C. Delano to Commissioner of Indian Affairs,

Washington, June 17, 1873, Reel 180, Frame 562, Office of Indian Affairs, Letters Received. R. L. Ream's complaint against the MK&T is on Reel 180, Frame 786, Office of Indian Affairs, Letters Received; see also R. L. Ream to P. P. Pitchlynn, Boggy Depot, Choctaw Nation, October 4, 1873, Reel 180, Frame 786, Office of Indian Affairs, Letters Received. See also H. Craig Miner, *The Corporation and the Indian* (Columbia: University of Missouri Press, 1976), 61–65; Bowden, "Choctaw Toll Roads and Railroads," 384–397.

8. Anna Ream and her husband had already attempted to jump the claim of William Chunn, another Choctaw citizen who had a coal claim adjoining that of Hailey and Dawson, but they were caught in the act and told to leave. Hailey nevertheless agreed to give Mrs. Ream one-quarter of his interest in the claim (deed dated April 2, 1875). Dawson relinquished his share of the claim to Hailey (deed dated April 20, 1875). Lewis conveyed his rights to Hailey, and Mrs. Ream and Hailey, Mrs. Ream, and William Chunn consolidated their respective claims into one, of which Hailey and Mrs. Ream each owned one-quarter and Chunn owned half. Hailey and Chunn then conveyed one-third of their interest in coal royalties to Mrs. Ream. See Choctaw Nation and Chickasaw Nation, *Memorial of the Choctaw and Chickasaw Nations to the Secretary of the Interior of the United States, Relating to Their Jurisdiction of Persons and Property under the Treaty of June 22, 1855* (Washington, D. C.: W. H. Moore, 1883), 1–4.

9. See biographical information about Fritz Sittel (Folder 1), correspondence about the establishment of the Choctaw Trading Company and contracts Sittel signed for railroad ties (Folder 5), information on lawsuits Sittel was involved in (Folder 11), and Wm. B. Pitchlynn's letter approving the application of Fritz Sittel to marry Malvina Pitchlynn, September 1, 1883 (Pitchlynn was the circuit clerk of Tobucksey County; Folder 13); all in Rogers-Neill Collection, Western History Collections, University of Oklahoma, Norman, Oklahoma (hereafter Rogers-Neill Collection).

10. E. S. Chaddick to Hon. G. W. Riddle, September 2, 1889, Folder 6, Rogers-Neill Collection.

11. J. F. Holden, "The B.I.T. The Story of an Adventure in Railroad Building," *Chronicles of Oklahoma* 11, no. 1 (March 1933): 644–650, 660–664.

12. Charles J. Kappler, *Indian Affairs: Laws and Treaties*, 5 vols. (Washington, D.C.: Government Printing Office, 1904–1941), 2:708.

13. "Act Requiring Permits for White Employees in the Nation, October 8, 1836"; "An Act Directing Chiefs to Assess a Tax on Licensed Traders, November 10, 1856"; An Act Regulating the Granting of Permits to Trade," November 20, 1867," all in Choctaw Nation, *Constitution and Laws of the Choctaw Nation: Together with the Treaties of 1855, 1865 and 1866* (New York: Wm. P. Lyon & Son, 1869), 149, 483–487.

14. U. S. Indian Agent Aaron Parsons reported to the commissioner of Indian affairs in 1873 that Choctaws were renting their lands to whites who paid county sheriffs for a license to rent; see A. Parsons to Hon. Edw. P. Smith, Boggy Depot, May 17, 1873, Reel 180, Frames 660–666, Office of Indian Affairs, Letters Received. See

also "An Act to Prevent Citizens of the Choctaw Nation from Leasing the Public Domain for Grazing and Other Purposes, Approved April 8, 1870," Box 2, Folder 19, Choctaw Nation Collection.

15. T. D. Griffith to Hon. A. R. Clum, November 4, 1871, Reel 179, Office of Indian Affairs, Letters Received; "A Proposed Act to Repeal the Act Approved November 20, 1867, Concerning the Granting of Permits for Trade, Approved October 28, 1872 [sic; 1871]," Box 3, Folder 20, Choctaw Nation Collection.

16. "An Act Regulating the Granting of Permits to Trade, Expose Goods, Wares or Merchandise for Sale within the Choctaw Nation, and to Reside within the Same, and for Other Purposes, Approved November 11, 1875," Box 7, Folder 14, Choctaw Nation Collection.

17. U.S. Department of the Interior, Office of Indian Affairs, *Annual Report of the Commissioner of Indian Affairs to the Secretary of the Interior for the Year 1876* (Washington, D.C.: Government Printing Office, 1876), 212. The Choctaw agency was the administrative unit of the Office of Indian Affairs. Indian agents reported on census statistics, among other things.

18. "An Act Providing Protection for Timber and Stone in the Choctaw Nation and for Other Purposes," Box 2, Folder 26, Choctaw Nation Collection.

19. Jeffrey Burton, *Indian Territory and the United States, 1866–1906: Courts, Government, and the Movement for Oklahoma Statehood* (Norman: University of Oklahoma Press, 1995), 109.

20. R. S. Stevens to F. A. Walker, MK&T, Sedalia, Missouri, February 12, 1873, Reel 180, Frame 831, Office of Indian Affairs, Letters Received.

21. R. S. Stevens to H. R. Clum, Acting Commissioner of Indian Affairs, September 25, 1873, Reel 180, Frames 865–868, Office of Indian Affairs, Letters Received.

22. John Bartlett Meserve, "Chief Coleman Cole," *Chronicles of Oklahoma* 14, no. 1 (March 1936): 9–18.

23. Coleman Cole to Editor of Vindicator, Executive Mansion, September 1, 1875, *The Vindicator*, September 4, 1875, Cole Collection.

24. Coleman Cole was born in Mississippi in 1800, son of Robert Cole, who later served as chief of the Apukshunnubbee District in 1824. Robert Cole was the son of a white man and a Chokchumma woman who had been adopted into the Choctaw Nation after the destruction of her tribe in warfare with the Chickasaws in the late 1700s. When Coleman Cole and his mother tried to establish their claims to land in Mississippi under the fourteenth article of the Treaty of Dancing Rabbit Creek, they were rejected; see "Petition of Coleman Cole," *Star Vindicator*, McAlester, Indian Territory, November 2, 1878, Cole Collection. Cole moved to Indian Territory sometime around 1845 and established a home in the Kiamichi Mountains. He served as county judge in Cedar County and represented the county in the General Council in 1850, 1855, 1871, and 1873.

25. "An Act Proposed Concerning the Citizenship of Persons Marrying Citizens of the Choctaw Nation. Approved Nov. 9, 1878," Box 10, Folder 46, Choctaw Nation Collection. The bill was passed by the council and approved on November 6, 1878.

26. "An Act to Prevent Leasing Lands to Non-citizens, Approved October 30, 1877," Box 9, Folder 37, Choctaw Nation Collection; also published in *Laws of the Choctaw Nation Passed at the Choctaw Councils of 1876 and 1877* (Atoka, Choctaw Nation: W. J. Hemby, Printer, 1878), 66.

27. "An Act to Sell Improvements Made by Non-citizens, Approved October 30, 1877," Box 9, Folder 38, Choctaw Nation Collection; "An Act to Sell Improvements Made by Non-citizens," in *Laws of the Choctaw Nation Passed at the Choctaw Councils of 1876 and 1877*, 65–66.

28. The resolutions are in Box 7, Folders 2 and 4, Choctaw Nation Collection; Gene Aldrich, "A History of the Coal Industry in Oklahoma to 1907" (Ph.D. diss., University of Oklahoma, 1952), 7.

29. "Message of Coleman Cole," *The Cherokee Advocate*, Indian Territory, October 17, 1877, Coleman Collection.

30. Choctaw Nation, *Constitution and Laws of the Choctaw Nation . . . 1866* (1869), 75. The punishment for selling any part of Choctaw Nation was death. Meserve, "Coleman Cole," 20–21; "Editorial on Coleman Cole," *Star Vindicator*, McAlester, Indian Territory, July 28, 1877, Cole Collection.

31. "Editorial on Coleman Cole," *Star Vindicator*, McAlester, Indian Territory, August 18, 1877, Cole Collection.

32. "Impeachment of Gov. Cole—Nolle Prosequi by the Senate," *Atoka Independent*, October 26, 1877; "Bills No. 6-7-8-9-10-11-12-13 of Coleman Cole," *Star Vindicator*, October 27, 1877, both in Cole Collection.

33. "Message of Coleman Cole," *The Cherokee Advocate*, Indian Territory, October 17, 1877, Cole Collection.

34. Meserve, "Coleman Cole," 20.

35. "An Act Prohibiting Non-Citizens from Engaging in Stock Business in the Choctaw Nation, Approved November 5, 1880," in *Acts and Resolutions Passed at the Regular Term of the General Council of the Choctaw Nation, October 1880, from Nos. 1 to 41 Inclusive* (Denison, Tex.: Dearing, 1880), 24–25.

36. "An Act to Prevent Cutting and Shipping Prairie or Wild Grass Hay out of the Choctaw Nation, Approved October 28, 1880," in ibid., 6.

37. Debo, *Rise and Fall*, 141–142.

38. Aldrich, "A History of the Coal Industry in Oklahoma to 1907," 11.

39. See the document signed by Dawes Commission chair Tams Bixby concerning the family's enrollment (Folder 6), Fritz Sittel to Edward Garthwaite Farish, September 16, 1895 (concerning the lease of oil rights to Edwin D. Chadick; Folder 7), a document from the law firm of Mansfield, McMurray, and Cornish giving Fritz and Malvina Sittel permission to trade horses covered by a mortgage to the firm (Folder 8), and documents relating to the property interests of the Sittels (Folder 11); all in Rogers-Neill Collection.

40. Choctaw Nation and Chickasaw Nation, *Memorial of the Choctaw and Chickasaw Nations to the Secretary of the Interior of the United States*, 4–14.

41. Ibid., 14–15.

42. The attorney general's opinion was issued on December 12, 1879; see ibid., 19.

43. "He Wants a Choctaw Wife," *The Indian Citizen*, April 5, 1900, Box 20, Folder 11, Green McCurtain Collection, Western History Collections, University of Oklahoma, Norman, Oklahoma (hereafter McCurtain Collection).

44. Dew M. Wisdom to the Commissioner of Indian Affairs, Muscogee, Indian Territory, September 30, 1893, in U.S. Department of the Interior, Office of Indian Affairs, *Annual Report of the Commissioner of Indian Affairs to the Secretary of the Interior for the Year 1893* (Washington, D.C.: Government Printing Office, 1893), 143.

45. *Proceedings of the Twelfth Annual Meeting of the Lake Mohonk Conference of Friends of the Indian* (New York: Lake Mohonk Conference, 1894), 27–34.

CHAPTER 9

1. *Congressional Record*, 43rd Cong., 2nd sess., January 19, 1875, 593.

2. John E. Semmes, *John H. B. Latrobe and His Times 1803–1891* (Baltimore, Md.: Norman, Remington Co., 1917), 541, 544; John H. B. Latrobe, "An Address to the Choctaw and Chickasaw Nations, in Regard to Matters Connected with the Treaty of 1866," 4, 9, Ayer Collection; *Claims against the Choctaw Nation*, 49th Cong., 2nd sess., February 28, 1887, S. Rep. 1978, 77. The Senate report called for an investigation of lawyers' fees in connection with judgments rendered on behalf of the Choctaws against the United States.

3. Copy of Cooper's false voucher, n.d., Reel 180, Frame 580, Office of Indian Affairs, Letters Received.

4. Ibid., Frames 582–583.

5. Ibid., Frame 585; In 1883, the Choctaw General Council reaffirmed the settlement of Cooper's accounts; see Bill No. 21, approved October 19, 1883, in *Laws of the Choctaw Nation Passed at the Choctaw Council at the Regular Session of 1883* (Sedalia, Mo.: Democrat Steam Printing House and Book Bindery, 1883); also in Box 15, Folder 31, Choctaw Nation Collection.

6. Charley (Charles Lombardi), Israel Folsom's Place, [to Peter Pitchlynn], October 10, 1868, Folder 2221, Pitchlynn Papers.

7. Mitchell contract, May 4, 1867, Folder 2177, Pitchlynn Papers.

8. W. David Baird, *Peter Pitchlynn: Chief of the Choctaws* (Norman: University of Oklahoma Press, 1972), 155.

9. E. S. Mitchell to Col. Peter P. Pitchlynn, Armstrong Academy, October 22, 1867, Folder 2189, Pitchlynn Papers.

10. William Norwood Brigance, *Jeremiah Sullivan Black: A Defender of the Constitution and the Ten Commandments* (Philadelphia: University of Pennsylvania Press, 1934), 120.

11. John McPherson, Stuttgart, Germany, to Chair of Committee on Indian Affairs, U.S. Senate, December 14, 1886, in *Claims against the Choctaw Nation*, 49th Cong., 2nd sess., February 28, 1887, S. Rep. 1978, 108–110.

12. *Claims against the Choctaw Nation*, 122–23.

13. Douglas H. Cooper, *Address and Memorial by Douglas H. Cooper, to the General Council of the Choctaw Nation Assembled* (Boggy Depot, C.N.: Vindicator Print, 1873).

14. Baird, *Peter Pitchlynn*, 158.

15. Brigance, *Jeremiah Sullivan Black*, 228; *Claims against the Choctaw Nation*, 6.

16. *Claims against the Choctaw Nation*, 5.

17. Ibid., 4.

18. Baird, *Peter Pitchlynn*, 161–62.

19. Israel Folsom to the Choctaw Council, Cottage Hill, C.N., October 14, 1867, Reel 177, Frames 19–22, Office of Indian Affairs, Letters Received.

20. As Mr. Hendricks said on the floor of the Senate, "Congress ought to live up to a bargain, fair and square, with the Indians"; *Congressional Globe*, 39th Cong., 2nd sess., February 23, 1867, 1811–1813.

21. *Claim by Choctaw Nation against United States*, 40th Cong., 2nd sess., February 1, 1868, H. Exec. Doc. 138, 1–3.

22. *Treaty with Choctaw Indians, to Accompany H.R. 1195*, 40th Cong., 2nd sess., July 6, 1868, H. Rep. 77, to accompany H.R. 1195.

23. *Congressional Globe*, 40th Cong., 2nd sess., May 30, 1868, 2707.

24. Ibid., 2709.

25. *Indian Appropriation Act*, 15 Stat. 223 (July 27, 1868).

26. *Congressional Globe*, 40th Cong., 3rd sess., February 3, 1869, 837–838.

27. The contract is in Folder 2240, Pitchlynn Papers.

28. Albert Pike, "To the Hon. The General Council of the Choctaw Nation: The Memorial of Albert Pike, Formerly of the State of Arkansas, and Now of the City of Washington, in the District of Columbia . . . October 1, 1869," 1, Ayer Collection.

29. *Congressional Globe*, 41st Cong., 1st sess., April 10, 1869, 718; *Memorial of P. P. Pitchlynn, Delegate of Choctaw Indians, on Bonds to be Issued under Treaty*, 41st Cong., 2nd sess., May 27, 1870, S. Rep. 178.

30. Letter of P. P. Pitchlynn Choctaw Delegate for Himself, and Co-delegates to the Senate's Committee on the Judiciary, February 1870, 8–9, Choctaw Papers, Ayer Collection, The Newberry Library, Chicago (hereafter Choctaw Papers).

31. *Congressional Globe*, 41st Cong., 2nd sess., June 18, 1870, 4208–4209.

32. *Congressional Globe*, 41st Cong., 2nd sess., July 12, 1870, 5483–5491. On July 13, Mr. Davis introduced a bill, S. 1058, which would have paid the award as a credit to the Choctaws on the books of the treasury at 4 percent, the interest to be used for the education of Choctaw children. The bill was referred to the Committee on Indian Affairs but was not reported; see *Congressional Globe*, 41st Cong., 2nd sess., July 13, 1870, 5531.

33. Baird, *Peter Pitchlynn*, 169; *Investigation of Indian Frauds*, 42nd Cong., 3rd sess., March 3, 1873, H. Rep. 98, 544.

34. *Memorial in Behalf of Choctaw Nation in Relation to Their Claim to the Net Proceeds of Their Lands Ceded to the United States by Treaty of Dancing Rabbit Creek, September 27, 1830*, 41st Cong., 3rd sess., January 17, 1871, H. Misc. Doc. 37, 12. Latrobe's memorial was referred to the House Committee on the Judiciary.

35. *Memorial of P. P. Pitchlynn, Choctaw Delegate, Carrying Out treaty Stipulations with Choctaw Indians*, 41st Cong., 3rd sess., February 6, 1871, S. Misc. Doc. 65. Pitchlynn's memorial was referred to the Senate Committee on the Judiciary.

36. *Opinion of Attorney General of the United States on Claim of Choctaw Indians to Issue of United States Bonds*, 41st Cong., 3rd sess., December 21, 1870, H. Exec. Doc. 25.

37. *Opinion of Attorney General of the United States on Claim of Choctaw Nation of Indians for $250,000 of United States Bonds*, 41st Cong., 3rd sess., January 5, 1871, S. Rep. 278.

38. Ibid.; *Choctaw Nation*, 41st Cong., 3rd sess., House Judiciary Committee, Report 41, February 27, 1871; 16 Stat. 570 (March 3, 1871).

39. Box 4, Folder 7, Choctaw Nation Collection.

40. "An Act Ratifying an Act of Congress of the United States, Appropriating Money to Pay Claimants under the 14th Article of the Treaty of 1830," in *Acts and Resolutions of the General Council of the Choctaw Nation, from 1852 to 1857, Both Inclusive* (Fort Smith, Ark.: Josephus Dotson, Printer for the Nation, 1858), 38.

41. *Choctaw Indian Claims*, 42nd Cong., 3rd sess., January 6, 1873, H. Exec. Doc. 69.

42. U.S. Congress, House Committee on Indian Affairs, *Investigation of Indian Frauds*, 42nd Cong., 3rd sess., March 3, 1873, H. Rep. 98, 71–72.

43. Ibid., 73.

44. *Letter from the Secretary of the Treasury, Accompanying A Report of the Solicitor of the Treasury Relative to the Claim of the Choctaw Indians, Known as the "Net Proceeds Claim,"* 42nd Cong., 2nd sess., June 7, 1872, S. Exec. Doc. 87, 3.

45. *Congressional Globe*, 42nd Cong., 2nd sess., June 8, 1872, 4432.

46. E. S. Mitchell to P. P. P., Boggy Depot, December 16, 1871, Folder 2502, Pitchlynn Papers; M. S. Temple to P. P. Pitchlynn, Armstrong Academy, October 14, 1872, Folder 2635, Pitchlynn Papers.

47. *Affairs in the Indian Department*, 41st Cong., 3rd sess., February 25, 1871, H. Rep. 39.

48. The Indian appropriation bill of the Forty-first Congress also restricted contracts without requiring the approval of the commissioner of Indian affairs.

49. *Journal, House of Representatives*, 42nd Cong., 2nd sess., January 8, 1872, House of Representatives, 123.

50. *Memorial of P. P. Pitchlynn, Delegate of Choctaw Nation, upon the Subject of the Claims of the Choctaw Nation to the Net Proceeds of Award of Senate of United States*, 42nd Cong., 2nd sess., April 2, 1872, H. Misc. Doc. 164.

51. *Letter of Secretary of Treasury on Payment of $250,000 in Bonds of United States to Choctaw Indians*, 42nd Cong., 3rd sess., January 22, 1873, S. Rep. 318.

52. Douglas H. Cooper, *Address and Memorial by Douglas H. Cooper, to the General Council of the Choctaw Nation Assembled* (Boggy Depot, C.N.: Vindicator Print, 1873).

53. U.S. Congress, House Committee on Indian Affairs, *Investigation of Indian Frauds*, 80.

54. Ibid., 81.

55. *Congressional Globe*, 43rd Cong., 3rd sess., February 4, 1873, 1082.

56. The Indian Appropriation Act of February 14, 1873 (17 Stat. 462) included a provision suspending action under acts of March 2, 1861, and March 3, 1871, and any payment for fees or rewards for service until further action by Congress.

57. Cooper, *Address and Memorial by Douglas H. Cooper*, 1.

58. Peter Pitchlynn, *Reply of Peter P. Pitchlynn, Choctaw Delegate, to a Libellous Pamphlet Published by Douglas H. Cooper* (Washington, D.C., 1873), 34.

59. Latrobe, "An Address to the Choctaw and Chickasaw Nations," 4, 9, 10–11.

60. Including, presumably, Pitchlynn; see Albert Pike, *Letter of Albert Pike to the Choctaw People* (Washington, D.C.: Cunningham & McIntosh, 1872), 23.

61. Walter Lee Brown, *A Life of Albert Pike* (Fayetteville: University of Arkansas Press, 1997), 460.

62. *Claims against the Choctaw Nation*, 91.

63. "An Act Entitled 'An Act Revoking a Certain Contract Known as Cochranes' Contract, and All Other Contracts Made by Any Choctaw Delegates,'" approved February 3, 1874, Box 6, Folder 4, Choctaw Nation Collection.

64. *Memorial of P. P. Pitchlynn on Claim of Choctaw Indians*, 43rd Cong., 1st sess, January 21, 1874, H. Misc. Doc. 89; *Right of Choctaw Nation of Indians to be Paid Money Awarded to It by United States Senate on 9 March 1859*, 43rd Cong., 1st sess., June 8, 1874, S. Misc. Doc. 121.

65. *Award in Favor of Choctaw Nation of Indians*, 43rd Cong., 1st sess., April 9, 1874, H. Rep. 391; *Choctaw Award*, 43rd Cong., 1st sess., May 20, 1874, H. Rep. 599.

66. *Congressional Globe*, 43rd Cong., 2nd sess., January 19, 1875, 592–593.

67. *An Act Making Appropriations for Sundry Civil Expenses of the Government for the Fiscal Year Ending June Thirtieth, 1875, and for Other Purposes*, 18 Stat., Rev. part 3, 230 (June 23, 1874).

68. *Congressional Globe*, 43rd Cong., 2nd sess., February 9, 1875, 1087–1088.

69. Ibid., 1087–1088, 1090, 1092–1093.

70. Peter P. Pitchlynn, "The Claim of the Choctaw Nation for the Net Proceeds of the Land Ceded by the Treaty Concluded at Dancing Rabbit Creek, September 27, 1830," Choctaw Papers, 1, 56.

71. Ibid., 22–23.

72. "A Memorial to the Government of the United States," May 29, 1876, Reel 183, Frame 32, Office of Indian Affairs, Letters Received; *Memorial on Choctaw Indian Claims*, 44th Cong., 1st sess., January 13, 1876, H. Misc. Doc. 40; *Memorial of Choctaw Nation Praying Settlement of Claim Arising under Treaty of 1855*, 44th Cong., 1st sess., January 6, 1876, S. Misc. Doc. 34.

73. The General Council had established its Court of Claims in 1859 in anticipation of the imminent payment of the Senate award; see "An Act Entitled 'An Act Defining the Duties and Powers of the Commissioners, the Jurisdiction of the Court of Claims, Fixing Their Pay, and for Other Purposes'" (approved October 21, 1859), in Choctaw Nation, *Constitution and Laws of the Choctaw Nation: Together with the Treaties of 1855, 1865 and 1866* (New York: Wm. P. Lyon & Son, 1869), 210–213; "An

Act Extending the Time for Holding the Court of Claims," Box 8, Folder 3, Choctaw Nation Collection.

74. "Memorial of Coleman Cole [November 30, 1875]," *The Vindicator*, October 11, 1876; and "Memorial of Coleman Cole," *The Indian Journal*, Eufaula, Creek Nation, April 26, 1877, both in Cole Collection; *Laws of the Choctaw Nation Passed at the Choctaw Councils of 1876 and 1877* (Atoka, Choctaw Nation: W. J. Hemby, Printer, 1878), 8–9; Untitled memorial to the U.S. government, Box 8, Folder 10, Choctaw Nation Collection.

75. "Coleman Cole Memorial to the United States Government," March 15, 1876, Reel 183, Frame 23, Office of Indian Affairs, Letters Received.

76. "Late letters from the Choctaw Nation inform me that the Principal Chief, Coleman Cole, has written you that the General Council has revoked the power conferred upon me by its authority to represent the Nation at Washington—an assertion which is destitute of any foundation in truth"; P. P. Pitchlynn to Hon. Z. Chandler, Secretary of the Interior, Washington, January 11, 1876, Reel 183, Frame 122, Office of Indian Affairs, Letters Received. See also P. P. Pitchlynn to U. S. Grant, Washington, January 8, 1876, Reel 183, Frame 127, Office of Indian Affairs, Letters Received.

77. *Choctaw Indians, Settlement of Claims under Treaty of 1830*, 44th Cong, 1st sess., May 15, 1876, H. Rep. 499.

78. *A Bill for the Relief of the Choctaw Nation of Indians*, 44th Cong., 1st sess., May 15, 1876, H. Rep. 499; *A Bill for the Relief of the Choctaw Nation of Indians*, 45th Cong., 1st sess., November 5, 1877, H. Rep. 980; *A Bill for the Relief of the Choctaw Nation of Indians*, 45th Cong., 2nd sess., February 26, 1878, H. Rep. 251; *A Bill for the Relief of the Choctaw Indians*, 45th Cong., 3rd sess., February 13, 1879; *An Act for the Ascertainment of the Amount Due the Choctaw Nation*, 21 Stat. 504 (March 3, 1881).

79. Baird, *Peter Pitchlynn*, 210–211.

80. Samson Holom, chair, Committee on Finance, letter recommending resolution for payment of $1,268 for final burial expenses and monument for Peter Pitchlynn to be paid to Mrs. Pitchlynn (approved November 7, 1884), Box 16, #59, Choctaw Nation Collection.

81. *The Choctaw Nation v. the United States*, 21 Ct. Cl. 59, 87 (January 25, 1886).

82. *An Act for the Ascertainment of the Amount Due the Choctaw Nation*, 21 Stat. 504 (March 3, 1881); *The Choctaw Nation v. the United States*, 21 Ct. Cl., 59.

83. *The Choctaw Nation v. the United States*, 21 Ct. Cl., 91, 103, 105.

84. *The Choctaw Nation v. the United States*, 21 Ct. Cl., 59. The actual breakdown of the award was $417,656 for claims under the fourteenth article, $42,920 for claims under the nineteenth article, $68,102 for eastern boundary lands, $51,993 for transportation and subsistence, $59,449 for unpaid annuities, and $18,000 for guns and ammunition, for a total of $658,120, less the $250,000 in cash paid in 1861.

85. *Choctaw Nation v. United States*, 119 U.S. 41 (November 15, 1886).

86. *Indian Appropriation Act 1889*, 25 Stat. 239 (June 29, 1888).

87. McKee admitted that other claimants were due almost $161,197: $147,057 plus a special appropriation of $14,140 for the estate of John T. Cochrane, passed by

the Choctaw General Council on February 15, 1889; see *Gilfillan v. McKee*, 159 U.S. 303 (1895).

88. U.S. Department of the Interior, Office of Indian Affairs, *Annual Report of the Commissioner of Indian Affairs to the Secretary of the Interior for the Year 1889* (Washington, D.C.: Government Printing Office, 1889), 211.

89. *McKee v. Lamon*, 159 U.S. 317 (1895); and *Gilfillan v. McKee*, 159 U.S. 303 (1895).

90. The court awarded the Pitchlynn heirs more money, but the Garland heirs received no more funds. Angie Debo concludes that the Net Proceeds Case "corrupted Choctaw politics for two generations"; see Debo, *Rise and Fall*, 73–74, 203–211.

91. *Claims against the Choctaw Nation*, 28.

CHAPTER 10

1. *Proceedings of the Third Annual Meeting of the Lake Mohonk Conference of Friends of the Indian, Held October 7 to 9, 1885* (Philadelphia: Sherman & Co., Printers, 1886), 43.

2. Janet O'Donnell, *The Dispossession of the American Indian, 1887–1934* (Bloomington: Indiana University Press, 1991), 2–4.

3. U.S. Department of the Interior, Office of Indian Affairs, *Annual Report of the Commissioner of Indian Affairs to the Secretary of the Interior for the Year 1889* (Washington, D.C.: Government Printing Office, 1889), 3.

4. *An Act to Provide for the Allotment of Lands in Severalty to Indians on the Various Reservations, and to Extend the Protection of the Laws of the United States and the Territories over the Indians, and for Other Purposes*, 4 Stat. 388 (February 8, 1887). Generally known as the Dawes Act or the General Allotment Act.

5. Richard Hofstadter, *The Age of Reform* (New York: Alfred A. Knopf, 1955), 11.

6. *Proceedings of the Fourth Annual Lake Mohonk Conference October 12, 13, 14, 1886* (Philadelphia: Indian Rights Association, 1887), 9.

7. "Editorial on a Proclamation of W. N. Jones," *The Caddo Banner*, December 22, 1893, Box 1, Folder 20, Wilson N. Jones Collection, Western History Collections, University of Oklahoma, Norman, Oklahoma (hereafter Jones Collection).

8. Alexandra Harmon, "American Indians and Land Monopolies in the Gilded Age," *The Journal of American History* 90, no. 1 (2003): 106.

9. Loring Benson Priest, *Uncle Sam's Stepchildren: The Reformation of United States Indian Policy, 1865–1887* (New Brunswick, N.J.: Rutgers University Press, 1942), 237–238; "An Act Entitled 'An Act to Provide for the Collection of Royalty on Stone Coal Lumber and Shingles That May Be Shipped Out of the Nation,'" Box 10, Folder 6, Choctaw Nation Collection.

10. D. S. Otis, *The Dawes Act and the Allotment of Indian Land*, edited by Francis Paul Prucha (Norman: University of Oklahoma Press, 1973), 43–44; H. Craig Miner, *The Corporation and the Indian* (Columbia: University of Missouri Press, 1976), 118–142. The Choctaw Nation had taken action to prevent leasing of tribal land to noncitizens. See "An Act to Provide for the Protection of the Public Domain," approved October 28, 1887, Box 19, Folder 12, Choctaw Nation Collection.

11. Otis, *The Dawes Act and the Allotment of Indian Land*, 6–7, 17–23, 181.

12. James D. Richardson, *A Compilation of the Messages and Papers of the Presidents*, 20 vols. (New York: Bureau of National Literature, 1917), 15:6672; Priest, *Uncle Sam's Stepchildren*, 223; Otis, *The Dawes Act and the Allotment of Indian Land*, 24.

13. Priest, *Uncle Sam's Stepchildren*, 224.

14. *Proceedings of the Third Annual Meeting of the Lake Mohonk Conference*, 51. Indians in contemporary society still make a point of adhering to "Indian time," meaning that an event starts when people show up, not when a published time is announced. Indian time continues to thwart Abbott's idea of civilization.

15. *Proceedings of the Twelfth Annual Meeting of the Lake Mohonk Conference of Friends of the Indian* (New York: Lake Mohonk Conference, 1894), 27–34.

16. *Indian Appropriation Act 1894*, 27 Stat. 645 (March 3, 1893); U.S. Department of the Interior, *Laws, Decisions, and Regulations Affecting the Work of the Commissioner to the Five Civilized Tribes, 1893 to 1906, Together with Maps Showing Classification of Lands in the Chickasaw, Choctaw, Cherokee, Creek, and Seminole Nations, and Recording Districts, Railroads, and Principal Towns of the Indian Territory* (Washington, D.C.: Government Printing Office, 1906), 11.

17. *Proceedings of the Twelfth Annual Meeting of the Lake Mohonk Conference*, 33.

18. U.S. Department of the Interior, Office of Indian Affairs, *Annual Report of the Commissioner of Indian Affairs to the Secretary of the Interior for the Year 1894* (Washington, D.C.: Government Printing Office, 1895), 27; Loren N. Brown, "Establishment of the Dawes Commission for Indian Territory," *Chronicles of Oklahoma* 18, no. 2 (1940): 171–181; Loren N. Brown, "The Dawes Commission," *Chronicles of Oklahoma* 9, no. 2 (June 1931): 71–105.

19. Angie Debo, *The Rise and Fall of the Choctaw Republic* (Norman: University of Oklahoma Press, 1934), 247.

20. "Message of W. N. Jones," *The Indian Citizen*, October 18, 1890, Box 1, Folder 1, Jones Collection. The fact that Jones was the richest man in the Choctaw Nation and had some 17,000 acres under fence led to a certain cynicism concerning his motives in resisting allotment. See "Editorial on W. N. Jones," *The Caddo Banner*, June 22, 1894, Box 1, Folder 27, Jones Collection.

21. "Editorial on W. N. Jones." *The Caddo Banner*, December 22, 1893, Box 1, Folder 20, Jones Collection.

22. U.S. Commission to the Five Civilized Tribes, *Annual Reports of 1894, 1895 and 1896, from March 3, 1893 to January 1, 1897* (Washington, D.C.: Government Printing Office, 1894–1896), 8.

23. "Act of April 2, 1894," Box 26, Folder 16, Choctaw Nation Collection.

24. U.S. Commission to the Five Civilized Tribes, *Annual Reports of 1894, 1895 and 1896*, 9–10.

25. Ibid. 7–10.

26. Ibid., 21–32.

27. Gene Aldrich, "A History of the Coal Industry in Oklahoma to 1907" (Ph.D. diss., University of Oklahoma, 1952), 76.

28. U.S. Department of the Interior, Office of Indian Affairs, *Annual Report of the Commissioner of Indian Affairs . . . 1894*, 74–79, 143–145.

29. Kent Carter, *The Dawes Commission and the Allotment of the Five Civilized Tribes, 1893–1914* (Orem, Utah: Ancestry.com, 1999), 6.

30. U.S. Commission to the Five Civilized Tribes, *Annual Reports of 1894, 1895 and 1896*, 60.

31. "Editorial on Green McCurtain," *The Talihina News*, Talihina, Choctaw Nation, July 18, 1895, Box 20, Folder 6, McCurtain Collection.

32. John Bartlett Meserve, "The McCurtains," *Chronicles of Oklahoma* 13, no. 3 (September 1935): 297–311.

33. "A Resolution Approved by Green McCurtain," *Fairland News*, Fairland, Indian Territory, July 26, 1895, Box 20, Folder 6, McCurtain Collection.

34. "Resolution Relative to Appointing a Committee to Confer with the Dawes Commission," approved October 21, 1895, Box 27, Folder 10, Choctaw Nation Collection.

35. U.S. Commission to the Five Civilized Tribes, *Annual Reports of 1894, 1895 and 1896*, 66–67.

36. *Report of the Committee to Meet with the Dawes Commission*, approved November 12, 1895, Box 27, Folder 60, Choctaw Nation Collection.

37. U.S. Commission to the Five Civilized Tribes, *Annual Reports of 1894, 1895 and 1896*, 67; Debo, *Rise and Fall*, 252.

38. U.S. Commission to the Five Civilized Tribes, *Annual Reports of 1894, 1895 and 1896*, 77–78.

39. Debo, *Rise and Fall*, 253; "News Item of Tuskahoma Party Nominating Green McCurtain," *The Purcell Register*, Purcell, Chickasaw Nation, I.T., May 29, 1896, Box 20, Folder 7, McCurtain Collection.

40. McCurtain's opponents were National Party candidates Jefferson Gardner, the incumbent chief; Jacob Jackson, the unsuccessful candidate in 1892; and Gilbert Dukes, Progressive Party candidate; see Carter, *The Dawes Commission and the Allotment of the Five Civilized Tribes*, 18.

41. "Message of Green McCurtain to the Members of the Senate and House of Representatives," *The Indian Citizen*, Atoka, I.T., October 8, 1896, Box 20, Folder 7, McCurtain Collection.

42. U.S. Commission to the Five Civilized Tribes, *Annual Reports of 1894, 1895 and 1896*, 84–85.

43. Ibid., 88–89; *Seventh Annual Report of the Commission to the Five Civilized Tribes to the Secretary of the Interior for the Fiscal Year Ended June 30, 1900* (Washington, D.C.: Government Printing Office, 1900), 11; Carter, *The Dawes Commission and the Allotment of the Five Civilized Tribes*, 16; "An Act Authorizing the Appointment of Commissioners, Fixing Their Pay and for Other Purposes," approved September 18, 1896, Box 28, Folder 4, Choctaw Nation Collection; Charles Francis Meserve, *The Dawes Commission and the Five Civilized Tribes of Indian Territory* (Philadelphia: Office of the Indian Rights Association, 1896), 17. Meserve reported that "money will buy

admission to the citizens rolls." An Indian woman charged that she paid $200 to members of the House of one tribal government to get on the rolls. The lower house approved her petition, but the upper house wanted $200 more.

44. U.S. Commission to the Five Civilized Tribes, *Annual Reports of 1894, 1895 and 1896*, 88.

45. Ibid., 97.

46. Ibid., 99.

47. U.S. Department of the Interior, Office of Indian Affairs, *Annual Report of the Commissioner of Indian Affairs to the Secretary of the Interior to the Secretary of the Interior for the Year 1897* (Washington, D.C.: Government Printing Office, 1897), 992–993.

48. Carter, *The Dawes Commission and the Allotment of the Five Civilized Tribes*, 19.

49. Kappler, *Indian Affairs: Laws and Treaties*, 1:647–656; *An Act for the Protection of the People of the Indian Territory and for Other Purposes*, 30 Stat. 505–513 (June 28, 1898) (the Curtis Act).

50. *Agreement with the Choctaw and Chickasaw*, 30 Stat. 93 (April 23, 1897).

51. "Message of Green McCurtain, to the General Council," *The Indian Citizen*, Atoka, I.T., October 7, 1897, Box 20, Folder 8, McCurtain Collection.

52. U.S. Commission to the Five Civilized Tribes, *Sixth Annual Report of the Commission to the Five Civilized Tribes to the Secretary of the Interior for the Fiscal Year Ended June 30, 1899*, in *Annual Reports of the Department of the Interior for the Fiscal Year Ended June 30, 1899*, Indian Affairs, Part II (Washington, D.C.: Government Printing Office, 1899), 10.

53. "An Act Ratifying and Confirming the Agreement between the Choctaw and Chickasaw Nations and the United States," Box 29, Folder 42, Choctaw Nation Collection.

54. *An Act for the Protection of the People of the Indian Territory and for Other Purposes*, 30 Stat. 495 (June 28, 1898). It is ironic that the bill's sponsor, Representative Charles Curtis, was himself a mixed-blood Kaw Indian. See William E. Unrau, *Mixed-Bloods and Tribal Dissolution: Charles Curtis and the Quest for Indian Identity* (Lawrence: University Press of Kansas, 1989).

55. "Letter of Green McCurtain," *The Indian Citizen*, August 3, 1898, Box 20, Folder 10, McCurtain Collection.

56. Debo, *Rise and Fall*, 262.

57. The United States assumed jurisdiction in matters of real estate and regulation of coal and asphalt and the crimes of homicide, embezzlement, bribery, embracery, breaches or disturbances of the peace, and carrying weapons; see "Letter of Green McCurtain," *The Indian Citizen*, August 17, 1898, Box 20, Folder 10, McCurtain Collection.

CHAPTER 11

1. Charles J. Kappler, *Indian Affairs: Laws and Treaties*, 5 vols. (Washington, D.C.: Government Printing Office, 1904–1941), 2:311.

2. Ibid., 706.

3. Samuel J. Crawford, *In the Matter of the Claim of the Choctaw and Chickasaw Nations on Account of Lands Ceded to the United States by the Treaty of 1866 before the Honorable United States Commission Created by Congress to Negotiate with the Five Civilized Tribes in the Indian Territory: Brief and Argument* (Washington, D.C.: Gibson Bros., 1897), 1–2, 7.

4. Robert Trennert, *Alternative to Extinction: Federal Indian Policy and the Beginnings of the Reservation System* (Philadelphia, Pa.: Temple University Press, 1975); see David La Vere, *Contrary Neighbors: Southern Plains and Removed Indians in Indian Territory* (Norman: University of Oklahoma Press, 2000).

5. Kappler, *Indian Affairs: Laws and Treaties*, 2:919.

6. See William T. Hagan, *Taking Indian Lands: The Cherokee (Jerome) Commission 1889–1893* (Norman: University of Oklahoma Press, 2003) for a complete account of the dispossession of tribes in the leased district and in northeastern Indian Territory.

7. Article 43, Treaty of 1866, in Kappler, *Indian Affairs: Laws and Treaties*, 2:929.

8. Kappler, *Indian Affairs: Laws and Treaties*, 1:955–958, 1010–1016.

9. Roy Gittinger, *The Formation of the State of Oklahoma, 1803–1906* (Berkeley: University of California Press, 1917), 152–159. The Land Run is still dutifully reenacted by students, Indian and white, in grade schools across the state of Oklahoma on April 22.

10. "A Proposed Act Authorizing the Appointment of Three Commissioners in Reference to the Leased District. Approved November 5, 1889," Box 21, Folder 4, Choctaw Nation Collection. The commissioners were Robert J. Ward, Henry C. Harris, and J. S. Standley, who were to receive $6 a day and 10 cents a mile for travel.

11. "Joint Resolution Approved December 23, 1889," Box 21, Folder 79, Choctaw Nation Collection.

12. Debate on H.R. 12106, *Congressional Record*, 51st Cong., 2nd sess., December 6, 1890, 183–191.

13. *Memorial of the Chickasaws Relating to Lands of the Choctaw and Chickasaw Nations West of the Ninety-eighth Meridian of West Longitude, with Accompanying Statement*, 51st Cong., 1st sess., March 19, 1900, S. Misc. Doc. 107.

14. Debo, *Rise and Fall*, 198; *Indian Appropriation Act 1892*, 26 Stat. 989, 1025 (March 3, 1891).

15. Robert J. Ward affidavit, April 4, 1891, in *Message from the President of the United States Relative to the Act to Pay the Choctaw and Chickasaw Indians for Certain Lands Now Occupied by the Cheyenne and Arapahoe Indians*, 52nd Cong., 1st sess., February 18, 1892, S. Exec. Doc. 42, 9. Payments were made to W. W. Hampton ($15,000), L. W. Oakes ($10,000), H. P. Ward ($5,000), Columbus Irwin ($2,500), Simon Nelson ($2,500), J. B. Jeter ($10,000), and G. T. Thibeau ($20,000); see *Congressional Record*, 56th Cong., 2nd sess., March 23, 1904, vol. 38, part 4, 3550.

16. U.S. Congress, House Committee on Indian Affairs, *Claims of J. F. McMurray: Hearings before the Subcommittee of the Committee on Indian Affairs, House of Representatives, Seventieth Congress, Second Session on H.R. 10741, December 12 to 21, 1928* (Washington, D.C.: Government Printing Office, 1929), 118. Hampton Tucker stated that

"Mr. Sypher's services were never worth very much, if anything, to the Choctaw Nation." Sypher was "a general and was a prominent Republican," and the Choctaw delegation counted on his political influence. His failure to deliver the claim led Tucker to conclude that "perhaps the Choctaw delegates was [sic] not the first delegation that ever came to Washington, either for the Indians or the whites, and picked out the wrong lobbyist." It also led the Choctaw Nation to cancel Sypher's contract, although it was Harrison's decision that thwarted his efforts. *Congressional Record*, 56th Cong., 2nd sess., March 23, 1904, vol. 38, part 4, 3359–3360.

17. *Message from the President of the United States Relative to the Act to Pay the Choctaw and Chickasaw Indians for Certain Lands Now Occupied by the Cheyenne and Arapahoe Indians*, 24–25.

18. Robert Owen to John Noble, November 6, 1891, in *Message from the President of the United States Relative to the Act to Pay the Choctaw and Chickasaw Indians for Certain Lands Now Occupied by the Cheyenne and Arapahoe Indians*, 24–25.

19. Ibid., 2.

20. *Document on Message of President on Choctaw and Chickasaw Indians*, 52nd Cong., 1st sess., April 13, 1892, S. Rep. 552.

21. "An Act Authorizing Distribution Per Capita of the Money Due the Choctaw Nation for the Sale of a Portion of the Leased District under Act of Congress Approved March 3, A.D. 1891," approved April 11, 1891, Box 23, Folder 28, Choctaw Collection.

22. Report of Leo E. Bennett, U.S. Agent, Union Agency, September 12, 1892, in U.S. Department of the Interior, Office of Indian Affairs, *Annual Report of the Commissioner of Indian Affairs to the Secretary of the Interior for the Year 1892* (Washington, D.C.: Government Printing Office, 1892), 260–262.

23. Ibid., 263.

24. "Message of W. N. Jones," *The Indian Citizen*, October 13, 1892, Box 1, Folder 7, Jones Collection.

25. Jeffrey Burton, *Indian Territory and the United States, 1866–1906: Courts, Government, and the Movement for Oklahoma Statehood* (Norman: University of Oklahoma Press, 1995), 182–184.

26. *Proceedings of the Tenth Annual Meeting of the Lake Mohonk Conference of Friends of the Indian 1892* (n.p.: Lake Mohonk Conference, 1892), 107.

27. *Memorial of the Choctaw Nation Relative to the President's Message, Dated February 17, 1892*, 52nd Cong., 1st sess., March 14, 1892, S. Misc. Doc. 95, 4.

28. Debo, *Rise and Fall*, 203.

29. *Proceedings of the Twelfth Annual Meeting of the Lake Mohonk Conference of Friends of the Indian* (New York: Lake Mohonk Conference, 1894), 31.

30. U.S. Department of the Interior, Office of Indian Affairs, *Annual Report of the Commissioner of Indian Affairs to the Secretary of the Interior to the Secretary of the Interior for the Year 1893* (Washington, D.C.: Government Printing Office, 1893), 88.

31. Burton, *Indian Territory and the United States, 1866–1906*, 91; U.S. Department of the Interior, Office of Indian Affairs, *Annual Report of the Commissioner of Indian Affairs . . . 1893*, 88–89.

32. U.S. Department of the Interior, Office of Indian Affairs, *Annual Report of the Commissioner of Indian Affairs . . . 1892*, 260–262.

33. "Letter of W. N. Jones to Hoke Smith, July 5, 1893," *The Indian Citizen*, July 20, 1893, Box 1, Folder 11, Jones Collection.

34. "Editorial on Message of Attorney General Hall to W. N. Jones," *The Purcell Register*, July 8, 1893, Box 1, Folder 13, Jones Collection.

35. "Letter of W. N. Jones to Hoke Smith."

36. "Editorial on W. N. Jones," *The Purcell Register*, July 14, 1893, Box 1, Folder 10, Jones Collection.

37. Debo, *Rise and Fall*, 173–174; Burton, *Indian Territory and the United States, 1866–1906*, 184.

38. Kappler, *Indian Affairs: Laws and Treaties*, 1:504.

39. *Indian Appropriation Act 1894*, 27 Stat. 645 (March 3, 1893); *Indian Appropriation Act 1896*, 28 Stat. 876 (March 2, 1895).

40. Halbert E. Paine, *The Choctaw Nation and the Chickasaw Nation, Claimants, vs. the United States and the Wichita and Affiliated Bands of Indians, Defendants: Brief for Claimants* (Washington, D.C.: Gibson Bros., 1896), 2:1.

41. Kappler, *Indian Affairs: Laws and Treaties*, 706–707, 919; *The Choctaw and Chickasaw Nations v. The United States and the Wichita and Affiliated Bands of Indians*, 34 Ct. Cl. 17 (1899), 3.

42. *An Act for the Protection of the People of the Indian Territory and for Other Purposes*, 30 Stat. 495 (June 28, 1898) (the Curtis Act).

43. *The Choctaw and Chickasaw Nations v. The United States and the Wichita and Affiliated Bands of Indians*, 34 Ct. Cl. 17 (January 9, 1899).

44. *U.S. v. Choctaw Nation; United States v. Choctaw Nation and Chickasaw Nation; Wichita and Affiliated Bands of Indians v. Choctaw Nation, Chickasaw Nation and United States; Choctaw Nation and Chickasaw Nation v. United States and Wichita and Affiliated Bands of Indians*, 179 U.S. 494, 548 (December 10, 1900).

45. The plenary power doctrine emerged in 1903 in the case of *Lone Wolf v. Hitchcock*. In that decision, the Court affirmed the ability of Congress to abrogate treaties based on the dependent status of tribes on the federal government. See C. B. Clark, *Lone Wolf v. Hitchcock* (Lincoln: University of Nebraska Press, 1994), 9.

46. "A Memorial to the Senate and House of Representatives of the United States Concerning the 'Leased Lands' of the Choctaw and Chickasaw," approved January 7, 1901, Box 35, Folder 9, Choctaw Nation Collection.

CHAPTER 12

1. Constitution of the Choctaw Nation of Oklahoma, June 9, 1983, available online at www.choctawnation.com/files/Constitution.pdf.

2. "An Act Conferring Citizenship upon Certain Beluksha Indians Therein Names," approved October 12, 1858; and "Creeks (McGilbery Family) Admitted to Citizenship," approved October 21, 1858, in Choctaw Nation, *Constitution and Laws*

of the Choctaw Nation: Together with the Treaties of 1855, 1865 and 1866 (New York: Wm. P. Lyon & Son, Printers and Publishers, 1869), 178–179 and 184, respectively.

3. "An Act Requiring County Judges to Take the Census," approved November 1855, in ibid., 492.

4. "An Act Directing and Authorizing the Appointment of a Committee by the General Council," approved October 19, 1876, in *Laws of the Choctaw Nation Passed at the Choctaw Councils of 1876 and 1877* (Atoka, Choctaw Nation: W. J. Hemby, Printer, 1878), 28–30; "Report of Special Law Committee Recommending Text of an Act Entitled 'An Act Directing and Authorizing the Appointment of a Committee by the General Council, Oct. 17, 1876,'" Box 8, Folder 17, Choctaw Nation Collection.

5. *Indian Appropriation Act 1897*, 29 Stat. 321 (June 10, 1896); U.S. Commission to the Five Civilized Tribes, *Annual Reports of 1894, 1895 and 1896, from March 3, 1893 to January 1, 1897* (Washington, D.C.: Government Printing Office, 1894–1896).

6. *Annual Report of the Commission to the Five Civilized Tribes to the Secretary of the Interior, 1898* (Washington, D.C.: Government Printing Office, 1898), 7.

7. Act of June 10, 1896 (29 Stat. L., 321), in Department of the Interior, *Laws, Decisions, and Regulations Affecting the Work of the Commissioner to the Five Civilized Tribes* . . . (Washington, D.C.: Government Printing Office, 1906), 12 ; U.S. Commission to the Five Civilized Tribes, *Annual Reports of 1894, 1895 and 1896*, 88–89.

8. Loren N. Brown, "The Choctaw-Chickasaw Court Citizens," *Chronicles of Oklahoma* 16, no. 4 (December 1938): 428; Kent Carter, *The Dawes Commission and the Allotment of the Five Civilized Tribes, 1893–1914* (Orem, Utah: Ancestry.com, 1999), 74. The Dawes Commission received applications from 1,418 individuals claiming membership on the Choctaw rolls. These were decided between December 1 and 8, the final days of the enrollment process. Applications generally included a number of family members. The commission decided favorably on 1,212 cases, encompassing 3,815 individuals. *Annual Report of the Commission to the Five Civilized Tribes to the Secretary of the Interior, 1898*, 7; see also Carter, *The Dawes Commission and the Allotment of the Five Civilized Tribes*, 21.

9. Judge William H. H. Clayton heard 245 cases in the Central District at South McAlester beginning in August 1897, and Judge Hosea Townsend of the Southern District at Ardmore heard 156 cases beginning on November 15, 1897; Carter, *The Dawes Commission and the Allotment of the Five Civilized Tribes*, 29.

10. *The Atoka Convention of Choctaw and Chickasaw Indians* (South McAlester, I.T.: Press of the South McAlester capital, n.d.), 5.

11. *Indian Appropriation Act 1899*, 30 Stat. 591 (July 1, 1898); Charles J. Kappler, *Indian Affairs: Laws and Treaties*, 5 vols. (Washington, D.C.: Government Printing Office, 1904–1941), 1:665; *Stephens v. Cherokee Nation*, 174 U.S. 445, 467 (May 15, 1899); Brown, "The Choctaw-Chickasaw Citizenship Court," 433.

12. "An Act to Provide for the Protection of the Choctaws and Chickasaws from the Citizenship Claims of Those Persons Known as Court Claimants," approved January 7, 1901, Box 35, Folder 5, Choctaw Nation Collection.

13. Ibid.

14. U.S. Congress, House Committee on Indian Affairs, *Claims of J. F. McMurray: Hearings before the Subcommittee of the Committee on Indian Affairs, House of Representatives, Seventieth Congress, Second Session on H.R. 10741, December 12 to 21, 1928* (Washington, D.C.: Government Printing Office, 1929), 272; "An Act to Provide for the Protection of the Choctaws and Chickasaws from the Citizenship Claims of those Persons Known as Court Claimants."

15. *Proceedings of Choctaw and Chickasaw Citizenship court in Connection with Compensation of Attorneys*, 60th Cong., 1st sess., March 10, 1908, S. Doc. 372, 5; *Seventh Annual Report of the Commission to the Five Civilized Tribes to the Secretary of the Interior for the Fiscal Year Ended June 30, 1900* (Washington, D.C.: Government Printing Office, 1900), 15–16.

16. *Indian Appropriation Act 1896*, 28 Stat. 876 (March 2, 1895); *Indian Appropriation Act 1897*, 29 Stat. 321 (June 10, 1896).

17. Kappler, *Indian Affairs: Laws and Treaties*, 1:313.

18. Since only 143 patents for land were issued out of some 600 cases heard by government commissioners from 1837 to 1843, it is clear that most of the Mississippi Choctaws never received a share of the tribe's land; see Ronald N. Satz, "The Mississippi Choctaw: From the Removal Treaty to the Federal Agency," in *After Removal: The Choctaws in Mississippi*, edited by Samuel J. Wells and Roseanna Tubby (Jackson: University Press of Mississippi, 1986), 3–32; *Laws of the Choctaw Nation . . . 1876 and 1877*, 13; *Indian Appropriation Act 1898*, 30 Stat. 83 (June 7, 1897).

19. Clara Sue Kidwell, "The Choctaw Struggle for Land and Identity in Mississippi, 1830–1918," in *After Removal: The Choctaw in Mississippi*, edited by Samuel J. Wells and Roseanna Tubby (Jackson: University Press of Mississippi, 1986).

20. "A Memorial to the Congress of the United States," approved December 24, 1889, Box 21, Folder 81, Choctaw Nation Collection.

21. *Winton et al. v. Amos et al.*, 255 U.S. 373, 379 (March 7, 1921); Angie Debo, *The Rise and Fall of the Choctaw Republic* (Norman: University of Oklahoma Press, 1934), 181.

22. *Winton et al. v. Amos et al.*, 255 U.S 380 (March 7, 1921); *Ninth Annual Report of the Commission to the Five Civilized Tribes to the Secretary of the Interior for the Fiscal Year Ended June 30, 1902* (Washington, D.C.: Government Printing Office, 1902), 13.

23. *Report of the Commission of the Five Civilized Tribes Relative to the Mississippi Choctaws*, 55th Cong., 2nd sess., H. Rep. 274, 6; Wm. O. Beall, Muskogee, to the Commissioner to the Five Civilized Tribes, April 14, 1914, Box 4, Folder 9, Patrick J. Hurley Collection, Western History Collections, University of Oklahoma, Norman, Oklahoma (hereafter Hurley Collection).

24. *Mississippi Choctaws, Rights to Choctaw Citizenship*, 54th Cong., 2nd sess., February 16, 1897, S. Doc. 129, 1–6; Memorial and Petition on Behalf of the Mississippi Choctaws, Charles Winton to the Secretary of the Interior [n.p., September, 1897]; *Mississippi Choctaws*, 54th Cong., 2nd sess., March 3, 1897, H. Rep. 3080, 1.

25. *Report of the Commission to the Five Civilized Tribes Relative to the Mississippi Choctaws*, 55th Cong., 2nd sess., February 3, 1898, H. Doc. 274, 2; *Indian Appropriation*

Act 1898, 30 Stat. 83 (June 7, 1897); *An Act for the Protection of the People of the Indian Territory, and for Other Purposes*, 30 Stat. 495 (June 28, 1898) (the Curtis Act).

26. *Indian Appropriation Act 1899*, 30 Stat. 495 (July 1, 1898).

27. *Report of the Commission to the Five Civilized Tribes to the Secretary of the Interior for the Year Ended June 30, 1905* (Washington, D.C.: Government Printing Office, 1905), 16, 92; *Eleventh Annual Report of the Commission to the Five Civilized Tribes to the Secretary of the Interior for the Fiscal Year Ended June 30, 1904* (Washington, D.C.: Government Printing Office, 1904), 18–19; *Winton et al. v. Amos et al.*, 255 U.S 373, 385, March 7, 1921.

28. Ninety-three applications, embracing 355 persons, were heard at Hattiesburg from December 17 to 22, 1900, mainly of full-blood Choctaws unable to speak English. Other hearings were held at Meridian, Philadelphia, Carthage, and Decatur throughout the spring of 1901. The Atoka office was opened on January 2, 1901; it heard 636 applications embracing 825 persons. The office at Meridian opened April 1, 1901; it heard 878 applications embracing 3,002 persons. From April 29 to May 4, 1901, the Philadelphia office heard 76 applications embracing 229 persons. From May 6 to 11, 1901, the Carthage office heard 56 applications embracing 203 persons. From May 13 to 18, the Decatur office heard 33 applications embracing 101 persons.

29. *Eighth Annual Report of the Commission to the Five Civilized Tribes to the Secretary of the Interior for the Fiscal Year Ended June 30, 1901* (Washington, D.C.: Government Printing Office, 1901), 19–21.

30. *Petition of the Mississippi Choctaws in Regard to an Act*, H.R. 8566, 56th Cong., 1st sess., S. Doc. 263, April 4, 1900, 1; *Indian Appropriation Act 1901*, 31 Stat. 221 (May 31, 1900).

31. Carter, *The Dawes Commission and the Allotment of the Five Civilized Tribes*, 75–76.

32. *Indian Appropriation Act 1901*; Department of Interior, *Laws, Decisions, and Regulations Affecting the Work of the Commissioner to the Five Civilized Tribes . . .*, 33–34; Carter, *The Dawes Commission and the Allotment of the Five Civilized Tribes*, 75–76.

33. *Eighth Annual Report of the Commission to the Five Civilized Tribes . . . 1901*, 19.

34. Ibid.; *Ninth Annual Report of the Commission to the Five Civilized Tribes to the Secretary of the Interior for the Fiscal Year Ended June 30, 1902* (Washington, D.C.: Government Printing Office, 1902), 25.

35. *Ninth Annual Report of the Commission to the Five Civilized Tribes . . . 1902*, 25.

36. Carter, *The Dawes Commission and the Allotment of the Five Civilized Tribes*, 85; U.S. Commission to the Five Civilized Tribes, *Eleventh Annual Report of the Commission to the Five Civilized Tribes to the Secretary of the Interior for the Fiscal Year Ended June 30, 1904* (Washington, D.C.: Government Printing Office, 1904), 19.

37. U.S. Department of the Interior, *Agreement with a Commission of the Choctaw and Chickasaw Nations*, 56th Cong., 1st sess., January 3, 1900, H. Doc. 221.

38. *An Act to Ratify and Confirm an Agreement with the Choctaw and Chickasaw Tribes of Indians, and for Other Purposes*, 32 Stat. 641 (July 1, 1902).

39. *Rights of Mississippi Choctaws in the Choctaw Nation: Memorial of the Full-Blood Mississippi Choctaws Relative to Their Rights in the Choctaw Nation*, 57th Cong., 2nd sess., April 24, 1902, S. Doc. 319, 1–4.

40. Ibid.

41. *Ninth Annual Report of the Commission to the Five Civilized Tribes . . . 1902*, 25.

42. Brown, "The Choctaw-Chickasaw Citizenship Courts," 440; *Proceedings of Choctaw and Chickasaw Citizenship Court in Connection with Compensation of Attorneys*, 60th Cong., 1st sess., S. Doc. 372, 2–5.

43. Carter, *The Dawes Commission and the Allotment of the Five Civilized Tribes*, 83.

44. It heard 128 cases at South McAlester and 131 cases at Tishomingo (the Chickasaw capital). It ended its work on December 10, 1904. Carter, *The Dawes Commission and the Allotment of the Five Civilized Tribes*, 83; *Report of the Commission to the Five Civilized Tribes to the Secretary of the Interior for the Year ended June 30, 1905* (Washington, D.C.: Government Printing Office, 1905), 11.

45. Carter, *The Dawes Commission and the Allotment of the Five Civilized Tribes*, 90.

46. "What the Choctaw People Saved by Defeating the 'Court Citizens,'" 1904, Box 27, Folder 4, McCurtain Collection.

47. Carter, *The Dawes Commission and the Allotment of the Five Civilized Tribes*, 84.

48. *Investigations of Indian Contracts*, 61st Cong., 3rd sess., February 28, 1911, H. Rep. 2273, 697.

49. McMurray lobbied Senator Orville Platt of Connecticut, Senator Allison of Iowa, Senator James K. Jones of Arkansas, Senator Morgan of Alabama, "and many others." For the passage of the supplementary agreement, see U.S. Congress, House Committee on Indian Affairs, *Claims of J. F. McMurray*, 243, 247; Carter, *The Dawes Commission and the Allotment of the Five Civilized Tribes*, 83. The work of the commission largely stopped during the hearings of the Choctaw-Chickasaw citizenship court. That court heard cases involving 3,487 people. It admitted only 161 and denied 2,792, offering its rulings by December 10, 1904.

50. *Indian Appropriation Act 1904*, 32 Stat. 982, 997 (March 3, 1903); *Winton et al. v. Amos et al.*

51. James D. Morrison, *Schools for the Choctaws* (Durant, Okla.: Choctaw Bilingual Education Program, Southeastern Oklahoma State University, 1978), 336.

52. "Editorials on G. W. Dukes and Green McCurtain," *The South McAlester Capital*, May 1, 1902, Box D29, Folder 39, Gilbert W. Dukes Collection, Western History Collections, University of Oklahoma, Norman, Oklahoma (hereafter Dukes Collection); "Interview with G. W. Dukes," *The Coalgate Courier*, July 3, 1902, Box D29, Folder 39, Dukes Collection.

53. "Election of G. W. Dukes," *The Wagoner Record*, August 9, 1900, Box D29, Folder 3, Dukes Collection.

54. "Editorial on Protest by G. W. Dukes," *The South McAlester Capital*, March 27, 1902, Box D29, Folder 29, Dukes Collection.

55. "Editorial on G. W. Dukes," *The Indian Journal*, Eufaula, January 25, 1901, Box D29, Folder 11, Dukes Collection.

56. Green McCurtain, "To the Choctaw and Chickasaw People," Box 27, Folder 6, McCurtain Collection.

57. "The Coal and Asphalt Question," published by the Supplementary Agreement Executive Committee, September 15, 1903 [*sic*; 1902], Box 27, Folder 7, McCurtain Collection.

58. "Proclamation of G. W. Dukes and D. H. Johnston," *The Holdenville Times*, August 16, 1902, Box D29, Folder 41, Dukes Collection; "Editorials on G. W. Dukes and Green McCurtain," *The South McAlester Capital*, August 28, 1902, Box D29, Folder 45, Dukes Collection.

59. "Proclamation of G. W. Dukes and P. S. Mosely," *The Indian Citizen*, October 2, 1902, Box D29, Folder 46, Dukes Collection.

60. "Choctaw Politics," *Twin Territories*, Muskogee, November 1902, Box D29, Folder 49, Dukes Collection; "Proclamation by G. W. Dukes," *Chickasaw Enterprise*, Pauls Valley, October 23, 1902, Box 20, Folder 13, McCurtain Collection.

61. U.S. Department of the Interior, Office of Indian Affairs, *Annual Reports of the Commissioner of Indian Affairs to the Secretary of the Interior for the Year 1903* (Washington, D.C.: Government Printing Office, 1903), 173–174; "News Item of G. W. Dukes," *The South McAlester News*, South McAlester, Ind. Ter., October 16, 1902, Box D29, Folder 47, Dukes Collection.

62. U.S. Department of the Interior, Office of Indian Affairs, *Annual Report of the Commissioner of Indian Affairs to the Secretary of the Interior for the Year 1903*, 174.

63. *An Act to Provide for the Final Disposition of the Affairs of the Five Civilized Tribes in the Indian Territory, and for Other Purposes*, 34 Stat. 137, 140 (April 26, 1906).

64. "Message of Gilbert W. Dukes," October 9, 1901, *The Indian Citizen*, October 17, 1901, Box D29, Folder 20, Dukes Collection.

CHAPTER 13

1. "Interview with Gilbert Webster Thompson," Vol. 46, 439, Indian-Pioneer Papers Collection, Western History Collections, University of Oklahoma, Norman, Oklahoma (hereafter Indian-Pioneer Papers Collection).

2. "Interview with Gilbert Webster Thompson," 6.

3. Carton 4, Frame 384, Choctaw Nation Papers, OHS.

4. "Interview with Gilbert Webster Thompson," 2.

5. D. C. Gideon, *Indian Territory, Descriptive Biographical and Genealogical Including the Landed Estates, County Seats etc., etc. with a General History of the Territory* (New York: Lewis Publishing Company, 1901), 301.

6. "An Act Granting G. W. Thompson, G. W. Dukes and J. H. McClure the Privilege to Have a Toll-Gate," approved November 2, 1892, Box 24, Folder 28, Choctaw Nation Collection.

7. Carton 41, vol. 230, 105, Choctaw Nation Papers.

8. "Interview with Gilbert Webster Thompson," 6.

9. Gideon, *Indian Territory*, 301–302; Carton 41, 242, Choctaw Nation Papers, OHS.

10. "Interview with Gilbert Webster Thompson," 4; "A Resolution Accepting the Report of G. W. Thompson, Captain of Militia, Second District," approved October 27, 1893, Box 25, Folder 63, Choctaw Nation Collection.

11. "An Act for the Relief of G. W. Thompson for Taking Care of the Capitol Building Repainting &c. Painting $90; Scrubbing, $50, 7 Cords Wood, $8.50, Miscellaneous Painting Supplies. Total $210.90," approved October 19, 1893, Box 25, Folder 37, Choctaw Nation Collection; "An Act for the Relief of Gilbert W. Thompson, for Work on Capital, $258.26," approved October 17, 1894, Box 26, Folder 34, Choctaw Nation Collection.

12. "An Act to Establish Two Boarding Schools and Erect a Building in Choctaw Nation," approved April 4, 1891, Box 23, Folder 2, Choctaw Nation Collection. This act allocated $40,000 for the schools.

13. Rex Francis Harlow, *Makers of Government in Oklahoma: A Descriptive Roster of Oklahomans Whose Influence and Activity Make Them Significant in the Course of Public Events in Their State* (Oklahoma City: Harlow Publishing Company, 1930), 709.

14. Carton 47, vol. 279, 39, Choctaw Nation Papers, OHS; Interview with Peter Hudson, July 20, 1967, T-284, 7, Doris Duke Indian Oral History Collection, Western History Collections, University of Oklahoma, Norman, Oklahoma (hereafter Doris Duke Collection).

15. *Minutes of the Twenty-first Annual Meeting of the Choctaw and Chickasaw Baptist Association Held with Armstrong Baptist Church, Blue County, Choctaw Nation, I.T., Commencing September 4, 1891* (Oklahoma City, O.T.: Baptist Publishing Company Print, 1891), 7.

16. *Minutes of the Twenty-fifth Annual Session of the Choctaw and Chickasaw Baptist Association, Held with the Rock Creek Baptist Church, San Bois County, Choctaw Nation, August 23 & 24, 1895* (South McAlester: Indianola Printing Co., Printers, 1895), 5.

17. Carton 51, Frame 15202, Choctaw Nation Papers, OHS.

18. Carton 47, vol. 283, 37, 63, Choctaw Nation Papers, OHS. The appointment as deputy sheriff was made on June 10, 1901; Carton 58, Frame 15102, Choctaw Nation Papers. The appointment as clerk and treasurer was made on October 1, 1902.

19. Theda Perdue, *Nations Remembered: An Oral History of the Five Civilized Tribes, 1865–1907* (Westport, Conn.: Greenwood Press, 1980), 185; "Josiah Billy Interview," Vol. 54, 390–392, Indian-Pioneer Papers Collection.

20. "Interview with Gilbert Webster Thompson," 6.

21. E. Hastain, *Index to Choctaw-Chickasaw Deeds and Allottments* (Muskogee, Okla.: E. Hastain, 1908–1910), 655–656, 1252–1253, 1259.

22. Kidwell family genealogy, privately published by Billy Dan Kidwell, July, 1991, 227; in author's possession.

23. Gene Plowden, *Those Amazing Ringlings and Their Circus* (Caldwell, Idaho: Caxton Printers, 1968), 119–121.

24. J. S. Murrow, a Baptist missionary, introduced the order into the Nation. Victor M. Locke, Jr., who was appointed governor in 1911, was also a Mason. See Frank

A. Balyeat, "Joseph Samuel Morrow, Apostle to the Indians," *Chronicles of Oklahoma* 35, no. 3 (Fall 1957): 297–314; Muriel Wright, "Old Boggy Depot," *Chronicles of Oklahoma* 5, no. 1 (March 1927): 10.

25. Albert Gallatin Mackey, *The History of Freemasonry, Its Legends and Traditions, Its Chronological History with William R. Singleton, the History of Its Introduction and Progress in the United States, the History of the Symbols of Freemasonry and the History of the S.S. Scottish Rite*, 7 vols. (New York: Masonic History Company, 1898), 6:1474–1475.

26. "Interview with Gilbert Webster Thompson," 6.

CHAPTER 14

1. Muriel H. Wright, "Origin of Oklahoma Day," *Chronicles of Oklahoma* 23, no. 2 (1945): 209; Muriel H. Wright, "The Wedding of Oklahoma and Miss Indian Territory," *Chronicles of Oklahoma* 35 (Fall 1957): 255–264.

2. Roy Gittinger, *The Formation of the State of Oklahoma, 1803–1906* (Berkeley: University of California Press, 1917), 198.

3. Thomas H. Doyle, "Single versus Double Statehood," *Chronicles of Oklahoma* 5, no. 1 (March 1927): 31; Seth K. Corden and W. B. Richards, comps., *The Oklahoma Red Book* (Oklahoma City, 1912), 2:xviii.

4. *Proposed State of Sequoyah*, 59th Cong., 1st sess., January 6, 1906, S. Doc. 143, 39.

5. Martha Gilmore to Gov. McCurtain, April 28, 1903, and Green McCurtain to Laura Harsha, April 3, 1903, both in Box 12, Folder 3, McCurtain Collection.

6. *Proposed State of Sequoyah*, 5.

7. *Coal Lands in Oklahoma: Message from the President of the United States Transmitting Reports Rendered in Connection with the Investigation to Determine the Extent and Value of the Coal Deposits in and under the Segregated Coal Lands of the Choctaw and Chickasaw Nations in Oklahoma*, 61st Cong., 2nd sess., February 28, 1910, S. Doc. 390 (Washington, D.C.: Government Printing Office, 1910), 120–121.

8. Doyle, "Single versus Double Statehood," 28.

9. Ibid., 33.

10. *Removal of Restrictions from Part of Lands of Allottees of Five Civilized Tribes*, 60th Cong., 1st sess., April 6, 1908, H. Rep. 1454, 1–2.

11. Gittinger, *Formation of the State of Oklahoma*, 203; "Proposed State of Sequoyah," 29, 30, 34; "Five Civilized Tribes Protest against Congressional Legislation Contemplating Annexation of Indian Territory to Oklahoma or Territorial Form of Government Prior to March 4th, 1906," Box 27, Folder 19, McCurtain Collection.

12. The Choctaw delegates were H. P. Ward, L. C. LeFlore, Hampton Tucker, and Henry Ansley; see Box 21, Folder 2, #3, McCurtain Collection.

13. In 1903, the Indian agent for Union Agency estimated a population of 70,000 Indians and 650,000 whites. *Annual Report of the Commissioner of Indian Affairs to the Secretary of the Interior for the Year 1903* (Washington, D.C.: Government Printing Office, 1904), 162.

14. *Addresses and Arguments by Prominent Men in Favor of Separate Statehood for Indian Territory* (Kinta, I.T.: Enterprise Print, n.d.), 4, Box 27, Folder 3, McCurtain Collection.

15. "Independent Statehood for Indian Territory, Five Civilized Tribes Executive Committee, To the Editor," a press release signed by W. H. Ansley, Chairman (Choctaw Nation), Alex Posey (Creek Nation), W. H. Murray (Chickasaw Nation), A. J. Brown (Seminole Nation), and Connell Rogers (Cherokee Nation), September 21, 1903, Box 12, Folder 3, McCurtain Collection.

16. *Proposed State of Sequoyah*, 24; "Editorial on Constitutional Convention," *The Muskogee Phoenix*, July 14, 1905, Muskogee Public Library, Muskogee, Oklahoma.

17. *Proposed State of Sequoyah*, 25–26.

18. Amos Maxwell, *The Sequoyah Constitutional Convention* (Boston: Meador Publishing Company, 1953).

19. "Proposed State of Sequoyah," 46.

20. Maxwell, *The Sequoyah Constitutional Convention*, 113.

21. Ibid., 99.

22. "Statement of Green McCurtain," *The Claremore Messenger*, February 27, 1903, Box 20, Folder 14, McCurtain Collection.

23. Gittinger, *Formation of the State of Oklahoma*, 212.

24. William H. Murray, "The Constitutional Convention," *Chronicles of Oklahoma* 9, no. 2 (June 1931): 126–138.

25. "Proposed State of Sequoyah," 42; Message of Theodore Roosevelt to Congress, December 5, 1905, in James D. Richardson, ed., *A Compilation of the Message and Papers of the Presidents*. Vol. 16. *1914.* (New York: Bureau of National Literature, Inc., 1917), 7400.

26. Corden and Richards, *The Oklahoma Red Book*, 2:356, 363.

27. *An Act for the Removal of Restrictions from Part of the Lands of Allottees of the Five Civilized Tribes, and for Other Purposes*, 35 Stat. 312 (May 27, 1908); Angie Debo, *And Still the Waters Run* (Princeton, N.J.: Princeton University Press, 1940), 166–169.

28. U.S. Department of the Interior, Office of Indian Affairs, *Annual Report of the Commissioner of Indian Affairs to the Secretary of the Interior for the Year 1908* (Washington, D.C.: Government Printing Office, 1908), 7.

29. *An Act for the Removal of Restrictions from Part of the Lands of Allottees of the Five Civilized Tribes, and for Other Purposes*, 35 Stat. 312 (May 27, 1908).

30. Gertrude Bonnin, Charles H. Fabens, Matthew K. Sniffen, *Oklahoma's Poor Rich Indians: An Orgy of Graft and Exploitation of the Five Civilized Tribes—Legalized Robbery* (Philadelphia, Pa.: Office of the Indian Rights Association, 1924).

31. U.S. Congress, House Committee on Indian Affairs, *Claims of J. F. McMurray: Hearings before the Subcommittee of the Committee on Indian Affairs, House of Representatives, Seventieth Congress, Second Session on H.R. 10741, December 12 to 21, 1928* (Washington, D.C.: Government Printing Office, 1929), 191.

32. Ibid., 231.

33. *Choate v. Trapp*, 224 U.S. 665, 679 (1912).

34. *Annual Report of the Commissioner to the Five Civilized Tribes . . . 1908*, 3; Debo, *And Still the Waters Run*, 159–202.

35. *Report of the Thirty-first Annual Lake Mohonk Conference of Friends of the Indian and Other Dependent Peoples, October 22d, 23rd and 24th, 1913* (n.p.: Lake Mohonk Conference of Friends of the Indian and Other Dependent Peoples, 1913), 22.

36. Warren K. Moorehead, *Our National Problem: The Sad Condition of the Oklahoma Indians* (n.p., 1913), 20–21; Debo, *And Still the Waters Run*, 225–229. Debo estimates the amount recovered at about $30,000.

37. Tanis Thorne, *The World's Richest Indian: The Scandal over Jackson Barnett's Oil Fortune* (Oxford: Oxford University Press, 2003). Although the major oil fields were in Creek and Seminole country, some were in Choctaw and Chickasaw country.

38. Bonnin, Fabens, and Sniffen, *Oklahoma's Poor Rich Indians*, 26–28.

39. U.S. Congress, House, Committee on Indian Affairs, *Five Civilized Tribes in Oklahoma: Hearings before the Subcommittee of the Committee on Indian Affairs, House of Representatives, Sixty-eighth Congress, First Session on H.R. 6900, March 22 and 28, 1924* (Washington, D.C.: Government Printing Office, 1924), 2–71.

CHAPTER 15

1. *Indian Appropriation Act 1905*, 33 Stat. 189, 209 (April 21, 1904).

2. "Report of Patrick Hurley," Box 12, Folder 3, Hurley Collection, 13; Chickasaws (November 17, 1905), Choctaws (November 21, 1905), Box 12, Folder 3, Hurley Collection.

3. U.S. Congress, House Committee on Indian Affairs, *Claims of J. F. McMurray: Hearings before the Subcommittee of the Committee on Indian Affairs, House of Representatives, Seventieth Congress, Second Session on H.R. 10741, December 12 to 21, 1928* (Washington, D.C.: Government Printing Office, 1929), 236; "Report of Patrick Hurley," 14.

4. *An Act to Provide for the Final Disposition of the Affairs of the Five Civilized Tribes in the Indian Territory, and for Other Purposes*, 34 Stat. 137, 142 (April 26, 1906).

5. *Investigations of Indian Contracts: Hearings before the Select Committee of the House of Representatives Appointed under Authority of House Resolution No. 847, June 25, 1910, for the Purpose of Investigating Indian Contracts with the Five Civilized Tribes and the Osage Indians in Oklahoma*, 61st Cong., 3rd sess., February 28, 1911, H. Rep. 2273, iii–iv.

6. *Coal Lands in Oklahoma: Message from the President of the United States Transmitting Reports Rendered in Connection with the Investigation to Determine the Extent and Value of the Coal Deposits in and under the Segregated Coal Lands of the Choctaw and Chickasaw Nations in Oklahoma*, 61st Cong., 2nd sess., S. Doc. 390, February 28, 1910 (Washington, D.C.: Government Printing Office, 1910), 29.

7. U.S. Department of the Interior, Office of Indian Affairs, *Annual Report of the Commissioner of Indian Affairs to the Secretary of the Interior for the Year 1907* (Washington, D.C.: Government Printing Office, 1907), 100. Senator Moses E. Clapp introduced a

bill in the Senate (S. 8286) to create the Choctaw-Chickasaw Coal, Oil, and Asphalt Land Company to manage and dispose of the resources, but the session ended before the bill could be acted upon.

8. *An Act to Provide for the Sale of the Surface of the Segregated Coal and Asphalt Lands of the Choctaw and Chickasaw Nations, and for Other Purposes*, 37 Stat. 67 (February 19, 1912).

9. "Memorial of the Principal Chief of the Choctaw Nation and the Governor of the Chickasaw Nation, to the Congress of the United States Asking for the Sale of the Segregated Coal and Asphalt Deposits Belonging to the Choctaw-Chickasaw Nations," Box 3, Folder 24, Hurley Collection.

10. *Authorizing the Purchase of Certain Interests in Lands and Mineral Deposits by the United States from the Choctaw and Chickasaw Nations of Indians*, 78th Cong., 1st sess., October 12, 1943, S. Rep. 463, 6; *An Act Providing for the Sale of Cole and Asphalt Deposits in the Segregated Mineral Land in the Choctaw and Chickasaw Nations, Oklahoma*, 40 Stat. 433 (February 8, 1918); *An Act Authorizing the Secretary of the Interior to Offer for Sale Remainder of the Coal and Asphalt Deposits in Segregated Mineral Land in the Choctaw and Chickasaw Nations, State of Oklahoma*, 41 Stat. 1107 (February 22, 1921); Angie Debo, *And Still the Waters Run* (New York: Gordian Press, 1966), 387.

11. Debo, *And Still the Waters Run*, 380.

12. *Sale of Coal and Asphalt Deposits in Choctaws and Chickasaw Nations, Oklahoma*, 71st Cong., 2nd sess., May 19, 1930, H. Rep. 1518; *An Act to Provide for the Leasing of the Segregated Coal and Asphalt Deposits of the Choctaw and Chickasaw Indian Nations, in Oklahoma, and for an Extension of Time within Which Purchasers of Such Deposits May Complete Payments*, 47 Stat. 88 (April 21, 1932).

13. Debo, *And Still the Waters Run*, 387.

14. *Choctaw Nation v. United States*, 91 Ct. Cl. 320 (1940).

15. U.S. Congress, Senate Committee on Indian Affairs, *Leasing of the Segregated Coal Deposits of the Choctaw and Chickasaw Nations in Oklahoma: Hearings before the Committee on Indian Affairs, United States Senate, 77th Congress, 2nd session, on S. 1542, a Bill to Authorize the Leasing of the Undeveloped Coal and Asphalt Deposits of the Choctaw and Chickasaw Nations in Oklahoma: February 2 and 3, and March 3, 1942* (Washington, D.C.: Government Printing Office, 1942), 7, 9.

16. Ibid., 74, 89.

17. *Appropriation Bill for Interior*, 58 Stat. 463, 483 (June 24, 1944); *Joint Resolution Providing for the Ratification by Congress of a Contract for the Purchase of Certain Lands and Mineral Deposits by the United States from the Choctaw and Chickasaw Nations of Indians*, 62 Stat. 596 (June 24, 1948).

18. "Every person who unlawfully cuts or aids or is employed in unlawfully cutting, or wantonly destroys, or procures to be wantonly destroyed, any timber standing upon lands of the United States, which, in pursuance of law, may be reserved or purchased for military or other purposes, shall pay a fine of not more than five hundred dollars, and be imprisoned not more than twelve months"; *Crimes Arising within the Maritime and Territorial Jurisdiction of the United States*, 18 Stat. 1044 (March 3, 1859).

19. "Report of John Q. Tufts, Union Agency, I.T., Muskogee, September 1, 1882," in U.S. Department of the Interior, Office of Indian Affairs, *Annual Report of the Commissioner of Indian Affairs to the Secretary of the Interior for the Year 1882* (Washington, D.C.: Government Printing Office, 1882), 88.

20. U.S. Department of the Interior, Office of Indian Affairs, *Annual Report of the Commissioner of Indian Affairs to the Secretary of the Interior for the Year 1880* (Washington, D.C.: Government Printing Office, 1880), xix; *Annual Report of the Commissioner of Indian Affairs to the Secretary of the Interior for the Year 1882* (Washington, D.C.: Government Printing Office, 1882), 104; U.S. Department of the Interior, Office of Indian Affairs, *Annual Report of the Commissioner of Indian Affairs to the Secretary of the Interior for the Year 1884* (Washington, D.C.: Government Printing Office, 1884), xvi; *Annual Report of the Commissioner of Indian Affairs to the Secretary of the Interior for the Year 1885* (Washington, D.C.: Government Printing Office, 1885), xxxiii.

21. *Eleventh Annual Report of the Commission to the Five Civilized Tribes to the Secretary of the Interior for the Fiscal Year Ended June 30, 1904* (Washington, D.C.: Government Printing Office, 1904), 46.

22. *Report of the Commission to the Five Civilized Tribes to the Secretary of the Interior for the Year Ended June 30, 1905* (Washington, D.C.: Government Printing Office, 1905), 36.

23. *An Act to Ratify an Agreement with the Indians of the Fort Hall Indian Reservation in Idaho, and Making Appropriations to Carry the Same into Effect*, 31 Stat., 672, 680 (June 6, 1900). This act referred the Leased District matter to the U.S. Court of Claims. See also "Message of Green McCurtain," *The Indian Citizen*, October 11, 1900, Box 20, Folder 11, McCurtain Collection.

24. Two tracts of timber land were withdrawn from allotment, one (1,373,324 acres) under the interior department's orders of December 3 and 8, 1906, and January 12, 1907. Tract 2 (10,801 acres) was withdrawn under an act of April 6, 1906 (34 Stat. 137). Tract 1 had 141,309,000 feet of hardwood and 1,430,857,500 feet of pine and was divided into twenty-four separate tracts for sale. Fifteen bids were received. Only Tract 2 had more than one bidder. The bids were rejected on May 15, 1912. Tract 2, in the southeastern part of Choctaw territory, contained about 3,000,000 feet of hardwood and 43,505,500 feet of pine. It was offered for sale on October 31, 1911, was appraised at $180,818, and sold for $287,000. See Hurley's semiannual report to Locke, November 28, 1912, 15, Box 12, Folder 2, Hurley Collection.

25. Sandra Faiman-Silva, *Choctaws at the Crossroads: The Political Economy of Class and Culture in the Oklahoma Timber Region* (Lincoln: University of Nebraska Press, 1997), 94–102.

26. William Sydney Coker, "Pat Harrison's Efforts to Reopen the Choctaw Citizenship Rolls," *Southern Quarterly* 3 (October 1964): 36–60.

27. Ibid., 36, 40; U.S. Department of the Interior, *Enrollment with the Five Civilized Tribes: Hearings before Subcommittee of the Committee on Indian Affairs, House of Representatives, Sixty-third Congress, Second Session on Bills for Enrollment with the Five Civilized Tribes: July 2, 1914* (Washington, D.C.: Government Printing Office, 1914), 3.

28. "H.R. 19213, To Reopen the Roll of the Choctaw-Chickasaw Tribe and to Provide for the Awarding of the Rights Secured to Certain Persons by the Fourteenth Article of the Treaty of Dancing Rabbit Creek of Date September 27, 1830," *Congressional Record*, 62nd Cong., 2nd sess., February 1, 1912, vol. 48, part 2, 1652.

29. "The Mississippi Choctaw," speech of Hon. Pat Harrison of Mississippi in the House of Representatives, December 12, 1912 (Washington, D.C., 1912), 2–3, 8–10, 16, Box 4, Folder 22, Choctaw Nation Collection.

30. *Condition of the Mississippi Choctaws: Hearing before the Committee on Investigation of the Indian Service, House of Representatives, Union, Mississippi, March 16, 1917* (Washington, D.C.: Government Printing Office, 1917), 2:117–178.

31. U.S. Department of the Interior, *Enrollment with the Five Civilized Tribes*, 2, 10–12.

32. *Papers and Reports Relating to Five Civilized Tribes*, 62nd Cong., 3rd sess., S. Doc. 1139, 27–37.

33. *Memorial of the Choctaw and Chickasaw Nations Relative to the Rights of the Mississippi Choctaws Submitted for Consideration in Connection with H.R. 19213* (Washington, D.C.: Government Printing Office, 1913).

34. Coker, "Pat Harrison's Efforts to Reopen the Choctaw Citizenship Rolls," 46.

35. *Report of the Thirty-first Annual Lake Mohonk Conference of Friends of the Indian and Other Dependent Peoples, October 22d, 23rd and 24th, 1913* (n.p.: Lake Mohonk Conference of Friends of the Indian and Other Dependent Peoples, 1913), 33–34.

36. *Reporting on H.R. 4536 to Reopen the Rolls of the Choctaw-Chickasaw Tribe and to Provide for the Awarding of the Rights Secured to Certain Persons by the Fourteenth Article of the Treaty of Dancing Rabbit Creek of Date Sept. 27, 1830*, 63rd Cong., 1st sess., vol. 50, part 1, May 1, 1913, H. Rep. 4536, 955.

37. Coker, "Pat Harrison's Efforts to Reopen the Choctaw Citizenship Rolls," 51.

38. *Indian Appropriation Act 1915*, 38 Stat. 600 (August 1, 1914).

39. Coker, "Pat Harrison's Efforts to Reopen the Choctaw Citizenship Rolls," 52–53.

40. *Appendix: Report to Reopen the Rolls of the Choctaw-Chickasaw Tribes, Congressional Record*, 63rd Cong., 3rd sess., January 2, 1915, vol. 52, part 6, 930.

41. Ibid.; Coker, "Pat Harrison's Efforts to Reopen the Choctaw Citizenship Rolls," 54.

42. Coker, "Pat Harrison's Efforts to Reopen the Choctaw Citizenship Rolls," 56–57.

43. Hurley, report to Cato Sells, December 15, 1915, in P. J. Hurley, *Choctaw Citizenship Litigation: Report of P. J. Hurley, National Attorney for the Choctaw Nation, to Hon. Cato Sells, Commissioner of Indian Affairs* (n.p., 1916), part 13, 10. The U.S. treasury had $7,432,353 in the Choctaw account and $1,143,638 in the Chickasaw account. The Choctaws could also claim deferred payments of approximately $6 million and the value of unsold land and other property was approximately $16,149,491, making the total Choctaw resource $31,503,954. There were 20,799 enrolled Choctaws and

6,304 Chickasaws; Part 14, "P.L. 80 (64th Cong.) Authorized payment of $300 per cap to Choctaws and $200 to Chickasaws," in Hurley's report to Sells.

44. Pat Harrison and Hampton Tucker to Hon. W. B. Pine, June 7, 1929, Box 11, Folder 3, Hampton Tucker Collection, Western History Collections, University of Oklahoma, Norman, Oklahoma (hereafter Tucker Collection). Senator King of Utah introduced two bills, S. 1196 and S. 1197, both entitled "A Bill Conferring Jurisdiction on the Court of Claims to Hear and Determine Certain Claims of Persons to Property Rights as Citizens of the Choctaw and Chickasaw Nations or Tribes."

45. Clara Sue Kidwell, "The Choctaw Struggle for Land and Identity in Mississippi, 1830–1918," in *After Removal: The Choctaw in Mississippi*, edited by Samuel J. Wells and Roseanna Tubby (Jackson: University Press of Mississippi, 1986), 64–93.

46. *Estate of Winton et al. v. Amos et al.*, 51 Ct. Cl. 284 (May 29, 1916). The court declined to rehear the *Amos v. Winton* case. See *Winton v. Amos*, 255 U.S. 373 (March 7, 1921).

47. The association's delegates were T. L. Howell, president; Ed Johnson, a prominent Chickasaw banker; and J. H. Miller, an intermarried citizen, stockman, merchant, and banker.

48. P. J. Hurley to W. K. Moorehead, Tulsa, April 10, 1913, 15–18, Box 16, Folder 7, Hurley Collection; Patrick J. Hurley to Hon. Victor M. Locke, Jr., Tulsa, January 1, 1913, Box 18, Folder 2, Hurley Collection.

49. *Suit in the Court of Claims by the Choctaw and Chickasaw (S. 8138) to Authorize the Choctaw and Chickasaw Nations to Bring Suit in the Court of Claims and for Other Purposes*, 62nd Cong., 3rd sess., January 15, 1913, S. Doc. 1007; "Memorial of the Choctaw and Chickasaw Indians with Reference to Their 'Leased District' to Accompany Bill (S. 8140) 'To Authorize the Choctaw and Chickasaw Nations to Bring Suit in the Court of Claims and for Other Purposes,'" in *Suits in the Court of Claims by the Choctaw and Chickasaw Indians*, 62nd Cong., 3rd sess., S. Doc. 1010.

50. *S. 8138 to Authorize the Choctaw and Chickasaw Nations to Bring Suit in the Court of Claims and for Other Purposes*, *Congressional Record*, 62nd Cong., 3rd sess., January 15, 1913, vol. 40, part 2, 3550; *S. 8140 to Authorize the Choctaw and Chickasaw Nations to Bring Suit in the Court of Claims and for Other Purposes*, *Congressional Record*, 62nd Cong., 3rd sess., January 15, 1913, vol. 49, part 2, 1535.

51. Hurley to Moorehead, April 10, 1913, 19.

52. U.S. Congress, House Committee on Indian Affairs, *Claims of Choctaw and Chickasaw Tribes (The Leased District), Hearing before the Committee on Indian Affairs House of Representatives, Sixty-eighth Congress, First Session on H.R. 9017, May 27 and 28, 1924* (Washington, D.C.: Government Printing Office, 1924), 14–15; Hampton Tucker to C. H. Victor, August 17, 1929, Box 8, Folder 12, Tucker Collection.

53. *H. Res. 301: A Resolution Providing for the Appointment of Seven Members of the House of Representatives to Inquire into Certain Claims of the Choctaw and Chickasaw Tribes of Indians, and for Other Purposes*, 69th Cong., 1st sess., June 18, 1926, vol. 67, part 10, 11610; "Resolution," Box 8, Folder 12, Tucker Collection.

54. Tucker to Victor, August 17, 1929.

55. Hampton Tucker to Hon. W. W. Hastings, Washington, January 23, 1930, Box 8, Folder 11, Hampton Tucker Collection; *Congressional Record*, 71st Cong., 3rd sess., February 4, 1931, vol. 74, part 4, 3969–3975; S. 2001: "Bill for the Relief of the Choctaw and Chickasaw Tribes of Indians of Oklahoma and for Other Purposes," 76th Cong., 1st sess., March 30, 1939; Box 8, Folder 12, Tucker Collection.

56. The president vetoed the Leased District payment on grounds of res adjudicate; see *Veto of Bill to Refer Claims of Choctaw Indians to Court of Claims*, 71st Cong., 3rd sess., February 30, 1931, S. Doc. 280; *Congressional Record*, 71st Cong., 3rd sess., February 20, 1931, vol. 74, part 6, 5575.

57. *The Choctaw and Chickasaw Nations v. The United States*, 88 Ct. Cl. 271 (January 9, 1939).

58. "Claims of Choctaw and Chickasaw Indians for Leased District, Oklahoma," 76th Cong., 3rd sess., June 3, 1940, S. Rep. 1743.

CHAPTER 16

1. Bentley Beams interview, April 23, 1969, T-433, 17, Doris Duke Collection.

2. Pierce Kelton Merrill, "The Social and Economic Status of the Choctaw Nation" (Ph.D. diss., University of Oklahoma, 1940), 49.

3. Angie Debo, *The Five Civilized Tribes of Oklahoma: Report on Social and Economic Conditions* ([Philadelphia]: Indian Rights Association, 1951), 8, 15, 17, 34.

4. Box 13, Rehabilitation—Choctaw Program, Tuskahoma Project, Record Group 75, E327, National Archives and Records Administration, Forth Worth Regional Archives (hereafter cited as Tuskahoma Project).

5. Address of William Durant, June 3, 1938, Tuskahoma Project, Box 14.

6. In 1881, the Choctaw Nation was the first Indian tribe to gain access to the Indian court of claims with the Net Proceeds Case; see Glen A. Wilkinson, "Indian Tribal Claims before the Court of Claims," *Georgetown Law Journal* 55 (December 1966): 512; *Choctaw Nation and Chickasaw Nation v. United States and Wichita and Affiliated Bands of Indians*, 21 S. Ct. 149 (December 1900).

7. Harvey D. Rosenthal, "Their Day in Court: A History of the Indian Claims Commission" (Ph.D. diss., Kent State University, 1976), 101, 137–138.

8. Subjects, Box 11, Folder 100, Elmer Thomas Collection, Carl Albert Congressional Research & Studies Center, University of Oklahoma, Norman, Oklahoma (hereafter Thomas Collection).

9. See the requests for per capita payments in Subjects, Box 11, Folder 60, Thomas Collection.

10. O. W. Folsom, McCurtain County, to Elmer Thomas, January 4, 1949, Box 11, Folder 100, Subjects, Thomas Collection.

11. Victor M. Locke, Jr., Oklahoma City, June 2, 1941 to Clerk, Committee on Indian Affairs, in U.S. Congress, Senate Committee on Indian Affairs, *Leasing of the Segregated Coal Deposits of the Choctaw and Chickasaw Nations in Oklahoma: Hearings*

before the Committee on Indian Affairs, United States Senate, Seventy-seventh Congress, Second Session, on S. 1542, a Bill to Authorize the Leasing of the Undeveloped Coal and Asphalt Deposits of the Choctaw and Chickasaw Nations in Oklahoma: February 2 and 3, and March 3, 1942 (Washington, D.C., Government Printing Office, 1942), 7, 8.

12. "Large Group Here Finds That Original Figure Still Intended," undated newspaper clipping from *Ada News*, Subjects, Box 11, Folder 100, Thomas Collection.

13. Harry J. W. Belvin to Ed Edmondson, Durant, December 28, 1967, Box 63, Folder 45, Departmental Files, Carl Albert Collection, Carl Albert Congressional Research & Studies Center, University of Oklahoma, Norman, Oklahoma (hereafter Albert Collection).

14. Harry J. W. Belvin, *Choctaw Tribal Structure and Achievement, August 18, 1948, to August 25, 1975* (Durant, Oklahoma: Choctaw Bilingual Education Program, Southeastern Oklahoma State University, n.d.)

15. *Choctaw Nation v. United States*, 91 Ct. Cl. 320 (1941).

16. *History of the Intertribal Council of the Five Civilized Tribes* (n.p.: n.d.), 3.

17. Belvin, *Choctaw Tribal Structure and Achievement*, 8.

18. Harry J. W. Belvin to Congressman Carl Albert, June 30, 1961, Box 51, Folder 29, Legislative Files, Albert Collection.

19. "Choctaws May Form Corporation," Box 40, Folder 61, Legislative Files, Albert Collection.

20. See Donald L. Fixico, *Termination and Relocation, Federal Indian Policy, 1945-1960* (Albuquerque: University of New Mexico Press, 1986) for a history and assessment of the termination policy.

21. *An Act to Supplement the Act of April 26, 1906 (34 Stat. 137), Entitled "An Act to Provide for the Final Disposition of the Affairs of the Five Civilized Tribes in the Indian Territory, and for Other Purposes,"* 73 Stat. 420 (August 25, 1959).

22. Carl Albert to Pete W. Cass, July 16, 1959, Box 40, Folder 58, Legislative Files, Albert Collection.

23. "Department Supports Choctaw Termination Bill Introduced in Congress at Request of Tribal Representatives," Press Release, April 23, 1959, Department of the Interior, Information Service, Albert Collection.

24. O. W. Folsom, McCurtain, Oklahoma, to Elmer Thomas, Senator, Washington D.C., January 4, 1949, Subjects, Box 11, Folder 100, Thomas Collection.

25. John O. Crow to Carl Albert, July 18, 1961, Box 51, Folder 29, Legislative Files, Albert Collection.

26. Harry J. W. Belvin to Carl Albert, March 2, 1964, Box 47, Folder 53, Departmental Files, Albert Collection; Area Director, Memorandum, Choctaw Fact Sheet and Questionnaire, Muskogee Area Office, July 21, 1966, Box 58, Folder 4, Departmental Files, Albert Collection.

27. "Statement of Harry J. Belvin, Principal Chief of the Choctaw Nation, on H.R. 18566, a Bill 'To Repeal the Act of August 25, 1959 with Respect to Final Disposition of the Affairs of the Choctaw Tribe,' before the Subcommittee on Indian Affairs of the United States Senate," Box 82, Folder 36, Departmental Files, Albert Collection.

28. Alvin Josephy, Jr., *Red Power: The American Indian's Fight for Freedom* (New York: American Heritage Press, 1971).

29. Robert K. Thomas, "Colonialism: Classic and Internal," *New University Thought* 6 (Winter 1966–1967): 37–44; Robert K. Thomas, "Powerless Politics," *New University Thought* 6 (Winter 1966–1967): 44–53.

30. Memorandum, June 2, 1965, Box 282, Folder 7, Fred R. Harris Collection, Carl Albert Congressional Research & Studies Center, University of Oklahoma (hereafter Harris Collection); John B. O'Hara to Mrs. Fred R. Harris, Norman, Oklahoma, September 16, 1965, Box 282, Folder 7, Harris Collection.

31. "Oklahoma Committee for Indian Opportunity," August 2, 3 [1965]; FRH to Bill, memorandum, June 2, 1965; O'Hara to Mrs. Harris, September 16, 1965, all in Box 282, Folder 7, Harris Collection.

32. Constitution and By-Laws of Oklahomans for Indian Opportunity, Inc., Box 282, Folder 5, Harris Collection.

33. Sarah Eppler Janda, "The Intersection of Feminism and Indianness in the Activism of LaDonna Harris and Wilma Mankiller" (Ph.D. diss., University of Oklahoma, 2002).

34. Maynard Ungerman, Chairman, Tulsa County Democratic Central Committee, to Senator and Mrs. Fred R. Harris, August 2, 1967, Box 284, Folder 16, Harris Collection.

35. Leon H. Ginsberg, School of Social Work, University of Oklahoma, to Senator Fred R. Harris, August 2, 1967, Box 284, Folder 16, Harris Collection; Neal McCaleb to LaDonna Harris, July 24, 1967, Box 284, Folder 16, Harris Collection.

36. "Cherokee and Creek Chiefs Defend BIA," *Muskogee Times Democrat*, July 1, 1970.

37. Report of Special Personnel Committee, Muskogee Area Office, July 25, 1967, Box 284, Folder 16, Harris Collection.

38. "Oklahomans for Indian Opportunity," Box 111, White House Central Files, Staff Member and Office Files: Leonard Garment, Nixon Presidential Materials, National Archives and Records Administration—College Park, Md.

39. Harry J. W. Belvin to William H. Bowman, Acting Deputy Director, Office of Program Development, Office of Economic Opportunity, November 21, 1969, Box 91, Folder 37, Albert Collection.

40. Oklahomans for Indian Opportunity Notebooks, personal collection of Daniel Cobb, Miami University, Oxford, Ohio.

41. "Choctaws Hold Firey Session," *Tahlihina American*, May 1, 1969, 1.

42. Harry J. W. Belvin to Honorable Carl Albert, February 16, 1971, Box 91, Folder 37, Departmental Series, Albert Collection; James J. Wilson, Director, Indian Division, Office of Indian Operations, Executive Office of the President, Washington, D.C., to Honorable Harry J. W. Belvin, Durant, Oklahoma, n.d., Box 91, Folder 37, Departmental Series, Albert Collection.

43. Harry Belvin to Ed Edmondson, December 28, 1967, Box 63, Folder 45, Departmental Series, Albert Collection.

44. "Local Indians Combat Termination Act," *McCurtain Weekly Gazette*, Idabel, Oklahoma, July 10, 1969, Box 76, Folder 61, Departmental Series, Albert Collection.

45. Harry J. W. Belvin to A. S. (Mike) Monroney, March 14, 1968, Box 70, Folder 46, Departmental Series, Albert Collection.

46. *Report No. 91–1151 of the House Committee on Interior and Insular Affairs*, Box 128, Folder 41, Legislative Series, Albert Collection.

47. "Statement of Senator Fred R. Harris before the Subcommittee on Indian Affairs of the Interior and Insular Affairs Committee," n.d., Box 82, Folder 38, Departmental Series, Albert Collection.

48. "Statement of Rep. Carl Albert before the Subcommittee on Indian Affairs of the Committee on Interior and Insular Affairs, May 14, 1970," Box 118, Folder 67, Legislative Series, Albert Collection.

49. *Hello Choctaw*, Box 82, Folders 39 and 44, Legislative Series, Albert Collection.

50. *Hello Choctaw . . . Halito Chahta*, August 30, 1970, Box 82, Folder 44, Departmental Series, Albert Collection.

51. *Hello Choctaw . . . Halito Chahta*, August 12, 1970, Box 82, Folder 39, Departmental Series, Albert Collection.

52. G. Mike Charleston, Constitution of the Choctaw Nation, Box 167, Folder 14, Page H. Belcher Collection, Carl Albert Congressional Research & Studies Center, University of Oklahoma, Norman, Oklahoma.

EPILOGUE

1. The ten counties are McCurtain, LeFlore, Haskell, Latimer, Pushmataha, Choctaw, Bryan, Atoka, Pittsburg, Coal, and part of Hughes County south of the Canadian River. See Constitution of the Choctaw Nation of Oklahoma, June 9, 1983, available online at www.choctawnation.com/files/Constitution.pdf.

2. The Atoka Agreement (1897), the Curtis Act (1898), the Supplementary Agreement of 1902, the 1906 act for the settlement of the affairs of the Five Tribes, the act of 1908 changing the status of lands based on degree of blood of the allottee, and the Oklahoma Indian Welfare Act of 1936 create a complex web of regulation around Indian land title in Oklahoma; see Veronica Velarde Tiller, *Tiller's Guide to Indian Country* (Albuquerque, N.M.: BowArrow Pubs., 2005), 824–825.

3. *Choctaw Nation v. Oklahoma*, 397 U.S. 620 (April 27, 1970).

4. *Cherokee, Choctaw, and Chickasaw Nations Claims Settlement Act*, 107th Cong., 2d sess., September 4, 2002, H. Rep. 107–632, ; *Indian Assistance Programs*, Public Law 107–331, December 13, 2002, Section 6.

5. Jennifer E. Pelphrey, "Oklahoma's State/Tribal Water Compact: Three Cheers for Compromise," *American Indian Law Review* 29 (2004–2005): 127.

BIBLIOGRAPHY

MANUSCRIPT COLLECTIONS

Bancroft Library, University of California, Berkeley
John Edwards Papers
Gilcrease Museum, Tulsa, Oklahoma
Peter Pitchlynn Papers
Houghton Library, Harvard University, Cambridge, Massachusetts
American Board of Commissioners for Foreign Missions, Papers, Series 18.3.4.
National Archives and Records Administration, College Park, Maryland
Nixon Presidential Materials
National Archives and Records Administration, Washington, D.C.
Office of Indian Affairs (Central Office), Register of Letters Received, 1824–1880, Record Group 75
National Archives and Records Administration, Fort Worth, Texas
Tuskahoma Project, Record Group 75
Newberry Library, Chicago
Choctaw Papers, Ayer Collection
Oklahoma Historical Society, Oklahoma City, Oklahoma
Choctaw Nation Papers
University of Oklahoma, Norman, Oklahoma
Carl Albert Congressional Research & Studies Center
Carl Albert Collection
Page H. Belcher Collection
Fred R. Harris Collection
Elmer Thomas Collection
Western History Collections
Choctaw Nation Collection
Coleman Cole Collection
Doris Duke Indian Oral History Collection

Gilbert W. Dukes Collection
Patrick J. Hurley Collection
Indian-Pioneer Papers Collection
Wilson N. Jones Collection
Cyrus Kingsbury Collection
Green McCurtain Collection
Peter Perkins Pitchlynn Collection
Rogers-Neill Collection
Hampton Tucker Collection
University of Texas at Austin
Gideon Lincecum Collection, 1821–1933

PRIMARY SOURCES

Acts and Resolutions of the General Council of the Choctaw Nation at the Called Sessions Thereof, Held in April and June 1858, and the Regular Session Held in October, 1858. Fort Smith, Ark.: Josephus Dotson, 1859.

Acts and Resolutions of the General Council of the Choctaw Nation, for the Year 1859. Fort Smith, Ark.: Printed at the Times Office for Campbell LeFlore, 1860.

Acts and Resolutions of the General Council of the Choctaw Nation, from 1852 to 1857, Both Inclusive. Fort Smith, Ark.: Josephus Dotson, 1858.

Acts and Resolutions Passed at the Regular Term of the General Council of the Choctaw Nation, October 1880, from Nos. 1 to 41 Inclusive. Denison, Tex.: Dearing, 1880.

American Anti-Slavery Society. *Slavery and the American Board of Commissioners for Foreign Missions.* New York: American Anti-Slavery Society, 1859.

American Board of Commissioners for Foreign Missions. *Report of the American Board of Commissioners for Foreign Missions, Compiled from Documents Laid before the Board at the Eighteenth Annual Meeting, Which Was Held in Middletown (Conn.), Sept. 14 and 15, 1826.* Boston: Crocker and Brewster, 1826.

————. *Report of the American Board of Commissioners for Foreign Missions, Presented at the Forty-eighth Annual Meeting, Held in Providence, Rhode Island, September 8–11, 1857.* Boston: T. R. Marvin & Son, 1857.

————. *Report of the American Board of Commissioners for Foreign Missions, Presented at the Forty-fifth Annual Meeting, Held in Hartford, Connecticut, September 12–15, 1854.* Boston: T. R. Marvin, 1854.

————. *Report of the American Board of Commissioners for Foreign Missions, Presented at the Forty-seventh Annual Meeting, Held in Newark, New Jersey, October 28–31, 1856 with the Minutes of the Special Meeting Held at Albany, New York, March 4–6, 1856.* Boston: T. R. Marvin, 1856.

————. *Report of the American Board of Commissioners for Foreign Missions, Presented at the Thirty-ninth Annual Meeting, Held in Boston, Massachusetts, Sept. 12–15, 1848.* Boston: T. R. Marvin, 1848.

————. *Report of the Committee on Anti-Slavery Memorials, September, 1845, with a Historical Statement of Previous Proceedings.* Boston: T. R. Marvin, 1845.

American State Papers: Documents, Legislative and Executive of the Congress of the United States. 38 vols. Series 2. *Indian Affairs.* 2 vols. Washington, D.C.: Gales and Seaton, 1832–1861.

Anderson, Rufus. *Memorial Volume of the First Fifty Years of the American Board of Commissioners for Foreign Missions.* 5th ed. Boston: Published by the Board, 1862.

The Atoka Convention of Choctaw and Chickasaw Indians. South McAlester, I.T.: Press of the South McAlester Capital, n.d.

Benson, Henry C. *Life among the Choctaw Indians, and Sketches of the South-West.* Cincinnati: L. Swormstedt and A. Poe, 1860; reprint, New York: Johnson Reprint Corporation, 1970.

Catlin, George. *Letters and Notes on the Manners, Customs, and Condition of the North American Indians . . . Written during Eight Years' Travel amongst the Wildest Tribes of Indians in North America. In 1832, 33, 34, 35, 36, 37, 38, and 39.* 2 vols. London: Tosswill and Myers, 1841; reprint, Mineola, N.Y.: Dover Publications, 1973.

Chahta okla i nanalhpisa nanapisa affami 1876 micha 1877, Aiena nanalhpisa tok oke. Atoka, Chahta yakni: W. J. Hemby, holisso ai ikbe, 1878.

Chahta oklahi nanulhpisa noshbobo micha nanvlhpisa: Mikmvt afamih 1837, 1855, 1865, 1866 kash nanitimapisa tok (treaties) aiena ho chata oklah nanvpisa chito vt vpisa toko anotaka hosh A. R. Durant, vt vlht uka yosh holisso achafa ilapa foki noke; Davis Homer micha Ben Watkins, apilvchi. Tullis, Teksis: J. F. Worley, 1894.

Chahta yakni ikastitushvn micha I nan vlhpisa Tokosowil ak o atobe. [Doaksville, 1852]: W. J. Hemby, holisso ai ikbe, 1878.

Choctaw Nation. *Constitution and Laws of the Choctaw Nation.* Park Hill, Cherokee Nation: John Candy, 1840.

————. *Constitution and Laws of the Choctaw Nation.* Park Hill, Cherokee Nation: Edwin Archer, 1847.

————. *Constitution and Laws of the Choctaw Nation.* Doaksville, 1852.

————. *Constitution and Laws of the Choctaw Nation: Together with the Treaties of 1837, 1855, 1865 and 1866.* Dallas, Texas: John F. Worley, Printer and Publisher, 1894; reprint, Wilmington, Del.: Scholarly Resources, Inc., 1973.

————. *Constitution and Laws of the Choctaw Nation: Together with the Treaties of 1855, 1865 and 1866.* New York: Wm. P. Lyon & Son, 1869.

————. *General and Special Laws of the Choctaw Nation Passed at the Regular Session of the General Council Convened at Chahta Tamaha, Oct.3rd and Adjourned Nov. 12th, 1881.* Denison, Tex.: Murray & Dearing, 1881.

————. *General and Special Laws of the Choctaw Nation Passed at the Regular Session of the General Council Convened at Tushka Homma, October 6 and Adjourned November 7.* Muskogee, [Indian Territory]: Indian Journal Steam Job Print, 1884.

————. *Laws of the Choctaw Nation Passed at the Choctaw Council at the Regular Session of 1883.* Sedalia, Mo.: Democrat Steam Printing House and Book Bindery, 1883.

———. *Laws of the Choctaw Nation Passed at the Choctaw Councils of 1876 and 1877.* Atoka, Choctaw Nation: W. J. Hemby, Printer, 1878.

The Choctaw Nation vs. the United States. Washington, D.C.: David M'Intosh, Printer, 1872.

Choctaw Nation. Chickasaw Nation. *Memorial of the Choctaw and Chickasaw Nations Relative to the Rights of the Mississippi Choctaws Submitted for Consideration in Connection with H. R. 19213.* Washington, D.C.: Government Printing Office, 1913.

———. *Memorial of the Choctaw and Chickasaw Nations to the Secretary of the Interior of the United States, Relating to their Jurisdiction of Persons and Property under the Treaty of June 22, 1855.* Washington, D. C.: W. H. Moore, 1883.

Cohen, Felix. *Handbook of Federal Indian Law.* Charlottesville, Va.: Michie Bobbs-Merrill, 1982.

Confederate States of America. *Message of the President, and Report of Albert Pike, Commissioner of the Confederate States to the Indian Nations West of Arkansas, of the Results of His Mission.* Richmond, Va.: Enquirer Book and Job Press, Tyler, Wise, Allegre & Smith, 1861.

Cooper, Douglas H. *Address and Memorial by Douglas H. Cooper, to the General Council of the Choctaw Nation Assembled.* Boggy Depot, C.N.: Vindicator Print, October, 1873.

Crawford, Samuel J. *In the Matter of the Claim of the Choctaw and Chickasaw Nations on Account of Lands Ceded to the United States by the Treaty of 1866 before the Honorable United States Commission Created by Congress to Negotiate with the Five Civilized Tribes in the Indian Territory: Brief and Argument.* Washington, D.C.: Gibson Bros., 1897.

Dwight, Ben. *Choctaw Social Welfare by Principal Chief Ben Dwight.* Washington, D.C.: Board of Indian Commissioners, 1931.

Flickinger, Robert Elliott. *The Choctaw Freedmen and the Story of Oak Hill Industrial Academy.* Pittsburgh, Pa.: Presbyterian Board of Missions for Freedmen, 1914.

Folsom, Israel. *Choctaw "Chata" Legends Told.* From Atoka Vindicator, Reprinted by Indian Citizen, 1983.

Gideon, D. C. *Indian Territory, Descriptive Biographical and Genealogical Including the Landed Estates, County Seats Etc., Etc. with a General History of the Territory.* New York: Lewis Publishing Company, 1901.

Hastain, E. *Index to Choctaw-Chickasaw Deeds and Allottments.* Muskogee, Okla.: E. Hastain, 1908–1910.

Hillyer, C. J. *Atlantic and Pacific Railroad and the Indian Territory.* Washington, D.C.: Gibson Bros., 1871.

Hitchcock, Ethan Allen. *A Traveler in Indian Territory: The Journal of Ethan Allen Hitchcock.* Edited by Grant Foreman. 1930; reprint, Norman: University of Oklahoma Press, 1996.

Hurley, P. J. *Choctaw Citizenship Litigation: Report of P. J. Hurley, National Attorney for the Choctaw Nation, to Hon. Cato Sells, Commissioner of Indian Affairs.* N.p., 1916.

Indian Territory. *Constitution of the State of Sequoyah*. Muskogee: Phoenix Printing, 1905.

Jefferson, Thomas. *The Writings of Thomas Jefferson*. Edited by Andrew A. Lipscomb. Washington, D. C.: Thomas Jefferson Memorial Association of the United States, 1905.

"Journal of the Adjourned Session of First General Council of the Indian Territory." *Chronicles of Oklahoma* 3, no. 2 (June 1925): 120–136.

"Journal of the General Council of the Indian Territory." *Chronicles of Oklahoma* 3, no. 1 (March 1925): 33–44.

Kappler, Charles J. *Indian Affairs: Laws and Treaties*. 5 vols. Washington, D.C.: Government Printing Office, 1904–1941.

Lanman, Charles. "Peter Pitchlynn, Chief of the Choctaws." *The Atlantic Monthly*, April 1870, 468–479.

McAdams, R. W. *Chickasaws and Choctaws; A Pamphlet of Information Concerning Their History, Treaties, Government, Country, Laws, Politics, and Affairs*. Ardmore, Indian Territory: Chieftain Print, 1891; reprint, Wilmington, Del.: Scholarly Resources, 1975.

McLaughlin, James. *Report of Inspector James McLaughlin on Bills for Enrollment with the Five Civilized Tribes, July 2, 1914*. Washington, D.C.: Government Printing Office, 1916.

Minutes of the Twenty-fifth Annual Session of the Choctaw and Chickasaw Baptist Association, Held with the Rock Creek Baptist Church, San Bois County, Choctaw Nation. August 23 & 24, 1895. South McAlester, Indian Territory: Indianola Printing Co., Printers, 1895.

Minutes of the Twenty-first Annual Meeting of the Choctaw and Chickasaw Baptist Association Held with Armstrong Baptist Church, Blue County, Choctaw Nation, I.T., Commencing September 4, 1891. Oklahoma City, O.T.: Baptist Publishing Company Print, 1891.

Möllhausen, Balduin. *Diary of a Journey from the Mississippi to the Coasts of the Pacific with a United States Government Expedition*. London: Longman, Brown, Green, Longmans, & Roberts, 1858.

Morrison, James D. *Seven Constitutions (Anumpa Ulhpisa Untuklo). Government of the Choctaw Republic, 1826–1906*. Durant, Oklahoma: Choctaw Bilingual Education Program, Southeastern Oklahoma State University, 1977.

Norris, Robert E. *Choctaw Census 1975: Results of the 1975 Census of the Choctaw Nation of Oklahoma*. Stillwater, Okla.: Geography Extension, Oklahoma State University, 1977.

Nuttall, Thomas. *A Journal of Travels into Arkansa Territory, During the Year 1819. With Occasional Observations on the Manners of the Aborigines*. Vol. XIII, *Early Western Travels*. Edited by Reuben Gold Thwaites. New York: AMS Press, Inc., 1966.

Oklahoma Indian Affairs Commission. *Oklahoma Indian Nations Information Handbook*. Oklahoma City: Oklahoma Indian Affairs Commission, 2002.

Paine, Halbert E. *The Choctaw Nation and the Chickasaw Nation, Claimants, vs. the United States and the Wichita and Affiliated Bands of Indians, Defendants: Brief for Claimants.* Washington, D.C.: Gibson Bros., 1896.

Pike, Albert. *Letter of Albert Pike to the Choctaw People.* Washington, D.C.: Cunningham & McIntosh Printer, 1872.

Pitchlynn, Peter P. *Remonstrance, Appeal, and Solemn Protest of the Choctaw Nation Addressed to the Congress of the United States.* Washington, D.C., 1870.

———. *Reply of Peter P. Pitchlynn, Choctaw Delegate, to a Libellous Pamphlet Published by Douglas H. Cooper.* Washington, D.C., 1873.

———. *Report of P. P. Pitchlynn, Choctaw Delegate, to His Excellency the Principal Chief and General Council of the Choctaw Nation, with Appendix Containing Correspondence on the Survey of the Chickasaw District, and Letter Addressed to the Secretary of the Interior Requesting a Survey of the Eastern Boundary Line of the Choctaw Nation.* Washington, D. C.: Cunningham & McIntosh, Printers, 1870.

———. *Papers Relating to the Claims of the Choctaw Nation against the United States Arising under the Treaty of 1830.* Washington, D.C.: A. O. P. Nicholson, 1855.

———. *Papers Respecting the Rights and Interests of the Choctaw Nation, and Their Relations with the United States, the Chickasaws and Other Indian Tribes.* Washington, D.C.: Geo. S. Gideon, 1855.

Proceedings of the Conference for the Indians of the Five Civilized Tribes of Oklahoma Held at Muskogee, Oklahoma, March 22, 1934, to Discuss the Wheeler-Howard Indian Bill. [Washington, D.C., 1934]

Proceedings of the Fourth Annual Lake Mohonk Conference October 12, 13, 14, 1886. Philadelphia: Indian Rights Association, 1887.

Proceedings of the Tenth Annual Meeting of the Lake Mohonk Conference of Friends of the Indian 1892. N.p.: Lake Mohonk Conference, 1892.

Proceedings of the Third Annual Meeting of the Lake Mohonk Conference of Friends of the Indian. Held October 7 to 9, 1885. Philadelphia: Sherman & Co., Printers, 1886.

Proceedings of the Twelfth Annual Meeting of the Lake Mohonk Conference of Friends of the Indian. New York: Lake Mohonk Conference, 1894.

Proposed Legislation for the Full-Blood and Identified Choctaws of Mississippi, Louisiana, and Alabama, with Memorial, Evidence, and Brief. Washington, D.C.: Judd & Detweiler, [1913].

Report of the Thirty-first Annual Lake Mohonk Conference of Friends of the Indian and Other Dependent Peoples. October 22d, 23rd and 24th, 1913. Lake Mohonk Conference of Friends of the Indian and Other Dependent Peoples, 1913.

Richards, W. B., comp. *The Oklahoma Red Book.* Vol. 2. Oklahoma City, 1912.

Richardson, James D. *A Compilation of the Messages and Papers of the Presidents.* 20 vols. New York: Bureau of National Literature, 1917.

Schermerhorn, John F. "Report Respecting the Indians Inhabiting the Western Parts of the United States." In *Collections of the Massachusetts Historical Society.* Vol. 2, second series. Boston, 1814; reprint, Charles C. Little and James Brown, 1846.

Scott, Robert N., H. M. Lazelle, George B. Davis, Leslie J. Perry, Joseph W. Kirkley,

Fred C. Ainsworth, John S. Moodey, and Calvin D. Cowles. *The War of the Rebellion: A Compilation of the Official Records of the Union and Confederate Armies.* 70 vols. Washington, D.C.: Government Printing Office, 1880–1901.

Smith, E. B. *Indian Tribal Claims: Decided in the Court of Claims of the United States, Briefed and Compiled to June 30, 1947.* 2 vols. Washington, D.C.: University Publications of America, [1976].

Smith, E. G., comp. *Indian Tribal Claims Decided in the Court of Claims of the United States, Briefed and Compiled to June 30, 1947.* 2 vols. Washington, D.C.: University Publications of America, Inc., [1947].

Stuart, John. *A Sketch of the Cherokee and Choctaw Indians.* Little Rock, Ark.: Woodruff and Pew, 1837.

Tocqueville, Alexis de. *Democracy in America,* Translated by George Lawrence. Edited by J. P. Mayer and Max Lerner. New York: Harper & Row, Publishers, 1966.

U.S. Congress. House. *Affairs in the Indian Department.* 41st Cong., 3rd sess., February 25, 1871. H. Rep. 39.

———. *Agreement with a Commission of the Choctaw and Chickasaw Nations.* 56th Cong., 1st sess., January 3, 1900. H. Doc. 221.

———. *Award in Favor of Choctaw Nation of Indians.* 43rd Cong., 1st sess., April 9, 1874. H. Rep. 391.

———. *Choctaw Award.* 43rd Cong., 1st sess., May 20, 1874. H. Rep. 599.

———. *Choctaw Indian Claims.* 42nd Cong., 3rd sess. January 6, 1873. H. Exec. Doc. 69.

———. *Choctaw Indians, Settlement of Claims under Treaty of 1830.* 44th Cong., 1st sess., May 15, 1876. H. Rep. 499.

———. *Choctaw Treaty—Dancing Rabbit Creek.* 26th Cong., 2nd sess., March 2, 1841. H. Doc. 109.

———. *Choctaw Treaty: Message from the President of the United States Transmitting a Report of the Secretary of War Relative to the Claims Arising under the Choctaw Treaty, in Compliance with a Resolution of the House of Representatives of the 31st of December Last.* 29th Cong., 1st sess., April 27, 1846. H. Doc. 189.

———. *Claim by Choctaw Nation against United States.* 40th Cong., 2nd sess., February 1, 1868. H. Exec. Doc. 138.

———. *Enrollment of Choctaws of Mississippi under Treaty of 1830.* 54th Cong., 2nd sess., March 3, 1897. H. Rep. 3080.

———. *Indian Claims in Mississippi, Petition of the Citizens of the State of Mississippi, Remonstrating against Indian Claims.* 24th Cong., 1st sess., February 1, 1836. H. Doc. 89.

———. *Investigation of Indian Frauds.* 42nd Cong., 3rd sess., March 3, 1873. H. Rep. 98.

———. *Investigations of Indian Contracts: Hearings before the Select Committee of the House of Representatives Appointed under Authority of House Resolution No. 847, June 25, 1910, for the Purpose of Investigating Indian Contracts with the Five Civilized Tribes and the Osage Indians in Oklahoma.* 61st Cong., 3rd sess., February 28, 1911. H. Rep. 2273.

———. *Land Claims, &c. under 14th Article Choctaw Treaty.* 24th Cong., 1st sess., May 11, 1836. H. Doc. 663.

———. *Leasing Coal and Asphalt Deposits of Choctaw and Chickasaw Nations in Oklahoma.* 76th Cong., 3rd sess., August 20, 1940. H. Rep. 2871.

———. *Memorial in Behalf of Choctaw Nation in Relation to Their Claim to the Net Proceeds of Their Lands Ceded to the United States by Treaty of Dancing Rabbit Creek, September 27, 1830.* 41st Cong., 3rd sess., January 17, 1871. H. Misc. Doc. 37.

———. *Memorial of P. P. Pitchlynn on Claim of Choctaw Indians.* 43rd Cong., 1st sess., January 21, 1874. H. Misc. Doc. 89.

———. *Memorial of P. P. Pitchlynn, Delegate of Choctaw Nation, upon the Subject of the Claims of the Choctaw Nation to the Net Proceeds of Award of Senate of United States.* 42nd Cong., 2nd sess., April 2, 1872. H. Misc. Doc. 164.

———. *Memorial of the Choctaw Indians of the State of Mississippi, to the Congress of the United States, by Andrew Hays, Agent.* 24th Cong., 1st sess., February 1, 1836. H. Doc. 119.

———. *On Claims to Reservations under the Fourteenth Article of the Treaty of Dancing Rabbit Creek, with the Choctaw Indians Communicated to the House of Representatives.* 24th Cong., 1st sess., May 11, 1836. H. Doc. 1523.

———. *Opinion of Attorney General of the United States on Claim of Choctaw Indians to Issue of United States Bonds.* 41st Cong., 3rd sess., December 21, 1870. H. Exec. Doc. 25.

———. *Petition of a Number of Citizens of Mississippi Praying Congress to Institute an Inquiry into the Claims of Choctaw Indians to Reservations under the Treaty of Dancing Rabbit Creek.* 24th Cong., 2nd sess., January 21, 1837. H. Doc. 91.

———. *Removal of Restrictions from Part of Lands of Allottees of Five Civilized Tribes.* 60th Cong., 1st sess., April 6, 1908. H. Rep. 1454.

———. *Repealing the Act of Aug. 25, with Respect to the Final Disposition of the Affairs of the Choctaw Tribe.* 91st Cong., 2nd sess., June 4, 1970. H. Rep. 1151.

———. *Report of the Commission to the Five Civilized Tribes Relative to the Mississippi Choctaws.* 55th Cong., 2nd sess., February 3, 1898. H. Doc. 274.

———. *Reports of Explorations and Surveys to Ascertain the Most Practicable and Economical Route for a Railroad from the Mississippi River to the Pacific Ocean.* 33rd Cong., 2nd sess., 1855. S. Exec. Doc. 78.

———. *Reservation of Minerals in Sales of Lands of Choctaw-Chickasaw Indians, Oklahoma.* 75th Cong., 1st sess., August 11, 1937. H. Rep. 1496.

———. *Reservations of Land under Fourteenth Article of Treaty of 1830 with the Choctaw Indians.* 25th Cong., 3rd sess., February 22, 1839. H. Doc. 294.

———. *Treaty with Choctaw Indians, to Accompany H.R. 1195.* 40th Cong., 2nd sess., July 6, 1868. H. Rep. 77.

U.S. Congress. House. Committee on Indian Affairs. *Claims of Choctaw and Chickasaw Tribes (The Leased District): Hearing before the Committee on Indian Affairs. House of*

Representatives, Sixty-eighth Congress, First Session on H. R. 9017, May 27 and 28, 1924. Washington, D.C.: Government Printing Office, 1924.

———. *Claims of J. F. McMurray: Hearings before the Subcommittee of the Committee on Indian Affairs, House of Representatives, Seventieth Congress, Second Session on H. R. 10741, December 12 to 21, 1928.* Washington, D.C.: Government Printing Office, 1929.

———. *Five Civilized Tribes in Oklahoma: Hearings before the Subcommittee of the Committee on Indian Affairs, House of Representatives, Sixty-eighth Congress, First Session on H. R. 6900, March 22 and 28, 1924.* Washington, D.C.: Government Printing Office, 1924.

———. *Investigation of Indian Frauds: Report of the Committee on Indian Affairs, Concerning Frauds and Wrongs Committed against the Indians, with Many Statistics of Value in the Management of Indian Affairs.* [Washington, D.C.: Government Printing Office], 1873.

U.S. Congress. House. Committee on Investigation of the Indian Service. *Condition of the Mississippi Choctaws. Hearing before the Committee on Investigation of the Indian Service, House of Representatives, Union, Mississippi, March 16, 1917.* Vol. 2. Washington, D.C.: Government Printing Office, 1917.

U.S. Congress. House. Judiciary Committee. *Choctaw Nation Entitled to Bonds under Treaty of 1866.* 41st Cong., 3rd sess., February 27, 1871. Report 41.

U.S. Congress. Senate. *Authorizing the Purchase of Certain Interests in Lands and Mineral Deposits by the United States from the Choctaw and Chickasaw Nations of Indians.* 78th Cong., 1st sess., October 3, 1943. S. Rep. 463.

———. *Claims of Choctaw and Chickasaw Indians for Leased District, Oklahoma.* 76th Cong., 3rd sess., June 3, 1940. S. Rep. 1743.

———. *Coal Lands in Oklahoma: Message from the President of the United States Transmitting Reports Rendered in Connection with the Investigation to Determine the Extent and Value of the Coal Deposits in and under the Segregated Coal Lands of the Choctaw and Chickasaw Nations in Oklahoma.* Washington, D.C.: Government Printing Office, 1910.

———. *Document on Message of President on Choctaw and Chickasaw Indians.* 52nd Cong., 1st sess., April 13, 1892. S. Rep. 552.

———. *Inquiry into Claims for Professional or Other Services Made upon Choctaw Nation on Account of Certain Judgments Rendered against United States.* 49th Cong., 2nd sess., February 28, 1887. S. Rep. 1978.

———. *Leasing of Undeveloped Coal Deposits, Choctaw and Chickasaw Nations Oklahoma.* 77th Cong., 2nd sess., March 11, 1942. S. Rep. 1157.

———. *Letter from the Secretary of the Treasury, Accompanying a Report of the Solicitor of the Treasury Relative to the Claim of the Choctaw Indians, Known as the "Net Proceeds Claim."* 42nd Cong., 2nd sess., June 7, 1872. S. Exec. Doc. 87.

———. *Letter of Secretary of Treasury on Payment of $250,000 in Bonds of United States to Choctaw Indians.* 42nd Cong., 3rd sess., January 22, 1873. S. Rep. 318.

———. *Memorial of P. P. Pitchlynn, Choctaw Delegate, Carrying Out Treaty Stipulations with Choctaw Indians.* 41st Cong., 3rd sess., February 6, 1871. S. Misc. Doc. 65.

———. *Memorial of P. P. Pitchlynn, Delegate of Choctaw Indians, on Bonds to be Issued under Treaty.* 41st Cong., 2nd sess., May 27, 1870. S. Rep. 178.

———. *Memorial of the Chickasaws Relating to Lands of the Choctaw and Chickasaw Nations West of the Ninety-eighth Meridian of West Longitude, with Accompanying Statement.* 51st Cong., 1st sess., March 19, 1900. S. Misc. Doc. 107

———. "Memorial of the Choctaw and Chickasaw Indians with Reference to Their 'Leased District' to Accompany Bill (S. 8140) 'To Authorize the Choctaw and Chickasaw Nations to Bring Suit in the Court of Claims and for Other Purposes.'" In *Suits in the Court of Claims by the Choctaw and Chickasaw Indians.* 62nd Cong., 3rd sess., S. Doc. 1010.

———. *Message from the President of the United States in Compliance with a Resolution of the Senate of the 13th October, 1837, in Relation to the Adjustment of Claims to Reservations under the 14th Article of the Treaty of 1830, with the Choctaw Indians.* 25th Cong., 2nd sess., December 19, 1837. S. Doc. 25.

———. *Message from the President of the United States Relative to the Act to Pay the Choctaw and Chickasaw Indians for Certain Lands Now Occupied by the Cheyenne and Arapahoe Indians.* 52nd Cong., 1st sess., February 18, 1892. S. Exec. Doc. 42.

———. *Memorial of the Choctaw Nation Relative to the President's Message, Dated February 17, 1892.* 52nd Cong., 1st sess., March 14, 1892. S. Misc. Doc. 95.

———. *Message from the President of the United States Transmitting a Communication from the Secretary of the Interior, in Reference to the Applications of the Chicago, Texas and Mexican Central, and the Saint Louis and San Francisco Railway Companies, for a Right of Way across the Lands of the Choctaw Nation, in the Indian Territory.* 47th Cong., 1st sess., December 15, 1881. S. Exec. Doc. 15.

———. *Message from the President of the United States Transmitting a Communication from the Secretary of the Interior, with Accompanying Papers, in Reference to the Bill of Choctaw Council, Approved November 10, 1881, Granting a Right of Way through the Choctaw Nation to the Saint Louis and San Francisco Railway Company, &c.* 47th Cong., 1st sess., January 9, 1882. S. Exec. Doc. 44.

———. *Message from the President of the United States Transmitting the Correspondence in Relation to the Proceedings and Conduct of the Choctaw Commission, under the Treaty of Dancing Rabbit Creek.* 28th Cong., 1st sess., January 30, 1844. S. Doc. 168.

———. *Mississippi Choctaws, Rights to Choctaw Citizenship.* 54th Cong., 2nd sess., February 15, 1897. S. Doc. 129.

———. *Opinion of Attorney General of the United States on Claim of Choctaw Nation of Indians for $250,000 of United States Bonds.* 41st Cong., 3rd sess., January 5, 1871. S. Rep. 278.

———. *Papers and Reports Relating to Five Civilized Tribes.* 62nd Cong., 3rd sess., April 22, 1912. S. Doc. 1139.

———. *Petition of the Mississippi Choctaws in Regard to an Act, H.R. 8566.* 56th Cong., 1st sess., April 4, 1900. S. Doc. 263.

———. *Proposed State of Sequoyah.* 59th Cong., 1st sess., January 16, 1906. S. Doc. 143.

———. "In Relation to the Location of Reservations under the Choctaw Treaty of the

27th of September, 1830." 23rd Cong., 1st sess., Public Lands No. 1230, April 11, 1834. In *American State Papers: Documents, Legislative and Executive of the Congress of the United States*. Vol. 2. *Indian Affairs*. Washington, D.C.: Gales and Seaton, 1832–1861.

———. *Report of the Secretary of the Treasury, in Compliance with a Resolution of the Senate Concerning the Location of the Choctaw Claims and Reservations*. 24th Cong., 1st sess., January 20, 1836. S. Doc. 69.

———. *Report of the Secretary of War—Information in Relation to the Contracts Made for the Removal and Subsistence of the Choctaw Indians*. 28th Cong., 2nd sess., February 7, 1845. S. Doc. 86.

———. *Report on Enrollment in Five Tribes: The Atoka Convention*. 60th Cong., 1st sess., March 9, 1908. S. Doc. 372.

———. *Right of Choctaw Nation of Indians to be Paid Money Awarded to It by United States Senate on 9 March 1859*. 43rd Cong., 1st sess., June 8, 1874. S. Misc. Doc. 121.

———. *Rights of Mississippi Choctaws in the Choctaw Nation. Memorial of the Full-Blood Mississippi Choctaws Relative to Their Rights in the Choctaw Nation*. 57th Cong., 2nd sess., April 24, 1902. S. Doc. 319.

———. *Suit in the Court of Claims by the Choctaw and Chickasaw (S. 8138) to Authorize the Choctaw and Chickasaw Nations to Bring Suit in the Court of Claims and for Other Purposes*. 62nd Cong., 3rd sess., January 15, 1913. S. Doc. 1007.

———. *Veto of Bill to Refer Claims of Choctaw Indians to Court of Claims*. 71st Cong., 3rd sess., February 30, 1931. S. Doc. 280.

U.S. Congress. Senate. Committee on Indian Affairs. *Leasing of the Segregated Coal Deposits of the Choctaw and Chickasaw Nations in Oklahoma: Hearings before the Committee on Indian Affairs, United States Senate, Seventy-seventh Congress, Second Session, on S. 1542, a Bill to Authorize the Leasing of the Undeveloped Coal and Asphalt Deposits of the Choctaw and Chickasaw Nations in Oklahoma, February 2 and 3, and March 3, 1942*. Washington, D.C., Government Printing Office, 1942.

U.S. Congress. Senate. Committee on Railroads. *Railroad through Indian Territory: Proceedings before the Committee on Railroads of the United States Senate Relative to the Bill (S. No. 60) "Ratifying the Act of the General Council of the Choctaw Nations of Indians Granting to the Saint Louis and San Francisco Railway Company Right of Way for a Railroad and Telegraph Line through the Nation."* Washington, D.C.: Government Printing Office, 1882.

United States. Bureau of the Census. Department of Commerce and Labor. *Thirteenth Census of the United States Taken in the Year 1910: Abstract of the Census, Statistics of Population, Agriculture, Manufactures, and Mining for the United States, the States, and Principal Cities with Supplement for Oklahoma Containing Statistics for the State Counties, Cities, and Other Divisions*. Washington, D.C.: Government Printing Office, 1913.

United States. Commission to the Five Civilized Tribes. *Annual Report of the Commission to the Five Civilized Tribes to the Secretary of the Interior*. Washington, D.C.: Government Printing Office, 1898.

———. *Annual Reports of 1894, 1895 and 1896. From March 3, 1893 to January 1, 1897.* Washington, D.C.: 1894–1896.

———. *Eighth Annual Report of the Commission to the Five Civilized Tribes to the Secretary of the Interior for the Fiscal Year Ended June 30, 1901.* Washington, D.C.: Government Printing Office, 1901.

———. *The Final Rolls of Citizens and Freedmen of the Five Civilized Tribes in Indian Territory. Prepared by the Commission and Commissioner to the Five Civilized Tribes, and Approved by the Secretary of the Interior on or Prior to March 4, 1907.* [Washington, D.C.: Government Printing Office, 1907].

———. *Eleventh Annual Report of the Commission to the Five Civilized Tribes to the Secretary of the Interior for the Fiscal Year Ended June 30, 1904.* Washington, D.C.: Government Printing Office, 1904.

———. *Ninth Annual Report of the Commission to the Five Civilized Tribes to the Secretary of the Interior for the Fiscal Year Ended June 30, 1902.* Washington, D.C.: Government Printing Office, 1902.

———. *Report of the Commission Appointed to Negotiate with the Five Civilized Tribes of Indians, Known as the Dawes Commission.* Washington, D.C.: Government Printing Office, 1895.

———. *Report of the Commission to the Five Civilized Tribes.* Washington, D.C. November 20, 1894.

———. *Report of the Commission to the Five Civilized Tribes to the Secretary of the Interior for the Fiscal Year Ended June 30, 1905.* Washington, D.C.: Government Printing Office, 1905.

———. *Report of the Commissioner to the Five Civilized Tribes to the Secretary of the Interior for the Fiscal Year Ended June 30, 1908.* Washington, D.C.: Government Printing Office, 1908.

———. *Report of the Commissioner to the Five Civilized Tribes to the Secretary of the Interior for the Fiscal Year Ended June 30, 1909.* Washington, D.C.: Government Printing Office, 1909.

———. *Report of the Commissioner to the Five Civilized Tribes to the Secretary of the Interior for the Fiscal Year Ended June 30, 1910.* Washington, D.C.: Government Printing Office, 1910.

———. *Report of the Commissioner to the Five Civilized Tribes to the Secretary of the Interior for the Fiscal Year Ended June 30, 1911.* Washington, D.C.: Government Printing Office, 1911.

———. *Report of the Commission to the Five Civilized Tribes to the Secretary of the Interior for the Fiscal Year Ended June 30, 1912.* Washington, D.C.: Government Printing Office, 1912.

———. *Report of the Commissioner to the Five Civilized Tribes to the Secretary of the Interior for the Fiscal Year Ended June 30, 1914.* Washington, D.C.: Government Printing Office, 1914.

———. *Report of the Superintendent for the Five Civilized Tribes to the Secretary of the Interior for the Fiscal Year Ended June 30, 1915.* Washington, D.C.: Government Printing Office, 1915.

———. *Seventh Annual Report of the Commission to the Five Civilized Tribes to the Secretary of the Interior for the Fiscal Year Ended June 30, 1900.* Washington, D.C.: Government Printing Office, 1900.

———. *Sixth Annual Report of the Commission to the Five Civilized Tribes to the Secretary of the Interior for the Fiscal Year Ended June 30, 1899.* Washington, D.C.: Government Printing Office, 1899.

———. *Tenth Annual Report of the Commission to the Five Civilized Tribes to the Secretary of the Interior for the Fiscal Year Ended June 30, 1903.* Washington, D.C.: Government Printing Office, 1903.

United States. Court of Claims. *Cases Decided in the United States Court of Claims.* Reported by James Hoyt. Washington, D.C.: Government Printing Office, 1949.

United States. Department of the Interior. *Agreement with a Commission of the Choctaw and Chickasaw Nations: Letter from the Acting Secretary of the Interior, Transmitting a Copy of an Agreement with a Commission of Choctaw and Chickasaw Nations.* Washington, D.C.: Government Printing Office, 1900.

———. *Enrollment with the Five Civilized Tribes: Hearings before Subcommittee of the Committee on Indian Affairs, House of Representatives, Sixty-third Congress, Second Session on Bills for Enrollment with the Five Civilized Tribes: July 2, 1914.* Washington, D.C.: Government Printing Office, 1914.

———. *Laws, Decisions, and Regulations Affecting the Work of the Commissioner to the Five Civilized Tribes, 1893 to 1906, Together with Maps Showing Classification of Lands in the Chickasaw, Choctaw, Cherokee, Creek, and Seminole Nations, and Recording Districts, Railroads, and Principal Towns of the Indian Territory.* Washington, D.C.: Government Printing Office, 1906.

———. *Report of Inspector James McLaughlin on Bills for Enrollment with the Five Civilized Tribes, July 2, 1914.* Washington, D.C.: Government Printing Office, 1916.

United States. Department of the Interior. Office of Indian Affairs. *Annual Report of the Commissioner of Indian Affairs to the Secretary of the Interior for the Year 1855.* Washington, D.C.: A. O. P. Nicholson, 1856.

———. *Annual Report of the Commissioner of Indian Affairs to the Secretary of the Interior for the Year 1856.* Washington, D.C.: A. O. P. Nicholson, 1857.

———. *Annual Report of the Commissioner of Indian Affairs to the Secretary of the Interior for the Year 1858.* Washington, D.C.: William A. Harris, 1858.

———. *Annual Report of the Commissioner of Indian Affairs to the Secretary of the Interior for the Year 1861.* Washington, D.C.: Government Printing Office, 1861.

———. *Annual Report of the Commissioner of Indian Affairs to the Secretary of the Interior for the Year 1865.* Washington, D.C.: Government Printing Office, 1865.

———. *Annual Report of the Commissioner of Indian Affairs to the Secretary of the Interior for the Year 1866.* Washington, D.C.: Government Printing Office, 1866.

———. *Annual Report of the Commissioner of Indian Affairs to the Secretary of the Interior for the Year 1869.* Washington, D.C.: Government Printing Office, 1870.

———. *Annual Report of the Commissioner of Indian Affairs to the Secretary of the Interior for the Year 1876.* Washington, D.C.: Government Printing Office, 1876.

————. *Annual Report of the Commissioner of Indian Affairs to the Secretary of the Interior for the Year 1880.* Washington, D.C.: Government Printing Office, 1880.

————. *Annual Report of the Commissioner of Indian Affairs to the Secretary of the Interior for the Year 1882.* Washington, D.C.: Government Printing Office, 1882.

————. *Annual Report of the Commissioner of Indian Affairs to the Secretary of the Interior for the Year 1884.* Washington, D.C.: Government Printing Office, 1884.

————. *Annual Report of the Commissioner of Indian Affairs to the Secretary of the Interior for the Year 1885.* Washington, D.C.: Government Printing Office, 1885.

————. *Annual Report of the Commissioner of Indian Affairs to the Secretary of the Interior for the Year 1889.* Washington, D.C.: Government Printing Office, 1889.

————. *Annual Report of the Commissioner of Indian Affairs to the Secretary of the Interior to the Secretary of the Interior for the Year 1892.* Washington, D.C.: Government Printing Office, 1892.

————. *Annual Report of the Commissioner of Indian Affairs to the Secretary of the Interior to the Secretary of the Interior for the Year 1893.* Washington, D.C.: Government Printing Office, 1893.

————. *Annual Report of the Commissioner of Indian Affairs to the Secretary of the Interior for the Year 1894.* Washington, D.C.: Government Printing Office, 1895.

————. *Annual Report of the Commissioner of Indian Affairs to the Secretary of the Interior for the Year 1903.* Washington, D.C.: Government Printing Office, 1903.

————. *Annual Report of the Commissioner of Indian Affairs to the Secretary of the Interior for the Year 1907.* Washington, D.C.: Government Printing Office, 1907.

Wheelock Academy. *Wheelock in Story and Song.* [Millerton, Okla., 1932].

Whipple, Amiel Weeks. *A Pathfinder in the Southwest: The Itinerary of Lieutenant A. W. Whipple during His Explorations for a Railway Route from Fort Smith to Los Angeles in the Years 1853 and 1854.* Edited by Grant Foreman. Norman: University of Oklahoma Press, 1941.

————, Thomas Ewbank, and William W. Turner. *Report upon the Indian Tribes: Explorations and Surveys for a Railroad Route from the Mississippi River to the Pacific Ocean.* Washington, D.C., 1854.

Whipple, Charles K. *Slavery and the American Board of Commissioners for Foreign Missions.* New York: American Anti-Slavery Society, 1859.

————. *The Relation of the A.B.C.F.M. to Slavery.* Boston: R. F. Wallcut, 1871.

Whitney, Asa. *A Project for a Railroad to the Pacific.* New York: George W. Wood, 1849.

Wood, George W. *Report of Mr. Wood's Visit to the Choctaw and Cherokee Missions, 1855.* Boston: Press of T. R. Marvin, 1855.

Wright, Alfred. "Choctaws, Religious Opinions, Traditions, etc." *Missionary Herald* XXIV (June 1828): 178–183, 214–216.

SECONDARY SOURCES

Abel, Annie Heloise. *The American Indian and the End of the Confederacy, 1863–1866.* Lincoln: University of Nebraska Press, 1993.

————. *The American Indian as Participant in the Civil War.* Cleveland, Ohio: Arthur H. Clark Company, 1919.

————. *The American Indian as Slaveholder and Secessionist: An Omitted Chapter in the Diplomatic History of the Southern Confederacy.* Cleveland, Ohio: Arthur H. Clark Company, 1915; reprint, Lincoln: University of Nebraska Press, 1992.

————. *The American Indian in the Civil War, 1862–1865.* Cleveland, Ohio: A. H. Clark, 1919; reprint, Lincoln: University of Nebraska Press, 1992.

————. *The American Indian under Reconstruction.* Cleveland, Ohio: Arthur H. Clark Company, 1925.

————. *The History of Events Resulting in the Consolidation of American Indian Tribes West of the Mississippi River.* Washington, D.C.: American Historical Association, 1906.

Akers, Donna. *Living in the Land of Death: The Choctaw Nation, 1830–1860.* East Lansing: Michigan State University Press, 2004.

Aldrich, Gene. "A History of the Coal Industry in Oklahoma to 1907." Ph.D. diss., University of Oklahoma, 1952.

Allen, Virginia R. "Medical Practices and Health in the Choctaw Nation." *Chronicles of Oklahoma* 48 (Spring 1970): 60–73.

Baird, W. David. "Are the Five Tribes of Oklahoma 'Real' Indians?" *Western Historical Quarterly* 21, no. 1 (February 1990): 5–18.

————. "Cyrus Byington and the Presbyterian Choctaw Mission." In *Churchmen and the Western Indians 1820–1920,* edited by Clyde A. Milner II and Floyd A. O'Neil, 1–40. Norman: University of Oklahoma Press, 1985.

————. *Peter Pitchlynn: Chief of the Choctaws.* Norman: University of Oklahoma Press, 1972.

————. "Spencer Academy, Choctaw Nation, 1842–1900." *Chronicles of Oklahoma* 45 (Spring 1967): 25–43.

Balyeat, Frank A. "Joseph Samuel Morrow, Apostle to the Indians." *Chronicles of Oklahoma* 35 (Fall 1957): 297–314.

Bell, Daniel. "Ethnicity and Social Change." In *Ethnicity: Theory and Experience,* edited by Nathan Glazer and Daniel P. Moynihan, 141–174. Cambridge, Mass.: Harvard University Press, 1975.

Belvin, Harry J. W. *Choctaw Tribal Structure and Achievement, August 18, 1948, to August 25, 1975.* Durant, Okla.: Choctaw Bilingual Education Program, Southeastern Oklahoma State University, n.d.

Bonnifield, Paul. "The Choctaw Nation on the Eve of the Civil War." *Journal of the West* 12 (1973): 386–387.

Bonnin, Gertrude, Charles H. Fabens, and Matthew K. Sniffen. *Oklahoma's Poor Rich Indians: An Orgy of Graft and Exploitation of the Five Civilized Tribes—Legalized Robbery.* Philadelphia, Pa.: Office of the Indian Rights Association, 1924.

Bowden, David. "Choctaw Toll Roads and Railroads." *Chronicles of Oklahoma* 44 (Winter 1996–1997): 384–397.

Bray, Alpheus Caswell. "A Story of the Building of the Railroads in the State of Oklahoma." Ph.D. diss., University of Oklahoma, 1923.

Brigance, William Norwood. *Jeremiah Sullivan Black: A Defender of the Constitution and the Ten Commandments*. Philadelphia: University of Pennsylvania Press, 1934.

Brown, Loren N. "The Choctaw-Chickasaw Court Citizens." *Chronicles of Oklahoma* 16, no. 4 (December 1938): 425–443.

———. "The Dawes Commission." *Chronicles of Oklahoma* 9, no. 2 (June 1931): 71–105.

———. "Establishment of the Dawes Commission for Indian Territory." *Chronicles of Oklahoma* 18, no. 2 (1940): 171–181.

Brown, Walter Lee. *A Life of Albert Pike*. Fayetteville: University of Arkansas Press, 1997.

Burton, Jeffrey. *Indian Territory and the United States, 1866–1906: Courts, Government, and the Movement for Oklahoma Statehood*. Norman: University of Oklahoma Press, 1995.

Carson, James Taylor. *Searching for the Bright Path: The Mississippi Choctaws from Prehistory to Removal*. Lincoln: University of Nebraska Press, 1999.

Carter, Kent. *The Dawes Commission and the Allotment of the Five Civilized Tribes, 1893–1914*. Orem, Utah: Ancestry.com, 1999.

Champagne, Duane. *Social Order and Political Change: Constitutional Governments among the Cherokee, the Choctaw, the Chickasaw and the Creek*. Stanford, Calif.: Stanford University Press, 1992.

Clampitt, Brad R. "'An Indian Shall Not Spill an Indian's Blood': The Confederate-Indian Conference at Camp Napoleon, 1865." *Chronicles of Oklahoma* 83, no. 1 (Spring 2005): 34–53.

Clark, C. B. *Lone Wolf v. Hitchcock*. Lincoln: University of Nebraska Press, 1994.

Clark, Ira Granville. "The Railroads and the Tribal Lands: Indian Territory, 1838–1890." Ph.D. diss., University of California, Berkeley, 1947.

Cobb, Daniel M. "'Us Indians Understand the Basics': Oklahoma Indians and the Politics of Community Action, 1964–1970." *Western Historical Quarterly* 33 (Spring 2002):41–66.

Cohen, Ronald "Ethnicity: Problem and Focus in Anthropology." *Annual Review of Anthropology* 7 (1978): 379–404.

Coker, William S., and Thomas D. Watson. *Indian Traders of the Southeastern Spanish Borderlands: Panton Leslie & Company and John Forbes & Company, 1783–1847*. Pensacola: University of West Florida Press, 1986.

Coker, William Sydney. "Pat Harrison's Efforts to Reopen the Choctaw Citizenship Rolls." *Southern Quarterly* 3 (October 1964): 36–60.

Cushman, H. B. *History of the Choctaw, Chickasaw and Natchez Indians*. Edited by Angie Debo. New York: Russell & Russell, 1962.

———. *History of the Choctaw, Chickasaw, and Natchez Indians*. 1899; reprint, Norman: University of Oklahoma Press, 1999.

De Rosier, Arthur H., Jr. "Pioneers with Conflicting Ideals: Christianity and Slavery in the Choctaw Nation." *Journal of Mississippi History* 21, no. 3 (1959): 174–189.

Debo, Angie. *The Five Civilized Tribes of Oklahoma: Report on Social and Economic Conditions.* [Philadelphia, Pa.]: Indian Rights Association, 1951.

———. *The Rise and Fall of the Choctaw Republic.* Norman: University of Oklahoma Press, 1934.

———. *And Still the Waters Run.* Princeton, N.J.: Princeton University Press, 1940.

Deloria, Vine, Jr., ed. *The Indian Reorganization Act: Congresses and Bills.* Norman: University of Oklahoma Press, 2002.

———, and Raymond Demallie. *Documents of American Indian Diplomacy.* 2 vols. Norman: University of Oklahoma Press, 1999.

Doran, Michael F. "Negro Slaves of the Five Civilized Tribes." *Annals of the Association of American Geographers* 68 (1978): 335–350.

Doyle, Thomas H. "Single versus Double Statehood." *Chronicles of Oklahoma* 5, no. 1 (March 1927): 31.

Dunkle, W. F. "A Choctaw Indian's Diary." *Chronicles of Oklahoma* 4, no. 1 (March 1926): 61–69.

Edwards, John. "The Choctaw Indians in the Middle of the Nineteenth Century." *Chronicles of Oklahoma* 10, no. 3 (1932): 392–425.

Eggan, Fred. *The American Indian: Perspectives for the Study of Social Change.* Chicago, Ill.: Aldine Publishing Company, 1966.

———. "Historical Changes in the Choctaw Kinship System." *American Anthropologist* 39, no. 1 (1937): 34–52.

Elkins, Stanley. *Slavery: A Problem in American Institutional and Intellectual Life.* 2nd ed. Chicago: The University of Chicago Press, 1968.

Evarts, Jeremiah. *Cherokee Removal: The "William Penn" Essays and Other Writings.* Edited and with an introduction by Francis Paul Prucha. Knoxville: University of Tennessee Press, 1981.

Faiman-Silva, Sandra. *Choctaws at the Crossroads: The Political Economy of Class and Culture in the Oklahoma Timber Region.* Lincoln: University of Nebraska Press, 1997.

Fischer, LeRoy H., and Jerry Gill. "Confederate Indian Forces outside of Indian Territory." *Chronicles of Oklahoma* 46, no. 3 (Autumn 1968): 249–284.

Fixico, Donald L. *Termination and Relocation: Federal Indian Policy, 1945–1960.* Albuquerque: University of New Mexico Press, 1986.

Foner, Eric. *Reconstruction: America's Unfinished Revolution, 1863–1877.* New York: Harper & Row, 1988.

Foreman, Grant. "The California Overland Mail Route through Oklahoma." *Chronicles of Oklahoma* 9, no. 3 (September 1931): 300–317.

———. *The Five Civilized Tribes.* Norman: University of Oklahoma Press, 1934.

———. *Indian Removal: The Emigration of the Five Civilized Tribes of Indians.* Norman: University of Oklahoma Press, 1972.

———. *Indians and Pioneers: The Story of the American Southwest before 1830.* Rev. ed. Norman: University of Oklahoma Press, 1936.

————. "A Journal Kept by Douglas Cooper of an Expedition by a Company of Chickasaws in Quest of Comanche Indians." *Chronicles of Oklahoma* 5, no. 4 (December 1927): 381–390.

————. *Marcy and the Gold Seekers: The Journal of Captain R. B. Marcy, with an Account of the Gold Rush over the Southern Route.* Norman: University of Oklahoma Press, 1939.

Franks, Kenny A. "The Confederate States and the Five Civilized Tribes: A Breakdown of Relations." *Journal of the West* 12 (July 1973): 439–454.

Galloway, Patricia. *Choctaw Genesis.* Lincoln: University of Nebraska Press, 1995.

Geertz, Clifford. *The Interpretation of Cultures.* New York: Basic Books, Inc., 1973.

Gibson, Arrell M. *The Chickasaws.* Norman: University of Oklahoma Press, 1971.

Gittinger, Roy. *The Formation of the State of Oklahoma, 1803–1906.* Berkeley: University of California Press, 1917.

————. "The Separation of Nebraska and Kansas from the Indian Territory." *Chronicles of Oklahoma* 1, no. 1 (January 1921): 9–29.

Goins, Robert Charles, and Danney Goble. H.4th ed. Norman: University of Oklahoma Press, 2006.

Graebner, Norman Arthur. "History of Cattle Ranching in Eastern Oklahoma." *Chronicles of Oklahoma* 21, no. 3 (September 1943): 300–311.

————. "The Public Land Policy of the Five Civilized Tribes." *Chronicles of Oklahoma* 23, no. 2 (Summer 1945): 107–118.

Gunning, I. C. *When Coal Was King: Coal Mining Industry in the Choctaw Nation.* N.p.: Eastern Oklahoma Historical Society, 1975.

Hagan, William T. *Taking Indian Lands: The Cherokee (Jerome) Commission, 1889–1893.* Norman: University of Oklahoma Press, 2003.

Hargrett, Lester. *A Bibliography of the Constitutions and Laws of the American Indians.* Cambridge: Harvard University Press, 1947.

Harmon, Alexandra. "American Indians and Land Monopolies in the Gilded Age." *Journal of American History* 90, no. 1 (2003): 106–133.

Hightower, Michael J. "Cattle, Coal and Indian Land: A Tradition of Mining in Southeastern Oklahoma." *Chronicles of Oklahoma* 62 (Spring 1984): 4–25.

History of the Intertribal Council of the Five Civilized Tribes. N.p.: n.d.

Hodder, Frank H. "The Genesis of the Kansas-Nebraska Act." *Proceedings of the State Historical Society of Wisconsin* (1912): 69–86.

————. "The Railroad Background of the Kansas-Nebraska Act." *Missouri Valley Historical Review* 12 (January 1925): 3–22.

Hofsommer, Donovan L., ed. *Railroads in Oklahoma.* Oklahoma City: Oklahoma Historical Society, 1977.

Hofstadter, Richard. *The Age of Reform.* New York: Alfred A. Knopf, 1955.

Holden, J. F. "The B.I.T.: The Story of an Adventure in Railroad Building." *Chronicles of Oklahoma* 11, no. 1 (March 1933): 644–650, 660–664.

Horsman, Reginald. *Expansion and American Indian Policy, 1783–1812.* [Lansing]: Michigan State University Press, 1967.

———. *Race and Manifest Destiny*. Cambridge: Harvard University Press, 1981.

Hoxie, Fred. *A Final Promise*. Lincoln: University of Nebraska Press, 1984.

Hudson, Peter. "Recollections of Peter Hudson." *Chronicles of Oklahoma* 10, no. 4 (December 1932): 501–521.

Janda, Sarah Eppler. "The Intersection of Feminism and Indianness in the Activism of LaDonna Harris and Wilma Mankiller." Ph.D. diss., University of Oklahoma, 2002.

Jenness, Theodora. "The Indian Territory." *Atlantic Monthly* 53 (April 1879): 444–452.

Johnson, Neil R. *The Chickasaw Rancher*. Stillwater, Okla.: Redlands Press, 1961.

Jordan, H. Glenn. "Choctaw Colonization in Oklahoma." In *America's Exiles: Indian Colonization in Oklahoma*, edited by Arrell Morgan Gibson, 16–33. Oklahoma City: Oklahoma Historical Society, 1976.

Josephy, Alvin, Jr. *Red Power: The American Indian's Fight for Freedom*. New York: American Heritage Press, 1971.

Kidwell, Clara Sue. "The Choctaw Struggle for Land and Identity in Mississippi, 1830–1918." In *After Removal: The Choctaw in Mississippi*, edited by Samuel J. Wells and Roseanna Tubby, 64–93. Jackson: University Press of Mississippi, 1986.

La Vere, David. *Contrary Neighbors: Southern Plains and Removed Indians in Indian Territory*. Norman: University of Oklahoma Press, 2000.

Lafferty, R. A. *Okla Hannali*. Garden City, N.Y.: Doubleday & Company, Inc., 1972.

Lincecum, Gideon. "Choctaw Traditions about Their Settlement in Mississippi and the Origin of Their Mounds." *Publications of the Mississippi Historical Society* 8 (1904): 524–542.

Lindquist, G. E. E. *The Red Man in the United States: An Intimate Study of the Social, Economic and Religious Life of the American Indian, Made under the Direction of G. E. E. Lindquist, with a foreword by Honorable Charles H. Burke*. New York: George H. Doran Company, 1923.

Linton, Ralph, ed. *Acculturation in Seven American Indian Tribes*. Gloucester, Mass.: Peter Smith, 1963.

Littlefield, Daniel F., Jr. *The Chickasaw Freedmen: A People without a Country*. Westport, Conn.: Greenwood Press, 1980.

Love, Wallace B., and R. Palmer Howard. "Health and Medical Practice in the Choctaw Nation, 1880–1907." *Oklahoma State Medical Association Journal* 63 (March 1970): 124–128.

Mackey. Albert Gallatin. *The History of Freemasonry, Its Legends and Traditions, Its Chronological History with William R. Singleton, The History of Its Introduction and Progress in the United States, the History of the Symbols of Freemasonry and the History of the S.S. Scottish Rite*. 7 vols. New York: The Masonic History Company, 1898.

Marsden, George M. *The Evangelical Mind and the New School Presbyterian Experience: A Case Study of Thought and Theology in Nineteenth-Century America*. New Haven, Conn.: Yale University Press, 1970.

Masterson, V. V. *The Katy Railroad and the Last Frontier*. Norman: University of Oklahoma Press, 1952.

Maxwell, Amos. *The Sequoyah Constitutional Convention*. Boston: Meador Publishing Company, 1953.

McLoughlin, William G. "The Choctaw Slave Burning: A Crisis in Mission Work among the Indians." *Journal of the West* 13, no. 1 (1974): 113–127.

Merrill, Pierce Kelton. "The Social and Economic Status of the Choctaw Indians." Ph.D. diss., University of Oklahoma, 1940.

Meserve, John Bartlett. "Chief Coleman Cole." *Chronicles of Oklahoma* 14, no. 1 (March 1936): 9–21.

———. "Chief George Hudson and Chief Samuel Garland." *Chronicles of Oklahoma* 20, no. 1 (March 1942): 9–17.

———. "Chief Wilson Nathaniel Jones." *Chronicles of Oklahoma* 14, no. 4 (December 1936): 419–433.

———. *The Dawes Commission and the Five Civilized Tribes of Indian Territory*. Philadelphia, Pa.: Office of the Indian Rights Association, 1896.

———. "Governor Benjamin Franklin Overton and Governor Benjamin Crooks Burney." *Chronicles of Oklahoma* 16, no. 2 (June 1938): 221–233.

———. "The McCurtains." *Chronicles of Oklahoma* 13, no. 3 (September 1935): 297–311.

Miner, H. Craig. *The Corporation and the Indian*. Columbia: University of Missouri Press, 1976.

———. "'Little Houses on Wheels': Indian Response to the Railroad." In *Railroads in Oklahoma*, edited by Donovan L. Hofsommer. Oklahoma City: Oklahoma Historical Society, 1973.

———. *The St. Louis–San Francisco Transcontinental Railroad: The Thirty-fifth Parallel Project, 1853–1890*. Lawrence: University Press of Kansas, 1972.

———. "The Struggle for an East-West Railway into the Indian Territory, 1870–1882." *Chronicles of Oklahoma* 47 (Spring 1969): 560–581.

———, and William E. Unrau. *The End of Indian Kansas: A Study of Cultural Revolution, 1854–1871*. Lawrence: Regents Press of Kansas, 1978.

Morehouse, Warren K. *Our National Problem: The Sad Condition of the Oklahoma Indians*. N.p., 1913.

Morgan, Lewis Henry. *Systems of Consanguinity and Affinity of the Human Family*. Lincoln: University of Nebraska Press, 1997.

Morrison, James D. *Schools for the Choctaws*. Durant, Okla.: Choctaw Bilingual Education Program, Southeastern Oklahoma State University, 1978.

———. "The Union Pacific, Southern Branch." *Chronicles of Oklahoma* 14, no. 2 (June 1936): 173–188.

Murray, William H. "The Constitutional Convention." *Chronicles of Oklahoma* 9, no. 2 (June 1931): 126–138.

Nesbitt, Paul. "J. J. McAlester." *Chronicles of Oklahoma* 11, no. 2 (June 1933): 758–764.

Nolen, Curtis L. "The Okmulgee Constitution: A Step towards Indian Self-Determination." *Chronicles of Oklahoma* 58 (Fall 1980): 264–281.

Nugent, Walter T. K. *Money and American Society, 1865–1880*. New York: The Free Press, 1968.

O'Brien, Greg, *Choctaws in a Revolutionary Age, 1750–1830*. Lincoln: University of Nebraska Press, 2002.

O'Donnell, James H., III. *Southern Indians in the American Revolution*. Knoxville: University of Tennessee Press, 1973.

O'Donnell, Janet. *The Dispossession of the American Indian, 1887–1934*. Bloomington: Indiana University Press, 1991.

"Okmulgee Constitution." *Chronicles of Oklahoma* 3, no. 3 (September 1925): 218–229.

Otis, D. S. *The Dawes Act and the Allotment of Indian Land*. Edited by Francis Paul Prucha. Norman: University of Oklahoma Press, 1973.

Perdue, Theda. *Nations Remembered: An Oral History of the Five Civilized Tribes, 1865–1907*. Westport, Conn.: Greenwood Press, 1980.

Pesantubbee, Michelene E. *Choctaw Women in a Chaotic World: The Clash of Cultures in the Colonial Southeast*. Albuquerque: University of New Mexico, 2005.

Philp, Kenneth R. *Termination Revisited: American Indians on the Trail to Self-Determination, 1933–1953*. Lincoln: University of Nebraska Press, 1999.

Plaisance, A. "The Choctaw Trading House—1803–1822." *Alabama Historical Quarterly* 16, nos. 1 and 2 (1954): 393–423.

Plowden, Gene. *Those Amazing Ringlings and Their Circus*. Caldwell, Idaho: The Caxton Printers, Ltd., 1968.

Presbyterian Historical Society. *American Indian Correspondence: The Presbyterian Historical Society Collection of Missionaries Letters, 1833–1893*. Westport, Conn.: Greenwood Press, 1978.

Priest, Loring Benson. *Uncle Sam's Stepchildren: The Reformation of United States Indian Policy, 1865–1887*. New Brunswick, N.J.: Rutgers University Press, 1942.

Prucha, Francis Paul. *Documents of American Indian Policy*. 2nd ed. Lincoln: University of Nebraska Press, 1990.

Rampp, Lary C., and Donald L. Rampp. *The Civil War in the Indian Territory*. Austin, Tex.: Presidial Press, 1975.

Redfield, Robert, Ralph Linton, and Melville J. Herskovits. "A Memorandum for the Study of Acculturation." *American Anthropologist* 38 (1936): 149–152.

Remini, Robert V. *The Legacy of Andrew Jackson: Essays on Democracy, Indian Removal and Slavery*. Baton Rouge: Louisiana State University Press, 1988.

"Report on the Five Civilized Tribes, 1897." *Chronicles of Oklahoma* 48 (Winter 1970–1971): 416–430.

Rister, Carl Coke. *Land Hunger: David L. Payne and the Oklahoma Boomers*. Norman: University of Oklahoma Press, 1942.

Roberts, Charles. "The Second Choctaw Removal, 1903." In *After Removal: The Choctaw in Mississippi*, edited by Samuel J. Wells and Roseanna Tubby. Jackson: University Press of Mississippi, 1986.

Rohrbough, Malcolm. *The Land Office Business: The Settlement and Administration of American Public Lands, 1789–1837*. New York: Oxford University Press, 1968.

Rosenthal, Harvey D. "Indian Claims and the American Conscience: A Brief History of the Indian Claims Commission." In *Irredeemable America: The Indians' Estate and*

Land Claims, edited by Imre Sutton, 35–70. Albuquerque: University of New Mexico Press, 1985.

———. "Their Day in Court: A History of the Indian Claims Commission." Ph.D. diss., Kent State University, 1976.

Satz, Ronald N. *American Indian Policy in the Jacksonian Era*. Lincoln: University of Nebraska Press, 1975.

———. "The Mississippi Choctaw: From the Removal Treaty to the Federal Agency." In *After Removal: The Choctaws in Mississippi*, edited by Samuel J. Wells and Roseanna Tubby. Jackson: The University Press of Mississippi, 1986.

Schultz, George A. *An Indian Canaan: Isaac McCoy and the Vision of an Indian State*. Norman: University of Oklahoma Press, 1972.

Sellars, Charles. *The Market Revolution: Jacksonian America, 1815–1846*. New York: Oxford University Press, 1991.

Semmes, John E. *John H. B. Latrobe and His Times, 1803–1891*. Baltimore, Md.: The Norman, Remington Co., 1917.

Sheehan, Bernard W. *Seeds of Extinction: Jeffersonian Philanthropy and the American Indian*. Chapel Hill: Published for the Institute of Early American History and Culture at Williamsburg, Virginia, by the University of North Carolina Press, 1973.

Spalding, Arminta Scott. "Cyrus Kingsbury: Missionary to the Choctaws." Ph.D. diss., University of Oklahoma, 1974.

Spoehr, Alexander. *Changing Kinship Systems: A Study in the Acculturation of the Creeks, Cherokee, and Choctaw*. Field Museum of Natural History Anthropological Series Publication 583. [Chicago, Ill.]: Field Museum of Natural History, 1947.

Swanton, John. *Source Material for the Social and Ceremonial Life of the Choctaw Indians*. Bureau of American Ethnology Bulletin No. 103. Washington, D.C.: Government Printing Office, 1931.

Thomas, Robert K. "Colonialism: Classic and Internal." *New University Thought* 6 (Winter 1966–1967): 37–44.

———. "Powerless Politics." *New University Thought* 6 (Winter 1966–1967): 44–53.

Thompson, Richard H. *Theories of Ethnicity: A Critical Appraisal*. New York: Greenwood Press, 1989.

Thorne, Tanis. *The World's Richest Indian: The Scandal over Jackson Barnett's Oil Fortune*. Oxford: Oxford University Press, 2003.

Tonkin, Elizabeth, Maryon McDonald, and Malcolm Chapman, eds. *History and Ethnicity*. Association of Social Anthropologists Monograph 27. London: Routledge, 1989.

Trennert, Robert. *Alternative to Extinction: Federal Indian Policy and the Beginnings of the Reservation System*. Philadelphia, Pa.: Temple University Press, 1975.

Unrau, William E. *Mixed-Bloods and Tribal Dissolution: Charles Curtis and the Quest for Indian Identity*. Lawrence: University Press of Kansas, 1989.

Wardell, M. L. "Southwest's History Written in Oklahoma's Boundary Story." *Chronicles of Oklahoma* 5, no. 3 (September 1927): 211–214.

Washburn, Wilcomb E. *The Assault on Indian Tribalism: The General Allotment Law (Dawes Act) of 1887*. Philadelphia, Pa.: J. B. Lippincott Company, 1975.

Wells, Samuel J., and Roseanna Tubby, eds. *After Removal: The Choctaws in Mississippi*. Jackson: University Press of Mississippi, 1986.

White, Richard. *Roots of Dependency: Subsistence, Environment, and Social Change among the Choctaws, Pawnees and Navajos*. Lincoln: University of Nebraska Press, 1983.

Wilkinson, Glen A. "Indian Tribal Claims before the Court of Claims." *Georgetown Law Journal* 55 (December 1966): 511–528.

Winsor, Henry M. "Chickasaw-Choctaw Financial Relations with the United States, 1830–1880." *Journal of the West* 12 (1973): 356–371.

Wright, James B. *Allen Wright, Minister of the Gospel: Scholar, Translator, Lexicographer, Educator, Principal Chief (Governor) Choctaw Nation and Gentleman*. McAlester, Okla.: [Democrat Print.], 1961.

Wright, Mike. "Indian Military 'Code Talkers.'" *The Oklahoma Observer* (November 10, 1986): 19.

Wright, Muriel H. "General Douglas H. Cooper, C.S.A." *Chronicles of Oklahoma* 32, no. 2 (Summer 1954): 142–184.

———. "Old Boggy Depot." *Chronicles of Oklahoma* 5, no. 1 (March 1927): 4–17.

———. "Origin of Oklahoma Day." *Chronicles of Oklahoma* 23, no. 3 (1945): 203–215.

———. "The Wedding of Oklahoma and Miss Indian Territory." *Chronicles of Oklahoma* 35 (Fall 1957): 255–264.

Wright, Muriel H., and Peter J. Hudson. "Brief Outline of the Choctaw and Chickasaw Nations in Indian Territory, 1820–1860." *Chronicles of Oklahoma* 7, no. 4 (1929): 386–413.

Wright, Muriel H., and George H. Shirk, eds. "The Journal of Lieutenant A. W. Whipple." *Chronicles of Oklahoma* 28, no. 3 (1950): 235–237.

Young, Mary Elizabeth. *Redskins, and Ruffleshirts: Indian Allotments in Alabama and Mississippi 1830–1860*. Norman: University of Oklahoma Press, 1961.

LAWS AND COURT CASES

U.S. Statutes

5 Stat. 513, 517. *Claims under the Treaty of Dancing Rabbit Creek. An Act to Provide for the Satisfaction of Claims Arising under the Fourteenth and Nineteenth Articles of the Treaty of Dancing Rabbit Creek, Concluded in September, One Thousand Eight Hundred and Thirty.* August 23, 1842.

5 Stat. 180. *Indian Appropriation Act*. March 3, 1837.

18 Stat. L. 1044. *An Act to Revise and Consolidate the Statutes of the United States. In Force on the First Day of December, Anno Domini One Thousand Eight Hundred and Seventy-three.*

21 Stat. 504. *An Act for the Ascertainment of the Amount Due the Choctaw Nation.* March 3, 1881.

24 Stat. 388. *An Act to Provide for the Allotment of Lands in Severalty to Indians on the Various Reservations, and to Extend the Protection of the Laws of the United States and the Territories over the Indians, and for Other Purposes.* February 8, 1887.

27 Stat. 645. *Indian Appropriation Act 1894.* March 3, 1893.

28 Stat. 876. *Indian Appropriation Act 1896.* March 2, 1895.

29 Stat. 321. *Indian Appropriation Act 1897.* June 10, 1896.

30 Stat. 83. *Indian Appropriation Act 1898.* June 7, 1897.

30 Stat. 495. *An Act for the Protection of the People of the Indian Territory, and for Other Purposes.* June 28, 1898.

30 Stat. 591. *Indian Appropriation Act 1899.* July 1, 1898.

31 Stat. 221. *Indian Appropriation Act 1901.* May 31, 1900.

31 Stat. 672, 680. *An Act to Ratify an Agreement with the Indians of the Fort Hall Indian Reservation in Idaho, and Making Appropriations to Carry the Same into Effect.* June 6, 1900.

32 Stat. 641. *An Act to Ratify and Confirm an Agreement with the Choctaw and Chickasaw Tribes of Indians, and for Other Purposes.* July 1, 1902.

32 Stat. 982, 997. *Indian Appropriation Act 1904.* March 3, 1903.

33 Stat. 189, 209. *Indian Appropriation Act 1905.* April 21, 1904.

34 Stat. 137, 142. *An Act to Provide for the Final Disposition of the Affairs of the Five Civilized Tribes in the Indian Territory, and for Other Purposes.* April 26, 1906.

37 Stat. 67. *An Act to Provide for the Sale of the Surface of the Segregated Coal and Asphalt Lands of the Choctaw and Chickasaw Nations, and for Other Purposes.* February 19, 1912.

47 Stat. 88. *An Act to Provide for the Leasing of the Segregated Coal and Asphalt Deposits of the Choctaw and Chickasaw Indian Nations in Oklahoma and for an Extension of Time within which Purchasers of Such Deposits May Complete Payments.* April 21, 1932.

58 Stat. 463, 483. *An Act Making Appropriations for the Department of the Interior for the Fiscal Year Ending June 30, 1945, and for Other Purposes.* June 28, 1944.

62 Stat. 596. *Joint Resolution Providing for the Ratification by Congress of a Contract for the Purchase of Certain Lands and Mineral Deposits by the United States from the Choctaw and Chickasaw Nations of Indians.* June 24, 1948.

U.S. Court of Claims

19 Ct. Cl. 243. *The Choctaw Nation of Indians v. the United States.* March 3, 1884.

21 Ct. Cl. 59. *The Choctaw Nation of Indians v. the United States.* January 25, 1886.

22 Ct. Cl. 476. *The Choctaw Nation v. the United States.* December 15, 1886.

22 Ct. Cl. 489. *Final Judgment in Net Proceeds Case.* December 15, 1886.

34 Ct. Cl. 17–168. *The Choctaw and Chickasaw Nations v. the United States and the Wichita and Affiliated Bands of Indians.* January 9, 1899.

38 Ct. Cl. 558. *The United States v. the Choctaw Nation et al.* April 27, 1903.

45 Ct. Cl. 154. *S. W. Peel v. Choctaw Nation and the United States.* January 31, 1910.

45 Ct. Cl. 618. *The United States v. Choctaw Nation, Chickasaw Nation, and Chickasaw Freedmen.* May 9, 1910.

47 Ct. Cl. 59–121. *Missouri, Kansas & Texas Railway Co. v. the United States.* December 4, 1911.

51 Ct. Cl. 284. *Estate of Winton et al. v. Amos et al.* May 29, 1916.

52 Ct. Cl. Rpt. 284. *Denied Rehearing of Winton Case.*

59 Ct. Cl. *Pitchlynn, Sophia C. et al. v. the Choctaw Nation.* June 9, 1924.

62 Ct. Cl. Rep. 458. *McMurray Claims against Choctaws and Chickasaws.* July 1, 1926.

75 Ct. Cl. 494. *For Value of Station Reservations Granted to Certain Railroads.* Dismissed June 6, 1932.

78 Ct. Cl. 837. *Balance of Compensation Allegedly Due for Cession of "Leased District" of the Choctaw-Chickasaw Reservation.* Dismissed October 9, 1933. No published decision.

81 Ct. Cl. 1. *Reimbursement for Per Capita Payments Made to Mississippi Choctaws.* Dismissed June 17, 1935; writ of certiorari denied November 25, 1935.

81 Ct. Cl. 63. *Value of Allotments to 466 Minor Children of Choctaw Freedmen and Proceeds from Sales of 21,134.95 Acres of Land out of the Choctaw and Chickasaw Reservation to Choctaw and Chickasaw Freedmen.* March 4, 1935.

83 Ct. Cl. 49. *Payment to Robert L. Owen for Services to Mississippi Choctaws.* April 6, 1936.

83 Ct. Cl. 140. *Apportionment of Certain Moneys on the Basis of Total Membership, Rather Than 3/4 to Choctaws and 1/4 to Chickasaws.* Dismissed April 6, 1936.

84 Ct. Cl. 644. *Apportionment of Certain Moneys on the Basis of Total Membership, Rather Than 3/4 to Choctaws and 1/4 to Chickasaws.* Writ of certiorari denied by Supreme Court. March 8, 1937.

88 Ct. Cl. 271. *The Choctaw and Chickasaw Nations v. the United States.* January 9, 1939.

90 Ct. Cl. 682. *Accounting of All Transactions between the United States and the Lessees of Coal and Asphalt Mining Rights in Tribal Land, and Collection of Royalties Allegedly Due from the Lessees.* Dismissed January 27, 1940. No published decision.

91 Ct. Cl. 320. *The Choctaw Nation v. the United States.* April 1, 1940.

121 Ct. Cl. 41. *The Chickasaw Nation v. the United States.* December 4, 1951.

128 Ct. Cl. 195. *The Choctaw Nation v. the United States.* May 4, 1954.

133 Ct. Cl. 207. *The Choctaw Nation v. the United States.* November 8, 1955.

U.S. Circuit Court Decisions
420 F. Supp. 1110, 1122–1123. *Harjo v. Kleppe.* D.D.C. 1976.

U.S. Supreme Court Decisions
119 U.S. 1. *Choctaw Nation v. United States.* November 15, 1886.

159 U.S. 303. *Gilfillan et al. v. McKee et al., McPherson v. Same.* October 21, 1895

159 U.S. 317. *McKee v. Lamon.* October 21, 1895.

174 U.S. 445. *Stephens v. Cherokee Nation.* Decided May 15, 1899.

179 U.S. 494. *U.S. v. Choctaw Nation, United States v. Choctaw Nation and Chickasaw Nation; Wichita and Affiliated Bands of Indians v. Choctaw Nation, Chickasaw Nation and United States; Choctaw Nation and Chickasaw Nation v. United States and Wichita and Affiliated Bands of Indians.* December 10, 1900.

193 U.S. 115. *U.S. v. Choctaw Nation*. February 23, 1904.

204 U.S. 415. *Wallace v. Adams*. February 25, 1907.

211 U.S. 249. *Garfield v. U.S. ex. rel. Goldsby*. November 30, 1908.

221 U.S. 286. *Tiger v. Western Investment Company et al.* May 15, 1911.

224 U.S. 665. *Choate v. Trapp*. May 13, 1912.

224 U.S. 448. *Mullen v. U.S.* April 15, 1912.

235 U.S. 37. *Missouri, Kansas, & Texas Railway Co. v. U.S.* November 9, 1914.

255 U.S. 373. *Winton v. Amos*. March 7, 1921.

397 U.S. 620. *Choctaw Nation v. State of Oklahoma*. April 27, 1970.

CPSIA information can be obtained
at www.ICGtesting.com
Printed in the USA
FFOW05n0013110214